URBAN DEVELOPMENT IN THE THIRD WORLD

URBAN DEVELOPMENT IN THE THIRD WORLD

Internal Dynamics of Lahore, Pakistan

Mohammad A. Qadeer

PRAEGER

PRAEGER SPECIAL STUDIES • PRAEGER SCIENTIFIC

Library of Congress Cataloging in Publication Data

Qadeer, Mohammad A.
  Urban development in the Third World.

  Bibliography: p.
  1. Urban policy—Pakistan.   2. Underdeveloped areas—
Urbanization.   3. Lahore (Pakistan)—Social conditions.
I. Title.
HT147.P25Q2   1983   307.7'64'0954143   82-15117
ISBN 0-03-061348-5   # 8728355

Published in 1983 by Praeger Publishers
CBS Educational and Professional Publishing
A Division of CBS, Inc.
521 Fifth Avenue, New York, New York 10175 U.S.A.

3456789 052 987654321

Printed in the United States of America

To my wife and children

Susan, Nadra, Ahmer and Ali.

PREFACE

Urbanization has received considerable attention from scholars and international advisory circles in the 1970's as a phenomenon of increasing proportion of a country's population living in cities. For the Third World, alarm bells have begun ringing as its urban populations have started to increase rapidly. Whether the Third World will be able to control and guide the process of urbanization remains in doubt; but there is no dearth of recipes. The question, then, arises how Third World cities accommodate burgeoning populations and continual growth despite severe problems. To answer this question one has to turn to the study of urban development, i.e., the social, economic and physical changes experienced by those cities and forces shaping the changes. Some very illuminating theories about the Third World's urban development have come forth recently, particularly from the neo-Marxist scholars; but there are very few empirical accounts of what actually happens when a city expands five to six times over the span of two decades. This book is a modest attempt to provide, through the case study of Lahore, Pakistan, insights into structural and operational processes triggered in a city by the expanding population on the one hand, and by the deliberate policies of development on the other. It focuses on the post-Independence period (1947-1980), and its analytical sights are trained on the internal dynamics arising from the contemporary developmental ethos and prompted by the International order in which the Third World is presently encased.

This book offers a somewhat unusual view of the phenomenon of urban development. It attempts to look at the actual workings and operation of institutions, organizations and programmes and not merely at their existence or absence. It attempts to uncover the order underlying daily transactions, and to observe structures of operations. It documents how packaged policies based on clichés of the West, the East or the United Nations end up having more or less the same effects. It explores the reasons for the prevailing state of affairs which can be summed up as 'the more things change, the more they remain the same.'

Though this book is about a specific city, its findings have bearings on the abiding issues of national development, i.e., continuity and change; modernity and dependence; overdeveloped state and underdeveloped polity, etc. The probing of the city has turned out to be a vehicle for charting the national terrain.

Wherever required vernacular (local) terms have been used to describe a phenomenon. Meanings of these terms have been spelled out often in parentheses or can be inferred from descriptions. Another point worthy of mention is that percentage totals in some tables may not add exactly up to 100. Small discrepencies arise from rounding procedures as well as inconsistencies of original data.

Lahore is my home city, so writing this book was, for me, an experience both deeply satisfying (for addressing the issues) and deeply painful (for uncovering unrelenting problems and inequities). Having lived through conditions described herein, I have experiential knowledge about the working of the city which has been very useful in this study. Yet my insights have been submitted to rigorous empirical criteria which hopefully will have eliminated any excesses of subjectivity. I believe that the outcome is a harmonious blend of tested hunches and objective knowledge which, if it raises questions about the current 'accepted knowledge' about the Third World's urban development will have fulfilled its promise.

For this study, I have received help, advice and encouragement from so many sources that I feel overwhelmed with intellectual and emotional debts. The initial idea for writing this book germinated in a series of lectures that Professor Robert Riddell invited me to give to the Development Studies Course at Cambridge University, England. I thank him for setting me on this path. Queen's University, my academic home, has been a very congenial place to pursue this study. Dr. Gerald Hodge, my colleague, friend, and Director of the School of Urban and Regional Planning, has been a continual source of encouragement and help. In the School's office, Mrs. Florence Gore and Mrs. Jacqueline Bell patiently bore my timely and untimely demands. Working in such a cooperative environment greatly facilitated my task. The Dean of the School of Graduate Studies and Research, Dr. Maurice Yeates, generously funded the production of this camera-ready copy. I am grateful for his interest as well as financial assistance.

On contracting to produce camera-ready copy for the publisher, I did not realize what I had undertaken. Mrs. Phyllis Bray's editorial help, mastery of the publisher's instructions and patient attention to detail, made it possible for me to produce an acceptable draft. I am very grateful for her help and guidance. Mrs. Deanna Speight meticulously typed the final copy on a word processor.

Professor Clarke Wilson, Mr. Wayne Myles, Dr. Mary Millar, Mr. Fayaz Baqir and Professor Elia Zureik of Queen's University reviewed drafts of various chapters and gave valuable suggestions. To Professor Azhar Zahar Butt of the Engineering University, Lahore, I am indebted in countless ways. There is much in this book that has been clarified and informed by his observations and explanations. He reviewed a few chapters of this book but his contributions pervade almost every section. Mr. Iftikhar Shabbir has been a source of continual moral and intellectual support, particularly on my field trips to Lahore. I also gratefully acknowledge the help of Professor Sattar Sikander, Mr. Abdur Rashid Shiekh, Mr. Tahir Rauf, Mr. Fazal Hussain and Mr. Inam-ul-Haque in collecting various bits of hard and soft data on which this book is based. Undoubtedly, I bear the responsibility for all the shortcomings of this book, despite such help from my friends.

My understanding of Lahore's traditions comes from growing up in the Walled City. Bazaar Sirianwala was an ideal neighbourhood to learn about the life in Lahore. I count myself extremely fortunate to have grown up in a family where traditions were appreciated, but change was not shunned. I acknowledge with love, the understanding and warmth of my mother, Maqbool Begum, brother and sister Mohammad Rauf and Khalida Zain, and of my father, Mr. Shamas-ud-din.

My wife and children prompted me to press on with writing both by their empathy and by frequent bursts of impatience. To them I owe much of what is valuable in my life.

CONTENTS

LIST OF TABLES

LIST OF MAPS AND FIGURES

URBAN DEVELOPMENT IN
THE THIRD WORLD

1
THE URBAN CRISIS
OF THE THIRD WORLD

On the long list of crises purportedly threatening the Third World, a new item has appeared in the 1970s, the urban crisis. This problem is not new although it has received much publicity recently. Demographers, urban planners and development experts started talking about the impending crises of Third World cities in the late 1950s and early 1960s [1]. In the 1970s, these predictions were taken up by international agencies and the conference circuits. Now in the 1980s, the urban crisis of the Third World is no longer a forecast. It has arrived.

As in the case of other crises of the Third World, the West (the United Nations, the United States Agency for International Development, the World Bank, etc.) has been in the forefront in heralding the arrival of the urban crisis. Two United Nations conferences, one on the environment in 1972 at Stockholm, and the other on human settlement (HABITAT) in Vancouver in 1976, have finally put a seal on the urgency of the Third World's urban crises. Now, hardly any account of the Third World's situation is complete without mention of its burgeoning cities and miserable squatters. Yet the realization in the Third World that there is an urban crisis has primarily emerged because of this Western concern and discussion. The problem is no less real because of its origin.

Third World cities are large, sprawling, lacking in jobs, houses, public services, and poorly financed and organized. As if these burdens were not enough, the populations of Third World cities are growing by as much as 5 to 10 percent per year. Almost every newspaper reader is now familiar with the street sleepers of Calcutta, the cemetery dwellers of Cairo, and the favela people of Rio de Janeiro. Similarly, it is common knowledge that these cities severely lack the basic necessities of community life. It boggles the mind to imagine how almost half the population of cities like Karachi, Bombay, Mexico, and Manila live without piped water or even latrines.

Numerically Third World cities are beginning to outgrow most of the prosperous western metropolises. Mexico City, Calcutta, Cairo, Buenos Aires and Sao Paulo are already rivaling New York, Tokyo and London in population. Barbara Ward estimated that by

1

mid-eighties, 147 of the 273 cities of a million or more population would be in the Third World [2]. The prospect of so many
people without jobs, houses, transport facilities, and even water
supply, triggers alarms of crises. The widening gap between the
resources and the needs of these cities is the cause of international concern with Third World urbanization.

A World Bank report articulates this dilemma in the following
terms:

> What most distinguishes the current urban problems of
> the developing countries is their scale and intensity.
> The severity of the problems reflects primarily the
> rapidity of overall population growth and acute shortage
> of resources with which to equip the additions of urban
> populations [3].

In order to appreciate the magnitude of the Third World's
urban problems, a few key statistics may be examined. Out of eight
million inhabitants of metropolitan Calcutta in 1971, 5.3 million
(67 percent) lived in squatter and slum communities [4]. About 75
percent of Ibadan's, and 60 percent of Bogota's residents were
living in slums in 1971. Karachi, Seoul, Jakarta, Cairo, Bombay,
are not faring much better. According to the estimates of the
United Nations about 25-40 percent of residents in these cities
live in squalid conditions. These figures convey a more vivid
account of the living conditions in these cities if they are converted into absolute numbers. Such computations reveal that
Calcutta had a backlog of almost a million houses. About half a
million people in Ibadan were making do without such elementary
urban facilities as piped water, toilets, and paved streets. And
these shortfalls are mere physical manifestations of urban problems. Employment, health, welfare, old age security, freedom from
tyranny, and human rights are equally non-existent in these
cities. A glimpse of the life in a Third World city is provided by
an account of Cairo's situation by the Prime Minister of Egypt. On
a tour of the city, he discovered: ". . . a forty percent failure
in street lighting, rat infested refuse heaps, and overflowing
sewers, pavements blocked by rubble, at one large hospital no
running water, and reports of nurses being beaten by doctors" [5].
If conditions now are unacceptable to meet the basic needs in
cities such as Calcutta, Karachi, and Cairo, what will it be like
in a decade or so when their populations would have multiplied two
to four times! This thought brings forth a feeling of alarm and a
sense of impending catastrophe. It is not an issue any more that
the cities of the Third World are in desparate straits. The question is how and why they have come to this fate. Some known
answers to this question are briefly discussed below.

TWO VIEWS OF THE CRISIS

Third World cities have been extensively discussed and docu-
mented. There are two distinct streams of literature about Third
World urbanism. One originates from city planners, administrators
and other professionals of practical bent. Usually their writings
are sponsored by an international agency of some kind. The United
Nations alone had published 950 documents on building, housing,
and city planning before even the outpourings from the HABITAT
Conference (1976). The World Bank has come late into the field of
urban development, yet its list of publications on housing and
city planning already runs into scores of titles. Such reports and
books present fairly reliable accounts of the poverty and misery
in the Third World but are usually deficient in identifying
reasons for the existence of these conditions. Generally the mood
in this literature is gloomy about the present situation but
eternally optimistic in suggesting solutions. There is also a
tendency to examine Third World problems in the current idiom.
Thus in the late sixties, when urban renewal was the main instrument of city planning, urban problems were attributed to decaying
city cores. By the mid-seventies, sites and services programmes
became favourites; squatters emerged as the cause of the Third
World's urban crisis.

A second stream of urban literature emerges from the labours
of academics and researchers. Geertz, McGee, Abu-Lughod, Friedmann, Santos are a few of the prominent contemporary figures in
this stream [6]. Their line of inquiry is characterized by ideological and methodological skirmishes, and their writings range
from ethnographic accounts of individual cities, to Marxian interpretations of the urban phenomenon. Some very exciting and dis-
cerning concepts have come out of these intellectual pursuits,
such as the culture of poverty, urban dualism, marginality,
dependence, etc. This literature is both rich and prolific. A
not-so-recent review essay on Third World urbanism lists 450
titles under references [7]. On one point the professional and
academic literature seems to agree that Third World cities have
monumental problems. The idiom of crisis is not much disputed in
any of the two streams of literature. They diverge from each other
in the identification of causes and in judgements about the
severity of the crisis. The official literature is more alarmist,
but also, as Myrdal says, incurably optimistic (if only those
countries would listen to the advice being offered!) [8]. The academic productions are more profound, often pointing to national
and international factors complicating (or causing) the urban
crisis, but usually devoid of workable strategies to alleviate
these conditions. However, one fact is indisputable: that cities
of the Third World have become intriguing and challenging
phenomena for analysis, and they present colossal problems both
for theoreticians and policymakers. At this point, let us briefly
explore the context of these problems.

THE CONTEXT OF THE URBAN CRISIS

When 30 to 50 percent of a city's population lacks clean
water or adequate shelter, it is a situation of crisis by norms of
human survival and decency. Such conditions become all the more
unacceptable if Hilton hotels, superhighways, suburban villas and
Wimpy bars continue to multiply, while piped water or public
transport remain in shambles. The cities of the Third World are
not afflicted with inaction and absence of developmental activity.
This point deserves to be noted because much of the literature
originating from the aid-agencies tends to convey the image that
little or nothing has been done to develop these cities. The facts
do not bear out this assumption. These cities have not suffered
from a lack of developmental efforts or planning and management
initiatives.

Most of these cities have the appearance of a gigantic construction site. There are boulevards being cut through shanty
towns, airports being expanded, skyscrapers growing up, and
trenches being dug to put in water, sewerage or telephone lines.
The experts from the World Bank or aid-agencies of the western
countries are to be found in these cities, advising on traffic
control, preparing master plans, computerizing local accounts,
drafting legislations for property taxation, installing modern
management systems, and so on. Almost every 'modern' institution
and programme finds its way into the Third World, be it family
planning campaigns, industrial research laboratories, atomic
energy agencies, institutes of appropriate technology, or whatever
else happens to be the fashion of the day. Most of this developmental activity has been promoted, aided (materially or concep-
tually) and applauded by the international agencies. Individual
entrepreneurship is equally manifest in these cities. The poor
manage to build themselves shelter, even if it does not meet
housing standards. Millions have managed to scrape marginal
livings through hawking, back yard manufacturing, recycling
rubbish, etc. In almost every large Third World city, literally
hundreds of thousands of new houses, streets and workshops have
been built by the ordinary people, while the local development
agencies were busy looking after the welfare of the privileged.

So despite these gigantic efforts, the results are dis-
appointing, particularly in terms of the quality of life. Programmes are implemented and chalked up as successes in annual
reports, yet the overall situation remains unaffected. New public
institutions and organizations emerge, but few tangible results
are visible. Administrative reforms are carried out, but bureaucratic inertia and corruption continue to increase. It is typically a situation where the more things change the more they
remain the same: a phenomenon of changing parts but persistent
system. Does this mean that these cities are in a state of chaos
as many observers seem to think? Let us turn briefly to this
question.

ORDER AND CHAOS IN THIRD WORLD CITIES

The idiom of crisis used in describing Third World cities tends to foster an image of pervasive chaos and disorder. This image is sustained by journalistic accounts and travellers' tales. Almost every newspaper reader (in the west) is likely to be familiar with accounts of buses bulging with chickens and commuters, telephones which maintain eerie silence, electricity that 'blacks out' at peak hours, traffic that observes no rules of the road, hospitals which are littered with garbage, and so on. These are typical descriptions of a Third World city. Foreign observers often find little order or reason in these situations. The civic life appears to be chaotic and unbearable. These conditions are undeniable. Yet life in these cities does have another side.

Third World cities are homes to millions of people. Hundreds of thousands converge on them every year from villages, with hopes of finding better living conditions. All this humanity could not be merely a rabble. Many of these cities are thriving centres of learning, arts and sciences. The point is that these are vibrant, pulsating and even innovative places in their own way. Such places could not be merely conglomerations of disorganized humanity. There is order and regularity; an order that may exact heavy social costs, yet order it is. The paradox of invisible order and visible chaos has not been acknowledged in the literature on Third World urbanism. For example, on the surface, the traffic in Tehran or Calcutta may look chaotic, but there are local rules of the road which escape a casual observer. In Tehran or Calcutta, one does not drive by traffic signals or by obligations to yield, but one drives by rules of precedence, i.e., who ever gets into a road space first proceeds first. To a local driver this order is obvious. This order may not be efficient or just, but that is another matter. The existence of an order cannot be denied. Thus, the first task for a researcher of a Third World city is to uncover the indigenous order and to outline its evolving form. Only by knowing the structure of a local social order can one begin to predict and direct the change.

THE PUZZLE

The foregoing brief discussion should dispel two common assumptions: first, that Third World cities are in a state of chaos; second, that they have not developed, and have suffered from public and private neglect. There is no basis for these assumptions on which Third World cities are generally judged. These cities manifest sustained and extensive developmental activity, yet their problems are multiplying geometrically. On questioning the validity of these assumptions, the focus of an inquiry in Third World urbanization shifts to the issue: why these cities are so burdened with problems despite extensive development and sustained action. This is the puzzle.

OBJECTIVES OF THE BOOK

This book proceeds from the assumption that Third World cities have not been lacking in developmental efforts. These efforts have produced peculiar results, wherein sectoral improvements are accompanied by deterioration or little change in the overall living conditions. The programmes have succeeded, but their objectives fail to materialize. This disparity between the efforts and the outcome is the point of departure of this book. It attempts to seek answers to questions such as: how a Third World city absorbs development; what structural changes occur in the social and economic organizations of a city with increasing population, commercialization, industrialization, and territorial expansion; how economic development creates jobs, yet fails to reduce unemployment; how a public housing programme spawns a squatter settlement. These questions suggest that there must be internal processes by which cities absorb change and development. The uncovering of these processes is the basic task in the study of the internal dynamics. It is to this task that the book is addressed.

Also implicit in the term internal dynamics is the assumption that this book will probe for those processes, forces and behaviours over which a local community has some 'control'. They arise from within a community or society, either as responses to external inducements or by themselves as evolutionary mutations of existing structures. Such a focus has been deliberately chosen so that the contemporary discussion about the Third World urbanization may proceed beyond the valid but circular notions of external dependency, foreign domination and burdensome world system. It is not that these notions are irrelevant, in fact they are very illuminating in explaining the reasons for the urban crisis. Yet these notions explain only the broader reality and their popularization has induced a vulgar form of 'blaming others' for national and local ills.

This book begins by conceding the existence of neocolonial domination and foreign control, and it proceeds to examine internal responses aroused by these forces. It is an attempt to search for factors that may lie within the purview of national and local politics. Undoubtedly it is an ambitious agenda for a modest effort. The book is regarded as an exploration of internal factors that might point out opportunities for reducing vulnerability to foreign influences.

THE CASE STUDY OF LAHORE

The foregoing arguments suggest that a clear understanding of the Third World's urbanism requires a close examination of the

MAP 1.1

PAKISTAN: PROVINCES AND CITIES

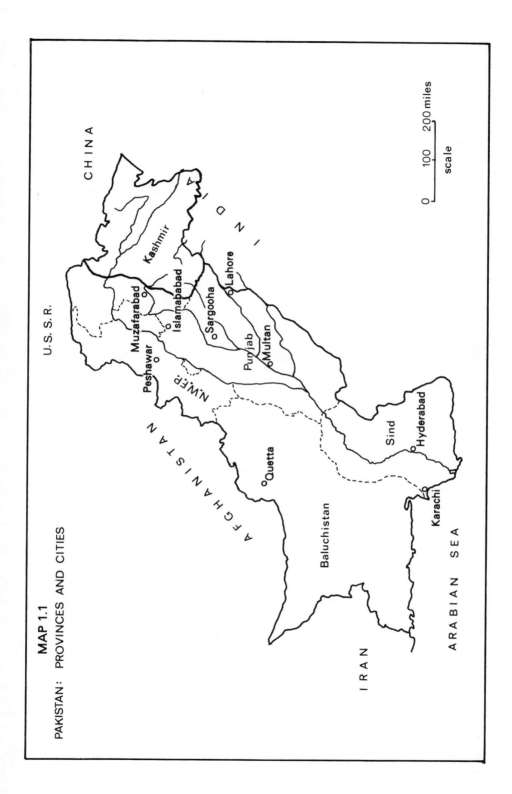

7

internal working of its cities. This knowledge can only be
obtained from a series of in-depth case studies. An examination of
Lahore's development in the post-colonial era (1947-80) would be
an appropriate beginning in this direction.

Lahore is the second largest city of Pakistan. It is a city
of about three million people (1981), yet it is an ancient city
dating back to the first millenium. It has undergone a dizzying
expansion in the past thirty years, both physically and demo-
graphically. It has all the usual problems of Third World cities,
despite continual public initiatives and private enterprise to
improve conditions. In a later chapter, these assertions will be
empirically validated. Presently the point to be emphasized is
that it presents the paradox: development that perpetuates underdevelopment. This is the starting point of our study. Lahore is a
representative Third World metropolis, therefore conclusions
emerging from an analysis of its development will illuminate the
process of Third World urbanism.

Lahore has been chosen as a case study also due to the
author's thorough and extended familiarity with the city. As the
latter chapters would indicate, the uncovering of the internal
dynamics of a city requires intimate knowledge of the economic and
physical changes, and of their respective social and political
contexts. On these scores, Lahore presented a special advantage to
the author.

NOTES

1. See for example, Bert F. Hoselitz, "The Role of Urban-
ization in Economic Development: Some International Comparisons,"
India's Urban Future, ed. Roy Turner (Bombay: Oxford University
Press, 1962); Philip Hauser (ed.), Urbanization in Asia and Far
East (Geneva: UNESCO, 1957).

2. Barbara Ward, The Home of Man (Harmondsworth: Penguin,
1976), p. 4.

3. World Bank, Urbanization sector paper (Washington, D.C.:
1972), p. 3.

4. Ward, The Home of Man, p. 3.

5. The Times (London, June 15, 1979), p. 7.

6. T. G. McGee, "Catalysts or Cancers? The Role of Cities in
Asian Society," in Urbanization and National Development, eds. Leo
Jakobsen and Ved Prakash (Beverly Hills: Sage Publications, 1971),
pp. 157-181; Clifford Geertz, Peddlers and Princes: Social Develop-
ment and Economic Change in two Indonesian Towns (Chicago:
University of Chicago Press, 1963); Janet Abu-Lughod, "Develop-
ments in North African Urbanism: The Process of Decolonization,"
in Urbanization and Counterurbanization, ed. Brian Berry (Beverly
Hills: Sage Publications, 1976), pp. 191-211; Milton Santos, The
Shared Space (London: Methuen, 1979); John Friedmann, Urbanization, Planning and National Development (Beverly Hills: Sage
Publications, 1973).

    7. John Friedmann and Robert Wulff, <u>The Urban Transition</u>
(London: Edward Arnold, 1976).
    8. Gunnar Myrdal, <u>Asian Drama</u>, Vol. I. (New York: Pantheon,
1968), p. 22.

2
INTERNAL DYNAMICS:
A THEORETICAL EXPLORATION

We cannot expect to discover the internal dynamics of Lahore unless we have some idea of what we are looking for and where to find it. Such an exploration must precede the empirical analysis of Lahore's situation. This chapter therefore is a review of the current theories and notions that purport to explain contemporary situations of Third World cities. It is not a review essay attempting to examine enduring theoretical themes or to catalogue the literature on urbanization. Nor is it an exercise in formulating a vigorous and testable model. It is an exploratory essay meant to identify concepts and deduce propositions from the current literature to organize empirical observations of the case study. As the material canvassed for this chapter is both wide ranging and divergent, main strands of discussion have been pulled together in the form of thematic propositions. These propositions will serve as sensitizing notions for empirical observations. They are not meant to be formal hypotheses for didactic testing.

DEFINING INTERNAL DYNAMICS

The term internal dynamics is not a standard concept referring to some widely understood phenomenon. It refers to a set of processes that underlie the changing economic, social and physical organization of a city. Its focus is on the change rather than on the state, on processes instead of structures, and it calls attention to functions rather than forms. In studying a city one is dealing with a preexisting system; therefore internal dynamics can be observed by examining the disturbances and accommodations resulting from a given change. For example, in a Third World city one may focus on finding out how public housing programmes produce squatters, or industrial development enhances unemployment, or physical development brings about skyrocketing housing prices. Such are the paradoxical processes of internal dynamics. Frank's lucid phrase, "development of the underdevelopment," captures the essence of such paradoxes [1]. In studying them, the focus is on the how and not on the what of an evolving structure. The internal

10

dynamics is observable in structures and processes precipitated by the impulses of change working through an urban system. The primary focus is on what happens within the system as it grows, expands, evolves or is reorganized. What new or revised structural arrangements emerge? What material changes occur and why? Whose interests are enhanced at the cost of whom? These questions guide the probing for internal dynamics. To seek answers to these questions, one looks at patterns of physical, economic and social changes in a city and attempts to uncover underlying processes. The realignment of social classes and institutions, the symbiosis of public and private realms, the interplay of economic production and distribution and the dialectic of tradition and modernity are the more obvious processes of the internal dynamics. These processes manifest tendencies variously described as evolution, equilibrium, dialectic and so on. At the scale of the city, such tendencies are not observable in pristine form. They appear in hybrid, contradictory, paradoxical, and not infrequently circular forms. Therefore, it is essential for a student of Third World cities to be open-minded and eclectic in outlook in order to comprehend processes of internal dynamics which may be simultaneously dialectical, equilibratory or evolutionary. With this brief introduction to the term internal dynamics, let us now turn to the literature to assess the present state of knowledge about its constituent processes.

THE FRAMEWORK OF VALUES: DEVELOPMENT

In the postcolonial era, the internal dynamics of a city (or society) has come to be examined in the perspective of development. It is one's view of development that provides the normative framework to assess and analyze the processes of internal dynamics. Therefore, a brief excursion into the field of concepts of development is called for.

In reference to cities, the term development is used with two different connotations. On the one hand, it refers to the building of roads, utilities, housing, industrial estates, shopping areas and other elements of the physical apparatus of a city. This is how city planners describe the development of a city, though lately institutional development has also come to be included in the term urban development. On the other hand, the meaning of the term development is rooted in the concept of economic development. What constitutes economic development has become a very debatable issue. Much ink has been spilled in defining the term. For a start, economic development can be defined as the increased production of goods and services by an economy. Accordingly, the economic development is equated with increasing Gross National Product (GNP). To increase GNP, savings and investments have to be stimulated, infrastructure improved, the labour force trained, bureaucracies streamlined, and markets reorganized. These are not pure economic tasks. They are matters pertaining to political,

organizational and sociological realms, and they call for social
transformation. The realization that development means, as Myrdal
says, "The movement of whole social systems upwards" [2] has
broadened the scope of the term.

Although the need to upgrade social institutions and attitudes had been conceded, and even, to some extent, the necessity
of wide distribution of economic gains, development was still conceived to be a process that worked from the top downwards. The
latter assumption was shattered by the experience of the 1960s.
The successful implementation of economists' models heightened
political tensions and widened social disparities in developing
countries. A decade of planned development made little dent in the
poverty of the Third World, despite high rates of GNP growth and
proliferation of airlines, Coca Cola factories, and Harvard
Advisory Groups. Mahbub ul Haq, the former Chief Economic Planner
of Pakistan, concedes that "A high growth (economic) rate has
been, and is, no guarantee against poverty and economic explosion." [3] The fact that mass poverty has to be directly attacked
came to be acknowledged, even by the World Bank. Mr. McNamara, the
former President of the World Bank, anointed the new definition of
development in the following terms: "They [governments] must be
prepared to give greater priority to establishing growth targets
in terms of essential human needs: in terms of nutrition, housing,
health, literacy and employment – even if it be at the cost of
some reduction in the pace of certain narrow and highly privileged
sectors whose benefits accrue to the few." [4]

The new definition of development began to lay stress on
people's needs, quality of life, distributional justice and
self-reliance, as much as on raising the GNP [5]. The incorpor-
ation of these themes in the concept of development signifies two
conceptual breakthroughs. One, it brings back the phenomenon of
development squarely into the intellectual realm of political
economy after being side-tracked for a decade in the arid, mystery
cults of economic models. Second, the new definitions of development are explicitly normative and break away from the so-called
value free stance of the social sciences. Now, the term development provides a set of criteria by which social change and
economic growth can be observed and assessed. Inherent in these
definitions are methodological approaches to chart the dynamics of
development.

Thus, a city's development is to be judged in terms of its
quality of life, in its provision for basic health, education,
housing and transportation services, in the reduction of social
inequalities, and in the expansion of its economic base. We can
begin by focussing on processes bearing on these dimensions as
they are the guideposts to the internal dynamics of a city.

CITIES AND NATIONS

Development theorists have been portraying the city as a

self-sustained entity which leads in the economic and social
transformation of a society. It is viewed as a growth centre which
reorders regional economies and transforms social structures. It
is assumed to be the driving wedge of modernization, at least for
the Third World [6]. This theme comes in different packages: in
the theory of deliberate urbanization, in the advocacy of national
urban strategy, and in the promise of growth centre strategy.
Whatever the development issue, the urban centre of one size or
the other is the answer [7]. The city as the instrument of
development is one of the most common themes of contemporary urban
literature. In this formulation, the city becomes the independent
variable and the society a dependant system. This is a contradic-
tion of the historical experience.

The explosive growth of cities in the Third World and the
mounting burdens of their poverty have cast doubts on the
modernizing role of Third World cities. Yet there is considerable
appeal in this notion and it continues to surface one way or the
other. Soja and Tobin believe that the development has to be geographically concentrated; hence the city is a prerequisite for
modernization [8]. Friedmann has postulated that polarized
development is an appropriate and natural order of modern spatial
systems [9]. Berry suggests that innovations filter down in an
urban heirarchy to generate the momentum of development [10].
These authors may be correctly reporting the contemporary Western
situation where a city is the locale of modern industrialism, but
in generalizing from European and American situations they are
being over enthusiastic if not ethnocentric.

Cities may be necessary but they do not constitute sufficient
condition for increased productivity, agglomeration economies,
capital accumulation and general uplifting of the welfare of their
inhabitants. The author found that urbanization in South Asia is
not bringing about any significant break with the impoverishment
of the past. The Westernization with which modernization is essentially synonymous was permeating only small segments of these
societies, i.e., the middle and upper classes [11]. Srinivas also
observed that "The western influences are greater in bigger towns,
but urbanism does not always result in westernism." [12] It is
being recognized that the urban norm, as Barbara Ward calls it,
fashioned in the West, is not being replicated in the East [13].

Instead, cities of the Third World, particularly the large
ones, have become centres of conspicuous consumption and imitative
Westernism. Their international links tend to dominate their
external roles. They act as conduits for foreign ideas and practices. Often they function as the agents of international
capitalism by serving as homes of multinationals. McGee identified
the dominant position of developed countries in determining the
role of Asian cities [14]. Perhaps Frank is the most illuminating
on this point. To him it appears that Third World cities have
played the role of managing agents for metropolitan countries. He
says that in contrast to the development of the world metropolis
which is no one's satellite, the development of the national and

other subordinate metropolises is limited by their satellite status [15]. Whether one subscribes to Frank's theory of dependency or not, one is compelled to take note of the over-whelming evidence that Third World cities are not hotbeds of development. They are turning out to be microcosms of their respective societies, which are mired in dependency, inaction and inequality. Even journalists working for the London Sunday Times conclude about cities of the Third World that: "Whether the argu-ments centre on promoting balanced national development by concen-trating on rural programmes, or on the urgencies of integrating the urban poor into the civic structure, they are tinged with a sense that cities are distortions, tragic parodies of the urban ideal." [16]

Some of the enthusiasts of the modernizing roles of cities are also changing their opinions [17]. The conclusion that Abu-Lughod and Hay arrived at is inescapable: "We assume that urban problems are merely manifestations in particular geographic sites of problems endemic to the entire society, but we also assume that urban areas offer a particularly vivid and concen-trated arena within which to see the operation of these larger forces." [18]

These observations suggest that the city per se is a neutral artifact. In progressive, self-reliant and vibrant societies, cities become crucibles of innovations and poles of development. In dependent and soft (as Myrdal calls them) states, cities become centres of conspicuous consumption and parasitic modernism [19]. This discussion leads to the following proposition:

Proposition 1: cities recapitulate in a heightened form the politico-economic processes of a society. Thus, the role of a city must be observed empirically according to its situation. This means that in order to observe the internal dynamics of a city, one has to be cognizant of the broader social and economic pro-cesses of the society-at-large.

At this juncture, one can ask the question whether there are any universal characteristics of cities. This question brings up the raging debate about the nature of the city.

THE NATURE OF THE CITY

On the surface, contemporary cities bear a close resemblance to each other, irrespective of where they are. A character of an Urdu short story paraphrases to the effect that "All cities are the same. If you have seen one, you have seen all. Each has avenues lined with plate glass windows, an airport, smoky indus-tries, slums, and quaint old towns." This description parallels the theoretical precepts that postulate a basic similarity of structures and functions among cities. Friedmann articulated this position by arguing that a city is a cross-cultural type: "All cities have a common way of life, that is characterized by varying degrees of social heterogeneity and cultural vitality, and by inventiveness, creativity, rationality and civic conscious- ness." [20] This mode of thinking was fostered by American sociologists of the early twentieth century, particularly those of the Chicago school. They said that a city possessed some universal attributes such as concentration of population, ethnic and social heterogeneity, high density and competition. To these attributes is credited the urban way of life comprised of anonymity, imper- sonality and segmentation of roles. These characteristics consti- tuted the archetype of a city. This notion has great resilience. It surfaces in many garbs: as the underpinning to the postulates of the modernizing role of cities, and as the basis for studies of comparative urbanism. In a previous section, we found that claims about the modernizing roles of cities are not sustained by the evidence from the Third World. Similar contradictions of the city as a universal type emerges from studies of the internal organ- izations of cities.

Close examination reveals that there are striking structural differences between cities; particularly noticeable are differ- ences between cities of the underdeveloped Third World and the industrialized West. Cities have often been classified on geo- graphical and sociological bases. Max Weber differentiated oriental from occidental cities on the basis of political incor- poration, fraternization, disruption of clans, and military compe- tence [21]. In recent times, Sjoberg postulated an urban typology wherein cities of low technology, limited mobility, sharp social cleavages, were branded as preindustrial [22]. It has become increasingly accepted that cities of the Third World differ from the Western cities in some fundamental way. Even Berry, a pro- ponent of cross-cultural regularities of urban systems, has con- ceded that urbanization of the Third World has produced different urban forms and social consequences [23]. For us, the disputation of the notion of the city as a cross-cultural type is only the starting point of the inquiry. Our interest lies in uncovering dimensions along which cities of one society differ from those of the others.

Underlying the Western theory of urbanism is the notion of urban-rural dichotomy. From Toennies' 'Gemeinschaft' versus 'Gesellschaft' to Redfield's folk-urban polarity is a long line of theoretical notions that point out the structural contrasts of rural and urban communities. The rigidity of this polarity has been softened over time with the introduction of the notion that rural-urban characteristics differ in the form of a continuum of values, rather as contrasting poles of opposing character- istics [24]. By this reasoning, a city is supposed to be a community based on industrial technology, characterized by high social mobility, nuclear families, smaller households, secondary relationships, etc., while a rural area is characterized by low technology, limited social mobility, consanguine families and pri- mary relationships, etc. This sociological typology supplemented

by central place theories of geography, constitute the foundations
of contemporary notions about the nature of cities.

The city as an ideal type is conceived to be the home of
modern man. It is a place bristling with formal organizations and
bureaucracies. It is a community of high social mobility and
heightened individualism. It is interest-based, achieve-
ment-oriented, and cosmopolitan in outlook. What is to be noted in
this description is that modernization and often development are
also described in these terms. Thus, there is an undercurrent that
regards the city as the repository of all that is modern, and
rural areas as vestiges of the past. This outlook is readily
transferred to analyses of Third World countries. By identifying
underdevelopment with rural areas and modernism with urban areas,
the contemporary theory implicitly becomes prescriptive. Urbanization is assumed to be the route to development and Western
urbanism becomes the model against which progress is measured.
This is a typical analytical approach to the study of urban
systems in the Third World. Yet it has not remained unchallenged.
Gans has found urban villagers in the heart of Boston, and Vidich
has found small towns as indistinguishable parts of the mass
society [25]. The author's studies of Canadian rural areas suggest
that sociologically, rural communities are not significantly
different from cities. The mass society envelops both [26].

Apparently what were identified as distinguishing characteristics of modern urbanism have turned out to be the features of
Western industrialism. Thus, the influence of the societal
settings is proving to be preeminent in defining the nature of
cities. Castells pointedly takes exception to the theoretical
stance of treating the city as an independent variable. Taking
issue with the thesis of urbanism as a way of life, he says that
it is "in fact the cultural expression of capitalist industrialization." [27] He suggests that "The study of a city can be conceived as the study of a 'society' as seen through a particular
spatial entity." [28]

Dependent Urbanism of the Third World

If a city is a locale where the social dynamics of a society
are enacted, then the study of a city must begin with the exploration of societal processes. But to understand the dynamics of
Third World societies, one has to examine the international and
national contexts, and this is the reason that the theories of
dependency and dualism have been found to be so illuminating. It
may be noted that in purely theoretical terms, dualism and
dependency are mutually contradictory: the former stressing an
internal structural condition, and the latter giving primacy to
foreign factors in explaining the underdevelopment of Third World
countries. Interestingly, observers of Third World cities have
found that the two processes are mutually complementary, and often
operate simultaneously. McGee has explicitly integrated the two

theoretical positions, and demonstrates how the two sectors of Asian urban economies are part of an all embracing system of "world metropolis – national metropolis – satellite relationship." [29] Citing Frank, he concludes that Asian cities' relationships to world metropolis – a manifestation of dependency – helps maintain a balance between dualistic bazaar and capitalist systems of production for a long time [30].

Dependency is a national condition. Dos Santos defines dependent relationships as "When some countries can expand through self-impulsion, while others, being in a dependent position, can only expand as reflecting the expansion of the dominant countries . . . the basis situation of dependence causes these countries to be backward and exploited." [31] It is the hegemony and primacy of foreign factors as determinants of social change in society that characterize dependency. Our concern is to identify the processes by which dependency is internalized by a society.

Frank, one of the leading dependency theorists, maintains that underdevelopment of the Third World is the direct result of the development of the colonial and industrial West [32]. Overall dependency theories suggest, as Chilcote summarizes, that:

(1) poverty is not due to feudal or traditional social systems, but to exploitative influences of international markets;
(2) the landowning aristocracy and the urban commercial bourgeoisie often align with the manufacturing bourgeoisie (no urban-rural conflict for them);
(3) interests of the dominant class are served by world imperialism, and therefore it is subservient to metropolitan commands, even if it harbours nationalist sentiments [33].

After political independence from colonial rule, the Third World has come under the influence of a new form of dependency, such as foreign financial and technical assistance, and branch plants of multinational corporations. The fact that in 1978 the less developed countries owed about $250 billion to foreign governments, commercial banks, and international agencies testifies to this new dependency. These debts have been largely incurred to sustain extravagant life-styles of the dominant classes in the Third World and to meet operational deficits of the Third World. There is an identifiable purpose in lending so generously to the developing countries. As Joan Robinson observes, "The underlying reason for giving, and in the form of loans, was not because donors needed their money back but because it enabled them to maintain the authority of the rule of the free market system." [34]

To sum up, it can be said that dependency may be viewed as a condition that permeates the social processes of a Third World country. It should not be viewed as a mechanical condition whereby foreign agents unabashedly dominate local politics and economic

life. It operates in subtle ways. It affects the productive process of a Third World country by encouraging the production of
those goods and services that cater to international markets at
costs favourable to metropolitan countries. Dependency lays the
framework of the terms of trade between a dependent country and
the metropolitan countries and, by corrollary, between various
sectors and corresponding social classes within a country.

On the consumption side, dependency promotes imitative and
ostentatious life-styles for a small minority of a country's population. It sharpens social inequalities and distorts national
priorities. Foreign goods become the prize possessions and a trip
abroad a persistent dream. In fact, dependency has far-ranging
effects on the consumption functions of a country's population.
Goods and services that satisfy demands of a small affluent
minority take precedence over the needs of the overwhelming
majority. Gradually the demonstration effect takes hold and
imitative Westernism becomes the dream of even those who can
barely afford to subsist. Dependency generates and reinforces
dualism through disparities of consumption patterns and
life-style. It splits apart a small but dominant segment of
society and pitches its interests against the interests of the
majority. By fostering an antagonistic internal class structure,
dependency leads to the perpetuation of the condition of underdevelopment. How the dependency sustains poverty is succinctly
described by Roberts:

> It is the chain of exploitative relationships that links
> the metropolitan country to the major city and dominant
> classes of the dependent country, and extends from these
> classes to traders and producers located in provincial
> towns, right down to the peasant producer or the land-
> less rural worker. At each stage of appropriation or
> expropriation, there must always be a class of people
> who derive advantage for their situation, and are pre-
> pared to act as agents in chanelling the local resources
> to the metropolis. The surplus that remains in the
> dependent country does little to stimulate development:
> the lifestyles and values of the dominant classes of
> land owners and merchants entail, it is claimed, that
> this surplus is consumed in luxury expenditures, rather
> than productive investment [35].

The foregoing discussion leads to the following conclusion:

Proposition 2: The main analytical task in studying Third World
cities is to uncover links in the chain of dependency observable
in transactions of power and resources that take place in the
market and in the political arenas. These transactions fractionate
the social structure and produce dualistic economic and social
organization. This is how externally induced dependency generates
internal dualism.

Dualism

The dualism of Third World societies has been recognized for a long time. It refers to the coexistence of two parallel economies, modes of production, and even cultures in a society: one, relatively large, impersonal, formal, relying on industrial technology and bureaucratic organizations; the second, family based, rooted in interpersonal relations, and using labour-intensive indigenous technology [36]. Dualism is the direct result of the penetration of capitalist economy into non-Western structures [37]. As an explanation of the underdevelopment of colonized countries, dualism may not stand critical scrutiny, as Frank maintains [38], but it is an accurate description of the existing situation in many of these countries. The overwhelming majority of people in these countries live in extreme poverty, earning meagre livelihoods as peasants or service workers attached to absentee landlords. They operate in a kind of household economy with little cash, obligatory exchanges, and reliance on clans for assistance and protection. This is the indigenous economy, and it coexists with a small but powerful parallel economy of import licenses, business corporations, bureaucratic enterprises, and industrial establishments. The modern economy has mostly emerged in the last 50-100 years under the direct influence of the colonial rule. This duality is the structural condition of many Third World economies which is equally evident in their cities.

From his observations of a Javanese town, Geertz postulated the dualistic model of bazaar and firm sectors, each of which represents a distinct mode of operation: the bazaar sector being comprised of "independent activities of a set of highly competitive traders who relate to one another mainly by means of an incredible volume of ad hoc acts of exchange," and the firm sector consisting of an economy "where trade and industry occur through a set of impersonally defined social institutions which organize a variety of specialized occupations with respect to some particular productive or distributive end." [39] These were penetrating observations for the early sixties. Geertz may have overstressed the ad hoc nature of transactions in the bazaar sector and the relative consistency of firm sector, but his contribution lies in perceiving the distinctions and parallelism of the two sectors.

After a lapse of a few years, the evidence about the dualism of Third World societies as well as cities began to mount. Mangin and Turner, independently, found that squatter settlements were not mere eyesores or conglomerations of unauthorized housing but socially cohesive and economically productive segments of urban fabric [40]. McGee took Geertz's formulation and turned it into a theory of Third World urbanism by grafting it with notions of dependency [41]. His work among hawkers of Hong Kong, Singapore, etc., brought evidence of the functional rationality of the bazaar sector [42]. Thus, the hawkers, squatters and other impoverished segments of a city's population began to be viewed in a new light. They are no longer looked upon as throwbacks to the tradition, burdens of the progress, or unassimilated ruralities. Instead, they are regarded as purveyors of a functional and creative economy under conditions of abject poverty.

Recently, economic and social activities of squatters, hawkers and other lower-class segments of a city's population have come to be described as the informal sector and correspondingly the term formal sector is applied to officially sponsored economic activities and organized institutions. Often the terms bazaar and informal and firm and formal are used interchangeably, though recently the informal-formal terminology has gained ground. Yet none of these terms are precise enough to constitute direct and mutually exclusive categories. Obviously hawkers, shanty towners, etc. have full blown social organizations, and on the other hand, the formal sector relies on traditional, informal and even ad hoc arrangements for many purposes. As Robinson says that "Some 'informal' activity may be considered parasitical or even criminal, but this is not unknown also in 'Formal' occupations." [43] There is a certain degree of overlap between the two sectors and their social organizations. The significant fact from our point of view is the recognition of the duality of Third World cities.

BAZAAR VERSUS FIRM SECTORS

At this juncture, let us examine in some detail the distinguishing features of each of the two sectors. Whatever terms are used to distinguish between the two, be it bazaar versus firm, formal versus informal, or organized versus unorganized, there are some identifiable characteristics of each. An ILO study succinctly distinguished between the two sectors in the following way [44]:

	Formal		Informal
a)	Difficult entry	a)	Ease of entry
b)	Frequent reliance on overseas resources	b)	Reliance on indigenous resources
c)	Corporate ownership	c)	Family ownership of enterprises
d)	Large scale of operation	d)	Small scale of operation
e)	Capital-intensive and often imported technology	e)	Labour-intensive and adapted technology
f)	Formally acquired skills often expatriate	f)	Skills acquired outside the formal school system

g) Protected markets   g) Unregulated and competitive
    (through tariffs, quotas   markets
    and trade licenses)

The two sectors are distinguished in terms of the type of ownership, scale, technology and size of firms, as well as markets.
Obviously, there are many more dimensions along which the two
sectors are being distinguished than those Geertz had initially
postulated.

     Hart has drawn attention to another dimension along which
both sectors, particularly the informal, can be further subdivided, i.e., legitimacy of income opportunities and economic
activities. Pawnbroking, smuggling, bribery, petty thefts, black
market, etc., are obvious examples of illicit activities
flourishing on a large scale in Third World cities [45]. Mazmudar
suggests the two sectors differ from each other in terms of: (1)
degree of protectiveness of employment; (2) wage differentials;
(3) ease of entry; and (4) mobility of workers. The formal sector
is protected; it offers regularity of work and earning, and
stability of jobs. The informal sector generally manifests con-
verse characteristics [46]. Economists seeking measurable indices
of the two sectors have reduced their distinction to the size of
the establishment [47].

     We can go on citing points of distinction between the formal
and informal sectors that have come to the fore through
observations in different settings. But a catalogue of such
factors serves no purpose. From our point of view, there are two
conclusions to be drawn from the ongoing discussion about the distinctions between the two sectors.

Proposition 3: The dualism of Third World urban economies is a
widely acknowledged fact. It is a structural condition of those
cities.
Proposition 4: Although the primary points of distinction between
the two sectors are readily identifiable, there are significant
situationally specific differences that may or may not be
generalized. The latter point has methodological implications. It
implies that a field study may begin with some theoretical precon-
ceptions about the nature of formal (firm) versus informal
(bazaar) sectors. but it should probe for specific features that
distinguish one from the other in a given country.

     Having realized the limitations of generalizing from observa-
tions of one country to another, let us consider the dimensions
along which the two sectors are known to differ most frequently.
Respective parameters of each sector identified above should be
viewed as continuum of values and not as mutually exclusive categories. For example, generally firm sector organizations are relatively large and impersonal, yet that does not mean that a small
firm will invariably belong to the bazaar sector. Boundaries
between the two sectors are fuzzy and each of these dimensions,

individually, will not distinguish one sector from the other. It
is the combination of these dimensions in a complex whole that
defines one or the other. At this point, we may turn to another
issue that has not been dealt with directly.

Dimension	Firm (Formal)	Bazaar (Informal)
Size of organization	Large-medium	Medium-small
Type of organization	Impersonal- bureaucratic	Familistic
Orientation	Economic	Economic-social- religious
Legitimacy	Formally legitimate, but widespread covert illegitimacy	Legitimate activities interspersed with illegitimate operations
Power	Dominant - controls resources and public policies	Subordinate, opportunistic
Production	Western, industrial products, catering to modern tastes	Indigenous goods and services

So far, the terms firm versus bazaar and formal versus
informal sectors have been used interchangeably. As the latter set
of terms evolved from the former, it is a valid procedure. The
terms formal versus informal have acquired a universal applicability. Now the researchers are discovering informal sectors in
rental districts of Montreal or the suburbs of New York [48]. The
point is that the formal-informal distinction is being extended to
the physical structure of cities, life-styles, and even subcultures. Such extensive use of the terms formal and informal has
lent them greater acceptability, compared with the terms firm and
bazaar. Yet semantically the two sets of terms may have some
divergent meanings.
    Formal-informal polarity suggests that the distinction
between the two sectors lies in the definitiveness of one and the
fluidity of the other. Yet this may not be the case, particularly
in old cities of Asia and Africa. What is dubbed as informal may
have very well defined and vigorous structures, e.g., the Iranian
bazaars which played such a significant role in the overthrow of
the Shah of Iran. On the other hand, it is a known sociological
fact that there is an informal organization paralleling almost
every formal organization. Therefore, to say that the formal
sector stands apart from the informal is to contradict this widely
observed fact. As much as the term informal sector is meant to

describe operations of hawkers and squatters, it is valid because
these activities are fluid and unstructured, at least in the early
phases. When the term is extended to the carpet merchants of
Tehran, or jewellers of Delhi, or butchers of Kano, whose
establishments go back many generations and whose operations are
patterned into a life-style, it ceases to be illuminating. Rotblat
observes about an Iranian provincial bazaar, that its "institutional patterns are the combination of elements from three
analytically distinct areas – economic, social and political.
Bazaar operations – including supply and consumption relationships, price determination, and the like – contribute to the
market place's economic character, while social influences – such
as non-economic interaction patterns and religion – structure the
economic relations and also link the market place to its broader
social context." [49] In the old cities (and countries) of Asia
and Africa, bazaar means indigenous but highly structured modes of
life in which economic activities, religious pursuits and social
relations are integrated into a cohesive whole. This mode of life
and the corresponding economic sector cannot be described as
informal. Even hawkers and domestics in such situations have
well-defined roles. It may not be so in the cities of Latin
America and thus the term informal may be more relevant in their
case.

The terms firm and formal sector pose less difficulty. They
can be used interchangeably because the referent is readily
identifiable, such as the Western inspired economy and mode of
life versus the indigenous social and economic organization. The
conclusion seems to be that bazaar-firm is a more appropriate
description for the old cities of Africa and Asia, and
formal-informal dichotomy is applicable to newly settled cities of
the New World. Yet it must be realized that there is a fair degree
of overlap between the two sets of terms. As the subject of this
study is Lahore, a city almost 1,500 years old, it may be appropriate to use the terms firm versus bazaar as descriptions of its
dualism.

Sectors and Circuits

At this juncture, the internal arrangement of each of the two
sectors might be explored briefly. The literature is generally
silent about this aspect. Yet each of these sectors is not internally homogeneous or even structurally cohesive. Each is discern-
ably divided into strata, differentiated by economic opportunities
and incomes, social power and prestige, and access to means of
production: in sum, in social classes. There is a vertical dimension that Santos explicitly recognizes [50]. He maintains that a
city may more appropriately be thought of as a combination of two
subsystems namely upper or modern circuit and lower circuit. This
diarchy arises from technological modernization which fosters new
structures and promotes identifiable consumption patterning by

social class and economic status. Each circuit is distinguished by
its activities and the section of population that is linked to it
by consumption and employment [51]. Santos points out that the
"fundamental difference between the activities of the upper and
lower circuits are of a technological and organizational nature.
. . . The upper circuit uses an imitative imported, high level and
capital-intensive technology, in the lower circuit, though technology is labour intensive and often either indigenous or locally
adapted, it often has considerable innovative potential." [52] For
our discussion, Santos' formulation implies that the two sectors
are further differentiated into layers according to respective
technological, organizational and consumption characteristics [53]. Overall the bazaar sector stands lower, in relation
to the firm sector, yet it does not mean that the top stratum of
the bazaar sector is lower than the base line of the firm sector.
As Figure 2.1 shows, the bazaar sector consists of an upper class
made up of wholesalers, merchants, proprietors of workshops, religious leaders, transporters, herbal doctors, etc. The distinguishing feature of this class is its rootedness in traditional
economy and social inheritance. The middle class is comprised of
self-employed artisans, shopkeepers, dairymen, skilled workers,
religious teachers. The lower class is made up of casual
labourers, apprentices, hawkers, domestics, cooks, etc. At the
bottom of the social heap are beggars, orphans, the handicapped,
jugglers, etc. The firm sector can be divided, similarly, in
social classes. One distinguishing feature of the firm sector is
that its top layer is comprised of the ruling class of the country
and at its base are legions of clerks, peons, industrial workers,
who stand almost at a level with the middle layer of the bazaar
sector.

Income, wealth, influence, resources, power and prestige are
distributed vertically in each sector, but they flow up and down a
sector, and between the two. These flows interrelate the two
sectors and integrate their constituent social classes into an
interdependent whole or circuits as Santos calls them. What items
flow is only one aspect of this complex exchange. Equally significant are the routes along which the flow takes place and those are
embedded in caste and class structures. Combining the social
strata with the sectorial duality, a stepped and oligarchic social
organization begins to be evident.

Proposition 5: The two sectors of a city's economy are organized
in layers, producing a hierarchy of circuits. The internal
dynamics of a city is to be observed in the evolving alignment of
these circuits under the influence of technological and social
changes.

Economy of Illicit Activities

Before concluding the discussion of the bazaar-firm sectors,

FIGURE 2.1

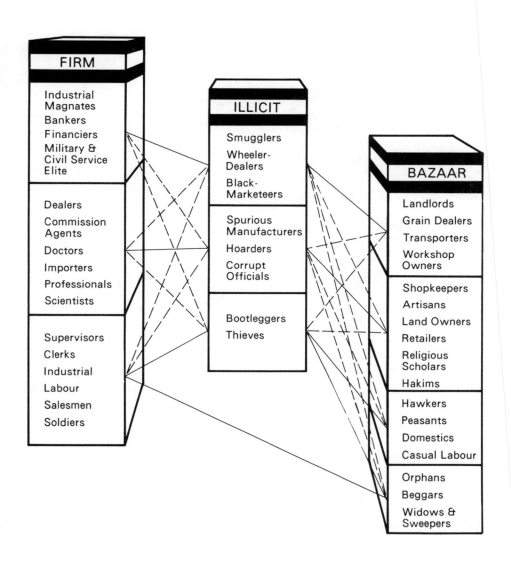

FIRM

Industrial Magnates
Bankers
Financiers
Military & Civil Service Elite

Dealers
Commission Agents
Doctors
Importers
Professionals
Scientists

Supervisors
Clerks
Industrial Labour
Salesmen
Soldiers

ILLICIT

Smugglers
Wheeler-Dealers
Black-Marketeers

Spurious Manufacturers
Hoarders
Corrupt Officials

Bootleggers
Thieves

BAZAAR

Landlords
Grain Dealers
Transporters
Workshop Owners

Shopkeepers
Artisans
Land Owners
Retailers
Religious Scholars
Hakims

Hawkers
Peasants
Domestics
Casual Labour

Orphans
Beggars
Widows & Sweepers

the scope of illicit activities needs to be commented upon.
Illicit activities range from petty thievery to kickbacks from
multinational corporations. Many of these activities are covert
operations of legitimate economic actors for example: bribery by
officials, black marketing by shopkeepers, tax evasion by industrialists, and so on. Often these covert operations become fairly
structured and regular (bribery, black marketing, racketeering,
etc.) but frequently they also remain ad hoc, one shot acts. All
in all, such activities thrive in environments of scarcity of
resources and opportunities, insularity of the ruling classes, and
the absence of accountability of public officials. Their primary
function is to provide surrogate markets for goods, services and
rights that become scarce. Illicit activities also take the form
of full-time occupations (smuggling, trade in contraband, spurious
manufactures, prostitution, thievery, gambling, etc.). If such
activities persist over a long time, they begin to coalesce into a
distinct economic sector operating in tandem with the other two
sectors. Saigon in the late 1960s is a case in point. Thus, the
operation of illicit activities has to be carefully assessed.
Often they complement the two sectors, but in some countries they
can take on the form of an autonomous third sector.

DYNAMICS OF DUALITY

     What has been outlined above is a structural model of a
Third World city. It suggests the existence of two parallel
sectors that are vertically stratified into circuits that cut
across sectional lines. The description also points out that there
is a considerable overlap and complementarity between the two
sectors. Yet this description portrays a static picture. Third
World cities are continually evolving, growing and developing.
This means that the above described structure is likely to be
jolted continually by forces of change. How this structure absorbs
such forces will now be examined.
     Sociocultural entities are systems of a kind. They maintain
fairly distinguishable boundaries and manifest regularity, as well
as continuity over time and space. Buckley maintains that sociocultural systems have morphogenic properties: their structures
internally change to maintain vitality and persistence of the
system [54]. It is the relation of a system to its environment
that remains steady, and not any particular structure. This is the
distinguishing feature of a sociocultural system according to
Buckley. This observation is germane to our discussion.
     In Third World cities, poverty, inequality and public
ineffectiveness persist, despite remarkable industrial development, housing expansion and large-scale public investment. The
duality survives despite continual interchange between the two
sectors. This suggests that the two sectors complement each other
and circuits help maintain the stability and persistence of both.
For example, development expands opportunities for professionals,

who in turn require the services of domestics, chauffeurs, gardeners, etc., which attracts labourers into the cities. Thus, new statuses are created all around, both in the firm sector and in the bazaar sector. New structures emerge, but interrelations among them remain intact. Santos points out that the dynamism of the two circuits is sustained by the imperatives of functional solidarity and structural antagonism [55]. An example can illustrate this point. The diffusion of transistor radios among the poor adds a new set of operations to the bazaar sector, to which the firm sector responds by product differentiation (fancier imports), and monopolization of manufacture and dealership. Thus, an economic activity is split up between two circuits, thereby allowing both to retain their positions and functions.

Theoretical explorations, so far, have revealed the structural features, e.g., dependency, dualism, etc. of Third World cities. The processes that sustain these structures will now be examined and the myriad of forms that they take will be explored. In the following sections, some ubiquitous processes that affect Third World cities are discussed, and their functions outlined.

Expansionism

Populations of Third World cities are increasing rapidly; too rapidly by many demographers' reckoning. Their economies are also expanding: their GNP grew at rates of 3–5 percent per year in the 1960s, and 2–3 percent in the 1970s. Industries are developing, agriculture is expanding, new schools, hospitals, houses and roads, etc. are being built all the time. These expansionary forces, demographic and economic, are affecting the internal structures of the cities profoundly. New households generate additional demands for goods and services and correspondingly precipitate new opportunities for production. This means that both sectors, bazaar and firm, are able to sustain and renew themselves.

As the bazaar sector caters mostly to the daily needs of people, increasing populations invariably mean expansion of existing economic activities. This expansion is not merely a ballooning phenomenon wherein existing facilities are being multiplied. It also means change in production functions and the introduction of new technologies, institutions and scale economies. For example, population increase leads to increased demand for milk, which in turn may induce increase of dairy herds in a city. This increase in dairy herds may necessitate starting up fodder shops, and might even promote refrigeration and veterinarian enterprises. The latter activities might fall in the firm sector, but their emergence will feed back into the backyard dairy business and raise the technological level of these operations in all sectors. The bazaar sector gains through the multiplication of milk shops and dairy herds, and from the introduction of new practices and enterprises. The old businesses became viable by adopting new practices, and new ones emerge to sustain the sector. This is an example of how expansionism modifies and thus sustains duality.

The firm sector also gains from the pervasive expansionism. Despite the fact that much of expansionism is multiplication of poverty, opportunities for high order activities are also precipitated. With mass demands, imports and manufacturing are stimulated which strengthen the firm sector.

Expansionism also allows some circulation of individuals between circuits and across sectors. This limited circulation sustains the overall system. It is the safety valve for ambition. For every one who realizes the dream of a comfortable existence, ten are infected with hope and are motivated to work within the system instead of seeking radical outlets. By changing and reorganizing continually, the two sectors survive intact. Without expansion, both would collapse.

Proposition 6: Expansionary thrusts of a city tend to produce a shifting equilibrium between various classes and sectors. They continually reconstitute these sectors thereby sustaining their distinctions and disparities.

Modernization

This term refers to a cluster of processes rather than to any one specific sequence or end state. Generally speaking, the Third World countries, and particularly cities in those countries, are borrowing Western technology, institutions, procedures and, most of all, consumption patterns. This phenomenon is worldwide. It is prompted by the necessity of applying modern technology to productive processes, by the dissemination of scientific knowledge, and by rising expectations of the masses. These trends set the stage for modernization.

Modernization operates within a particular sociopolitical framework and thus takes specific forms. Colonialism first brought the Western and Eastern cultures in contact with each other but it was not a relationship of equality or choice. It was an unequal relationship between dominating and dominated states. Thus the roots of contemporary modernization lie in this matrix of unequal exchange. Westernism became synonymous with modernization and progress came to mean imitation of the Western ways. This legacy has persisted into the postcolonial era. Even in theory, modernization is difficult to disentangle from Westernization.

At a very generic level, modernization refers to the dynamism of a society. A progress or change oriented sociocultural system is essentially a modernizing society [56]. It can be argued that ideally this process may be rooted in the indigenous ethos of a society, and it does not have to be Western inspired. Modernization could grow out of tradition. At least this is the view of theorists who are labouring to rise above Western ethnocentrism with which earlier definitions of modernization were tinged. For example, Moore has recently revised his view and now maintains that modernization is a form of development wherein a society moves from simple and multicentred structures to centralized and complex organizations [57].

These attempts to neutralize the term modernization and divest it of a close identity with the process of Westernization, have had limited success. Operationally, modernization has meant Westernization, and that too of the imitative variety. Shopping malls, multinational corporations, Coca Cola or television networks continue to be identified as concrete manifestations of modernization. Yet this modernization has inherent limitation. It runs against national values and traditions sooner or later, and its emphasis on imitation of Western ways is bound to run into resource constraints. Poor countries cannot provide refrigerators or television sets for everybody and thus the modernization comes to be identified as the way of life of the privileged.

Two distinct life-styles emerge, indigenous and modern. These are evident in dress, food, housing and facilities of the rich and the poor. Many times it amounts to two cultures. This duality is most pronounced in cities where it can be vividly observed even in physical structures and architecture.

Proposition 7: Contemporary forms of modernization favour a small minority at the cost of the well-being of the masses. The more imitative Westernism spreads, the greater is the cleavage between the rich and the poor. Modernization as commonly practiced is a process of sustaining and perpetuating the dual life-styles and modes of operation.

Reincorporation of Traditions

The bedrock of every society is its traditions. A nation's social structure and economic organization develop around its traditional values and norms, division of labour, and modes of production. Although it is fashionable to depict traditional societies as static, undifferentiated, lacking in specialization, and relatively homogeneous, the reality is very much at variance from this preconception. Traditions are tested responses of a society to the challenges of life. As the challenges vary, the responses change accordingly, though with some time lag and not without much experimentation. Traditions absorb borrowings as well as inventions. This absorption is a two-way process. The new elements are seldom incorporated in their original forms. They are modified and revised. In turn, traditional ways also undergo changes in accommodating new elements.

The role of tradition in promoting and directing social changes has not been fully acknowledged. Gusfield, among others, has argued that a traditional society is not a monolithic and homogeneous social structure. He maintains that "tradition adapts to modernization in specific contexts," and old ways are "not

misplaced by new changes." He particularly cautions against "the
all too common practice of pitting traditions and modernity
against each other as paired opposites and the neglect of the
mixture and blend" of the two that frequently occurs [58]. These
arguments point out that tradition and modernity act on and react
to each other. New technology, artifacts and behaviours ushered by
modernity trigger reassertion of tradition. Some new items are
rejected, others incorporated; some traditional ways are obliter-
ated and others realigned to accommodate change. It is this
dialectic which produces the unity of opposites that is so often
visible in Third World countries: an irrigation dam or nuclear
plant inaugurated with the blessings of astrologers, a planned new
city where cows roam freely, a taxi driver who recites prayers
while speeding through red lights: these are examples of the
blending of opposites. Such phenomena testify to the resilience of
tradition and its capacity to accomodate the new.

The process of revival of tradition goes hand in hand with
the phenomenon of borrowing from abroad that has been called
modernization. Whenever the foreign cultural elements begin to be
very disruptive and blatantly divisive, the resurgence of tradition takes a violent form. In such situations, the tradition
becomes the rallying ground of resistance against new institutions
and practices. What normally is a steady trend of revision of
traditions, in situations of disruptive social change turns into a
revivalist movement.

Proposition 8: Traditions accommodate and assimilate new cultural
elements and evolve ways of dealing with unprecedented situations.
Yet they become obstructive if the change is socially too disruptive. In a specific situation, modernity and tradition continually
interpenetrate each other. This process of mutual adaptation is
the key to an understanding of the outcomes of the dialectical
interaction.

Capitalistic Transformation

Third World societies are being transformed from precapitalist to commercial-industrial nations. This transformation
started under colonial rulers and has accelerated with the independence of these countries. It has not turned out to be a smooth,
linear path. Instead, this transformation is taking place sequen-
tially and selectively. New productive activities and sectors are
fashioned in a contemporary capitalistic-corporate world and
established activities (commerce, agriculture, crafts, etc.) are
being brought into the cash nexus. Many traditional features of
agrarian economies have proven to be functional for emerging
commercialism (e.g., large land holding), and thus helped promote
capitalistic transformation, whereas numerous new productive
activities and consumption patterns incorporate traditional modes
of operation and division of labour. This give and take between

the precapitalist and capitalist modes of production creates a
spiral transformation. Yet there is a clear line of evolution. The
economies of these countries, particularly their cities, are being
commercialized. This process can be described, in the vivid
language of Marx and Engels, as (1) ". . . constant revolution-
izing of production, uninterrupted disturbance of all social conditions, everlasting uncertainty and agitation . . .;" (2) "giving
of a cosmopolitan character to production in every country . . .;"
(3) "agglomeration of population, centralization of means of production and property;" (4) "economical and political sway of the
bourgeois class." [59]

     In contemporary times, only those activities which cater to
the demands of the privileged are brought under the influence of
modern technology. It is in these niches of a nation's economy
that the firm sector takes hold, and from this base it dominates
the bazaar sector. The bazaar sector becomes restratified. The
petty bourgeoisie of the bazaar sector successfully combines the
greed, enterprise and opportunism of modern capitalism with the
clannish values of the traditional order. Bazaar bourgeoisie can
be distinguished from managers, professionals and industrialists
that constitute the upper echelons of the firm sector in terms of
outlook, life-style, interests, and even dress [60]. The firm
sector bourgeoisie imbibe Western modes of operation and
life-styles, whereas their counterparts in the bazaar sector represent an updated version of the traditional way of life. Sometimes their political styles are also different. For example, the
bazaar bourgeoisie played a very significant role in the downfall
of the Shah of Iran, while most of the firm sector middle and
upper classes were benefiting from the Shah's white revolution.
The point to be noted is that even among bourgeoisie in the Third
World there are divergent interests.

     Some writers have viewed bazaar versus firm sector bourgeois
as two faces of a singular process: capitalistic penetration in
precapitalist societies. McGee regards Third World cities in this
light. He compares the bazaar sector to Chayanov's formulation of
peasant economy, and has recently put forth the hypothesis that
Third World cities constitute a distinct form of production, i.e.
peripheral capitalism, which consists of (1) a combination of
capitalist and noncapitalist modes of production under the
hegemony of the first mode, and (2) a combination of these two
modes in which one is grafted onto another, and which is characterized by a series of foreign introduced leaps, rather than
entirely domestic evolution [61]. The interplay between capitalist
and precapitalist (indigenous) modes of production has been presented as a process of dissolution and conservation of the precapitalist mode of production. While there is much in this formulation that captures the secular trends in the urbanism of Third
World countries, it is too much influenced by studies of one
stratum of the bazaar sector, such as hawkers. There is as much
amalgamation of the old and the new as the battle for the dissolution or conservation of one and the other. The carpet merchants of

Tehran and jewellers of Delhi have not been operating in a peasant economy. They represent the upper strata of bazaar capitalism, which has existed for a long time and has been continually incorporating useful modern practices without casting their traditional moorings.

Without getting bogged down by the notions of peripheral capitalism, or precapitalist economy, it is enough to note that development is reordering economic organizations of Third World cities, in particular, by fractionating otherwise cohesive traditional economy, and by interjecting capitalistic and postindustrial modes of operations. The firm and bazaar sectors come to have distinct though complementary spheres of operations, and their internal hierarchy reflects these differences. The bourgeoisie of the bazaar sector may have common class interests with the bourgeoisie of the firm sector, but they also compete with each other for economic rewards and power.

Thus, capitalistic transformation of Third World urban economies brings about a specialization by product. It fractionates local economies and promotes segmentalization of social classes by sectoral affiliation. As Lipton says, "the LDC's (Less Developed Countries) conflicts and inequalities are often more important within Marx's classes than between them." [62]

In a later section, the nature of social relations that emerge from this segmentalization will be discussed. Presently it is enough to describe this condition. One last point that needs to be made in this connection is that the socialistic approaches followed in the development of Third World countries have not produced much different results. In Nasser's Egypt or Nrere's Tanzania, public corporations and governmental bureaucracies constitute the firm sector with almost similar results, i.e., duality, dependence, etc. This is state capitalism in the guise of socialism.

Proposition 9: Transformation of traditional economies into cash based, impersonal, capitalistic mode of transaction is the most common modern process. It fractionates society along class lines and creates interests that are distinguished by life-styles and modes of operation.

Privatization

One of the dimensions of capitalistic transformation of Third World societies is the increasing emphasis on private, not necessarily individual, possessions and pursuits. This process is ubiquitous and stands out against the traditional communal order. Human societies operate in two complementary realms, public and private. The relative proportion of the two realms varies from society to society, and for the same society over time. Agrarian societies are primarily organized around public or communal dimensions. Clan, caste, village, or neighbourhood are their basic social units. An individual's life is organized around religious obligation, communal responsibilities and customary exchange. The group, rather than the individual, is the unit of production and consumption, and often of ownership. All in all, the collectivist aspect of life is dominant, whereas the private dimension is secondary. This is a broad description of the historical structure of most of the Third World societies.

Modern societies are built on values of private ownership, privacy and individualism. The emerging social organization lays stress on the private realm and the public dimension is minimized, particularly in the market economies. The development of Third World countries has meant a wholesale transferrence of these values and institutions. A few examples will illustrate this point.

Communal lands are being turned into individual holdings in the name of modernizing land tenure. Housing facilities that normally consist of a family's living quarters, communal bath, and guest rooms, and public arrangements for latrines, albeit a mixture of public and private facilities, are being privatized in the form of self-contained dwellings for a nuclear family. Similarly, the motor car, telephone, job, tax laws and family mores, by and large promote privatization of life. These are the usual manifestations of the process of privatization. In Third World countries, privatization takes many forms: abandonment of communal obligations and assertion of privileges; breaking down of clans and of communities into families and emergence of friendship networks of common material interests; appropriation of the communal property for individual or family use and neglect of public facilities; encashment of communal privileges and trusts for private benefits and, most of all, the ethics of greed and grab. The process of privatization in the Third World is not synonymous with the process of individualization. It is the process of realignment of public versus private responsibilities and privileges. It is also the process of the restructuring of social organizations into kindred groups, extended families and associational cliques.

Proposition 10: In Third World cities, the production and consumption of conventional communal goods (and services) are being privatized. Social arrangements to share certain facilities and services are giving way to small groups wanting to have exclusivity and monopoly of the collective goods.

Decommunalization and Recommunalization

Third World societies are undergoing social transformation. The cohesion and primacy of the traditional clans and tribes are yielding to the fluidity of new social networks. These changes are pervasive, but they appear in a concentrated and heightened form in cities. It is in cities that one can observe vividly the erosion of the old order and the emergence of the new social

organization. The question, then, is what is the form and structure of the emerging social organization.

Industrialization and urbanization are supposed to bring
about an individualistic, formal, interest-based, achieve-
ment-oriented, universalistic and secular social organization.
This is the wisdom of sociology. It has been challenged in the
Western as well as in the Third World context. The evidence from
the Third World cities contradicts these sociological propositions
all the more convincingly. Costello records the persistence of
family ties and religious commitment in Middle Eastern
cities [63]. Little describes the phenomenon of tribal
associations that have emerged in African cities as social organizations of migrants [64]. These observations suggest that African
and Asian urban social organizations are not recapitulating
characteristics that have been attributed to Western cities. But
it does not mean that those social structures remain unchanged. In
fact, the range and variety of the changes are very impressive and
often innovative.

Old communal ties are being eroded, but in their place new
social relations are emerging to reconstitute the social order.
There are some discernible trends in this process of
decommunalization and recommunalization. Social units are becoming
smaller, relatively uniform by class and ethnicity and interest.
But cohesiveness, interdependence, loyalty and emotional warmth
continue to be distinguishing features of the emerging social
units. The traditional communities are giving way to family
groups, kindred brotherhoods, and friendship cliques, often of
similar interests and social standing. In an exploration of professions in Pakistan, the author found them to be organized like
clans. Professionals and civil servants of similar social standing
were found to be bonded in sorts of brotherhoods, bearing intense
emotional and symbolic meanings [65]. What this example illustrates is the phenomenon of reconstitution of social bonds to
recapitulate the characteristics of a community. These bonds do
not normally take the form of an interest group or association.
They are more inclusive than a typical medical association or
snooker club for example. The emerging social units are bound in
emotional ties, brotherly feelings, and mutual support obligations. They are organized, usually, along class and ethnic lines.
Srinivas describes the structure of such units in India, in the
following terms: "The social network of an educated, white-collar
South Indian or Bengali who is living away from his linguistic
area does not include many people who speak a different language,
but those who speak his language will perhaps preponderate in it.
To obtain a seat in a school or college, or a job for a relative
or fellow townsman, he may have to approach a Hindi or
Punjabi-speaker, but he does this usually through intermediaries
who speak his own language." [66] There are two deductions to be
drawn from these observations: (1) urbanism does not lead to individualization; in a city, ethnicity acts as a social cement and
even the secular and educated middle class tends to gravitate

towards people of similar linguistic-cultural background, and (2) within these ethnic categories, there is a process of banding together by social class. These bonds constitute the bases of new social organizations. Functionally, this process of recommunalization serves the conventional functions of a clan. It creates a mutual support group through which an individual obtains a job, house, access to a school or hospital. This group also acts as the new tribe for mate selection, recreation and emotional support.

From the perspective of the social structure of a city as a whole, the emerging communities tend to sharpen social differences and compartmentalize the communal order. With the proliferation of social units delineated by ethnicity, social standing, occupation, and language, a city becomes a conglomeration of villages, as some observers call it. The kaleidoscopic variety of life-styles in a Third World city are vivid reminders of the process of recommunalization and sectorization. This is the social ecology of a Third World city. It has to be uncovered to understand urban dynamics.

Proposition 11: Social organizations of Third World cities are undergoing restructuring. From clan based social groups, they are turning into brotherhoods of shared economic and ethnic interests. They are becoming smaller in size, looser in interdependence but retain emotive cohesiveness. Urban social structures in the Third World are not turning into interest-centred coalitions.

Distribution of Power and Resources

Who gets what, and who pays for it? This is a fundamental issue for every human society, be it developed or underdeveloped. Rewards in a society are distributed along the lines of its power structure. This realization has prompted a new line of inquiry in the study of the urban development process. Harvey's Social Justice and the City is a seminal work that raised the issue of equity in urban systems [67]. This idea has recently bloomed into a full-fledged analytical approach wherein the outcomes of the process of development are examined as a function of power relations pervading in a society or community. Those who wield power reap rewards, and not necessarily those who need, deserve or have worked for them. Those who hold the power appropriate the rewards of development and become in turn more powerful. These notions underlie the power analysis approach. This approach has been very fruitful in exploring the reasons for the success or failures of specific development policies such as land reforms, urban development, etc.

The processes of distribution of power and appropriation of resources have a very significant influence over the spatial forms and public economies of cities. Decisions about the production of public goods and regulation of economic activities are generally guided by the interests of the powerful. Even public programmes

that are manifestly meant to serve the poor effectively turn out
to be beneficial to the influential. For example: the slum
improvement and public housing programmes have accomplished,
mostly, the removal of the poor from commercially valuable central
city sites; urban community development has primarily created new
job opportunities for the educated elite; industrial incentives
have given employers a free hand to run sweat shops. Whatever
little advantage filters down to the poor is mopped up through the
black market, bribery and nepotism. The access of the poor to the
fruits of development is regulated by time/distance costs, by
bureaucratic rules, procedures, and by eligibility criteria. As
Pahl says, "social gate keepers who help to distribute and control
resources and locational conditions, lay the basis for differential access of varying social strata to urban resources and facilities." [68] He maintains that the organizations that control
people's access to urban resources (power structures and bureaucratic elite), are the independent variables determining the distribution and use of resources [69].

For the Third World, some broad patterns of the structuring
of power can be identified. There is the traditional power elite
rooted in the preindustrial economy, such as landlords, religious
leaders and merchants. Upper strata of the bazaar sector represent
this segment of the power structure. Since colonial times, arching
over the traditional power elite are the landlord politicians,
industrialists, senior bureaucrats and army generals. Usually,
even these power wielders band together in clan-like configurations. These two power structures, though operating in tandem,
occasionally come into conflict. Sometimes, charismatic leaders
arise through popular movements to shake the power structures. Yet
the history of the past three decades in the Third World suggests
that the upper and middle classes have a great capacity to stay in
control.

As the economic base of a country changes, the professional
bureaucrats and entrepreneurs begin to gain influence. Roberts
observes that the urban economies in the Third World are being
increasingly organized "in such a way that exceptional premiums
are obtained by capital and by technical and skilled labour." [70]
The urban elite comes to have power as well as riches as a country
follows the path of development. Occasionally it might suffer
temporary reversals, but the secular trend is towards the
entrenchment of the urban elite's interests and privileges. This
trend is further reinforced by increasing technological and organizational complexity of a city. For example, the introduction of
public transport in a Third World city increases its dependence on
Western technological imports on the one hand, and lends power to
the managers and operators on the other. They become central to
the smooth functioning of the city. Development brings forth a new
power alignment, and redistributes privilege and rewards among
various segments of the dominant class. It changes the relative
social standings of the influential and contributes to the
reorganization of the power structure. But it does not necessarily

bring about a more egalitarian social structure. It essentially improves the fortunes of one segment of the ruling classes at the cost of the other, and vice versa. Economic scarcities and institutional imperatives keep the vast majority of the population in perpetual poverty.

Proposition 12: (1) In contemporary Third World cities, services and benefits are distributed according to the social alignment of power, and (2) the process of urban development favours the professionals, bureaucrats and urban capitalists.

SUMMARY AND CONCLUSIONS

This chapter presents an overview of theories and concepts that illuminate the internal dynamics of Third World cities. Such a review is not merely a scholastic ritual that primarily enhances the author's credibility. It is a necessity in this case, because there are so many conflicting points of view and rival theories. Also, it is meant to identify and deduce concepts and propositions that would guide our empirical tasks.

The term internal dynamics is a broad and imprecise one. It is as much an implicit statement of intentions as a pointer to a specific phenomenon. It emphasizes the processes which produce the present paradoxical conditions in Third World cities. It draws attention to the internal factors and to the penetration of international and national impulses in an urban system. The explicit focus on internal processes is meant to counterbalance current theoretical preoccupation with the external factors (colonialism, etc.) as the sole determinant of the Third World urban problems.

The overwhelming weight of the present evidence, conceptual as well as empirical, upholds the proposition that Third World cities are lodged in a state of dependence and that they are split up into two or more parallel economies and subcultures. Although these theories are now common knowledge, they bear reiteration because of the competing formulations that stress development to be a linear evolutionary process wherein poverty and inequality are necessary social costs along the way. It is essential to stress that this point of view is intellectually indefensible and politically discredited. This chapter argues that dependency and dualism are not static structural conditions. They are dynamic and functionally entrenched situations. They appear in a myriad of forms. Furthermore, it shows that the two broad parallel economies are divided in vertical layers. There are upper and lower rung activities grouped in circuits in both the bazaar and firm sectors. This hierarchy within each sector is a source of further fractionation of urban social structures. Thus, a Third World city is a kaleidoscope of life-styles and economic interests. Bazaar merchants who are millionaires have status and life-styles distinct from those of the executive of a Toyota dealership or army generals.

   Similar distinctions of life-styles and economic roles can be
observed among the poor: peons in the post office are relatively
more modern than hawkers or matchmakers of the traditional mode.
The two polar economies are not autonomous; they are complementary
to each other. Their interaction is symbiotic, rather than competitive. The illicit activities (black market, smuggling, bribery
and kickbacks) further link the two sectors together. In a Third
World city, the illicit activities have a significant function.
They foster conspicuous consumption and privatization of public
resources. All in all, the chapter points out that the two
parallel modes of operation themselves are continually evolving.

   If the social structures of Third World cities are horizon-
tally and vertically fractionated, then how are these being held
together. This question led to an investigation of the ubiquitous
processes of internal dynamics: the expansionist thrusts lent by
population and territorial growth; the social cleavages resulting
from Westernism; the reincorporation of tradition; the spread of
the cash nexus and capitalistic transformation of productive and
distributive relations; the tendency towards privatization of
life-styles and communal goods; the decommunalization of traditional social bonds and emergence of new brotherhoods of shared
interests, and the mutually reinforcing relationship between power
structures and development efforts. Many of these processes
counteract each other and there are dialectical relationships
among them. By counterbalancing each other in complex ways, they
help promote a dynamic social integration. Dependency coexists
with duality; bureaucratization proceeds along with castism, and
atomic technology appears alongside thriving voodoo practices.
These apparent contradictions are manifestations of the interpenetration of the old and new orders. Beneath the so-called urban
chaos is a social order based on a shifting balance among social
classes, clans, life-styles and territorial interests. This
balance is manifest in land uses, distribution of public facilities and other indices of quality of life of a city. This chapter
has explored these issues, and provides a catalogue of concepts
and propositions that can serve as guideposts in charting an
empirical study.

   Development is a normative process. It cannot be reduced to a
positive so-called value-free science, and this applies to urban
development also. At the outset, this chapter outlines the
standards by which development is to be assessed: improved quality
of life; reduction of social inequalities; increased
self-reliance; greater production and meeting people's basic
needs. Whether a specific process is leading towards or away from
these objectives is the overall criterion by which Lahore's
specific situation will be judged. These norms will be the yard-
sticks of this study. With this orientation, the postcolonial
developments in Lahore will be examined beginning with an investigation of the patterns of social change in Pakistan.

NOTES

1. Andre Gunder Frank, "The Development of Underdevelopment," in Dependence and Underdevelopment, ed. James D. Cockcroft (New York: Anchor Books, 1972), pp. 3-18.

2. Gunnar Myrdal, Asian Drama, Vol. III (New York: Pantheon, 1968), p. 1864.

3. Mahbub ul Haq, The Poverty Curtain (New York: Columbia University Press, 1976), p. 32.

4. Robert S. McNamara, "Annual Speech to the Board of Governors," Sept. 1972, quoted by Mahbub ul Haq, ibid., pp. 9-10.

5. The revised view of development offered by Dudley Seers includes not only the growth of economy but also decline of inequality, unemployment, poverty and better redistribution (of incomes and power) and self-reliance. Dudley Seers, "The New Meaning of Development," International Development Review 3 (1977): 3-5.

6. John Friedmann, "The Role of Cities in National Development," in Systems of Cities, ed. L. S. Bourne and J. W. Simmons (New York: Oxford University Press, 1978), pp. 72-73.

7. Towns and villages have been proposed as anchors of rural development and cities suggested as regional growth poles. These are some of the policy roles suggested for urban centres. See Dennis A. Rodinelli and Kenneth Ruddle, Urbanization and Rural Development (New York: Praeger Publishers, 1978).

8. Edward W. Soja and Richard J. Tobin, "The Geography of Modernization: Paths, Patterns, and Processes of Spatial Change in Developing Countries," in Third World Urbanization, eds. Janet Abu-Lughod and Richard Hay, Jr. (Chicago: Maaroufa Press, 1977), pp. 158-159.

9. John Friedmann, "A General Theory of Polarized Development," in Growth Centers in Regional Economic Development, ed. Niles Hanson (New York: The Free Press, 1972), pp. 82-107.

10. Brian J. L. Berry, "Hierarchical Diffusion: The Basis of Developmental Filtering and Spread in a System of Growth Centers," in Growth Centers in Regional Economic Development, ed. Niles M. Hansen (New York: The Free Press, 1972), p. 50.

11. Mohammad A. Qadeer, "Do Cities 'Modernize' the Developing Countries: An Examination of the South Asian Experience," Comparative Studies in Society and History 16 (1974): 282.

12. M. N. Srinivas, Social Change in Modern India (Berkeley: University of California Press, 1969), p. 66.

13. Barbara Ward, "Epilogue," in The Exploding Cities, eds. Peter Wilsher and Rosemary Righter (London: Andre Deutsch, 1975), p. 209.

14. T. G. McGee, The Urbanization Process in the Third World. Explorations in Search of a Theory (London: G. Bell, 1971).

15. Frank, "The Development of Underdevelopment" in Dependence and Underdevelopment, p. 9.

16. Peter Wilsher and Rosemary Righter, The Exploding Cities (London: Andre Deutsch, 1975), p. 116.

40

URBAN DEVELOPMENT

17. See for example John Friedmann's revised opinion about
the role of cities in John Friedmann and Flora Sullivan, "An
Absorption of Labor in the Urban Economy: The Case of Developing
Countries," in Regional Policy, Readings in Theory and Applica-
tions, eds. John Friedmann and William Alonso (Cambridge: M.I.T.
Press, 1975), pp. 494-501.

18. Janet Abu-Lughod and Richard Hay Jr. (ed.), Third World
Urbanization (Chicago: Maaroufa Press, 1977), p. 7.

19. By soft state, Myrdal meant complex social conditions
prevailing in South Asia whereby "national governments require
extraordinarily little of their citizens. There are few obligations either to do things in the interest of the community or to
avoid actions opposed to that interest." Myrdal, Asian Drama, vol.
II pp. 895-896.

20. City as a crosscultural type means "that there are no
fundamental differences between industrial and preindustrial
cities." John Friedmann, "Cities in Social Transformation," in
Regional Development and Planning, eds. John Friedmann and William
Alonso (Cambridge: M.I.T. Press, 1964), p. 359.

21. Max Weber, The City (New York: The Free Press, 1958),
pp. 91-118.

22. Preindustrial city as a universal type is supposed to be
small, more of a governmental and religious centre than a commercial hub, divided in ethnic enclaves, dominated by an elite and
organized in guilds and kin based economic units. Gideon Sjoberg,
The PreIndustrial City (New York: The Free Press, 1960), pp.
323-328.

23. Brian Berry, The Human Consequences of Urbanization (New
York: St. Martin's Press, 1973), p. 74.

24. See for example, Ferdinand Toennies, "From Community and
Society," in Social Change, eds. Amitai Etzioni and Eva
Etzioni-Halevy (New York: Basic Books, 1973), pp. 54-62; Robert
Redfield, Peasant Society and Culture (Chicago: University of
Chicago Press, 1965); Horace Miner, "The Folk-Urban Continuum," in
Cities and Society, eds. Paul K. Hatt et al. (Glencoe: The Free
Press, 1957), pp. 22-34.

25. See for example, Herbert J. Gans, The Urban Villagers
(New York, The Free Press, 1962) and Arthur J. Vidich, Small
Town in Mass Society (New York: Garden City Press, 1968).

26. Mohammad A. Qadeer, "Issues and Approaches of Rural Community Planning in Canada," Plan Canada 19 (1979): 109-110.

27. Manuel Castells, "Is There an Urban Sociology," in
Urban Sociology: Critical Essays, ed. C. G. Pickvance (London:
Tavistock Publications, 1976), p. 54.

28. Ibid., p. 56.

29. McGee, The Urbanization Process in the Third World, pp.
168-169.

30. Ibid., p. 170.

31. Dos Santos, "The Structure of Dependence," American
Economic Review 60 (May 1970): 236.

32. Frank, "The Development of Underdevelopment," in

Dependence and Underdevelopment, pp. 3-4.
    33. Ronald H. Chilcote, "Dependency: A critical synthesis of
the   literature,"   in   Third World Urbanization,   eds.   Janet
Abu-Lughod and Richard Hay, Jr. (Chicago: Maaroufa Press, 1977),
pp. 134-135.
    34. Joan Robinson, Aspects of Development and Underdevelop-
ment (Cambridge: Cambridge University Press, 1979), p. 94.
    35. Bryan   Roberts,   Cities of Peasants   (London: Edward
Arnold, 1978), p. 14.
    36. For a survey of the topic of duality, see Harold Brook-
field, Interdependent Development (London: Methuen, 1975).
    37. C. Furtado, "Elements of a Theory of Underdevelopment -
the underdeveloped structures," in Underdevelopment and Development, ed. Henry Bernstein (Harmondsworth: Penguin Books, 1973),
p. 34.
    38. Frank,   "The   Development   of   Underdevelopment,"   in
Dependence and Underdevelopment, p. 4.
    39. Clifford Geertz, Peddlers and Princes: Social Develop-
ment and Economic Change in Two Indonesian Towns (Chicago:
University of Chicago Press, 1963), pp. 28-29.
    40. William Mangin, "Latin American Squatter Settlements: A
Problem and a Solution" Latin American Research Review 2, 3
(Summer 1975): 65-98; John Turner, "Uncontrolled Urban Settlement:
Problems and Policies," in Gerald Breese, The City in Newly
Developing Countries (Englewood Cliffs, N.J.: Prentice-Hall,
1969), pp. 507-537.
    41. McGee, The Urbanization Process in the Third World.
    42. T. G. McGee and Y. M. Yeung, Hawkers in Southeast Asian
Cities (Ottawa: International Development Research Centre, 1977).
    43. Robinson, Aspects of Development and Underdevelopment,
p. 6.
    44. International Labour Organization (ILO), Employment,
Incomes and Equality: A Strategy for Increasing Productive Employment in Kenya (Geneva: 1972), p. 6.
    45. Keith Hart, "Informal Income Opportunities and Urban
Employment in Ghana," The Journal of Modern African Studies 11
(1973): 69.
    46. Dipak Mazmudar, "The Urban Informal Sector," World
Development 4 (1976): 656-657.
    47. The informal sector has been treated as equal to small
scale economic activities (e.g. workshops, hawkers, etc.) for ease
of measurement. Although this is an inadequate procedure, it is
widely used by economists. See for example, Stephen Guisinger and
Mohammad Irfan, "Pakistan's Informal Sector," in The Journal of
Developmental Studies 16 (1980): 413.
    48. Roger G. Krohn, et al., The Other Economy (Toronto:
Peter Martin Associates, 1977), pp. 2-10.
    49. Howard J. Rotblat, "Social Organization and Development
in an Iranian Provincial Bazaar," Economic Development and
Cultural Change 23 (1975): 293.
    50. M. Santos, The Shared Space (London: Methuen, 1979),

Figure 1, p. 19.
    51. Ibid., p. 19.
    52. Ibid., pp. 20–21.
    53. It may be noted that Santos rejects the notion of urban dualism because of its emphasis on production and neglect of distribution and employment. As our discussion takes into account urban systems as a whole, we can skirt around his antagonism to the notion of dualism.
    54. Walter Buckley, Sociology and Modern Systems Theory (Englewood Cliffs, N.J.: Prentice-Hall, 1967), pp. 58–62.
    55. Santos, The Shared Space, p. 197.
    56. S. N. Eisenstadt, "Reflections on a Theory of Modernization," in Nations by Design, ed. Arnold Rivkin (New York: Anchor Books, 1968), pp. 56–57.
    57. Wilbert Moore, "Modernization as Rationalization: Process and Restraint," in Essays on Economic Development and Cultural Change in honor of Bert F. Hoselitz, ed. Manning Nash. Economic Development and Cultural Change, Supplement 25 (1977): 29–42.
    58. Joseph R. Gusfield, "Tradition and Modernity. Misplaced Polarities in the Study of Social Change," in Social Change, ed. Eva Etzioni-Halevy and Amitai Etzioni (New York: Basic Books, 1973), pp. 333–341.
    59. Karl Marx and Friedrich Engles, "The Communist Manifesto," in Essential Works of Marxism, ed. Arthur P. Mendel (New York: Bantam Books, 1961), pp. 16–18.
    60. The term bourgeoisie is used here to refer to middle and upper classes. In Marxist literature fine terminological distinctions are argued about. Petty bourgeoisie is considered to be a separate class than bourgeoisie: the former term being applied to merchants of the traditional sector and the latter reserved for the modern middle class of managers, professionals and traders, etc.
    61. T. G. McGee, "Conservation and Dissolution in Third World City: the shanty town as an element of conservation," Development and Change 10 (1979): 6–9.
    62. Michael Lipton, Why Poor People Stay Poor (London: Temple Smith, 1977), p. 109.
    63. V. F. Costello, Urbanization in Middle East (London: Cambridge University Press, 1977), p. 56.
    64. Kenneth Little, West African Urbanization (Cambridge: Cambridge University Press, 1965), pp. 66–83.
    65. Mohammad A. Qadeer, "Some Indigenous Factors in the Institutionalization of Professions in Pakistan," in Pakistan in Transition, ed. W. H. Wriggens (Islamabad: University of Islamabad Press, 1975), pp. 136–144.
    66. M. N. Srinivas, Social Change in Modern India (Berkeley: University of California Press, 1969), pp. 139–140.
    67. David Harvey, Social Justice and the City (London: Edward Arnold, 1973).
    68. R. E. Pahl, Whose City? (Harmondsworth: Penguin Books,

1975), p. 201.
    69. Ibid., pp. 201–204.
    70. Roberts, Cities of Peasants, p. 122.

3

THE SOCIAL ECONOMY OF PAKISTAN

A city is a fragment of the national fabric. It captures, undoubtedly in a heightened form, basic elements of both the continuity and change in a society. To understand the internal dynamics of a city, an appreciation of its societal context is essential. This proposition has been amply discussed in the preceding chapter. In this chapter, the post-Independence directions of social change and economic development in Pakistan will be briefly examined to outline the countrywide trends that affect Lahore [1].

INTRODUCTION TO PAKISTAN

Pakistan is a country with an area of 310,000 square miles, and a population of about 83 million (1981). It forms the western quarter of the Indo-Pakistan subcontinent in Asia. It lies in a semiarid zone at the western margin of the monsoon region. Although Pakistan has some of the world's loftiest mountains and is buffered by the Himalayan and Hindu Kush ranges on the northern and western borders, most of the land mass is a flat plain. Pakistan has very variable weather. Hot summers (April to June) are followed by the humid heat of monsoons in July and August. From October to January, winter sets in, bringing temperatures ranging from 45-50°F in the north, to 75-80°F in the south along the coast.

Pakistan consists of four provinces, namely Baluchistan, North West Frontier Province (N.W.F.P.), the Punjab, and Sind, and a part of the disputed territory of Kashmir and the northern tribal areas. The four provinces of Pakistan are not mere administrative units. They are distinct cultural areas, each having a different language (or languages), customs, folklore and myths.

The province of Punjab is the most populous. About 57 percent of Pakistan's population lives there on 25 percent of the nation's land. This seemingly innocuous statistical fact has turned out to be very weighty in the affairs of Pakistan. Apprehensions about the Punjab's domination have continually bedevilled the politics

of Pakistan. The Punjab is an extensively irrigated farming area
(27 million cultivatable acres). It is also dotted with industries, public establishments, military cantonments, which make it
a relatively prosperous area. The capital of Pakistan, Islamabad,
is in Punjab and the province is the home base of the army which
consumes almost 40 percent of the federal budget. Lahore, the city
that is the object of this case study, is the capital of Punjab.

Sind also has an agricultural economy. Its lands are being
increasingly brought under cultivation with new irrigation schemes
(about 13.7 million acres under cultivation in 1972). Karachi, the
largest city of Pakistan (estimated population 6 million in 1980)
is a port in Sind province, and its capital [2]. It is the commercial and industrial hub of Pakistan. Yet Karachi stands apart from
the rest of the province, both culturally and economically.
Karachi is a cosmopolitan city that has become predominantly the
home of Urdu speaking refugees from northern India, whose outlook,
language, and economic activities are in contrast with the
indigenous Sindis.

The North Western Frontier Province (N.W.F.P.) is the homeland of Pushto-speaking Pathans. It is an arid, mountainous region
of limited agricultural and industrial activity. Baluchistan is
territorially the largest province but, in terms of population,
the smallest province of Pakistan. It is a rugged and barren area
of bare mountains and dry plateaus. Balachis, Pathans and Brohis
inhabit this province with a sprinkling of settlers from other
parts of Pakistan. Baluchi and Pushto are the two common tongues.

All in all, Pakistan is a multicultural society. Yet the
recognition of this fact has eluded Pakistan. Its eastern half,
now Bangladesh, broke away in 1971 after a popular insurrection
and Indian intervention. This cataclysmic event was the culmina-
tion of almost 20 years of political wrangling over the issues of
provincial autonomy and recognition of regional cultures and
languages. Pakistan split into two countries due to the inability
of its rulers to accommodate regional economic and cultural
aspirations. Malik, in analyzing the reasons for the breaking away
of Bangladesh, concludes that, "The two parts of Pakistan could
hardly have hoped to evolve a homogeneous Pakistan nationalism. At
best, East and West Pakistan might have developed an enduring
partnership, but the opportunity for this was lost during
President Ayub's semidictatorial regime." [3] To some extent the
same conditions continue to prevail in contemporary Pakistan. It
is against this historical background that the smaller provinces
continue to resent the economic and political domination of the
army and the civil bureaucracy (which are perceived to be essentially of Punjab origins), and of a Karachi's commercial and
industrial elite.

POLITICAL DEVELOPMENTS

At this point, the ideological and political bases of

Pakistan as a nation might also be examined. What holds it together? Pakistan came into being in August 1947 as an independent nation when Britain relinquished its colonial rule in India. It was created because of the persistent and widely shared demand of Indian Muslims for a separate homeland. Muslims viewed themselves as a separate nation on the basis of their religious and cultural differences from the Hindu majority of undivided India. Muslims were also economically a repressed minority. Under British rule this disparity was acutely felt by the Muslim aristocracy and the emerging urban middle classes. They visualized a more fulfilling future in a country of their own. An overwhelming majority of Muslims, peasants and urban craftsmen, labourers, etc., were also enthusiastic supporters of the demand for Pakistan. They were burdened by usurous indebtedness to Hindu moneylenders, and were imbued with anticolonial feelings. To them, an independent Muslim state appeared as the embodiment of national liberation. Thus the interests of almost all social classes of Muslims converged toward a common demand for a separate independent country. Mulsim majority areas were carved out of colonial India to constitute Pakistan. Such areas could be found in two separate clusters: parts of Bengal and Assam provinces in the east, and four provinces that now constitute Pakistan in the west, separated by a 1,000 miles of hostile India.

Pakistan of the 1970s is the second version of those aspirations of Indian Muslims. It consists of what was the western wing of the bifurcated Pakistan created in 1947. East Pakistan fulfilled its inclination to be liberated from the control of what was popularly described as the Punjab-dominated federal state by becoming the state of Bangladesh in 1971.

Pakistan has lived through a variety of political systems in its chequered history of 32 years. From Independence in 1947 until 1958, it was a nominal parliamentary democracy ruled by a group of Muslim leaguers who were prominent in the independence struggle. By and large, it was a democracy of a self-perpetuating clique. No national elections were held, and the parliamentarians continued to appoint and reappoint each other. Yet there was a certain freedom of expression and a facade of parliamentary accountability. This phase also witnessed the emergence of the civil service and the army as the kingmakers. Two prime ministers and a governor-general stepped into these positions directly from the civil service. Others were beholden to a clique of senior civil and military officers. During this phase Pakistan also became a full and often overenthusiastic member of defence alliances promoted by the United States.

In October 1958 the then army Commander-in-Chief, Ayub Kahn, staged a coup and instituted the first national rule by martial law. In 1962, he legitimized his rule by introducing indirect elections and a controlled democracy, and by forming a political party. By 1968, Ayub and his basic democracies had become intolerable. A popular uprising in the form of widespread riots brought down his regime in 1969. The ten years of Ayub's regime witnessed a spurt in the economic development activity and was hailed in the foreign press as a model for developing countries. Yet it collapsed like a house of cards under the burden of its own contradictions.

Ayub handed over the power to his protégé, the Commander-in-Chief of the army, Yahya Khan. Yahya Khan's two and a half years of martial law is known for two major events. He recreated the four provinces (Punjab, Sind, N.W.F.P. and Baluchistan) as political administrative units after about eight years of Ayub's experiment of merging them into one province. The first nationwide elections on the basis of adult franchise were held in 1970. From these elections, populist left-leaning parties emerged victorious.

In former East Pakistan (Bangladesh), Mujib's Awami League swept the electorate on promises of obtaining Bengal's fair share of economic and political powers. In the Punjab and Sind, Bhutto's Pakistan People's Party won a commanding majority on the strength of its Islamic democratic socialist platform. In the N.W.F.P. and Baluchistan, the secular, mildly socialist, National Awami Party and its allies obtained a majority of seats on platforms of social justice for the two depressed provinces. All in all, the 1970 elections registered a popular preference for parties of social justice and regional autonomy. Islamists won some seats in Karachi, and in a few urban constituencies of Punjab. They could only command the preference of urban businessmen and middle-class professionals. The grand alliance between impoverished Muslim masses, landlords and urban bourgeoises that Jinnah put together to create Pakistan came completely apart in 1970. The newly rich and respectable, particularly in cities, espoused the Islamic order and the masses agitated for prosperity and justice. This social cleavage has sharpened with time.

Yahya's regime came to an end with the humiliating defeat of Pakistan's army in East Pakistan in November 1971. It terminated the direct rule of the military-bureaucratic structure.

From 1971 to 1977, Bhutto ruled Pakistan as the leader of a majority party. It was nominally a democratic era: national and provincial assemblies were functioning, opposition parties were operating, though under severe restraints. But it was also a personalized rule wherein all power and wisdom originated from Bhutto. Despite a personalized rule, Bhutto articulated the people's demands and symbolized their hopes. His socialist rhetoric, expedient policies and autocratic ways made his rule both popular and oppressive. Large industrial establishments, banks and insurance companies were nationalized. Public corporations mushroomed. American influence was muted, but dependence on Arab and Iranian aid became the mainstay of the national economy. Bhutto's autocratic democracy also fell due to mass protests. Using the 1977 elections as an opening, Bhutto's opponents, particularly the Islamic party (Jamaat-i-Islami) put together a coalition that took advantage of the simmering discontent with Bhuttoism and brought down his government through mass protest. Thus the third army regime was inaugurated in June 1977.

The martial law regime of General Zia-ul-Haq attempted to legitimize itself by raising the banner of Islam. It vowed to introduce Islamic order, which as a motherhood statement is not disputed in Pakistan. What specific meanings were put on this goal became a matter of divided loyalties and sectional struggles. The post-1977 Islamic order in practice turned out to be an attempt to maintain the privilege and the power of a small minority, i.e., civil and army officers, city merchants and capitalists, who also happen to be Punjabis and Urdu speaking Karachites. Qureshi concludes a review of the Zia regime's Islamic measures with this statement: "If there has been any increase [in liberty and the security of the citizen] resulting from the Islamic laws it is in the capacity of the government to intimidate and repress citizens." [4] There are signs that such an Islamic order commands very little enthusiasm, if any.

It must be obvious by this brief resumé of Pakistan's political history that it is a country of many divisions and cleavages. The masses, rural as well as urban, demand a just, progressive and prosperous social order. Whereas the military, bureaucratic establishment and its middle-class supporters find in the populace a threat to their newly won prosperity. Cutting across these social-ideological divisions are regional/provincial interests and aspirations. Around regional causes the rich and the poor come together, and that is why regional uprisings have proven to be potent in temporarily restraining the ruling classes.

This is the national political background against which the political economy of Lahore is to be explained. A few noteworthy points from this description are recapitulated.

(1) Pakistan is politically a very turbulent country. Three entrenched, autocratic regimes have been brought down by mass uprisings.

(2) Since 1970, the cleavage between the masses and middle and upper classes has come out in the open. Sometimes it takes the form of a contest between Islamic and socialist orders and at others it bursts forth as a clash of sectional interests.

(3) Pakistan's politics has been turning in circles, from military dictatorship to populist autocratic rule and back to military rule. It has been a vicious circle with little movement towards resolution.

(4) Major forward movement in national development has come from coalitions of interests cutting across provincial boundaries, but the failure to meet regional aspirations has brought down such coalitions.

With these observations in mind, the changes that Pakistan's social structure has undergone since 1947 will be examined.

SOCIAL STRUCTURE

The term social structure refers "to the patterns discernible in social life, the regularities observed, the configurations detected; but there is little agreement on the scale and focus of these patterns and regularities." [5] Of primary interest are those configurations of social statuses which constitute the organizational framework of the economy, i.e., class configurations, alignment of power and division of labour. The social structure of Pakistan will be examined in these terms.

Family is the basic social unit in Pakistan. It is a unit of production and an organization to take care of the old, sick, and unemployed. It is also a source of identity and social status for an individual. A cluster of families constitutes a clan or Baradari (endogamous kin group) which, in turn, combines into tribes and castes, and at a still broader level makes up provincial ethnolinguistic groups. Organizationally, all these structures are patriarchal, patrilineal, and patrilocal. Pakistan is a collectivist as opposed to an individualistic society. By and large, an individual's social standing, economic opportunities, psychological well-being and conjugal alliances are determined by the status of his family. An individual is fully encased in obligations, privileges, and a network of complementary behaviours and rituals prescribed by familistic norms.

Pakistan is often described as an open social system which is free of caste barriers. It is argued that Islam does not allow caste or racial discrimination, and its social system is built on the ethos of human equality before God. This is a statement of the ideal. In reality Pakistan's society is organized along caste, tribe and ethnic lines. Marriage is within a Baradari and clan. Support in finding a job or dealing with bureaucracy and succor in adversity comes from kinsmen. A superior or inferior place in the social hierarchy depends on clan standings. It is not the father's name, but the tribal or clan title that usually makes the last name of a Pakistani. Clans tend to be local or regional in scope. For example, Chaudhries or Janjuas submerge into 'Punjabi' as the ethnolinguistic category and Yousafzais or Shinwaris are subsumed under the title Pathans at the provincial level. This dovetailing of kin and clan groups into provincial social structures makes provinces natural cultural areas.

Social Classes

The Muslims of undivided India were predominantly farmers, peasants, craftsmen and labourers. There was also a small urban white-collar class consisting of clerks, students and a sprinkling of lawyers, doctors and civil officers.

The Muslim upper class was essentially based in rural areas as landlords and tribal chiefs. There was a vacuum in the Muslim urban upper strata. Independence removed Hindu competitors and opened the opportunities for making fortunes and gaining influence quickly. Senior civil officers and politicians became the wielders of power in the new country. Merchants who first started new businesses and industries became the economic elite.

Much of the post-Independence economic development took place under the government's patronage. Private fortunes were nurtured through import licences, tax holidays, subsidized foreign exchange, favourable labour laws, and protected markets. Thus, from the beginning, there was an intertwining of the administrative, commercial and industrial elites. Army generals retired to become industrial magnates overnight [6]. Senior civil servants appropriated newly irrigated lands. For example, Shibli lists 28 names among whom are generals and federal secretaries who were allotted large tracts of land in Sind and Punjab [7]. Thus the upper stratum that emerged after Independence was formed by the convergence of economic and political powers. Undoubtedly a majority of Pakistan's new elite have acquired this status almost as a windfall of Independence, yet it has not been a free-for-all process. With few exceptions of cases of rags to riches, most of Pakistan's nouveau riche had access to the state powers one way or the other.

Alavi has very perceptively identified the special role of the state in the post-colonial society. He says that the state "is relatively autonomous and it mediates the competing interests of the three propertied classes - the metropolitan bourgeoisie, the indigenous bourgeoisie, and the landed classes [8]. He goes on to outline the pivotal role of the bureaucratic-military oligarchy who act as the repository of the powers of the state and as mediators and arbitrators between all of the propertied classes. As he outlines, "None of the propertied classes dominates state apparatus, therefore the bureaucratic military oligarchy in a post-colonial society has a relatively autonomous role." [9] The predominance of officers in Pakistan's ruling elites is appropriately explained by Alavi.

From the middle strata downward, Pakistan's social structure is bifurcated into the traditional or bazaar versus modern or firm groupings. There are traditional bourgeoisie whose social status and economic opportunities are derived from their positions in clans and occupational castes. Religious priests, bazaar traders, propertied farmers, tribal notables, and village headmen, etc., belong to this group. They are safad posh who are small propertied men who historically have been the middlemen both economically and politically.

The second distinguishable middle-class group is rooted in the firm sector of the economy. It consists of middle management executives, junior army and civilian officers, professors, journalists, engineers, doctors, lawyers, etc. They are affluent but not wealthy, influential to the extent of being able to obtain their share of advantages, but not dominant enough to affect public policies. Their power and status are based on their achieved organizational roles and their influence derives from their occupational credentials.

The working class in Pakistan is also broadly bifurcated along sectoral lines. Peasants, farm workers, artisans, herdsmen, matchmakers, cooks, carpenters, etc., mostly those whose occupations are prescribed according to castes, operate in personalized and ritualized bazaar modes. Clerks, petty officials, factory workers, students, etc. are engaged in relatively more fluid, monetized, impersonal and open occupations, typical of the modern sector. The two parallel streams of the working class have similar economic burdens and opportunities.

There is also a vast mass of landless farmers, casual unskilled labourers, beggars, unemployed, old, blind, widows and orphans who have no regular means of livelihood. They constitute a social stratum even below the working class, living a prey to hunger, disease and deprivation. Their numbers run in the millions. Pakistan does not have full social security coverage and no provision for old age pensions or unemployment insurance. This means that there is little succour for the unfortunate. Theirs is a subservient existence. They may work hard, yet are entirely at the mercy of one or another individual. Family and clan are their only source of security in life, hence this class has entrenched familistic structures.

By now, the contours of Pakistan's social structure should be visible. Major discernible social groupings seem to be aligned along three dimensions: (1) economic class, (2) regional-ethnic-clan, and (3) sectoral affiliation and life-style. The first two dimensions are self-evident, the third category requires some explanation.

In both rural and urban areas there are two broad sectors, along the lines of the modes of operation characterized as bazaar and firm. Similar incomes earned from the two sectors result in distinct differences of social relations, life-styles and outlooks.

The modern life-style is patterned after Western modes of living and consumption patterns. The urban white-collar class is the primary practitioner of this life-style. To wear western style pants, neckties, to have breakfast of toast, jam and tea, to aspire to a bungalow and furnishings, are some of the distinguishing features of this life-style. In the local vernacular, this life-style is described as up-to-date.

In contrast to the modern is the traditional life-style associated with the bazaar type of production. The rituals, obligations and privileges of the extended family constitute the behavioural framework of this life-style. A localist orientation, an indigenous shrewdness, commitment to ritualistic aspects of religion, preference for conventional housing, food, dress, and furnishings, indifference to schooling, are some of the discernible characteristics of this life-style. It must be pointed out that the traditional life-style must not be associated with the poor only. Village landlords, city merchants, entrepreneurial artisans are the guardians of this subculture. The two life-styles are rooted in respective modes of production, and consequently reflect economic roles as much as social standings.

Lest it may be concluded from the above description that the two life-styles are poles apart and exist in exclusion of each other, it must be emphasized that their differences are not merely those of consumption patterns and cultural artifacts, but of the overall configuration of the constituent elements. There are overarching social institutions that permeate both. For example, marriage patterns, norms about women's status and dress, religious beliefs and practices and food habits are similar. The modern is not entirely European in these respects, and the traditional is not customary 17th century culture. They are two cultural com- plexes of differing emphasis and ethos, but considerable interdependence.

One can visualize Pakistan's social structure as a pyramid, whose vertical axis is divided into social classes, horizontal into ethnolinguistic groups, and depth into the modern and traditional life-styles. The permutations and combinations of these three dimensions have produced a complex mosaic of social classes in Pakistan. For example, Baluchi tribal chiefs are poli- tically influential but so traditional in outlook and values as to form a distinct section of the upper class, whereas impoverished government clerks of Punjab who "drink tea and speak English" are an identifiable segment of the lower classes. Such are the varia- tions within the social classes. How have these groups fared eco- nomically? This question leads us to the next section.

                            Income Distribution

Pakistan is among the world's poorest countries. Yet there is visible affluence. Karachi and Lahore are jammed with cars and scooters. Travel agents advertise group flights to Singapore for the New Year's revelries. Obviously poverty is not everybody's destiny and many are immune from its burdens. To observe systema- tically the relative economic standings of the various social classes, income distributions must be examined.

Bergen was the first to analyze the distribution of household incomes in Pakistan [10]. He found that the lowest 40 percent of urban households were receiving only 16 percent of income. Conversely the top 20 percent were obtaining 43-52 percent of income. The distribution of urban incomes was more skewed than the rural incomes. A recent comparable study does not exist, though a few attempts were made to estimate incomes in selected sectors. For example, Khan found that real wages of industrial labour in (West) Pakistan in 1963/64 were 90.1 percent of those in 1954, a decline that he interprets as an indication of increasing inequality of urban incomes [11].

Naseem's exploration of mass poverty yielded the following estimates [12]:

TABLE 3.1

Persons Below the Poverty Line

Year	Urban		Rural	
	Below Rs 375/ annual income		Below Rs 300/ annual income	
	Population	Number	Population	Number
1963–64	70.0	8.7	60.5	23.5
1969–70	58.7	10.0	59.7	26.5

Source: S. M. Naseem, "Mass Poverty in Pakistan: Some Preliminary Findings," The Pakistan Development Review 12 (1973): 322–325, Tables I and III.

The above table shows a staggering proportion of Pakistan's population (60–70 percent) living below the estimated poverty line. It also shows that although the proportion of the poor had slightly declined in the decade of the 1960s (more notably in urban areas), their numbers have increased considerably over the Ayub's decade of development. Naseem concludes that, "Although urban per capita incomes are considerably higher than rural per capita incomes, and the rural-urban disparity has worsened over time, the problem of urban poverty has become more serious. The concentration of income and expenditure in the urban areas is higher than in the rural areas, and has been getting worse over time. The cost of living in the urban areas is rising faster than in the rural areas. Urban consumption levels of essential food items are also lower, and there is a much higher caloric deficienty in the urban areas than in the rural area." [13] There are many methodological limitations which render estimates of poverty less than precise, and the actual number varies considerably with the definition of poverty and at what income level is the poverty line drawn [14]. Without getting dragged into economists' methodological disputes, it is obvious for our purposes that a preponderant share of national income goes to about 20 percent of the population, and almost half of Pakistan's population has continued to live in poverty. This inequality may have been slightly reduced over the past 30 years, yet the number of poor has been continually increasing [15].

Relative Gains and Losses of Various Classes

If the poverty has not been substantially mitigated despite continual, though uneven, development, then who are the benefici-

aries of development. This question was partially answered by none
other than the celebrated architect of the decade of development,
Mahbub ul Haq, who coined the phrase that 20 families controlled
"two thirds of the industrial assets, 80 percent of banking and 70
percent of insurance." [16] A subsequent study by Amjad in 1974,
comparing industrial concentration in Pakistan between 1960 and
1970, found that there was a slight decline in concentration
between the two points. Whereas in 1960, 13 industrial houses
controlled 30 percent of private assets, in 1970 they controlled
27 percent [17]. Bhutto's policies of nationalization (1971-77)
have had a small deconcentration effect, particularly in the
banking and insurance sector, but overall the position of the top
30-40 industrial-merchant houses remained eminent [18].

The story of the rise of industrial oligopolies is very
interesting, but is outside the scope of this study [19]. The
point to be noted is that Dawoods, Saigols, Habibs and Adam Jis,
etc., were merchant capitalists who migrated to Pakistan from
India and were given liberal privileges, subsidies and incentives
to establish industries. Within a short span of 10-15 years, the
main contours of industrial capitalism were established and these
proverbial 20 families emerged as the beneficiaries of Pakistan's
industrial development.

Pakistan inherited a small but powerful landlord class which
dominated the economic and social life of rural areas. A few
thousand absentee landlords holding estates of hundreds of acres
each "owned 50% of the available land in Punjab, a little less
than 50% in N.W.F.P., and over 80% in the Sind." [20] This summa-
tion of the situation is from none other than Ayub Khan, the
former President of Pakistan (1958-69).

Rural landlords are not merely an economic class, but they
represent a social institution. It is a way of life wherein a
landlord commands through economic and customary compulsions the
labour and loyalty of a large number of peasants, tenants, craftsmen, etc. Traditionally, landlords were virtual rulers of their
respective domains. It is therefore not a surprise that land
reforms to redistribute lands among tiller farmers have remained
high on the agenda of popular demands. It was therefore expedient
for every regime in Pakistan to make a show of land reforms. Thus,
Pakistan has gone through four major land reform programs without
much effect on the rural social structure. While the land reforms
may have been ineffective, rural areas have undergone many changes
on account of secular demographic and economic trends. There has
been a successive subdivision of land. Shrewd landlords have
transformed their farms into commercial enterprises through
mechanization and the green revolution. Landlords have also
invested in business and urban real property. Many have become
industrialists. The population pressure, commercialization of
agriculture, increasing peasant militancy, incipient industrialization, have eroded the landlords' dominant position in the
farming sector. Yet they retain considerable hold over the political and social life of villages.

The most notable development since Independence is the emergence of a sizeable upper middle/upper class consisting of civil servants, army officers, doctors, engineers, managers, etc. This class has greatly benefited from post-Independence development. Its ranks have swelled with the expansion of the state apparatus, industrialization, continual increase of the army, and other processes of national development. This class has turned out to be more influential and powerful than its economic role might have suggested. Thrice in the history of Pakistan, army and civilian officers have staged coups and instituted martial law rule, and in other times when the elected governments were supposed to be ruling, the officers' class retained considerable control over the decision-making process.

The visible incomes of members of the managerial, professional and officers classes do not necessarily afford them an opulent life-style. The salaries of the highest category of civil servants (i.e. high court judges, central secretaries) are at best 12 times those of the lowest (peons, porters, workers). Yet the "perks" of office and possible gains from bribery, nepotism, and manipulation of rules are so extensive that the real economic status of this class is comparable to landlords and industrialists. Officers are some of the most conspicuous consumers. A good part of this life-style is afforded from illicit earnings and abuse of public offices. There have been periocic, politically inspired, selective purges of officers to weed out corruption. Ayub Khan suspended 303 officers and Bhutto Dismissed 1,300 at the begining of his regime. Yet such purges have had little effect and the fortunes of the officer class have continually increased since Independence, though its powers have fluctuated with the fall and rise of political governments.

The foregoing description suggests that the beneficiaries of development in Pakistan have not been a single group. Industrialists, rural landlords, merchants and officers have been the main beneficiaries. Some circulation of elites, and a certain degree of vertical mobility, particularly from the lower middle to upper middle ranks of professionals, officers and managers, has taken place. Faces of the beneficiaries have changed, but new entrants to the ranks of the privileged have quickly assumed the characteristics of the ruling class. Maddison's opinion of 1971 is also, by and large, valid at the beginning of the 1980s: "The main beneficiaries of independence have been, a) bureaucracy and military, who have enjoyed lavish privileges and have grown considerably in number, b) the new class of industrial capitalists, c) professional people whose numbers have grown rapidly, and d) landlords." [21] This observation raises the question to which we now turn: how has economic development affected the working class.

The affluence of the privileged and poverty of the masses have remained in sharp contrast, despite increased production and economic development of the last 30 years. While the peasants may have acquired transistor radios, the privileged now vacation

abroad; clerks may be riding bicycles, the officers have become
land speculators. The relative positions have remained unaltered,
though the material base of each class has changed.

The recent mass exodus of skilled workers to the Middle East
has introduced a new thrust to change in the social structure. The
conventional caste and class hierarchy is being severely strained.
Sweepers are earning in the Middle East three to four times the
incomes of their erstwhile middle-class patrons. It is not likely
that they will continue to be subservient for long. The same will
be the case with other workers. There were about 800,000
Pakistanis working abroad whose remittances amounted to $1.7
billion in 1979/80, though an additional $1.0 billion was
estimated to have flowed in through unofficial channels (the
latter incidentally also is an indicator of the scale of the
illicit sector in Pakistan) [22]. Although the migration of
workers to the Middle East and Europe provides substantial foreign
exchange and lowers unemployment, its most pronounced effects have
been in the sociological realm. There are shortages of workers,
even in villages, which have strained landlord-tenant relationships. Occupational caste barriers are breaking down. Family
structures are being realigned. There is an increasing number of
female heads of households as the men have gone abroad to work.
Modern consumer goods such as refrigerators, colour television
sets, etc., have ceased to be the exclusive possessions of the
rich. Airports are flooded with illiterates as the privileged are
wont to say.

Some of the traditional symbols of modernity have ceased to
be exclusive. Yet on the other hand, there is a revival of traditional practices and values; be they 'slaughtering a lamb to cele-
brate a home visit' or the reinstitution of marriages among
cousins. These are symptoms of the dialectic of modernization and
nativistic revivalism. And they indicate convulsive social
changes. The age old rigidity of Pakistan's social structure has
been breached by 30 years of independence and new opportunities.
What will come of it is not so clear yet. Economic development has
altered the material base of the social structure and has
unleashed the forces of change. What economic changes has Pakistan
undergone since Independence? This will be analyzed in the
following section.

STRUCTURE OF THE ECONOMY

An overview of Pakistan's economic output is provided in
Table 3.2. Pakistan is among the countries classified as the
poorest by the United Nations. In 1980, the per capita income in
Pakistan was $280 (Rs. 2837) in current prices, which is low even
by the standards of developing countries whose average for that
year was $540. Pakistan's per capita income was about 60 percent
that of Egypt, 33 percent of Korea, and 25 percent of Malaysia. At
the present rate of economic growth, it will take almost 30 years

to attain the national income level that Egypt has at present.

Table 3.2 shows that Pakistan's Gross Domestic Product (GDP) increased more than four times, and its per capita gross income has increased by almost 89 percent in constant prices over a 30 year period. This growth has been accompanied by visible structural changes in the economy. Agriculture's share in the GDP has continually declined, whereas the contributions of the manufacturing, construction, utilities and transport sectors have increased since Independence. These are symptoms of incipient industrialization. The share of large-scale manufacturing in the GDP has increased almost fivefold. Overall the secondary and tertiary sectors have undoubtedly expanded at rates much faster than agriculture. In 1979-80, agriculture was contributing about one-third of the GDP, which had declined in proportionate terms since 1949-50; despite a one and one-half times increase in actual output. The industrial and service sectors have grown faster than agriculture, thereby altering the structural profile of the economy.

The economic development of Pakistan has proceeded in three distinct phases, each corresponding to a political era. The first decade (1948-58) was a period of unstable parliamentary rule wherein refugees were settled, administration organized, and urgently needed infrastructure was laid to stimulate industrial development. During this phase the GDP increased by 36 percent in constant prices. The second phase consisted of Ayub's martial law rule and basic democracy (1958-69). This was the phase of an unabashed capitalistic model of development. "Robber barons", Papanek's term for new industrialists and bankers, were extended government backing to exercise their entrepreneurial talent [23]. It was also an era of Pakistan's military alignment with the U.S., and consequently of generous foreign aid. Two five-year plans were prepared and implemented under the guidance of the Planning Advisory Group from Harvard University. This era witnessed a 92 percent increase in the GDP led by almost a doubling of the outputs of large scale industry, construction, and banking and insurance.

The third phase began under adverse circumstances after the separation of East Pakistan. Although this decade began and ended with coups led by the army, about five and a half years (1972-77) of Bhutto's rule characterizes this decade. Proclaiming socialism as his economic creed, Bhutto initially nationalized heavy industries, banks and insurance companies and in 1976, out of political expediency, flour mills and ginning factories were taken over. During Bhutto's rule, a government corporation was established for every conceivable activity. While civil services thrived in Ayub's era, under Bhutto's people's regime their economic role and job opportunities further expanded. Since the reinstitution of military rule (1977) after Bhutto's downfall, the policy has shifted once again and many taken-over industries have been returned to previous owners and private enterprise has been given a prominent role.

TABLE 3.2

Structure of Output at Constant Factor Cost
(1959–60 Prices)

Sector/Activity	Gross Domestic Product (GDP) (percent)			
	1949/50	1959/60	1969/70	1979/80
Agriculture	53.2	45.8	38.9	31.6
Mining & Quarrying	0.0(3)	0.0(2)	0.0(5)	0.0(6)
Manufacturing				
Large scale	2.2	6.9	12.5	10.8
Small scale	5.5	5.1	3.5	4.6
Construction	1.4	2.6	4.2	5.4
Electricity & Gas	0.0(3)	0.0(6)	1.9	3.1
Transport, storage,				
communication	5.0	5.6	6.3	6.8
Wholesale & retail trade	11.9	12.5	13.8	13.7
Banking & insurance	0.1	0.1	1.8	2.9
Ownership of dwelling	5.1	4.9	3.4	3.1
Public Administration				
& defence	7.0	6.2	6.4	10.2
Services	7.7	8.3	6.7	7.4
	100.0	100.0	100.0	100.0
Gross Domestic Produce				
(Rs. Millions)	12,389	16,826	32,336	50,189
Percentage Increase		35.8	92.1	55.2
Net Factor Income from				
rest of world	–18	–23	+2	+3004
Gross National Product				
(Rs. Millions)	12,380	16.803	32,338	53,193
Per Capita Gross				
Income (Rs.)	351	373	542	663

Source: Pakistan Economic Survey, 1979–80 (Islamabad: Finance
Division, 1980), Table 2–1, Statistical Annexure, pp.
9–11.

Overall in the decade of the 70s, the GDP increased by 55
percent, led by the construction, electricity, gas, banking and
public services. The pace of industrial development slowed down in
this phase. Another distinguishing feature of this decade was the
emergence of workers' remittances from abroad as a significant

component of invisible exports, and as a source of foreign
exchange. The net factor income from the rest of the world came to
be in the black to the tune of Rs. 3 billion per year.

To give some concrete impressions of Pakistan's economic
growth, production figures for a few selected goods over a 30 year
period are reported in Table 3.3.

TABLE 3.3

Output of Selected Goods

Goods	Output			
	1949–50	1959–60	1969–70	1979–80*
Wheat (thousand tons)	3,924	3,909	7,294	10,870
Sugar (thousand tons)	17	84	610	514
Cotton Cloth (million square mets.)	46.3	455.0	606.5	250
Bicycles (thousand units)	---	---	161.3	211.4
Cement (thousand tons)	39,500	982	2,656	2,417
Mild Steel Products (thousand tons)	---	---	180.0	278.6

* 1979–80 figures are provisional estimates.

Source: Pakistan Economic Survey, 1979–80   (Islamabad: Finance
         Division, 1980), Tables 3.3 and 4.2.

It is evident that substantial gains have been registered in
the production of essential goods since Independence. Whereas the
population grew by about 131 percent between 1951–80 (from 34
million to 82 million), the production of wheat increased by 177
percent, sugar output increased 30 times, the production of cloth
registered a 500 percent increase by 1968–69 but has suffered setbacks in the last decade, cement's production increased 700
percent. Consumer durables industries, such as bicycles and steel
products, have come up in the past 20 years. The industrial growth
in Pakistan proceeded initially at a rapid rate to work off the
large gap between supply and demand for consumer goods [24]. Once
the impetus for import substitution had been used up, the spate of
industrial growth decelerated (after 1955) and intermediate and
capital goods industries began to be developed. Guisinger concludes that Pakistan ". . . has made the transition from
'inward-looking' policies to 'outward-looking' policies that promote exports." [25]

Despite fluctuating output, it seems that the secular trend

in Pakistan has been towards increasing the share of the secondary and tertiary sectors. It is no more a feudal-agrarian economy. Instead it has become a rudimentary industrial economy, producing consumer goods and processing agricultural outputs.

Modes of Operation

Paralleling the bifurcation of life-styles is the duality of economic organization in Pakistan. The first is the traditional prescriptive system of economic transactions, of which the most evolved form is the village communal economy. It is a caste based division of labour wherein the lower castes serve the upper classes as an obligation and in return obtain a meagre but prescribed share from the annual harvest. The social relations and economic exchanges between various castes are indistinguishable. It is a system of patron-client network. In urban areas, this economy takes the form of family enterprises, artisan workshops and service castes. There are few written laws, although customary expectations regulate mutual rights and obligations. Most of the small businesses, neighbourhood stores and services such as cooking, arranging marriages and funerals are carried out in this mode. In these economic transactions are overlays of social obligations and customary exchanges in kind at prescribed occasions. This mode of operation characterizes the bazaar sector.

The firm sector operates primarily on a cash basis through supposedly impersonal transactions. Modern corporations, public agencies, large factories, banks, etc., are the constituent units of the firm sector. It would be correct to say that most of the production in Pakistan occurs in the bazaar mode. Robinson and Abbasi conclude from an analysis of underemployment data that "Pakistan is still largely a rural, agricultural, family enterprise-oriented economy. At most, a third of the employed labour force works in the modern sector under conditions approximating a labour-market wage bargaining situation. Most of the rest, in agriculture and trade, work within a family-based economic unit. That is, the 'employees' qualify for employment in these enterprises by blood, marriage, previous family interconnections and other customarily defined family ties." [26] This conclusion is remarkably borne out by Guisinger and Irfan, in a study of Pakistan's informal sector. They estimate that "70 percent of Pakistan's urban labour force is employed in the informal sector." [27] They found that about 35 percent of employment in manufacturing was of informal mode, community and social services (55 percent), whereas agriculture, trade and construction were overwhelmingly (80-100 percent) informal activities [28]. Both studies are based on data collected in the early 70s. These estimates indicate the share of the bazaar (informal) sector after Pakistan's economy had undergone some degree of industrialization. Obviously the bazaar sector capitalized on the opportunities offered by the post-Independence development.

Two points can be deduced from the preceding description. First, the organizational unit for economic purposes in Pakistan remains predominantly a familistic group. Such a unit operates on the principle of optimizing the earnings, as well as meeting social obligations. Its transactions are personalized, book-keeping is minimal, capital is limited and family members are an abundant source of labour. Public regulations and tax laws are seldom observed by such enterprises. Second, these production units, though predominantly small and of low level of technology, are neither immune to riches nor resistant to change. Since Independence, the bazaar enterprises have adopted numerous practices that are beneficial: the example of electronic calculators may be very vivid. Illiterate traders have very readily learned how to use these electronic aids for haggling over prices.

It is interesting to note that even large firms are organized along familistic lines. For example, the famous 20 families which owned most of Pakistan's industries at the end of the 1960s originated from four clans, i.e., Chinoti, Shiekhs, Bhora and Memons. Given that the predominant economic organization in Pakistan is a family enterprise, it is amazing that policymakers seldom recognized this empirical fact. The development strategies continue to be conceived as if Pakistan was the land of individualistic ethos and impersonal social relations.

Shadow Economy of Corruption

Corruption is not a mere occasional exception to normal economic activities in Pakistan. It is so extensive and entrenched that it can almost be described as a distinct sector. Bribery, kickbacks, smuggling, black market and spurious manufacturing are its various manifestations. It is very difficult to estimate the overall share of corruption in the national economy. Yet it would not be far-fetched to say that about 25-30 percent of the national product circulates through illicit channels. For example, there are fixed rates of commissions that administrators and engineers are assumed to be entitled to as kickbacks on public capital works. The president of Lahore's Government Contractors' Association alleged (1981) that those commissions added up to at least 20 percent of the estimated cost of a project [29]. For almost every public activity there are set rates. What bribes are to be paid to obtain a passport quickly or fix a parking ticket are secrets that can be learned on one visit to the respective agencies. Almost all cities of Pakistan have well known Bara, markets where smuggled goods can be bought. Adulteration or spurious manufacture of foreign products, and a black market of meat, sugar, vegetable oil and other daily necessities are extensive.

Corruption essentially is a form of transfer payments. Resources already budgeted for various goods and services are funnelled into the black market and bribery. The smuggling and spurious manufacture could also have income effects as additional

goods and services are produced or traded which could add to the
domestic product. Although corruption permeates all social strata,
as a rule corruption is an encashment of the authority; therefore
its scale must increase in direct proportion to the authority and
power. For example, a chief engineer's share of kickbacks would be
larger than that of a site supervisor. It means that the distributional effects of corruption would be regressive.

A notable effect of corruption is on the consumption side. It
promotes conspicuous consumption and alters demand functions which
in turn, distort production priorities. In Pakistan, the earnings
from corruption increase the demand for new homes, restaurants,
entertainment outlets, travel and jewellery. They also reinforce
the traditional practices of lavish marriage feasts and dowries.
Thus corruption paradoxically expands the modern upper circuit,
while simultaneously reviving old customs. If a large proportion
of the national product circulates through illicit channels, the
obviously developmental policies conceived in disregard of these
practices will be ineffective.

INSTITUTIONAL EVOLUTION

The development of Pakistan's economy is modest compared to
its needs and aspirations. Yet the ethos of development has been
established. People's expectations about better living conditions
have been raised. A small minority has visibly gained prosperity,
if not the good life. For each one who has prospered, there are
scores whose hopes have been raised. So much of the individual's
affluence is visibly the product of corruption that everyone's
success is suspect. These features of development have lent it an
aura of a lottery. One person may strike rich by obtaining an
import license for scarce items, and another's son may land a job
in Saudi Arabia, bringing respectability to the family. Development has remained a string of episodes and projects. It has not
ushered in a new social order based on criteria of achievement and
individual rights, yet it has cracked the traditional order. These
conditions have profoundly affected social mores. Traditional clan
obligations have weakened, and a certain form of entrepreneurial
individualism has come to characterize social relations. Yet an
individual has to mobilize and use all his contacts to succeed
economically, which makes him dependent upon kinsmen, clansmen,
and friends.

In the realm of public institutions, development appears to
have more persistence and pattern. Almost every contemporary
development idea and practice has been imported in Pakistan under
public aegis. For example, administrative reforms to make public
agencies responsive to developmental tasks have been an abiding
concern of each regime. Every time there has been a change of
regime in Pakistan, a civil service reform commission has been
constituted to reorganize the public administrative system. Similar commissions have been periodically instituted for education,

family, labour, and constitutional reforms. The recommendations of these commissions may not have been followed in total, but the recurrent acts of establishing such task forces indicate the deliberateness with which the successive regimes have gone about developing new and reforming existing institutions. To take the example of public administration, the innovative and reform measures undertaken since 1947 include the formation of a pool of senior officers for economic tasks, the introduction of the section officers scheme on the American administrative model to streamline secretariat procedures, the institution of lateral entry methods of recruiting middle level civil servants, and the establishment of programming-budgeting procedures and in-service training academies. Yet these measures did not improve the efficiency and responsiveness of the civil services.

Many observers believe that the overall performance of the public bureaucracies has declined over the years; certainly bribery, neglect of duties, and sheer incompetence have continued unabated. So much so that a governor of the Punjab province admitted recently in exasperation that "80 percent of funds allocated for development purposes are wasted, pocketed and embezzled." [30] All those measures to modernize public administration have essentially kept up a momentum of change without bringing about any substantive improvement. They imbibed forms of modernity but failed to incorporate its functions. Undoubtedly these measures acted as band-aids to the tottering administrative system.

Rural Development programmes offer another example of irrelevant institutional development wherein forms are emphasized and substance ignored. Such programmes have come to mean a new set of officials and offices every time a measure is instituted. Local notables immediately calculate what they can get out of a programme, and become available to be coopted as citizens' leaders. Thus, the officials and notables together appropriate funds and monopolize the benefits. So predictable are these patterns that locals who benefit from them remain almost the same, no matter what new twist is given to a programme. One of the few comprehensive evaluations of these programmes suggests that beneficiaries are middle- and upper-middle class entrepreneurs. [31] They are town merchants, commercial farmers, teachers, clerks and other petty rural officials [32].

This narrative suggests that the development efforts benefit middle-class entrepreneurs and other respectables. It is not a surprising finding. The development in Pakistan has been conceived in the Western middle-class idiom. To benefit from it, resources, knowledge and power are needed. Development has been a process of benefiting the bourgeoisie, whether it takes the form of administrative reforms or mobilization for rural development.

Myrdal arrived at the same conclusion: "All the significant policy measures of agricultural uplift adopted by the government – whether technological or institutional – have tended to shift the power balance of the rural structure in favour of the privileged

classes." [33] Similar results are observable for other success
stories of Pakistan's development, such as the green revolution,
mechanization of agriculture, technical education, or new towns.
Managerial and professional careers have opened up, thus creating
a small but visible managerial class. Exclusive housing estates,
cars and separate schools, clinics and clubs shelter this class
from the scarcities of daily life and create for them a distinct
circuit of production and consumption. Opportunities for jobs as
industrial labour have expanded, and a large number of workers
have found jobs, but not the privileged existence obtainable by
officers.

Any account of the development of new institutions will be
incomplete without a mention of Bhutto's socialist policies. By
nationalizing major industries and banks, Bhutto's regime provided
another expansionary thrust to the opportunities of the upper
middle class, without bringing corresponding social gains in productivity and efficiency. This experience suggests that the
strategy of economic development is not a simple matter of
choosing between public or private sectors. It poses a challenge
to design institutions and organizations that are responsive to
the people's needs, and are efficient as well as innovative.

Since Independence, Pakistan has experienced a significant
increase in the service sector. For example, the number of high
schools has increased from 408 in 1947-48 to 3,464 in 1979-80; and
universities increased from two to 15 in this period. The number
of doctors increased from 1,014 in 1948 to 19,922 in 1977.
Increases of similar scale have been registered in the numbers of
hospitals, houses, mileage of roads, telephones, radio stations,
etc. There is scarcely any modern activity for which a public
agency or institute does not exist. To name a few: Atomic Energy
Commission, Building Research Laboratories, Transport Studies
Cell, Institute of Hydrocarbons, Institute of Brain Research,
Social Sciences Research Centre, Manpower Commission, and Family
Planning, etc. Almost every day there are national and
international conferences being held, regurgitating familiar
clichés. These are the manifestations of development, yet these
institutions imitate Western organizational models. They imitate
the form but seldom the purpose of their Western prototypes. They
create jobs and expand the opportunities for administrators and
professionals, but they produce little social utility. They are
hollow institutions. An example may illustrate this point. Scientific research institutes have been established with great pride
to assist in the economic and social development. Such agencies
employ literally legions of officers and directors and spend
lavishly on their training abroad. Yet none of the enduring problems of Pakistan, be they low cost housing or prospecting for
minerals, has been adequately examined by these institutions.
Science remains a prestige symbol of modernity, and not an instrument of problem solving. This is another example of the hollowness
of the new imitative institutions. Foreign aid particularly
contributes to the development of such institutions.

SOCIAL RELATIONS OF PRODUCTION AND CONSUMPTION

Economic development enhances productive capacities of a
society, introduces new technologies, alters consumption patterns,
and affects the relative statuses of its constituent groups. Such
changes take place irrespective of whether they are desired or
not. The sociological questions thus are: whose opportunities are
enhanced, and at whose cost, and what organizational changes are
thus initiated? These questions have come to be of primary concern
in planning.

In Pakistan, a modern bureaucratic mode has been emphasized
as the organizational framework for development. Instead of
upgrading and modernizing family workshops and artisans' coopera-
tives, packaged industrial plants were installed by public or private limited companies. Along with technology, the organizational
form has also been copied out of the European textbooks. Yet, in a
poor and familistic society, the preconditions for its functioning
do not exist. Thus the so-called modern organization becomes the
job bank and service agency for the educated, the capitalists, the
fixers, and the wheeler-dealers.

On the consumption side also, new goods and services have
been delivered in forms that only the privileged and resourceful
can make use of. Hospitals where medicines are to be bought,
doctors to be bribed, and patients to be cared for by relatives,
are obviously not for the poor. Similarly, the dropout rate of
50-60 percent in primary schools speaks for the irrelevance of
this elementary service for the poor in its present form. It must
be understood that the mere availability of goods and services
does not necessarily mean that general welfare is being enhanced.
How and to whom these are being made available is the crucial
issue. In all these respects, the middle and upper classes have
benefited to the detriment of the poor. Economic development has
turned out to be a process of embourgeoisation or, more
appropriately, a process of turning out brown sahibs.

Pakistan's economic and social evolution since Independence
has proceeded along the lines initially set by the British. It
breaks open the traditional symbiotic social structure, separates
the middle and upper classes from the poor masses, and creates a
segregated and privileged life-style for the select few.
Pakistan's social structure and economy have been split into upper
and lower circuits. The development has expanded the upper circuit
at the cost of the lower circuit. This hierarchy exacerbates
regional discord. Cities of the Punjab province and Karachi have
manifestly become the locale of the upper circuit, thereby
highlighting the contrast with the dismal living conditions of
Baluchistan and the interior Sind.

The upper circuit is primarily sustained by the state
apparatus. The civil and military officers constitute the single
most powerful segment of the upper circuit, and they protect their
interest vigorously. The periodic coups in Pakistan are exercises
in preservation of privileges for the upper circuit. The recent

Islamic resurgence among the educated, urban middle class and the army reflects the Weberian situation. The newly rich and powerful are attempting to protect their new status by justifying it as the divine reward.

Social changes occurring in Pakistan have proceeded along three lines: (1) extension of the cash nexus, (2) splitting apart of the customary social structure and disruption of mutual obligations, and (3) privatization of consumption and production. Communal ways of living are being supplanted by contractual privatized modes of operation. Ahmad observes that the effects of land reform and other agricultural development measures have been: "a) to create tenants, artisans, and landless labourers who are linked to their landlords through cash payments that derive from the operation of market forces, rather than through the sharing of a subsistance crop, b) to increase the proportions of labourers who are hired for short periods, as opposed to tenants and artisans having long-term ties to their landlords; and c) to impoverish tenants, artisans and landless labourers and widen the gap between their incomes and those of the more prosperous landlords." [34] Similar trends can be observed in cities in more heightened form.

SUMMARY AND CONCLUSIONS

Pakistan is an ancient land, though it is a new country. It has been continually inhabited for the last 5,000 years. Pakistan's social organization is rooted in historical caste structures, and its agrarian economy has been encased in an intricate division of labour with landlords in command.

Pakistan's four provinces have distinct ethnic-linguistic identities and manifest significant variations of economic production, customs and mores, and social structure; yet they share a common Islamic ethos embodied in Pakistan as a nation. The balance between regional and national interests has always been precarious. Pakistan has been ruled, mostly, by military-bureaucratic cliques who preferred a centralized rule. This preference triggered a cataclysmic separation of Pakistan's eastern half in 1971, and it continues to be a source of regional discontent. Pakistan is politically a very aroused nation. In the 30 years of independence, three entrenched governments have been brought down by popular uprisings. Pakistan has had a chequered political history. It moved from a parliamentary democracy to military rule and guided democracy, another military rule, war and military defeat, to five years of Islamic socialism, and back to the military rule.

Economically, Pakistan inherited a traditionalist agrarian economy. Over the period of 32 years, it has undergone modest industrialization and steady, though limited, economic development. Per capita gross income has increased 89 percent in constant prices, the share of the manufacturing sector in the national output has doubled, and public facilities and services have expanded.

Even visually it is evident that there is a proliferation of goods and services, compared to the pre-Independence days. Yet Pakistan remains one of the poorest countries in the world.

Pakistan's economic development has broken the so-called 'cake of tradition'. Yet most of the benefits have gone to the privileged and the powerful. The development has expanded the income opportunities of the engineers, doctors, civil servants, merchants, industrialists, etc., and has provided goods and services which, by and large, serve their demands. The overwhelming majority of people have remained impoverished, and have even been deprived of traditional modes of obligatory support.

Economic development has also brought about extensive institutional changes. The proliferation of public and private corporations, the expansion of the army, multiplication of public agencies, are obvious examples of the post-colonial development. Although these institutions replicate the Western forms, they do not function in the same way. They provide middle class jobs, and produce goods and services that often are inaccessible to the poor. The state takes care of the influential through development, and the poor are left to compete in the market.

The overwhelming majority of Pakistan's population is comprised of peasants, labourers, casual workers, etc. The social cleavages arising from development have thrust the poor into an economy of subsistence. Their transactions have been monetized to a great extent, though not completely, and their traditional rights have eroded.

Economic development has fragmented Pakistan's economic and social structures into broad but interconnected sectors and circuits, the firm versus bazaar sectors on the one hand which are further subdivided in upper and lower circuits. Extensive illicit activities further sharpen this cleavage. The cities are the primary locale of the firm sector, and the effects of development visibly concentrated there. Therefore, in cities, the contrasts between the poor and the affluent are most vivid.

Pakistan is not being transformed into a modern society despite the increasing stock of the so-called modern institutions and artifacts. There are more doctors, yet the health standards are declining; there are more schools, yet the literacy rate has not significantly increased; there are more cars, houses, telephones and factories, but everything is scarce for the growing number of seekers. These are the effects of segmental and imitative development. The irony of the situation is that this form of development reduces the quality of life even for the upper class. The institutional disarray has a feedback effect on the whole system eroding its regularity and dependability. Even the rich cannot live in peace if the garbage is not picked up and the electric supply breaks down every day.

NOTES

1. The emphasis on both economic and social organization is deliberate. This approach called social economics is said to be a branch of applied economics, wherein social issues are analyzed in the context of economic goals, and it also examines social context and consequences of economic behaviour. See Walter Hagenbuch, Social Economics (Cambridge: James Nisbet & Co., 1958), pp. 2–9. Also, see Gary Gappert and Harold M. Rose (eds.), The Social Economy of Cities (Beverly Hills: Sage Publications, 1975), pp. 20–29.

2. Karachi's population estimate reported The Economist Intelligence Unit, Quarterly Economic Review of Pakistan, Bangladesh and Afghanistan. Annual Supplement (London: 1980), p. 6.

3. Hafeez Malik, "Problems of Regionalism in Pakistan," in Pakistan in Transition, ed. Howard Wriggens (Islamabad: University of Islamabad Press, 1975), p. 123.

4. Saleem Qureshi, "Islam and Development: The Zia Regime in Pakistan," World Development 8 (1980): 573.

5. Peter M. Blau, "Introduction: Parallels and Contrasts in Structural Inquiries," in Approaches to the Study of Social Structure, ed. Peter M. Blau (London: The Free Press, 1975), p. 3.

6. One of the most illuminating accounts of the collaboration between the officers and the new industrialists is provided by A. R. Shibli, 22 Khanawaday (Twenty-Two Families) (Lahore: People's Publications, 1972).

7. A. R. Shibli, Pakistan Kay Dahi Khuda (Pakistan's Rural Lords) (Lahore: People's Publications, 1973), pp. 75–77.

8. Hamza Alavi, "The State in Post-Colonial Societies: Pakistan and Bangladesh," in Imperialism and Revolution in South Asia, eds. Kathleen Gough and Hari P. Sharma (New York: Monthly Review Press, 1973), p. 148.

9. Ibid., p. 159.

10. A. Bergan, "Personal Income Distribution and Personal Savings in Pakistan, 1963–64," The Pakistan Development Review (1967): 202–04.

11. Azizur Rahman Khan, "What has been happening to real wages in Pakistan," in Growth and Inequality in Pakistan, eds. Keith Griffin and A. R. Khan (London: MacMillan, 1972), Table 9.1 and p. 243.

12. S. M. Naseem, "Mass Poverty in Pakistan: Some Preliminary Findings," The Pakistan Development Review 12 (1973): 322–325, Table III.

13. Ibid., p. 328.

14. G. B. S. Mujahid, "A Note of Measurement of Poverty and Income Inequalities in Pakistan: Some Observations on Methodology," The Pakistan Development Review 17 (1978): 365–377.

15. Like most discussions of economic conditions, income distributions are also subject to divergent interpretations. Depending on an analyst's political perspective, the same data can

yield signs of hope or forebodings of gloom. The debate about Pakistan income distribution is also not without controversy. Guisinger and Hicks conclude from calculations of Gini coefficients that "income inequality did not deteriorate over the 1963-71 period." Stephen Guisinger and Norma L. Hicks, "Long Term Trends in Income Distribution in Pakistan," World Development 6 (1978): 1272. We are in agreement with their substantive point that 'growth and equality are not necessarily inimical objectives' (p. 1279). Yet the non-deterioration of income distribution in an era of economic growth does not mean that the existing disparities are acceptable on welfare criteria.

16. Mahbub ul Haq, The Poverty Curtain (New York: Columbia University Press, 1976), p. 6.

17. Rashid Amjad, Industrial Concentration and Economic Power in Pakistan (Lahore: South Asian Institute, University of the Punjab, 1974), p. 70.

18. Ibid., pp. 56-57.

19. As mentioned above (7), a very illuminating account is given by A. R. Shibli.

20. M. Ayub Khan, Friends Not Masters (New York: Oxford University Press, 1967), p. 87.

21. Angus Maddison, Class Structure and Economic Growth (London: George Allen and Unwin, 1971), p. 137.

22. The Economist Intelligence Unit, Quarterly Economic Review of Pakistan, Bangladesh and Afghanistan. Annual Supplement, 1980, p. 6.

23. G. Papanek, Pakistan's Development: Social Goals and Private Incentives (Cambridge: Harvard University Press, 1967), pp. 54-55.

24. Stephen R. Lewis, Jr., Economic Policy and Industrial Growth in Pakistan (London: George Allen & Unwin, 1969).

25. Stephen E. Guisinger, "Patterns of Industrial Growth in Pakistan," The Pakistan Development Review 15 (1976): 14.

26. Warren C. Robinson and Nasreen Abbasi, "Underemployment in Pakistan," The Pakistan Development Review 18 (1979): 329.

27. Stephen Guisinger and Mohammad Irfan, "Pakistan's Informal Sector," Journal of Development Studies 16 (1980): 413.

28. Ibid., p. 413.

29. Pakistan Times, Lahore, February 18, 1981, p. 3.

30. Viewpoint, Lahore, July 31, 1980, p. 14.

31. Mohammad A. Qadeer, An Evaluation of the Integrated Rural Development Programme (Islamabad: Pakistan Institute of Development Economics, 1977), p. 62.

32. Ibid., p. 72.

33. Gunnar Myrdal, Asian Drama, Vol. II (New York: Pantheon, 1968), p. 1367.

34. Saghir Ahmad, "Peasant Classes in Pakistan," in Imperialism and Revolution in South Asia, eds. Kathleen Gough and Hari P. Sharma (New York: Monthly Review Press, 1973), pp. 207-208.

4
LAHORE: GROWTH AND CHANGE

Lahore is an historic city. It has a recorded history of about 1,000 years, though references to its existence can be traced to antiquity. Yet what it has become in the past 30 years makes it almost a new city. It is new in the sense that it has undergone a metamorphosis physically as well as socially. It has grown from a somnolent provincial capital of half a million people in 1947 to a bustling metropolis of almost 3 million by 1981; from a city known for its gardens, literary salons, fairs and festivals, to a place of shopping plazas, noisy traffic and sprawling suburbs. Only three decades ago, it was a cohesive community where poverty, though pervasive, was tempered by familistic bonds and caste obligations. Today it is a conglomeration of fissured neighbourhoods, wealthy suburbs and squatter clusters. This transformation has taken place essentially under the developmental thrust that has accelerated since Independence. In this chapter, the main sequence of this transformation will be described as evident from the patterns of demographic and physical growth; the two significant indices of urban development. The material is organized in the chronological order of historical periods.

HISTORY

Cities are like trees, they may add new branches, shed old limbs and burst into new forms, but they remain attached to their roots. Lahore may have undergone a metamorphosis but its character has been shaped by its history. Historically, the city dates back to the year 990 A.D. [1] though there are allusions to its existence in the documents of the second century A.D. and in Hindu legends of the pre-Christian era [2]. Lahore may have originated in antiquity, but its evolution has been determined essentially by nine centuries of Muslim rule in India. It is an Islamic city both physically and culturally [3]. This is not to suggest that only Muslims have lived in it or even ruled it. It is only that the Islamic Turko-Iranian ethos had a dominant influence in the evolution of the city. The Walled City is the historical core of

70

Lahore. Its labyrinthian streets, clan quarters, congregational squares, bustling bazaars, turquoise mosques, imposing walls, gates and ramparts are living testimony to its Islamic heritage. Lahore always was the seat of Punjab suzerainty as long as an emperor was reigning in Delhi but, at the first sign of a decline of imperial authority, Lahore would become the capital of a transitory sovereign state. Thus, one way or the other, it has remained the centre of northwestern India and, now, Pakistan.

The Muslim Rule

Nine centuries of Muslim rule in India encompassed nine different imperial dynasties. Each succeeded the other by conquest and was in turn conquered by new invaders from central Asia. As the major city on the road to Delhi from the northwest, Lahore was the first prize for every invader. Thus its fortunes ebbed and flowed with these dynastic changes. Each conquerer initially brought death and destruction to the city but, as his rule took hold, Lahore regained its status and prosperity. Of all the rulers, the Moguls (1526-1729 A.D.) have had the most significant influence on the development of Lahore [4]. They made Lahore almost the second capital of India. It became a royal residence where Mogul emperors spent some time every year. They built mosques, gardens, palaces and held court. The city walls were built in 1584-1598 by Emperor Akbar and his successor, Emperor Jehangir, is buried here. The famous Shalimar garden was built by Shah Jehan in 1642, and the Badshahi Mosque (1673) was Aurengzeb's legacy to the city. These monuments have survived to the present day and are a source of Lahore's distinction as a city of gardens. Moguls not only bestowed an enduring architectural heritage on the city, but also laid the bases for its social organization.

Mogul social order was based on a military-administrative hierarchy wherein nobles were appointed as local vassals responsible for providing a prescribed number of soldiers to the imperial army, collecting revenue and administering an area. This social order resembled European feudalism. The Mogul urban social order was similarly based on territorial-communal principles. Cities were divided into quarters or districts, each inhabited by a tribe or clan or a guild fraternity under the patronage of a noble family. These neighbourhoods were villages of a kind wherein rich and poor were knit together through customary obligations and privileges. There were also commercial districts and market bazaars specializing in commodities such as jewels and spices. Lahore was also organized along these lines.

Within the walls of Lahore there were, originally, nine such quarters and, according to an estimate, 27 quarters of varying sizes constituted suburbs towards the east-southeast of the city [5]. The genesis of these quarters can be deduced from names of streets and neighbourhoods that are still current in the Walled City. Such expressive names as the neighbourhood of "the manor of

Kabli Mal," or street names such as "Street of arrow-makers" or "Bazaar of bow carvers," or the "Street of Bila the pigeon keeper" are obviously suggestive of the social origin of these areas. The suburban quarters were essentially summer gardens of the nobility which were not so substantial to outlast the collapse of the Mogul Empire.

The Colonial Period (1849-1947)

While Moguls laid the physical and social framework of Lahore, the British brought it into modern times. With the defeat of the Sikhs, who ruled Punjab for about a century after the Moguls, the province was incorporated into British India (1849). Lahore once again became the seat of the provincial government and the headquarters of the northern military garrison. Thus began an era of systematic exposure to Western influences that continues unabated. The British literally built a new town for themselves towards the south and southeast of the Walled City. This became known as the Civil Lines, though now it is the core of the city. It was built as the locus of British civilian administrators. Here were the offices, homes, clubs and shops comprising the total living environment of the British officers. In time the Indian officials and professionals also began to live in this area.

A wide, tree-lined boulevard known as the Mall became the spine of the Civil Lines. It was called the cool road by the Lahoris because of its spaciousness and greenery. Along this spine were built most of the new buildings of the British administration: the Governor's House (1849), the High Court (1889), Central Telegraph office (1880), the University Hall (1876), the General Post Office (1912). These buildings are not only monuments commemorating the rule of a new dynasty, but also symbols of social institutions and practices that came with the British. The British government also built railways, introduced public transport, established schools, hospitals and other appurtenances of modern life. In the 1860s the British built a cantonment for troops at a distance of five miles from the Civil Lines. All these modern measures and practices altered the face of Lahore. It became three towns in one.

A new idiom of the good life was introduced in Lahore. The bungalow, the flush toilet, wide roads, the club and the cricket ground became the necessities of life. Obviously this life-style could only be available to the rich and influential, primarily in the Civil Lines. In the old city and surrounding villages, where the majority lived, there were few changes. Thus began the process of dualization of life-style and economy that divides the city of the elite from the indigenous town of the masses. It is even evident in the road and traffic patterns. Rudduck, an Australian town planner, remarks that the roads built by the British were designed to "enable Sahibs to drive sedately from office to house or club," [6] and little notice was taken of existing street

patterns and traffic needs creating "a dual and conflicting system
of roads and traffic representing, as it were, two different cultural phases." [7]

Before concluding this historical account, some comments
about the effects of the British colonial rule are in order. The
British conquest represents a watershed in Indian history. It laid
open the Indian subcontinent to Western influences. Through the
British raj many beneficial modern practices and institutions were
introduced in colonial India: public health and sanitation, roads
and railways, etc. These innovations profoundly altered the Indian
society and accelerated the pace of social change. Yet these
institutions and facilities remained the prerogative of the gentry
who actively cooperated with the British. For the majority of
Indians, the changes seeped down so slowly that they could hardly
be observed. The British transformed the life of a small ruling
elite, and turned them into an island of modernity in a sea of
tradition and poverty.

Whether India would have modernized without British rule is a
question only for speculation. If Turkey, Iran and Saudi Arabia
are any examples, then obviously Western technology and institutions sooner or later are diffused in countries which were not
directly colonized. Yet it is not necessary that the adoption of
modern technology should bring about a recapitulation of Western
social structures. As much as Lahore provides any evidence, the
grafting of modern ways over a traditional economy and society
sets in train processes of social fragmentation and dualization.
In a later chapter, the dynamics of these processes will be discussed at length; at this point it is enough to identify their
origins.

After Independence (1947–   )

With the partition of British India into the independent
states of India and Pakistan in 1947, Lahore underwent another
historic convulsion. Hindus and Sikhs, about 40 percent of the
city's population, migrated to India and a proportionate number of
Muslims came from India as refugees. This massive turnover of the
population jolted the social cohesiveness and cultural homogeneity
of the city. People of unfamiliar dialects and different tongues
settled in Lahore. Although the Muslim refugees took over houses
and businesses left by Hindus and Sikhs, they did not entirely
recreate the social and economic life of pre-Independence Lahore.
Hindus had dominated the wholesale trade, large-scale industry and
white-collar professions, and their departure left a vacuum in
these sectors. Furthermore, Lahore became a border city (the
Indo-Pakistan border is only 20 miles away) and this situation
engendered a feeling of insecurity in the early years. There was
periodic talk of shifting the capital of Punjab Province from
Lahore to another city inland. All these factors inhibited the
development of Lahore for almost a decade after Independence

(1947). Gradually the uncertainties and disruptions engendered by Independence were overcome. Its position as the provincial capital remained unaltered, even during the 1954–69 period when four provinces were merged into a single province of West Pakistan. By the late 1950s, Lahore had begun to attract industries and economic activity picked up, whereas its historical role as the administrative and commercial capital of the Punjab was never lost.

POPULATION GROWTH

Lahore has grown almost 14 times in size since the beginning of the twentieth century. From a population of 202,964 in 1901, it grew to a population of 2,920,000 in 1981. These census figures generally underestimate populations, due to enumeration difficulties [8]. Not only has Lahore become a metropolis with a multimillion population, but its rate of growth has been accelerating (Table 4.1). With the exception of the 1941–51 decade, the annual rate of population growth has been steadily increasing [9].

TABLE 4.1

Population Growth

Year	Population	Yearly Rate of Growth (percentage)
1901	202,964	
1911	228,687	1.3
1921	281,781	2.3
1931	429,747	5.3
1941	671,659	5.6
1951	849,333	2.6
1961	1,296,477	5.3
1972	2,165,372	6.1

Source: Pakistan Statistical Year Book 1977 (Karachi: Statistics Division, Government of Pakistan, 1978).

The population of Pakistan grew at rates of 1.8, 2.4 and 3.6 percent respectively for the decades 1941–51, 1951–61, and 1961–72 [10]. These two sets of figures suggest that Lahore's population has been increasing at almost twice the rate of Pakistan's population. Population forecasts of Lahore have been prepared by three different methods (see Appendix A of the chapter), and the medium projections suggest that Lahore is likely to have a population of about 3 million in 1981, and 5 million by 1990, and about 8 million by 2,001. These are undoubtedly staggering prospects. They vividly portray not only what is going to happen to the city, but what has been happening: a population almost doubling every decade. With an overwhelming majority of the population newly born, the historic components of city life will be less and less significant. There was never a Lahore as big and burgeoning as now, and it is becoming bigger every day.

Lahore in the National Urban System

In the urban system of Pakistan, Lahore ranks second among cities and towns (see Appendix B). It was the biggest city of the area now constituting Pakistan until 1947. After Independence, Karachi was designated as the first capital of Pakistan, and much of the new commercial and industrial activity gravitated to it making it the top ranking city. Karachi and Lahore are the two primate cities that stand at the apex of Pakistan's urban hier-archy, and they are a class apart. Cities of third and lower ranks are proportionately much smaller than these two [11]. Yet the rank order (not ratios of sizes) of Pakistan's urban system has remained remarkably stable since the beginning of the twentieth century. The Spearman rank correlation coefficients for consecu-tive decades are 0.8 or above, and statistically significant (see Appendix B).

This relative stability of the rank order of Pakistan's cities is an indication that they have grown in tandem, despite the domination by Karachi and Lahore. Pakistan's cities and towns may not conform to rank size rules but they manifest a significant continuity in relative positions [12]. This characteristic sug-gests that Lahore attained a preeminent position in the urban system early, and has retained it for three decades.

Does this mean that the city has pulled in large numbers of rural migrants, as is often thought to be the case of Third World cities? To answer this question, factors contributing to popula-tion growth will be analyzed.

Population Composition

Lahore's population is a reasonable replica of the national population in terms of age and sex distributions.

Pakistan, like many other Third World countries, has a high sex ratio (more males per 100 females) and a large proportion (43 percent or so) of population in younger age groups (Table 4.2 and Figure 4.1). More males per 100 females in Pakistan is attributed to underenumeration of females and relatively higher mortality rates of females due to childbirth and sexist values [13]. Sex ratios for Lahore were four to six percentage points higher than those of Pakistan, yet Lahore's population seems to be moving

close to Pakistan's norm of the sex ratio, as evidenced in a convergence trend for 1972. Pakistan and Lahore were very close in
terms of proportions of children in their populations (Figure
4.1). This comparison of the two populations is meant to point out
that Lahore's demographic characteristics recapitulate most of the
national features and the city is, thus, a representative of
societal trends. This conclusion has a bearing on the question of
whether Lahore is growing primarily by natural increase or largely
by in-migration from rural areas.

TABLE 4.2

Age and Sex Distribution

	Sex Ratio		Population Below 15 Years of Age (percentage)	
	Pakistan	Lahore	Pakistan	Lahore
1961	115	126	42.4	42.1
1972	114	119	42.9	42.7

Source: Population Census of Pakistan, District Census Reports,
          Lahore, 1961 and 1972.

Fertility and Mortality

Pakistan's crude birth rate was estimated to be 44 per thousand and death rate 15 per thousand for the period 1970-75 [14].
The crude death rate has been declining since the beginning of the
twentieth century, and fell more precipitously in the period
1950-60 [15]. Control of epidemics started the downward trend in
death rates, which was accelerated by the dissemination of modern
medical practices. Pakistan's crude birth rate has shown little,
if any, decline. More refined measures of fertility, such as Total
Fertility Rate (births per woman) or Age Specific Fertility Rate
(births per woman of reproductive age) have also remained relatively stable. A study of rural-urban fertility differential has
revealed a startling pattern, in that "the Total Marital Fertility
Rate was slightly higher in urban areas than in rural areas." [16]
Furthermore, younger women in urban areas are reproducing at
higher rates than their counterparts in rural areas [17]. This
finding is contrary to the normal expectation that urban areas
would manifest lower fertility rates. There seems to be no difference in age of marriage and in the number of children born to
females in Lahore and Karachi on the one hand, and a rural dis-

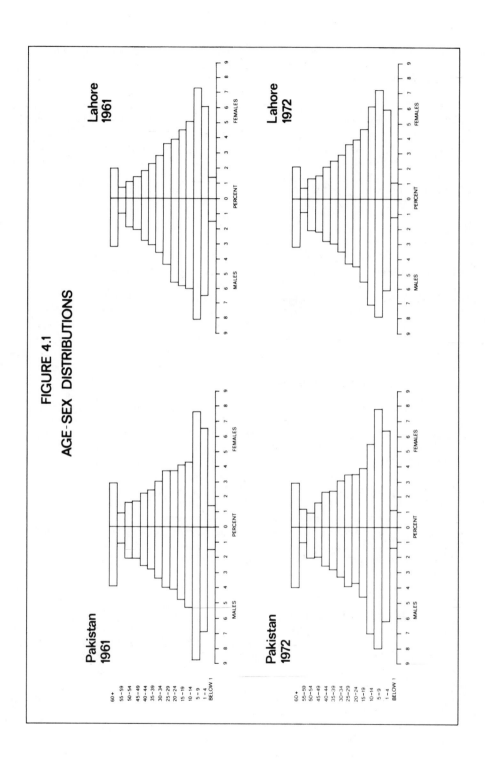

FIGURE 4.1
AGE-SEX DISTRIBUTIONS

trict on the other [18]. With fertility in cities being the same
as in rural parts of Pakistan, and mortality slightly lower [19],
it is likely that the rate of natural growth of population in
cities like Lahore will be higher than the country as a whole.
These observations suggest two conclusions. One, that Pakistani
cities are not manifesting demographic trends that are normally
associated with urbanism. Second, the foregoing observations cast
doubt on the notion that Third World cities grow primarily by
attracting rural immigrants. This question calls for an examination of relative contributions of in-migration and natural
increase to the growth of the population in Lahore.

Natural Increase versus In-Migration

During the period 1961-72, Lahore's population grew by
873,265 persons. During the same period (11.7 years), the population of Pakistan increased at the geometric rate of 3.6 percent,
predominantly through natural increase [20]. Applying this rate to
Lahore's 1961 population, it is estimated that Lahore would have
had a population of 1,960,983 by the time of the 1972 census, if
there had been no migration [21]. On subtracting the estimated
population from the population reported in the 1972 census
(2,165,372), the difference thus obtained (204,389) can be
attributed to the in-migration.

The foregoing calculations suggest that migration has played
a significant but not primary role in the growth of Lahore's population. This observation is in line with Helbock's findings about
Lahore being a moderately growing city, with only 13.2 percent of
population in 1961 being migrants from other parts of
Pakistan [22]. To confirm further the conclusion about the moderate contribution of migration to Lahore's growth, a complicated
statistical test on 1961 and 1972 census data was carried out.
Details of this test are given in Appendix C of this chapter. This
test, the "shift-share analysis," essentially decomposes the
increments of decennial populations into growth versus movement
factors. As Appendix C indicates, the test confirms that in-migration had a significantly small contribution to the increase of
Lahore's population for the two periods.

The analysis of census data on mobility further affirms and
illuminates this conclusion.

It is evident from this table that refugees from India who
came in 1947 were the only sizeable group which were not born in
Lahore. It is very revealing to note that between 1961 and 1973,
the proportion of Lahore's population born in the city increased
by almost 12 percent and, correspondingly, the proportion of
people born in India and in the rest of the province declined.
This finding implies that the local born population was increasing
at a higher rate than those born elsewhere.

Lahore has maintained a consistent pattern of growth: a large
proportion of the increase from natural increase, and about 25-30

percent of the population increase contributed by in-migration. All in all, it is an important finding because it contradicts a popular assumption that Third World cities are bursting at the seams because of the flood of rural poor [23]. Lahore, at least, does not uphold this assumption, and it may turn out to be the case for other cities if a similar analysis is carried out.

TABLE 4.3

Place of Birth

Lahore's Population	Lahore City	Rest of Punjab Province	India	All Other Places	Total
1961					
Total population	56.9	10.5	28.5	4.1	100%
males	54.9	11.3	29.2	4.6	100%
females	59.5	9.5	27.6	4.4	100%
1973					
Total population	68.3	9.6	16.9	5.2	100%
males	67.1	9.6	17.1	6.2	100%
females	69.8	9.6	16.6	4.0	100%

Sources: 1961:   Population of Pakistan, 1961, District Census Report, Lahore (Karachi: Census Organization, 1965), Table 10, pp. iv-14/iv-5.

1973:   Housing, Economic and Demographic Survey Vol. II, Part III. Statistical Tables Punjab, 1973 (Islamabad: Census Organization, no date), Table 12, pp. 134-137.

PHYSICAL DEVELOPMENT

Two separate local governments constitute the city of Lahore: the Lahore municipality, and the Cantonment. The total area of the city is about 160 square miles [24]. The city occupies a flat plain which is devoid of any natural features that could lend visual and topographical variety to the site. It is an alluvial plain formed by the deposits of the Rivers Ravi and Sutluj and their tributaries. The Ravi River flows along the northwestern boundary of the city, and its seasonal floods have inhibited the city's growth towards the north and northwest. Climatically, Lahore is in a semiarid zone of searingly hot summers (mean May temperature 102°F) and vigorous winters (mean minimum temperature 45°F), interspersed with monsoon and westerly rains. The city has

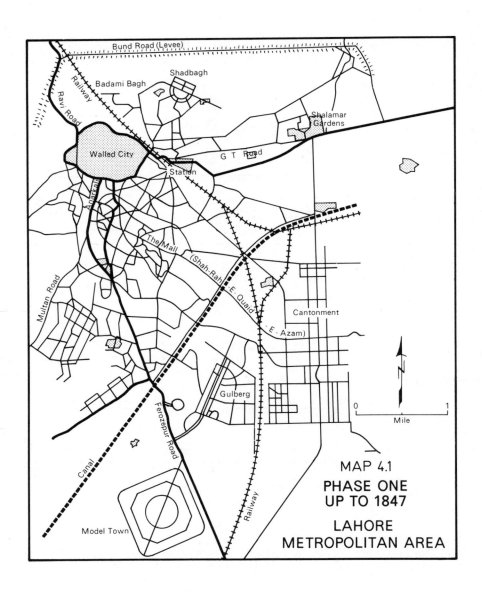

Bund Road (Levee)

Railway

Ravi Road

Badami Bagh

Shadbagh

Shalamar Gardens

Walled City

G T Road

Station

The Mall

(Shah-Rah)

E. Quaid

E. Azam)

Multan Road

Cantonment

Anarkali

Gulberg

Canal

Ferozepur Road

Railway

Model Town

0   1
Mile

N

MAP 4.1
**PHASE ONE
UP TO 1847**

**LAHORE
METROPOLITAN AREA**

been fanning out, historically, towards the east and south-south-east.

Lahore is a city that perhaps can be described more appropriately as a federation of neighbourhoods, markets and special districts, each highly individual in character. Functionally as well as architecturally, these neighbourhoods reflect consecutive historical stages of the city's growth. From a suburban model town to the "Street of well diggers," almost all period pieces continue to thrive in the mosaic called Lahore. To convey a systematic account of the city's growth, a brief sketch of major physical developments will be helpful given in chronological order.

Pre-British City

In the first half of the nineteenth century, Lahore was ruled by Sikhs. It was a period of internecine fights, invasions and economic decline. Most of the Mogul residences and gardens outside the city walls were abandoned when their owners took refuge in the city to be safe from brigands. In 1849, when the British took over Lahore, they acquired a city that had retreated behind its walls. A few villages along the main highways were all that had survived of the Mogul metropolis (Map 4.1).

The architectural idiom of the Walled City is a threestorey house covering 100 percent of its lot, having a flat roof, high walls, screened balconies and, frequently, a light well. Along the main streets, houses have shops at the ground floor. Houses are crammed together along narrow alleys, sometimes so narrow that three persons cannot stand shoulder to shoulder. With the exception of a few market squares, open space is almost nonexistent. Overall density in the Walled City is about 500 persons per acre. Lest it be thought that the Walled City is essentially a residential area, it should be noted that there are numerous historical markets that are beehives of commercial, often wholesale, activities. There are separate markets and bazaars for jewellery, utensils, fabric, blankets, grains, spices and even a district of courtesans.

The Walled City was shaped by the Mogul social system. It evolved as a mosaic of socially cohesive and functionally specialized neighbourhoods. As these neighbourhoods were inhabited primarily by a specific clan or occupational caste, they tended to be specialized in one or the other activity. For example, Rarra was the district of oil-makers and blacksmiths lived in Mochi Gate. Lahore, thus, is not unlike other subcontinental cities which, according to Brush, have "segregation by commodity in business areas, and by socio-economic or religious groups in residential areas" but which lack "a clean cut separation of residential land use from business or industry." [25] This is the city that the British took over with the conquest of Punjab.

British Contributions

On taking over Lahore, the British were confronted with the problem of finding suitable quarters for the Imperial army and civilian officers since the Walled City was unsafe, crowded and unsanitary. They also wanted to be segregated from the local populace. The Civil Lines was their contribution to the physical stock of Lahore. Wide and relatively straight roads, a rectangular layout, freestanding detached houses (called bungalows) surrounded by a lawn, and separation of commercial and residential areas were the distinguishing characteristics of the Civil Lines.

This idiom of urban development was new for the India of those days. It broke with almost a millenium of past sociological and architectural traditions. King calls it the colonial urban settlement [26]. Apart from introducing these new habitational norms, the British built railways, established hospitals, schools, churches, postal and telecommunication systems.

For the Imperial army, a separate town, called the Cantonment, was built at a distance of five miles from the Civil Lines. It anticipated the principles of Garden City planning by almost half a century. With wide tree-lined boulevards, parade grounds and parks, rectangular layout and a functional self-containment, the Cantonment forged another urban form.

These British contributions have laid the path for the development of Lahore (Maps 4.2 and 4.3). The city's street names commemorate memories of British soldiers (Chamberlain) and administrators (Brandeth, Cooper, Cust, Lake, Hall, Nisbet, etc.) [27]. Its architecture is indelibly British colonial, as exemplified by the secretariat, the university, the railway station, etc.

With the development of Civil Lines and Cantonment, the city became almost three towns in one. The old city retained its own native bazaars and neighbourhoods. The Mall road eventually emerged as the axis of the British Civil Lines area. The Cantonment had its own bazaars for the native soldiers and markets for the British officers. Thus, colonial rule led to the emergence of two sociophysical idioms: European and indigenous. These in time have come to differentiate the rich from the poor, and to some extent, the educated from the illiterate.

The insularity of these two sectors began to be breached in the latter part of the British rule (1920-47). The British administration was Indianized, particularly in the lower ranks. Legions of locals became government clerks, accountants, revenue officers, engineers, doctors, lawyers, etc. They constituted the new middle class which served as the bridge between the old and the new social order. They could not be content to live in the crowded and filthy gullies of the old city, but were not affluent enough to afford a Kothi (a bungalow). Their demands prompted the emergence of a new house type and an updated version of indigenous neighbourhoods. The new house was a modern version of the traditional home. These houses were laid in rectangular grids along streets wide enough to accommodate a car or horse drawn carriage. Main streets were wider and lined with shops. This new indigenous urban form found expression in neighbourhoods that sprang up in a broad swath through the Civil Lines area. In these New Indigenous Communities, segregation by religious groups continued to persist. Krishan Nagar, Gowal Mandi, Mohni Road, Ram Nagar, were modern Hindu neighbourhoods, and correspondingly Islamia Park, Faroog Gunj, Garhi Shahu were predominantly Muslim residential areas. It might be noted that while these middle-class communities were seg-regated along religious lines, areas of upper-class bungalows were fairly well integrated.

While Breese, King, Brush and other observers of Indian cities have identified the Walled City, Civil Lines and Cantonment as the three distinct urban forms, they have overlooked the evolu-tion of the New Indigenous Communities as updated versions of the traditional architectural forms [28]. The latter represent a syn-thesis of the functional elements of the indigenous and the European house types and urban forms.

By the time the British relinquished their rule in 1947, Lahore had become a mosaic of urban forms. At least four distinct urban physical idioms could be found: (1) the Walled City, (2) New Indigenous Communities, (3) the Civil Lines, and (4) the Canton-ment. These urban forms continually interplay to produce a myriad of residential patterns. Independence further accelerated the pro-cesses of evolution and integration of these urban idioms.

The Physical Developments Since Independence

By the time Pakistan came into being (1947), Lahore was well on the way to becoming a metropolis, at least in terms of physical infrastructure. The road network was in place. A public water supply system had been laid out. There were schools, hospitals, a local bus service, and a radio broadcasting station. The municipal corporation had been functioning for decades, and a separate public body, the Lahore Improvement Trust (LIT) was in existence for city planning and development. All in all, the physical and institutional bases of a modern civic order had been laid.

Immediately after Independence, resettlement of Muslim refugees from India became the urgent task. Almost half of the city had been vacated by Hindus and Sikhs, and their homes and businesses were available for distribution among refugees. It took about five years to complete the initial phase of resettlement. New construction started after the stock of the evacuee property was used up. The LIT initiated schemes for the development of sub-urban subdivisions, and thus stimulated the process of the city's expansion. Two of these early development schemes, Samanabad and Gulberg, were located towards the south and southeast of the city, and they defined the direction of its future growth. Another LIT subdivision, ShadBagh, was located to the north of the city (an area subject to floods), but it did not stimulate the same base of

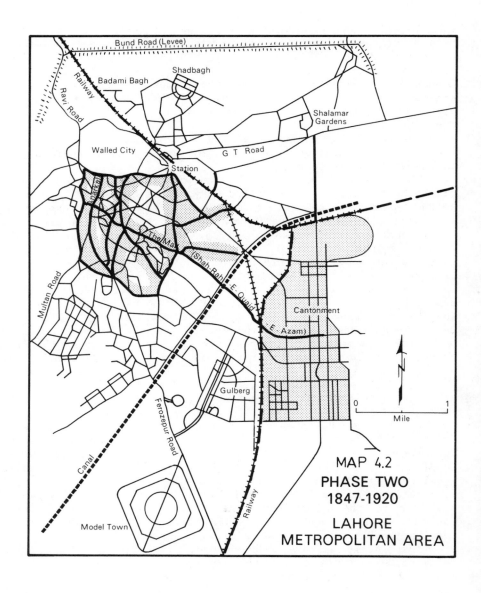

Bund Road (Levee)

Railway

Ravi Road

Badami Bagh

Shadbagh

Shalamar Gardens

Walled City

G T Road

Station

The Mal(Shah-Rah E. Quaid

Multan Road

E. Azam)

Cantonment

Gulberg

Ferozepur Road

Canal

Railway

Model Town

MAP 4.2
PHASE TWO
1847-1920

LAHORE
METROPOLITAN AREA

N

0   1
Mile

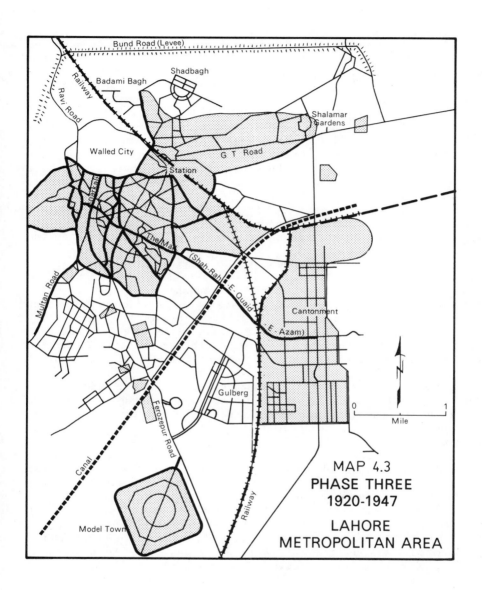

Bund Road (Levee)

Railway

Ravi Road

Badami Bagh

Shadbagh

Shalamar Gardens

Walled City

G T Road

Station

The Mall

Multan Road

(Shah-Rah-E- Quaid

E Azam)

Cantonment

Gulberg

Ferozepur Road

Canal

Railway

Model Town

0   1
Mile

N

MAP 4.3
PHASE THREE
1920-1947

LAHORE
METROPOLITAN AREA

development as those to the south.

By 1980, the LIT and its successor, Lahore Development Authority (LDA), had started 58 land development projects. Some were small commercial relocation projects, such as a new fruit and vegetable market; others were large suburban development schemes sited over 1,000 to 1,500 acres, and meant to promote multifunctional communities, e.g., Gulberg, Iqbal Town, etc. All in all, up to 1979, the public bodies had developed 38,844 residential lots, averaging about 1,214 lots per year [29], whereas, according to the LDA's own estimates, about 60,000 housing lots per year were required to meet the city's housing needs [30]. Obviously, public efforts fell far short of the people's needs. Furthermore, the LIT (and later LDA) concentrated on developing lots for bungalows, and thus catered to the demands of the rich and the influential, leaving the overwhelming majority of the population to the vagaries of the market. Yet these schemes profoundly affected the development of Lahore.

The LIT's land development schemes defined the lines of the city's development. To serve these areas, new water storage towers, electric grids and telephone exchanges were built, which often meant that the surrounding areas could also be serviced. Thus, these schemes became the magnetic poles attracting development. Another impact of these schemes was in setting norms of good living. A bungalow became synonymous with decent living and, for each one who realized this dream, the expectations of thousands of others were raised.

Lest it be assumed that planned schemes were the main instruments of Lahore's development, it must be stated that massive additions to the city's housing stock occurred through private, unplanned and often unapproved and unregistered home building. People have individually built homes, carved out streets, cajoled and bribed officials to extend them electricity, water and other community services. The cumulative result of these individual incremental effects has appeared in the form of vast neighbourhoods of new indigenous mode.

These neighbourhoods have appeared on tracts of land left over by the expanding city. Contrary to Western practice, the public agencies leapfrog to virgin lands in the periphery, and the private builders do the infilling. This has been the pattern in Lahore. For example, in developing Samnabad, the LIT bypassed vacant land closer to the city, which has been gradually built up into the communities of Rasool Park and Naya Mozang. Similar back tracking and infilling has occurred throughout the city. For example, Begumpura, Sultan Pura, Habibullah Road, Ghari Shahu, are other such neighbourhoods which have grown in the interstices of the Civil Lines. By and large the poor could not find shelter even in these areas. They had to resort to their own devices.

After Independence, squatter clusters, locally called Katchi Abadi, have become numerous and visible to the point that they now constitute a distinct mode of habitation. Here live the poor, the unsettled refugees and recently, the migrants from rural areas [31]. Katchi Abadis or squatter communities are clusters of one- to two-room mud or thatched houses erected on lands of uncertain titles. The term Katchi in the local vernacular means impermanent or easily dissolvable, and it epitomizes their legal status. Yet, over time, these clusters have become almost as permanent as any other new neighbourhoods. Not only the old Katchi Abadis have gradually become permanent, but new ones continue to emerge as house rents and prices keep on rising. According to estimates prepared in 1964, there were about 30,000 people living in squatters' clusters, but by 1979 the number of clusters had increased to 133, accommodating about 700,000 persons [32].

Before 1947, it was not uncommon to find mud houses in Lahore. There was a form of compound house where small one-room shacks were lined around a small yard, serviced by common latrines and a well or stand pipe. Such houses were called Ahatas, literally meaning enclosure, and were essentially built by enterprising landlords for renting to transient labourers and workers in small craft shops. In one sense, Katchi Abadis have replaced Ahatas. The homeless build shacks on public or disputed lands, often without any formal lay-out. Over time, squatters' clusters are improved, as residents gain some modicum of prosperity and status. By the time a second generation grows up in a Katchi Abadi, it is beginning to look like any other working class neighbourhood.

The industrial expansion stimulated demand for workers' housing in Lahore. As housing shortages increased and prices escalated, more and more labourers and workers were left no choice but to band together to build and retain flimsy shacks. Periodic demolition raids by the authorities and denials of basic community services, aroused Katchi Abadi residents into agitation and protests. Belatedly, the government took notice of this situation, and a few low-income housing projects were initiated. The largest of these projects was started in 1962, and is a satellite town called Lahore Township towards the southeast of the city at a distance of about 15 miles from the city. Lahore Township was planned as a self-contained industrial workers' community on a 3,000 acre site meant to provide 10,000 low income houses (locally called quarters). A number of self-help community improvement projects were also carried out. Yet there was such a backlog of unmet housing needs that these projects served the relatively more affluent among the workers. Katchi Abadis kept on expanding, despite these efforts.

As Ayub's regime was brought down by urban protests in which the poor played a significant part, Bhutto's government (1971-77) was more tuned to the rumblings of Katchi Abadis. It encouraged residents to establish cooperative societies and inhibited police excesses that often took the form of 'raid and raze' Katchi Abadis. In 1973, the provincial government passed a law establishing ceiling prices for land acquired for housing schemes. In Lahore, a People's Planning Project was launched to assist residents of Katchi Abadis in identifying their needs, and in pre-

paring plans for neighbourhood improvement. The LDA and the Provincial Housing Ministry were required to institute improvements
proposed by the People's Planning Project.

These measures brought a sense of stability and a feeling of
self-confidence in Katchi Abadis [33]. Although there were some
rudimentary improvements in the provisions of public services, the
most noteworthy achievement of this period was the public acceptance of the need to give land titles to squatters. With Bhutto's
downfall, the political mood took another turn and the People's
Planning Project was disbanded. Yet, Katchi Abadis had become too
potent a political force to be overlooked. The task of regular-
izing and improving Katchi Abadis has been assigned to the LDA
which has established a separate directorate for developing
Katchi Abadis. By 1980, 32 abadis (clusters) were said to have
been provided with public water, electricity and paved streets, at
a cost of about Rs. 132 million over a three-year period [34].

Commercial Areas

Lahore is a city whose various sections not only were
developed in different time periods, but were also meant to be
self-contained to serve disparate social groups, economic functions, and technologies. To appreciate this process of parallel
but not hierarchical commercial development in various sections of
the city, a description of distinguishable sections of the city
will be helpful.

Almost everywhere in the Walled City, main thoroughfares are
lined with shops offering daily merchandise. At the next level are
commodity markets (Mandis) and bazaars: the jewellers bazaar; the
grain market; the copperware bazaar; and there is even a bazaar
for "Lambs' Heads and Feet". These are specialized markets that
serve the whole city and not just the Walled City. These are areas
of specialized commercial land uses, but their specialization lies
in commodities, and not in activities. This commercial structure
dates back to pre-British days, and it reflects a real segregation
of occupational clans and other cohesive social structures.

The British introduced the practice of separating commercial
areas from homes. This was not only a transplantation of a
European town planning notion, but also an expression of their
rigid, formal and highly differentiated life routines wherein
work, play, home and shopping were compartmentalized. Yet soon a
hybrid form of commercial establishments emerged: local shops
selling imported goods. Anarkali bazaar, that links one of the
gates of the Walled City to the western end of the Mall, became
the centre of this modernized indigenous commercial activity and,
to this day, it remains a thriving and glittering commercial area.
If one were to designate one focal point of the city, probably the
junction of Anarkali and the Mall would be the most appropriate.

Since Independence (1947), Lahore has experienced an accelerating tempo of commercial development. This is the result of

expanding population and consequently demand, but also a property boom has hit the city, inducing a large scale conversion of old bungalows and houses to shops, and commercial centres. The development of commercial properties has proceeded with, as well as without, public consent. Public bodies responsible for the development of the city, the LDA, Municipal Corporation, and the Cantonment Board, have developed commercial zones in the new housing schemes. The liberty market in Gulberg has become the centre of the modern sector of the city, where Van Heusen shirts or Sony video games are sold. Similar commercial areas have been developed in other schemes. What is to be noted is that these developments are differentiated by quality of goods, modes of operation and clientele. They have been planned as replicas of British shopping arcades, and the North American commercial centres. These are the official developments.

The unofficial commercial development constitutes the bulk of new shops built in Lahore since Independence. In this category fall two forms of commercial properties. First, most of the large bungalows along main roads in Civil Lines, and even in new housing estates, have been converted to showrooms, restaurants, offices and shopping plazas. These conversions proceeded incrementally and essentially in defiance of the city's zoning bylaws. Second, the vast mazes of shopping streets, bazaars and hawkers' sheds that have sprung up in the New Indigenous Communities. These shopping areas contain retail establishments of neighbourhood and convenience store types. These developments almost remain unnoticed by the public agencies, not to speak of approval and planning. Not infrequently they are built over sidewalks and open spaces thus constituting what locally are known as encroachments.

Industrial Development

Lahore's industrial activity manifests the same variety of modes of operation and locations as its residential and commercial land uses. The Walled City has craft shops and small manufacturing establishments at locations that go back to pre-British days. Usually these establishments are interspersed in residential areas, though there are some historic clusters of bangle-makers, copper and wood workers, binders and packagers, and furniture makers in close proximity to relevant markets and bazaars.

The British did not encourage the industrialization of Punjab in any systematic way. Yet the building of railways, roads and other public works fostered small scale milling, lathing and molding workshops at the outskirts of the Walled City near the railway station. Another industrial concentration emerged in the Badami Bagh area to the north of the Walled City. The railway engineering works (1918) also became a major manufacturing employer in the city.

Since 1947, Lahore has become a major industrial node of the country. Factories manufacturing bicycles, textiles, rayon,

fertilizer, chemicals, pharmaceuticals, have located along the
main highways radiating out of the city. The LIT developed an
industrial estate in Gulberg, and the provincial Ministry of
Industries has planned zones of small industries. In the industrial sector, two parallel processes of development are evident.
International and national corporations have been officially
encouraged to establish plants, and much of the public effort has
been addressed to this sector. At the same time, craft shops,
small workshops and backyard manufacturing units have sprung up
throughout the city, often without public approval. So much so,
that some illicit manufacturing operations are reported as being
carried out in the rented bungalows of Gulberg, Samnabad and other
high class residential areas. The overall outcome of the ongoing
industrial development is that there are five concentrations of
heavy industry, and a high degree of intermixing of industries,
shops and houses in most parts of the city.

Company Housing

No account of Lahore's physical development can be complete
without mention of houses built by public agencies and private
corporations for accommodating their employees. Numerically these
houses would constitute a significant proportion of the standard
housing stock. Much more important is their demonstration effect.
They symbolize the exclusivity and the privilege that an appointment in these agencies can bring. The beginning of company housing
estates goes back to the early days of the British raj. The
English officers on a tour of duty had to be provided with accommodation and other accoutrements of the British gentry: clubs,
orderlies, etc. This necessity led to the development of government officers' residences (GOR estates) and Mayo Gardens (railway
officers' estates). These two estates are still the most
salubrious residential areas of Lahore. Palatial houses, acres of
lawns, tall trees, immaculately maintained roads and streets, the
awe of exclusivity combined to make them the most coveted
addresses.

The practice of providing exclusive housing estates for the
officers has continued after Independence. Since 1947, every major
governmental agency has built or acquired houses for officers.
Recently, universities, research institutes and private corporations have also become major developers of housing estates to
accommodate their staff. For the lower staff, such as supervisors,
clerks and peons, there are also some company-provided houses.
Railways are the most generous in this respect, followed by the
post office, provincial secretariat and public corporations.
Houses of the lower staff are known as quarters, a term suggesting
the spartan accommodation of the foot soldiers. These quarter
estates are of varying standards, some are two- to three-bedroom,
single-storey detached houses, and others are clusters of the
one-room and courtyard variety. Obviously these quarters are

allotted according to the rank of the staff member. Recently, three- to four-storey walk-up apartment buildings are being built for the lower staff. Locationally, company houses used to be clustered in the railway colony near the station, and in parts of the Civil Line area. After Independence, the proliferation of public agencies and their uncoordinated way of providing houses have resulted in the emergence of company housing clusters almost all over the city.

Reprise of Physical Development

The foregoing account of Lahore's development portrays a city throbbing with activity and energy. Although the organized development activity was limited in scope, the sheer weight of the pressing needs impelled people to take matters in their hands, irrespective of discouragements posed by shortages of serviced land, unavailability of facilities, and obstructive bureaucracies. People have individually bought, bribed, blustered and even begged for themselves, homes, shops and shelters. The cumulative result of these exertions is an explosive growth of the city. Over the last 30 years the population has approximately quadrupled, numbers of houses approximately tripled, the areal expanse has doubled, if not more. These are manifestations not only of the expansion, but also of the development of the city in that it has been transformed economically, physically and socially.

Lahore's physical growth has proceeded in periodic waves of leaping out and filling in. The River Ravi on the west and north, and the Indian border to the east have inhibited the expansion of the city in these directions. Lahore has expanded along south-southeastern axes, though lately the low income communities have begun developing even to the north and east. This outward thrust has been paralleled by filling in of vacant lands and open spaces in developed areas. Lahore's development has taken the form of three distinct physical idioms or patterns: (1) Planned Housing Estates and multi-functional townships and suburbs, (2) New Indigenous Communities, and (3) Katchi Abadis or squatter clusters. Add to these three community development idioms the Walled City and Civil Lines and Cantonment, ahatas and quarters of workers, and the city's kaleidoscopic form becomes evident. The city is a federation of functionally, socially and physically disparate communities. Within a few hundred yards one can pass from a village setting of mud huts and buffalos to an air conditioned shopping plaza reminiscent of the North American suburbs. Various functional and architectural idioms have evolved in tandem. It is a city where spatial specialization is not by activity or function, but by commodity and clientele. Land uses are generally mixed and segregation of activities does not survive too long intact, despite the best intentions of town planners.

The city has evolved physically by a dialectical interplay of indigenous and Western modes of living. It has also developed

under two distinct sets of influences: official and unofficial.
The official mode of development tends to be the modern corporate
idiom that serves the educated and the influential. The unofficial
entrepreneurship is in individualistic, indigenous and revivalist
modes that cater to the needs of middle and low income segments of
the population and of the merchant class.

How has all this development affected the quality of life in
Lahore? To answer this question, the two indices of physical
improvement, housing trends and community services, will be
examined.

HOUSING CONDITIONS

The massive physical development described in the preceding
section essentially was an expression of people's struggle for
shelter. Was there any improvement in housing standards of the
city, or did all the buildings merely keep the status quo? To
answer this question we turn to census housing data which are
available for the decade 1961-72.

TABLE 4.4

Housing Conditions, 1961-73

Structural Conditions	Houses			
	1961		1973	
	Number	Percent-age	Number	Percent-age
Wall Materials				
cement/baked bricks				
(pucca)	171,441	88.3	310,937	90.3
mud/thatch (katcha)	22,735	11.7	33,534	9.7
Total	194,176	100.0	344,471	100.0
Roof Materials				
concrete, baked tiles/				
cement (pucca)	50,597	26.1	121,256	35.2
wood/mud/thatch				
(katcha)	143,579	73.9	223,215	64.8
Total	194,176	100.0	344,471	100.0

Note: Categories reported in this table have been reconstituted
        from wall and roof material data.

Sources: Census of Pakistan, 1961, Lahore District Report, Table

14; Housing (Karachi: Census Organization, no date);
Economic and Demographic Survey 1973, Vol. II, Part III,
Statistical Tables, Punjab, Table 2 (Islamabad: Census
Organization, no date).

A striking fact observable from the table is that almost
150,000 houses were added to the city's housing stock between 1961
and 1973, about a 77 percent increase. This volume of home
building gives an annual rate of about 12,500 new houses per year.
In absolute terms it is an impressive rate of home building,
though in comparison to the housing needs it falls woefully short.
According to the estimates of the Lahore master plan (1964),
73,310 dwelling units were needed at that time. In 1979, the World
Bank sponsored a new structure plan project which estimated a
minimum need of 25,000 house units per year [35]. By comparing
these two sets of data, it can be readily concluded that this
massive housing development was still meeting 50 percent or less
of the need.

The quality of housing registered little, if any, gains in
this period. Table 4.4 indicates that the proportion of houses
with pucca walls increased by two percent during the period
1961–73, though the proportion of houses with pucca roofs seems to
have increased a bit more, i.e., nine percent. These figures have
been obtained by combining commensurate categories, and are liable
to some error. Also, the 1973 figures were based on a sample
survey, whereas the 1961 data were census count. Given these
reservations about the data, it would seem that there was
negligible improvement in the overall proportion of standard
houses in the city's housing stock, despite 130 percent and 80
percent increases in the numbers of houses with pucca roofs and
walls respectively. Obviously the number of Katcha houses
increased as much or more as the pucca houses.

Another illuminating aspect of house building activity in
Lahore is revealed by counterposing two bits of information. It is
estimated that about 12,500 dwellings per year were built in
1961–73. The Lahore master plan (1964–65) estimated that about
1,500 building permits per year for new dwellings were being
issued by local authorities [36]. Comparison of the two figures
suggests that only 12 percent of the houses were being built with
public approval. This is a hint about the scale of unauthorized
building activity. It is unlikely that the situation would have
changed substantially since that time.

Census data on other indices of the housing quality (e.g.,
crowding, water supply, latrine in a house) are nonexistent.
Sample surveys of housing conditions have been taken for various
purposes. On examining this evidence, it appears that there has
been little improvement in living conditions over the past 30
years. A city-wide sample survey to obtain data for Lahore's
master plan in 1962 revealed that 12 percent of the houses did not
have latrines, 54 percent lacked bathrooms, 55 percent were without a kitchen, and 27 percent did not have electricity [37].

No comparable survey has been done since then. The housing situation in the mid-70s can be observed from the information culled from studies of individual neighbourhoods. Estimates of Lahore's squatter population in 1980 ranged between 500,000 to 700,000; even the lower figure would mean that about 17 percent of the population was living under substandard conditions [38]. Most of the squatter clusters lack water supply, drainage, sewerage, etc. Often the situation in older and working class areas is not much better. For example, a survey of a neighbourhood in the Walled City (1979) found that 31 percent of households averaging four to six members were living in one-room dwellings. Only half of these households had a separate latrine [39]. A similar survey in a New Indigenous Community revealed that households averaging 6.5 persons were living in semi-pucca houses that had 1.3 rooms on the average [40]. Putting these bits of information about the housing condition in the city's three predominant areas, it seems that 50-60 percent of the population was living in katcha and semi-pucca overcrowded houses, sharing latrines and baths with other households and not infrequently without electricity and/or indoor plumbing. This picture of housing conditions in 1980 shows little qualitative improvement since 1962, the year for which city-wide survey data are available. Although the number of standard houses has almost tripled, and many exclusive bungalow estates have appeared all over the city, the proportion of sub-standard houses has not decreased since the 1960s. As they say, the more things change, the more they remain the same.

FACILITIES AND SERVICES

This account of Lahore's development would be incomplete without a description of the expansion of public facilities and services. At the outset, it must be said that data about facilities and services are scantier even than the housing counts. Agencies responsible for their delivery and regulation often pay little attention to systematic data collection and are reluctant to release information, if they do have any. The following item by item account has been carefully gleaned from newspaper reports and interviews.

Water Supply

Like most other contemporary civic facilities, the basic framework for piped water supply in Lahore was laid by the British. A water storage and pumping station was built at the highest point inside the Walled City in the 1920s. From thereon the system has gradually expanded. The city's water supply is drawn from underground aquifers at depths of 90 to 130 yards. It appears that there is plentiful water to draw upon, as these aquifers are continually replenished by the seepage from the

rivers and canals, and by the monsoons. The Lahore Municipal Corporation and the Cantonment Boards have been responsible for the
water supply and sewerage for respective jurisdictions. In 1967,
the LIT took over the water supply function from the municipal
corporation, and in 1973 a public agency known as the Water and
Sanitation Authority (WASA) was created to consolidate and expand
such facilities in accordance with a comprehensive plan prepared
by American consultants. Some sections of the city have private
tube wells to supply water: the railway's estates, hospitals and
other large institutional complexes, and the suburbs of Model
Town. Even the municipal system is not a centralized operation. It
is comprised of a network of wells and water towers for respective
neighbourhoods. By 1964, the municipality was running 100 tube
wells and supplying about 27 million gallons per day [41]. The
system has been steadily expanding, particularly to service the
housing estates developed by LIT/LDA. By 1980, WASA was supplying
130 million gallons of water per day from 143 tube wells through
about 1,200 miles of pipelines [42].

Over a period of about 15 years, the public water supply had
increased by about 400 percent. Yet from various estimates, it is
evident that the proportion of population served has not increased
significantly. About 60 percent of the population continues to be
served by the public water supply. This suggests that the consumption of water by those connected with the public supply system
would have gone up proportionately more than the increase in their
number. The rest of the population makes do with water from private wells, stand pipes, and by hauling over long distances.

Sewerage and Drainage

Lahore's sewerage and drainage system was initially designed
in 1937 by an English engineer, Mr. Howell. The flatness of the
ground and periodic river floods pose obstacles for the drainage
of the city. Lahore has been divided into seven sewerage and four
drainage districts. The waste water and the runoff are discharged
into the river. A flood protection levee (bund) has been built
(1955) to the north and west of the city. Effluents are pumped
across the bund whenever necessary. According to WASA, about
100,000 houses in the municipality had sewerage connections in
1979, constituting 25-30 percent of the housing stock. The rest of
the city had open drains and arrangements for collection of night
soils. As regards drainage, the director general of LDA, in a
press statement in February 1980, revealed that about 200 miles of
drain channels were needed in the municipal area, whereas only 50
miles of such networks existed, 20 miles of which had been built
since 1947, and another 20 miles of channels were being constructed [43]. This suggests an increase of about 40 percent in
the channeling capacity since Independence. Overall the development of drainage and sewerage has been slower than other public
services. Every rainy season brings large areas of the city under

pools of stagnant rain water.

Electricity and Telephones

Some older persons recall the excitement with which people from the Walled City used to go to the Mall to look at the first row of street lights in the early twenties. The electricity was brought to the city by a private company known as the Lahore Electric Supply Company. During World War II, the Punjab government took over the operation of the company and integrated the city's electric system into an hydroelectric grid. These arrangements continued till 1961, when a public corporation with the acronym WAPDA (Water and Power Development Authority) was created to promote the development and management of water and power resources of the country. WAPDA has proceeded to expand electric generation capacity and to build a countrywide transmission and supply grid. It has built hydroelectric dams, and has vastly expanded the electrical generating capacity. Lahore is served from this national grid.

According to the data reported in Lahore's master plan, "in 1962 the per capita consumption of basic load was 28.6 kilowatts, and it was projected to increase to 42 milowatts by 1985." [44] About 40 percent of electric supply in 1962 was consumed by industry, and 30 percent by households [45]. By 1979, the number of consumers (households, industries, etc.) was 350,000 [46]. If the proportion of residential to industrial–commercial consumers has remained approximately the same as in 1962 (i.e., 30 percent), then it means that in 1979 about 100,000 to 110,000 households had electric supply. This estimate suggests that about one-third of the houses in Lahore would have had electricity in 1979. Undoubtedly a large proportion of local population was still without electric supply, yet these figures suggest a four to five times increase since Independence.

Lahore had about 5,000 telephone connections in 1947. By 1978, there were about 40,000 telephones [47], an almost 700 percent increase. Six new telephone exchanges had been built by 1978, mostly to serve the new housing estates. Apart from the expansion of the capacity for telephone connections, long distance and overseas direct dialing facilities have been provided. From this brief analysis, it is evident that facilities such as telephones and electricity that are privately consumed have developed more rapidly than the community services that could not be individually appropriated, such as sewerage and drainage. This observation also applies to new facilities such as gas supply and television.

Gas Supply

The provision of piped natural gas as a fuel is a new feature of post-Independence Lahore. It was not available in British days.

With the discovery of a large field of gaseous hydrocarbons in Sui
(Province of Baluchistan), a network of pipelines was laid to
bring gas to cities like Karachi and Lahore. In Lahore, the gas
became available in 1965-66, and since then its supply expanded to
the point that, by 1980, it has displaced wood and charcoal as the
main cooking fuel. In 1979, there were 100,000 gas consumers [48],
industrial as well as residential, and cylindered gas was available for the use of those whose homes were not connected to gas
pipes. The piped gas could only be available in newly developed
areas. The older parts of the city were too congested to lay
pipes.

Schools and Dispensaries

The civic life in a city depends on the availability of
health, education and recreation services. This is why a city is
almost inconceivable without schools, hospitals, playgrounds, etc.
Being an ancient city, Lahore has had provision for such facilities. The herbal system of medicine, popularly called the Greek
system, reached its zenith under the Mogul rule, though names of
practicing physicians can be identified from records as old as
1160 A.D. [49]. The Mogul emperors employed physicians in their
courts, and encouraged them to provide medical care for the populace. Within the Walled City there is a neighbourhood called
Physicians' Bazaar, which was so named because generations of
physician families practiced there. Similarly, there was an
Islamic system of schooling centred on mosques and tombs. Persian
was the language of instruction, and the curriculum was comprised
primarily of Arabic, logic, history, etc. With the advent of the
British rule, a sharp break with traditional systems of medicine
and education occurred. The British established the provincial
Department of Education in 1856, and started Punjab University in
Lahore in 1869. A high school run by the American Mission was
started in the historic building known as Rang Mahal (palace of
colours) within three years of the establishment of British rule
in 1852 [50]. In 1860, a medical college was started in Lahore,
and a hospital was opened [51]. Establishment of these institutions is indicative of the dispatch and design with which the
British proceeded to transform the social order in Lahore and
colonial India as a whole. The old maktabs (educational institutions), the traditional medicine and the historic curriculum were
quickly displaced. They receded to the unofficial sector. The
modern institutions and practices drove the traditional facilities
and services into private and voluntaristic realms. The pre-British schools and colleges became religious madrassah (centres of
studies) for the training of priests and the traditional medicine
became the art of individual healers, though later, with the
resurgence of indigenous nationalism, a voluntary Islamic Council
started a college of traditional medicine in 1926. The dualization
of education and health into an upper and recognized modern cir-

cuit, and a lower and unofficial traditional circuit, is the noteworthy consequence of the British rule.

From the beginning of the British rule in 1849, the number of
schools, colleges and hospitals have continued to increase with
the expanding population. Hindus were the first to take to the
modern education and professions. Philanthropists and communal
welfare societies established schools, colleges and dispensaries.
Muslims, after an initial reluctance, began to realize the need
for modern facilities. In 1884, the Anjuman-i-Hamiat-i-Islam
(Association for Islamic Self-Help) was founded. It established
the first high school (1885), and subsequently a college (1892),
the Islamia College, which eventually became one of the centres
for the Muslim independence movement. The provincial Department of
Education established schools, degree colleges, a teachers'
training institute, the Engineering College, and the medical,
dentistry and veterinary colleges. Separate schools and colleges
for girls were also established. Lahore municipality was responsible for primary education, and it built schools throughout the
city. Similarly, the municipality's responsibility for public
health and control of epidemics found expression in the form of
out-patient dispensaries, maternity and child health centres, and
epidemic diseases hospitals. Thus, by 1945, Lahore had 98 primary
schools, 45 high schools, nine general degree and professional
colleges, one university, 14 hospitals and 14 dispensaries [52].

Since Independence, there have been two to ten times the
increase in education and health facilities. Hospitals increased
to 17 by 1965, and one more medical college has been established.
The number of out-patient dispensaries increased from 14 in 1945
to 42 in 1962, and 98 in 1979, almost six times an increase since
Independence [53]. Similar scales of increase in schools and
colleges are evident. Schools increased from 143 in 1945 to 451 in
1965, and about 50 new schools a year on the average have been
established since then [54]. All in all, the population of Lahore
increased by about 300 percent between 1947 and 1979, whereas
schools, colleges, dispensaries and hospitals increased by about
500 percent and more. Most of the post-Independence development
has been publicly sponsored.

Radio and Television

Radio broadcasting has been a public monopoly since its first
introduction in the 1920s. Lahore radio station was established in
the early 1930s. After Independence, the Pakistan government
increased channels and established new broadcasting stations in
other cities. A television station was established in Lahore in
1964. This was a new service and it has expanded very rapidly.
Within a decade, Lahore's skyline has been dotted with TV
antennas.

Parks and Playgrounds

Lahore used to be known as the city of gardens. The famous Shalimar gardens and the tomb-gardens of Jehangir are living examples of the Mogul legacy that earned the city this name. There was also a circular park around the walls of the old city. The British restored these monuments and parks to overcome the depradation that decades of invasions, insurrections and instability had wrought. They also enhanced the heritage of the city by building parks, college and school playfields, gymnasiums, clubs and golf courses, and the zoo. The Lawrence Garden (170 acres), Minto Park (110 acres), Race Course (120 acres), Golf Course (125 acres), Railway-stadium and Golf Course (136 acres) are some of the notable British contributions. Although most of these large parks and playgrounds have remained untouched, the post-Independence building boom has swept away many open spaces, tot-lots, and playfields. According to estimates prepared by Lahore's town planners, there were 2.6 acres of open space per 1,000 persons in 1946, which had decreased to 1.8 acres per 1,000 persons by 1964 [55]. By 1980, many open spaces had been encroached upon by squatters or public and private entrepreneurs.

After Independence, land for parks and playfields was set aside in planned schemes. A number of highbrow prestigious recreational complexes have even been developed. A cricket stadium (124 acres) and a parade and exhibition ground known as Fortress Stadium (85 acres) are obvious additions to the public amenities of Lahore since Independence. All in all, the open space is being used up in the old and poor section of the city, whereas new amenities are being developed in the spacious, affluent suburbs. Once again, development has visibly taken place, only it has occurred primarily to suit the preferences of the firm sector and affluent suburbanites.

CONCLUSIONS AND COMMENTARY

This chapter presents an analysis of two visible indices of Lahore's development, i.e., population and physical growth for the post-colonial period. Little evidence is required to convince someone of the massive population growth of a Third World city like Lahore. Its population grew almost five times over a 33 year period (1947-81). It is not the growth of population that was surprising. What the analysis revealed as unexpected is the fact that the city grew more from the natural increase of the resident population than by migration from rural areas. After all, the poor ruralities cannot be blamed entirely for the city's woes. There is a demographic explanation of this observation. Pakistan's urban areas are benefiting from declining mortality without experiencing the falling fertility rates that are normally assumed to accompany urbanism. This is the reason for an higher than average rate of natural increase in urban areas. Migration is contributing about

25 percent of population increase in Lahore, but it is not the cause of explosive population growth.

The examination of the data on Lahore's physical development also contradicts the general assumption that Third World cities have suffered from lack of public action and private initiative. In Lahore, home building has averaged about 12,000 houses per year since 1961. Schools and dispensaries have increased four to six times since 1947. Community services such as water supply, electricity, telephones, radio and television have also registered increases of 200-500 percent. Some of these facilities have expanded at twice the rate of population. A look at the maps in this chapter would indicate the extent to which the city has fanned out, almost two to three times since Independence.

All this developmental effort has not been episodal. It is the outcome of deliberate policies, public programmes and relentless private exertion. On the public side, two master plans for land uses, water, sewerage and drainage have been prepared. The creation of the LIT, WASA, and subsequently their merger in the LDA as a super agency to supervise Lahore's development; the formation of an urban transport corporation to manage local bus services, the establishment of the House Building Finance Corporation and the Building Research Station to facilitate home building, are all obvious examples of institutional development. Undoubtedly with changes in national political culture, development programs have swung back and forth between market guided and public initiated approaches. For example, Ayub's regime concentrated on infrastructure development and institution building, Bhutto's regime experimented with people's participation in planning, cooperative housing, sites and services for squatters, and control of land prices. The interesting fact is that with these politico-ideological cycles, fashionable ideas of both the right and the left have been tried. Schools have been nationalized, milk plants established, a factory to produce indigenous bread (roti) has been operating since 1974. All in all, there has not been a dearth of developmental effort of the type normally advocated in city planning literature. Almost every development cliché has swept through Lahore. The private efforts have been equally vigorous and pervasive. Even squatter settlements are a proof of people's capability to create housing out of nothing. Lahore cannot be described as a city suffering from inaction and neglect. Perhaps the same is the story in other cities of the Third World.

All this development has not significantly improved the quality of life in Lahore. Housing quality data indicate that the proportion of houses with mud roofs and lacking in latrines, baths or electricity has not substantially changed, despite massive home building over the last 20 years. The sheer expanse of the city has increased so much that it is now more exasperating to go from home to work, despite numerous reorganizations of the bus system, promises of a circular railway, periodic traffic master plans and proliferation of cars, scooters and minibuses. A sprawled and high

density city requires more community services. What is not necessary in a small town becomes public necessity in a big city.
People in Lahore could make do without latrines, as long as they
could reach out to the fields in a hurry; latrines become a public
necessity in a metropolis. These are the threshold effects of
growth. Thus, despite the impressive expansion of community
facilities, more people have come to require public services that
were not necessary a decade or two ago.

This chapter reveals a noticeable pattern in the development
of community services. Facilities and services that can be privately appropriated and which cater to the modern elite sectors
have increased to a far greater degree than those that are indivisible and partake of the characteristics of public goods. For
example, radio, television, telephones, modern housing and
stadiums, etc. have increased 500-600 percent, whereas drainage,
sewerage, water supply and open spaces (for common uses) have
expanded by 100-200 percent. This is a characteristic of contemporary development in the Third World.

Lahore has developed in two distinct metaphors: (1) modern-
Western, as symbolized by bungalow architecture, shopping centres
and Western dress, and (2) the indigenous, an updated version of
the traditional house taking the form of a town house, the family
store and local garb. This developmental polarity gives rise to a
myriad of forms and functions through continual differentiation
and periodic synthesis. The modern sector is not entirely upper
class, though it is predominantly so, and the indigenous is not
necessarily the domain of the poor. The quarter (one room,
one-storey house) is the modern abode of the lower class that
includes industrial workers, clerks, inspectors, engineering
supervisors, etc. Whereas the indigenous form of development
embraces the life-style of the traditional affluent such as a
millionaire grain dealer who lives in a modest house in an old
neighbourhood, the point of this illustration is that the indigenous versus the Western are not entirely poles of social class,
though there is an aura of upper class around the Western, and a
symbolism of subordination around the indigenous. These two
life-styles and physical forms take on many subtle variations, and
they are continually colliding and coalescing to produce a variety
of architectural forms and life-styles. The city is divided into
neighbourhoods or districts of very divergent physical and social
structures, almost to the point of being towns within the city.
Each district has a character, a central area, and even a hierarchy of activities. There are not many citywide central functions. Lahore does not have a downtown in the North American sense
of the term. It is a city that is a federation of districts.

This chapter also vividly documents the duality of the
development process. The official corporate sector leads and sets
the norms of development without making them realizable for the
majority of the population.The unofficial market-induced processes
provide for the uncatered needs. For example, it is estimated that
only 12 percent of houses in Lahore were built with official

approval; obviously the preponderance (88 percent) were
unapproved. House building is a functional response to the official neglect of pressing housing need. Yet the infrastructure laid
to serve the official sector makes it feasible for the unofficial
sector to operate. The bribery and corruption, thus, became adap-
tive to self-serving official policies. The dialectic of relationships between the two sectors will be examined later. Now it is
enough to appreciate the overall outcome of their operations.

APPENDIX A

POPULATION FORECASTS

     Forecasting is an uncertain science. A forecast can be pre-
cise and accurate only if the phenomenon being forecast is stable
and persistent. In forecasting the population of a city, the
objective for undertaking such an exercise has to be borne in
mind. Obviously greater precision and accuracy is desired when
attempting to estimate future demand for housing or jobs; whereas
a forecast meant to provide a general overview of the future population trends can be less demanding. The objective of this study
is to estimate the probable future size of Lahore, so that forces
bearing on its development and the quality of life could be understood. Three different methods have been applied to obtain a
series of forecasts that will give a range of projected populations of Lahore.
     Before presenting these forecasts, it may be worthwhile to
look at Figure 4.2 that shows the trend of population growth in
Lahore since 1901. It is obvious that Lahore's demographic curve
approximates an exponential function with an increasing slope of
the curve. It can be visually inferred from the graph that the
rate of population growth has accelerated since 1951, and the city
has entered a new demographic phase. Thus, in projections, weight
will be given to the post-1951 rates of population growth and
their derivatives.

Projections Based on Moving Averages

     Table 4.5 presents the census counts for the years 1901 to
1972, and the yearly rates of increase for successive decades. As
the 1941-51 period had some unique occurrences (exchange of populations between India and Pakistan, and disruptions caused by the
communal riots as well as the Independence), it has been treated
as an exception. The moving average for successive decades is
given in Column 5 of Table 4.5. Assuming that the rate of population growth of Lahore during the next three decades will increase
by the same proportion (three percent) as it did during the past
four decades, 1931-72, the moving averages for the period

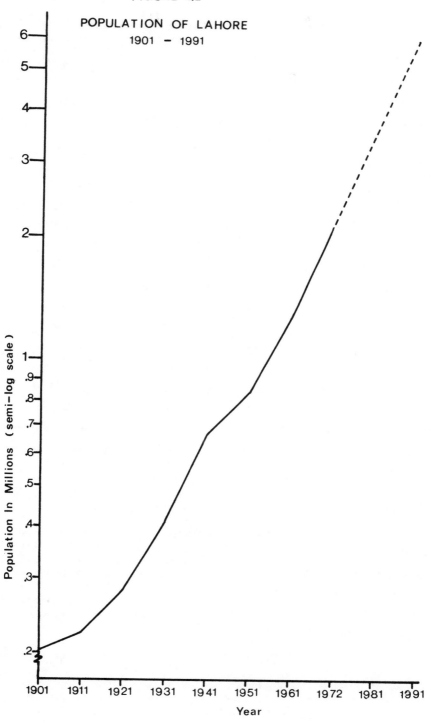

FIGURE 4.2

POPULATION OF LAHORE
1901 − 1991

Population In Millions (semi-log scale)

Year

103

1972–2001 have been projected in Column 5. Applying these moving averages to the base year populations, it appears that Lahore could have a population of about 3.3, 5.1 and 8.2 millions respectively in the years 1981, 1991, and 2001.

TABLE 4.5

Population Growth: Lahore

Year	Population	Decennial Increase	Average Yearly Increase	Moving Average
1901	202,964			
1911	228,687	25,723	1.3	
1921	281,781	53,094	2.3	
1931	429,747	147,966	5.3	
1941	671,659	241,912	5.6	5.4
1951	849,333	177,817	2.6	
1961	1,296,477	447,144	5.3	5.4
1972	2,165,372	868,859	6.1	5.6

Projected Population

Year	Population	Decennial Increase	Average Yearly Increase	Moving Average
1981	3,298,000	1,128,265	5.7	5.8
1991	5,078,900	1,780,923	5.4	6.0
2001	8,227,900	3,148,936	6.1	6.2

Source: Pakistan Statistical Year Book   (Islamabad: Statistical Division, 1978).

Graphic Extrapolation

The population data for the 1901–72 period were plotted on a semilog graph and the curve thus obtained was extrapolated for the successive decades of the period 1972–2001. Reading the respective values of the Y-axis (Figure 4.2), Lahore's population could be 3.6 million in 1981, 6 millon in 1991, and about 10 million in the year 2001. These estimates appear to be on the high side; they reflect the relatively greater influence of the most recent rates of population growth (i.e., the decades of 1952–72).

Regression Analysis

As the population growth curve approximates an exponential function, the population data were converted into natural log figures and regressed on time. This exercise yielded the following equation to fit the curve.

Log y(pop) = 11.8 + 0.0355X (No. of years)

The equation has an R^2 value of 99.3, which is almost a
perfect fit and it is statistically significant at 99.5 percent
level -(DF=4). Estimating the future populations of Lahore on the
basis of the equation, the following figures were obtained:

Year	Projected Population
1981	3,087,276
1991	4,550,748
2001	6,707,923

Comparison of Forecasts

The population estimates obtained from the above described
three methods vary considerably. In the following table, these
estimates have been arrayed in descending order (from high to low)
for each of the three periods:

Forecast Population (millions)

Year	High	Medium	Low
1981	3.6	3.3	3.1
1991	6.0	5.1	4.6
2001	10.0	8.2	6.7

High forecasts as yielded by the method of graphic extrapolation, the medium being obtained from moving averages, and the low
forecasts came from the regression equation.

APPENDIX B

PAKISTAN'S URBAN SYSTEM

Forty-one cities and towns of Pakistan have been arranged
according to their rank sizes in Table 4.6, for successive decades
from 1901 to 1972.

The Spearman rank correlation coefficients for the successive
decades are the following:

Decade	Correlation Coefficient (r)	Z value
1901–41	.8070	5.12
1941–51	.8906	5.69
1951–61	.9484	6.00
1961–72	.9148	5.89

This test shows that the rank order of Pakistani cities has remained very stable over these seven decades. Cities of lower ranks in the early part of the century have continued to be of lower order subsequently, and vice versa. It is an indication of the stability of Pakistan's urban hierarchy and a proof that growth of towns of different sizes has proceeded in a proportionate order.

TABLE 4.6

Rank Order Distribution of Cities in Pakistan

City	Rank				
	1901	1941	1951	1961	1972
Peshawar	3	4	8	7	8
Mardan	31	18	16	15	15
D. I. Khan	9	14	20	28	34
Kohat	11	16	22	23	31
Abbottabad	26	29	35	40	40
Bannu	23	20	36	39	42
Charsadda	18	27	37	33	41
Nowshera Kalan	24	17	21	30	37
Lahore	1	1	2	2	2
Rawalpindi	4	3	3	6	5
Multan	5	5	5	5	6
Faisalabad	25	9	6	4	3
Sialkot	7	6	7	9	9
Gujranwala	12	8	9	8	7
Sargodha		22	11	10	10
Jhang Maghiana	14	15	13	13	13
Kasur	16	13	14	17	18
Sahiwal	29	21	15	16	17
Gujrat	17	26	17	20	20
Bahwalpur	19	19	19	14	14
Burewala		39	40	38	36
Chiniot	20	23	23	27	29
Jhelum	21	24	25	22	32

Khanewal		35	26	24	30
D. G. Khan	15	25	27	26	27
Okara		38	28	18	19
Rahim Yar Khan		40	41	31	25
Hofizabad	30	34	32	37	33
Sheikhupura		30	33	32	21
Kamalia	28	36	34	36	38
Wah Cantt			31	34	16
Kamoki		37	39	41	39
Karachi	2	2	1	1	1
Hyderabad	6	7	4	3	4
Sukkur	10	10	12	12	11
Shikarpur	8	12	18	21	28
Mirpur Khas	32	32	23	19	22
Nawabshah		33	29	29	23
Larkana	22	28	30	25	26
Jocobabad	27	31	38	35	35
Quetta	13	11	10	11	12
Islamabad					24

Source of data: Pakistan Statistical Year Book, 1977   (Islamabad:
                  Statistical Division, 1978).

APPENDIX C

DETERMINING THE COMPONENTS OF POPULATION GROWTH:
SHIFT-SHARE ANALYSIS

Has Laore grown by attracting large numbers of rural migrants? This question arises on examining the accelerating rate of
population growth since 1951. Often a five or more percent annual
increase of a city's population is assumed to be the result of
massive in-migration from rural areas. Does this assumption hold
true empirically? To answer this question, a shift-share analysis
has been applied to the 1961-72 population data of Lahore. The
shift-share analysis was devised by Perloff and Dunn to sort out
reasons for differential [56] rates of regional economic growth in
the United States. Its underlying logic is simple and convincing.
It postulates that a region's economic performance is determined
by two sets of conditions: (1) the industry mix effect, and (2)
the competitive effect. A region may grow (or decline) due to the
differential rates of growth of its industries compared with the
nation as a whole. It may have fast or slow growing industries
which lend their respective characteristics to the regional
economy. Alternatively, it may attract (or lose) greater shares of
an industry from the national stock, which reflects the competitive advantage of a region. The national rates of growth for each
industry serve as the standards by which shifts are measured, and

the principle of proportionality is applied to judge the share of a region [57].

Hodge and Paris have adapted this method to identify factors that lead to differentials in rates of regional population growth [58]. The regional population increase over a decade is decomposed in two factors: (1) the structural component (the tendency of a region to grow slow or fast because of its own population structure), and (2) the regional component (the tendency for a region's growth rate to be influenced by factors not accounted for in its population structures, e.g., migration). This formulation is algebraically represented by the equation $D_i = S_i - R_i$

> where D_i = Difference in the growth rate of a region, i, and
> a nation or a province, p
> S_i = Structural Component
> R_i = Regional Component

To calculate S_i and R_i, a hypothetical growth rate for the region is computed. This is the growth rate that would have occurred for the region if each of its population groups had grown at the same rate as the corresponding age groups in the province (or nation).

The hypothetical growth rate is obtained by multiplying the number in each age group in the region at the start of the time period, by the rate of increase in the time period of the corresponding age cohort of the nation, and then averaging out these age-wise estimates.

$$P_i^h = \frac{\Sigma J \; G_J \, n_{iJ}}{\Sigma J \, n_{iJ}}$$

> where P_i^h = hypothetical growth rate of the region, i, in the period;
> G_J = growth rate of a specific national age group over the period, J;
> n_{iJ} = number of persons of an age group in region, i, at the beginning of the period J.

Thus, P_i^h is an average rate of expected population growth in a region if its component age groups grow at the corresponding national rates.

The Structural Component (S_i), then, is the hypothetical regional rate minus provincial rate of growth of population P;

$$S_i = P_i^h - P$$

and Regional Component (R_i) is actual regional growth rate (pi) minus the hypothetical rate P_i^h

$$R_i = p_i = P_i^h$$

Lahore's population growth in the period 1961-72 was factored into Structural and Regional components with the aid of the computer programme developed by Hodge and Paris.

Pakistan was used as the standard area against which Lahore's population growth was compared. This procedure yielded the following results:

P   (Pakistan's rate of growth 1961-72) = 65.58

pi (Lahore's rate of growth 1961-72)   = 67.36

P_i^h (Hypothetical rate for Lahore)   = 72.30

Si (Structural Component)   = 6.72

Ri (Regional Component)   = -4.94

The low minus value of the regional component suggests that migration and other unique factors (not inherent in the age distribution of Lahore's 1961 population) made little contribution to the rate of growth of Lahore's population in this period. This finding confirms our earlier observation that migration was secondary to natural increase as a factor in Lahore's high rate of population growth in the 1960s.

NOTES

1.   Shuja-ud-din, "Siyasi and Saqafati Tarigh" Urdu (Political and Cultural History), NaQoosh, special issue on Lahore's political, cultural, religious and literary history, February 1962, p. 126.
2.   Mohammad Baqar, "Lahore," NaQoosh, February 1962, pp. 29-32.
3.   Middle Eastern Islamic cities constitute an architectural idiom characterized by narrow lanes, labyrinthian layout, covered bazaars, densely packed houses with high walls, interior courts, and screened balconies, mixed land uses, central mosques, and market squares. Janet Abu-Lughod, "Contemporary Relevance of Islamic Urban Principles," Ekistics 47 (1980): 9.
4.   G. Rudduck, Urban Biographies (Karachi: Planning Commission, Physical Planning and Housing Study 19, 1965), p. 107.
5.   Syed Muhammad Latif, Lahore: Its History, Architectural Remains and Antiquities (Lahore: New Imperial Press, 1892), p. 84.
6.   Rudduck, Urban Biographies, p. 114.
7.   Ibid., p. 113.
8.   Under-numeration of population in a census is a problem almost everywhere (witness the rash of court challenges by cities such as New York, Detroit, etc. to the 1980 census counts of their populations in the U. S.). In Pakistan, poor records of home

addresses, illiteracy and reluctance to reveal names and/or numbers of one's family members, particularly females, pose unusual difficulties for census enumerators. Afzal estimates that 6-8 percent have remained uncounted in census populations (see Mohammad Afzal, The Population of Pakistan (Islamabad: Institute of Development Economics, CICRED series monograph, 1974)). Lahore's City Planners assumed that the city's population was under-numerated by 6.15 percent and 3.22 percent in 1961 and 1972 censuses respectively. Under-enumerations are not central to the objectives of this study, because it is concerned with longitudinal trends and rates of change which are not likely to be much affected, assuming that the scale of under-enumeration did not vary considerably from census to census. Any corrections of under-enumerations are rendered all the more difficult in this case because there are no estimates of the under-count by small areas such as a city.

9. The decade 1941-51 was exceptional. The Independence of Pakistan, large scale in- and out-migration of populations and communal riots disrupted the secular trend.

10. Afzal, The Population of Pakistan, p. 2.

11. Richard W. Helbock, "Urban Population Growth in Pakistan, 1961-72," The Pakistan Development Review 14 (1975): 320.

12. Heitmann et al. suggest that rank-size rule may be relevant after an urban system has reached a steady state over a long time. See George Heitmann et al., "A Note on the Rank-Size Rule and Future Urban Growth Patterns in Pakistan," The Pakistan Development Review 16 (1977): 465.

13. Karol J. Krotki, "Population Size, Growth and Age Distribution: Fourth Release for the 1961 Census of Pakistan," The Pakistan Development Review 3 (1963): 305.

14. Afzal, The Population of Pakistan, p. 5.

15. Ibid., pp. 17-18.

16. Zeba Ayesha Sathar, "Rural-Urban Fertility Differential," The Pakistan Development Review 18 (1979): 249.

17. Ibid., p. 249.

18. Afzal, The Population of Pakistan, p. 14.

19. Naseem Iqbal Farooqi and Iqbal Alam, "Provisional Abridged Life Tables," The Pakistan Development Review 13 (1974): 341.

20. Afzal, The Population of Pakistan, p. 2.

21. Lahore's population is a close approximate of Pakistan's population profile. See Figure 4.1 for comparisons of age-sex distribution.

22. Richard W. Helbock, "Differential Urban Growth and Distance Considerations in Domestic Migration Flows in Pakistan," The Pakistan Development Review 14 (1975): 55-56.

23. For example, see World Bank, Urbanization, Sector Paper (Washington, D.C.: 1972), and Barbara Ward, The Home of Man (Harmondsworth: Penguin Books, 1976).

24. Lahore Urban Development and Traffic Study (LUDTS) Final Report: Volume I. Urban Planning (Lahore: Lahore Development

Authority, 1981), Preliminary Draft, p. 2.

25. John E. Brush, "The Morphology of Indian Cities," in India's Urban Future, ed. Roy Turner (Berkeley: University of California Press, 1962), p. 60.

26. Anthony D. King, Colonial Urban Development (London: Routledge and Kegan Paul, 1976), p. 17.

27. H. R. Goulding, Old Lahore, Reminiscences of a Resident, 1924 (Lahore: Lahore Universal Book, 1976), p. 34.

28. For example, see Gerald Breese, Urbanization in Developing Societies (New Jersey: Prentice Hall, 1966); Brush, The Morphology of Indian Cities.

29. Lahore Urban Development and Traffic Study, Mansooba-E-Lahore, Preliminary Report (Lahore: Lahore Development Authority, 1979), p. 12.

30. Ibid., p. 12.

31. Mahmood Zaman, "Katchi Abadis: How did it Begin," Viewpoint October 19, 1980, p. 18.

32. Ibid., p. 18.

33. Mian Muhammad Iqbal, "Participation of Local Organizations in Planned Improvement of Katchi Abadis," in Proceedings of the National Seminar on Planning for Urban Development in the Developing Countries, with Special Reference to Pakistan, ed. Sattar Sikander (Lahore: Dept. of City and Regional Planning, University of Engineering and Technology, 1978), pp. 180–181.

34. Mahmood Zaman, "Katchi Abadis: Recognised and Developed," Viewpoint October 26, 1980, p. 18.

35. Lahore Urban Development and Traffic Study (LUDTS), Mansooba-E-Lahore, Preliminary Report (Lahore: LDA, 1979), p. 14.

36. Government of West Pakistan, Directorate of Town Planning, Master Plan for Greater Lahore, Final Draft (Lahore: The Master Plan Project Office, 1964), p. 60.

37. Ibid., p. 55.

38. Estimates of squatter populations can only be approximations in view of the fluidity of the situation. The range suggested at this point is based on estimates of Lahore Urban Development and Traffic Study, Mansooba-E-Lahore, 1979, p. 14 and Zaman, "Katchi Abadis: How did it Begin," p. 18.

39. Lahore Development Authority, Summary of Findings: Socio-Economic Survey of Walled City of Lahore (Mimeographed) (Lahore: 1979).

40. Lahore Development Authority, "Summary of the Findings," Socio-Economic Survey of Gujjarpura, Lahore (mimeographed) (Lahore: 1979).

41. Government of West Pakistan, Master Plan for Greater Lahore, p. 83.

42. Viewpoint, April 13, 1980, p. 14.

43. Pakistan Times, Feb. 7, 1980, p. 5.

44. Government of West Pakistan, Master Plan for Greater Lahore, p. 91.

45. Ibid., p. 91.

46. Lahore Urban Development and Traffic Study, Mansooba-E-

Lahore, Preliminary Report, p. 16.

47. Data supplied to the author by the General Manager,
Telephone and Telegraph Department, Lahore.

48. Lahore Urban Development and Traffic Study, Mansooba-E-
Lahore, p. 16.

49. Hakim Mohammad Musa, "Atbas," NaQoosh, Special Issue on
Lahore, 1962, pp. 798–838.

50. Goulding, Old Lahore, p. 24.

51. Yousaf Jamal Ansari, "Angrazi Dor Ki Chund Tameerat"
some British monuments ; and Waheed-ul-Hasan Hashmi "Colleges",
NaQoosh, Special Issue on Lahore, 1962, p. 673 and p. 692.

52. Government of West Pakistan, Master Plan for Greater
Lahore, Appendices 12–16.

53. Lahore Urban Development and Traffic Study, Mansooba-E-
Lahore, p. 22.

54. Ibid., p. 25.

55. Government of West Pakistan, Master Plan for Greater
Lahore, p. 73.

56. H. Perloff and Edgar S. Dunn, Regions, Resources and
Economic Growth (Baltimore: The John Hopkins Press and Resources
for the Future, 1960).

57. Donald A. Krueckeberg and Arthur L. Silvers, Urban
Planning Analysis: Methods and Models (New York: John Wiley &
Sons, 1976), p. 418.

58. This section paraphrases Hodge and Paris' description of
their method. See Gerald Hodge and Jacques D. Paris, "Population
Growth and Regional Development: Implications for Educational
Planning," in Demography and Educational Planning (Toronto:
Ontario Institute for Studies in Education, Monograph series no.
7, 1969), pp. 254–255.

5
THE URBAN ECONOMY

Lahore is not a stagnant community where increasing population has merely multiplied poverty and misery. Undoubtedly, it is a city of mass poverty, but this condition is as much the result of planned development as of public indifference. Acts of commission have flouted norms of efficiency, equity and welfare more often than acts of omission. This is only a generalized and overarching observation, whereas this chapter probes much more than that. It is addressed to such questions as: What are the post—Independence trends in the production of goods and services in Lahore? How have the city's productive capacities developed since Independence? What are the sectoral components of the local economy? Where are economic activities located within the city? What public policies and market processes have promoted the observed patterns of development? and finally, How have consumption levels changed?

It must be noted that there are three distinct sets of tasks: (1) to analyze and describe the structure of local economy; (2) to uncover longitudinal trends of the economic structure; and (3) to explain the social meanings of these patterns (i.e., to determine whether they are leading to a more efficient, satisfying and equitable economy). All these tasks will be attempted, but their fulfilment will vary according to the availability of evidence and theoretical guidance.

North American urban economics is concerned with the concentration of people and economic activities in geographical space and it deals with topics such as factor pricing, space utilization and size of city [1]. Nurtured in the neoclassical tradition, it has become almost a science of mystification where arguments revolve around elasticities of space consumption and mathematical functions that fit density gradients of various characteristics [2]. This chapter is only peripherally concerned with such issues. The urban economics that this chapter attempts to analyze is Thompson's "little economy." [3] It views a city as a local labour market which is also a subnational unit of production and a community of consumers. Broadbent defines an urban system "as a pool of labour – a relatively self-contained area where a whole

community can and does enter into common production and consumption processes on a daily basis." [4] This concept of a city's
economy is fundamental to the questions raised in the chapter and
it underlies the approach commonly followed in studying Third
World cities.

ECONOMIC BASE

    The economic base of a city is comprised of goods and ser-
vices, produced in it [5]. Lahore always has had a mixture of
activities (i.e., manufacturing, commercial, and administra-
tive-religious). From the eleventh century A.D. onward, it has
been the capital of the Punjab and could be assumed to be
specialized in administrative activities. Yet even in the nineteenth century, at a time of political instability and decline,
oil lamps, candles, soap, fabrics, glass, and copper and iron
wares manufactured in Lahore were in demand in far-off places [6].
British rule ushered in the modern industrial era, and the city
became the centre of repair workshops for railway-carriages and
locomotives, and the headquarters of a military garrison. These
public initiatives spawned metal fabricating, molding and lathing
industries, mostly through the upgrading of traditional smithies.
Paralleling the expansion of its industrial base, Lahore also
became the centre of administrative, health and educational services. Its hospitals, colleges and the High Court served the whole
province, thereby diversifying its economic base.

TABLE 5.1

Distribution of Work Force

Industry	Percentage of Work Force		
	Lahore Metropolitan Area	Pakistan (urban)	Location Quotient (LQ)[a]
Agriculture	9.27	6.20	1.49
Manufacturing	17.60	25.74	0.67
Utilities (electricity, gas)	1.18	1.27	0.89
Construction	10.50	6.41	1.63
Trade (wholesale/ retail/hospitality)	24.70	25.93	0.95
Transport – Communication	9.80	10.34	0.95
Finance – Real Estate	2.00	2.31	0.86
Services (community/ personal)	24.40	21.26	1.14
Total	100.00	100.00	

<u>Note a</u>:   Location Quotient is obtained by dividing figures of a
            cell in column (2) by corresponding figures under column
            (3).

<u>Sources</u>:   Labour force data for Lahore taken from Lahore Urban
            Development and Transportation Study, <u>Mansooba-E-Lahore</u>
            Interim Report (Lahore: LDA, 1979), p. 9; data on Pakis-
            tan from Government of Pakistan, Pakistan Statistical
            Year Book 1977 (Karachi: Statistics Division, 1978), p.
            17.

All in all, Lahore has largely remained a city of many economic
activities, without becoming too specialized in any one. This is
evident from Table 5.1 which reports Location Quotients (LQ), a
measure of degree of specialization and export base, for various
activities [7]. Table 5.1 reveals that Lahore's economy has a fair
mix of all activities, and it approximates Pakistan's urban economic profile. Most LQ's are relatively close to 1.00, which indicates conformity to the national norm. Employment figures for construction and agricultural activities in Lahore are proportionally
higher than corresponding figures for Pakistan, indicating a
degree of specialization. Yet this observation also reveals limitations of applying concepts of economic base to a Third World
city. Both these activities are meant for local consumption, and
high LQ's do not reflect export capabilities of these activities
as much as they indicate a high level of production for local
demand. For example, the high LQ for agriculture reflects the fact
that Lahore is surrounded by a belt of vegetable gardens, and dispersed in its neighbourhoods are buffalo and cow herds. Table 5.1
also indicates that employment in manufacturing is about eight
percentage points less than the comparable norm for Pakistan. The
meaning of this observation will be explored later. At present, we
may note that, overall, the economy is neither overly specialized
in any one activity nor lacking any industry to a significant
degree.
      The profile of Lahore's economy can also be observed from
Table 5.1. Almost 50 percent of the local labour force is engaged
in services and trade, a figure which is comparable to the corresponding proportion for Canadian metropolises, where 48 percent of
the labour force was engaged in similar activities in 1971. Yet
this comparison poses a paradox. Lahore, a poor city of rudimentary health, educational, and recreational services, has the same
proportion of its labour force engaged in services and trade as
post-industrial Canadian cities. This high (compared to its stage
of development) proportion of tertiary workers in Lahore is indicative of the phenomenon of tertiarization that McGee, Peatie and
others have observed in Third World cities, i.e., absorption of
kin in family enterprises through minute subdivision of tasks [8].

TABLE 5.2

Non-Agricultural Labour Force
Lahore, 1961 and 1977

| Industry | Labour Force | | | |
| | 1961 | | 1977 | |
	Number	Percent- age	Number	Percent- age
Manufacturing	104,045	30.4	135,461	19.4
Construction	13,305	3.9	81,111	11.6
Transport – Storage	32,205	9.4	76,038	10.9
Public Utilities	3,542	1.0	8,831	1.2
Trade	63,788	18.6	190,412	27.3
Finance, Insurance, etc.	2,809	0.8	15,605	2.2
Community/Personal Services	119,139	34.8	188,835	27.1
Not working but looking for work	3,387	0.9		
Total	342,220	100.0	696,293	100.0
Agriculture/Mining[a]	977	---	75,128	---
Grand Total	343,197		771,421	

Note a: 1961 data are for the city, and 1977 for the metropolitan
         area which includes the vegetable garden belt; hence a
         relatively large number of agricultural workers are
         reported in 1977 data.

Source: Pakistan Census of Population 1961, Census Bulletin on
         Non-Agricultural Labour Force by Industry (Karachi: Cen-
         sus Commissioner, undated); Lahore Urban Development and
         Traffic Study, Mansooba-E-Lahore, Interim Report (Lahore:
         LDA, 1979), p. 9.

        Statistical data about Lahore are sparse and crude. The city
has not been divided into districts or tracts for census purposes.
Censuses are not taken regularly, and they are neither comprehensive nor consistent. Government documents are often inaccessible
and special purpose surveys lack comparability. Despite these
handicaps, a rough profile of Lahore's employment distribution at
two points in time is provided by Table 5.2, giving both a view of
the structure of the local economy and an idea of how it has
changed.
        Lahore had almost three-quarters of a million economically
active workers in 1977. Leaving aside agricultural activities, it

can be observed that in 1977 about 54 percent of workers were
engaged in trade and services. Their proportion had not changed
since 1961, though employment in trade had expanded by 200
percent. Over these 18 years, Lahore seems to have experienced 103
percent increase in overall employment, which indicates a gross
average rate of economic expansion of five to seven percent per
year and a net rate (minus the average yearly rate of population
growth) of approximately -1.1 percent per year. The low negative
rate of employment change indicates that the city economy did not
expand enough (or barely could - given the benefit of doubt for
limitation of data) to keep up with the increasing population. Yet
in absolute terms it registered impressive gains; e.g., construction employment increased 600 percent and trade 200 percent. The
rate of growth of employment in manufacturing seems to be low,
whereas trade, construction, and services continue to be the
leading industries of Lahore. This pattern of economic development
is characteristic of Third World cities where the poor create
their own jobs through hawking, casual labour, and sharing in
family enterprises. The authors of the 1977 data estimate that
almost 68 percent (527,000) of gainfully engaged workers were in
what they called the unorganized sector.

   To sum up, it can be said that Lahore's economy has maintained considerable structural consistency over time. It has
remained a multifunctional city with trade and services being
dominant productive activities contributing about 46 percent of
Gross Metropolitan Product [9]. Since Independence, it has
experienced considerable economic expansion, as evidenced by the
growth of a gainfully engaged labour force; yet this development
has not put its economy ahead of the increasing population. The
local economy is being tertiarized essentially in the bazaar mode.
These are answers to questions about the structure of the city's
economy and its evolutionary trends. For further illumination of
the organization of the economy and the distribution of activities
within the city, specific activities need to be examined in
detail.

MANUFACTURING

   The contemporary city is the home of modern industries. A
city offers the infrastructure, the skilled labour force, and the
advantages of a concentration of activities (linkages and external
economies) and people (markets, etc.), all of which make it an
attractive locale for manufacturing establishments. The economic
underdevelopment of the Third World arises, essentially, from the
inadequate industrial base. The urban crisis of the Third World is
to a large extent the phenomenon of burgeoning cities with no
corresponding industrial capacities to provide goods and jobs. It
would, therefore, be illuminating to examine the development of
manufacturing activities in Lahore.

   It has been noted that, compared to other activities, manufacturing employment expanded slowly in Lahore between 1961 and 1977. Yet, in absolute numbers, Lahore's industrial development is spectacular. This observation is based on data about the number and size of industrial establishments in Lahore, which were derived from the Directory of Registered Factories [10].

In 1978, Lahore district had 888 registered factories (almost 26 percent of the factories in the province) with an employed labour force of 61,109 (18 percent of provincial industrial employees). In numbers of factories as well as employees, Lahore ranked topmost among 21 districts of the province. By these measures, Lahore can be classed as the most industrialized district of the province. About 90 percent of these factories were established after 1947, incontrovertible evidence of spectacular industrial development since Independence.

Did this development occur steadily over the 30 year period or did it happen in "boom and bust" cycles? Table 5.3 demonstrates that Ayub's decade of development (1959-69) was a period of accelerated industrial development but only to a small degree. During this period, 283 new factories were started, whereas in 1949-59, 255 factories were started, and in 1970-78 (Bhutto's era) 256 new establishments came into being. Overall, Lahore has had a steady rate of industrial development. On average, about 26 new registered factories (small as well as large) per year have been coming on stream. Bhutto's nationalization policies did not decelerate the rate of development, and Ayub's preceding era of free enterprise was not a period of explosive development. A steady and consistent rate of industrial development is evident. The factories tend to be medium in size, averaging 67 workers per establishment compared to 96 workers per factory for Punjab. This is the pattern of recent industrialization in Lahore.

TABLE 5.3

Registered Factories in Lahore

| Type of Industry | Starting Period | | | | | | | |
| | Pre-1947 | | 1947-58 | | 1959-69 | | 1970-78 | |
	No.	%	No.	%	No.	%	No.	%
Consumer Goods	43	47.3	115	45.1	138	48.8	125	48.8
Intermediate Goods	6	6.5	43	16.9	36	12.7	32	12.5
Investment Goods	42	446.2	97	338.0	109	338.5	99	338.7
Total	91	100.0	255	100.0	283	100.0	256	100.0

Source: Derived from data in Directory of Registered Factories in the Punjab (Lahore: Government of the Punjab, 1978).

What goods do these factories produce? The answer to this question
is provided by the data in Table 5.3. Two observations can readily
be made. First, industrial production in Lahore was bipolar: a
large proportion (48 percent) of output consisted of consumer
goods, and a slightly lower but significant proportion consisted
of investment goods (38 percent). In concrete terms, the two sets
of goods manufactured in Lahore were food, apparel, textiles, and
leather goods on the one hand, and tools, pipes, engines, and
steel bars, etc., on the other. Second, there is a remarkable consistency in the distribution of new factories by the type of goods
produced. The proportion of new factories producing investment,
intermediate, and consumer goods respectively in the three
post-Independence periods remained almost constant. This remarkable consistency in the rate and mix of establishment of new factories signifies that Lahore's industrial development was
self-sustaining. It appears to be all the more so in comparison
with Pakistan's pattern of industrialization.

Pakistan's industrial development has proceeded in three
phases. The virtual absence of any industries at the time of Independence led to the rapid development of consumer-goods industries, to work off demand and supply disequilibrium, as Lewis
aptly described [11]. From 1955 onward, the linkage effects began
to be evident, fostering intermediate and capital goods industries
which peaked around the mid-1960s. Since the late 1960s, the
public sector has become prominent in industrial development, and
many capital goods industries with a long gestation period have
been started [12] (e.g., steel mills, defence industries, heavy
machinery complexes). Simultaneously, small enterprises of consumer-goods industries were established privately. These national
phases do not seem to have worked through Lahore's economy, which
has remained on a low-key, steady course. This divergence from
national trends is an indication of the relative autonomy of the
city's industrial economy.

Bases of Industrial Self-Sustenance

Paradoxically, Lahore's steady industrial growth results from
its unique position as the provincial capital and from the
resilience of its traditional social structure. Whatever industrial development has taken place is the outcome of a process
wherein local entrepreneurs responded to new demands by establishing workshops and factories which relied on the plentiful
supply of skilled labour ensured by hereditary occupational
castes. Being a big city and the seat of provincial government,
Lahore has also been a beneficiary of public expenditures which
stimulated demand for manufactured goods.

An idea of the scale of public expenditures can be gained
from the fact that the provincial government alone disbursed about
Rs. 1.5 billion per year for development in the 1970s. Lahore is
the hub of this developmental activity. Here, construction con-

tracts are let out, equipment and materials are tendered, planning and management of projects are centred. Even kickbacks and bribes paid for projects in other districts flow into the city. These factors stimulate demand for industrial goods, for both consumption and investment. Lahore's position in the settlement hierarchy, the size of its market, and its political and administrative clout lend stability to its economy. While the country at large may be experiencing a slump in industrial activity, Lahore (and Karachi) stays on a steady course by attracting a larger share of shrinking development expenditures.

On the supply side, Lahore has many intrinsic strengths that have also helped its industrial development. This is where the positive role of the traditional social structure is evident. Lahore is inhabited by occupational caste groups that historically specialize in specific occupations, e.g., carpenters, goldsmiths, weavers, etc. These castes are not guilds in the European sense of the term, but their occupational exclusivity has been sustained by a system of prescribed obligations and privileges characteristic of the subcontinental Jajmani system [13]: a blacksmith would consider it unbecoming to work as a weaver, and vice versa. These occupational castes have been sources of steady supply for the skilled labour force. Post-Independence development accelerated the monetization and commercialization of their operations; yet occupational specialization of castes has remained relatively undisturbed. Enterprising members of these caste groups have established family workshops and factories which operate like a clan. Workers are often kin, though, in larger establishments of 10 to 20 workers, non-relatives may also be employed. Owners work with their hands alongside employees. An owner is both a <u>mistri</u> (master craftsman) and <u>ustad</u> (teacher) for workers who are not mere paid employees but also apprentices learning the trade. There is an aura of patriarchy in these relationships. Lest all this may sound too romantic, it must be noted that working conditions in these factories are poor, job security is nonexistent, and child labour common. Some mutual obligations and clan ties partially mitigate these hardships.

These workshops represent a commercialized evolution from household production units and Lahore's industrial development is largely due to them. This mode of industrialization has produced such well-known success stories as the blacksmithies of Railway Road. While the economic planners of Pakistan were busy inviting foreign companies and subsidizing new industrial capitalists, these worker-entrepreneurs were sustaining the "green revolution" by manufacturing diesel pumps and tubewells. By the late 1960s when members of the affluent class had become numerous enough to constitute a submarket, and air conditioners and refrigerators had become items of household use for them, some of the workshops switched to manufacturing components. The point is that these craft-enterprises have demonstrated a canny inventiveness and flexibility in responding to market demand. They have proven to be the backbone of Lahore's industrial base, however small it may be.

Other data further illustrate the role of these workshops in Lahore's industrial development. From the Directory of Registered Factories, it was found that almost 90 percent of Lahore's factories were owned either by individuals or by partnerships, indications of a personalized pattern of ownership. On the other hand only 6.5 percent (48 out of 887) were corporations of one kind or another. An overwhelming majority (87 percent) of factories were low-capital enterprises, i.e., up to Rs. 500,000 in fixed assets in 1978. The mean value of fixed assets per factory was Rs. 300,000, if nine large establishments are excluded, and, even if those are counted for computational purposes, the mean value still turns out to be only Rs. 451,000. To give an idea of the value of these assets, it may be noted that a modern three- to four-bedroom house in Lahore cost about Rs. 400,000 in 1978. The mean capital (fixed assets) per worker was Rs. 10,000, a quarter of the price of a new Toyota car in 1978.

This evidence clearly indicates that the registered factories in Lahore, though numerous, were mostly small, labour-intensive family enterprises of low overhead and minimal capital. They represent a bazaar mode of operation that characteristically brought some affluence but not social status to the owner-entrepreneurs. They remain owner-worker enterprises, though they have manifested opportunistic flexibility and inventiveness. They also train workers for the large industrial establishments.

The preceding discussion should not lead to the playing-down of the role of large industrial establishments. By 1978, about 20 percent (168 out of 887) of Lahore's registered factories employed 50 or more workers, which, by the city's standards, makes a large establishment. There were eight establishments employing more than 1,000 workers each. Only 13 percent of large establishments were of pre-Independence vintage. The proportion of new large factories in each phase generally remained the same (about 15 percent), except for Ayub's era (1959-69), when it was 24 percent. Large registered factories operate as corporations in the firm mode.

In terms of employment, large establishments provide the bulk of industrial jobs. They essentially produce public ultilities infrastructure: railways, electricity, irrigation, etc., though a few public enterprises of the Bhutto era, such as Roti and milk plants, were exceptions to this pattern.

At the outskirts of the Lahore metropolitan area along the national highway, a ribbon of industries has emerged, among them are some large establishments, such as the Herculus Fertilizer Plant and Ithad Chemicals. All in all, there is an implicit division of markets. The large establishments concentrate on investment and infrastructural goods, while the small bazaar sector establishments produce what cannot be supplied by large factories: investment goods (lathes) or consumer goods (fans and taps). Bazaar sector establishments operate in that segment of the market which has not been appropriated by the firm sector. There is as well a lower layer of the bazaar sector. The small establishments referred to so far are registered factories which are a cut above the backyard workshops, small household production units, and artisan manufacturers. These unregistered manufacturing units could easily number up to another 10,000 [14].

The preceding account of the structure of Lahore's manufacturing establishments is intended to provide evidence to support the hypothesis that the traditional social structure proved an asset in establishing a steady course for Lahore's industrial development. Local workers and entrepreneurs responded to the opportunities of expanding demand. The state played a significant intermediary role by fuelling the demand and providing the infrastructure. Monopoly capitalists generally settled around, but not in, Lahore.

Location of Industries

From the pattern of distribution of factories in the city, significant factors in its industrial development can be deduced. Observations of locational patterns provide answers to questions about the relative roles of bazaar versus firm modes of operations. Before analyzing Lahore's industrial location patterns, two points must be elucidated. First, Pakistan remains an under-industrialized country, despite rapid strides after Independence. Of the little industrialization which has occurred, the lion's share has gone to Karachi, which is a port and was the capital of the country till 1959. The rest of the country has drawn mostly the industries that rely heavily on argricultural and mineral raw materials, such as sugar and textile mills, cement plants, and fertilizer and chemical factories. The economics of their location require that they be situated near bulk sources of raw materials. With tax incentives and licensing procedures, such plants have been directed towards underdeveloped regions and away from large cities. For example, in the Punjab the two most backward districts, Mianwali and Muzzafargarh, have only large plants. Due to locational requirements and public policies, heavy industries have shied away from Lahore City, though some have settled along main highways at a distance of 10 to 15 miles from Lahore in adjoining districts to enjoy tax holidays, escape workers' agitation, and at the same time benefit from Lahore's assets and amenities. Lahore's locational assets are plentiful skilled labour, an entrepreneurial spirit, banking and financial services, the availability of trained professional and managerial staff, a large consumer market, and its status as the seat of political and administrative power and hub of a transportation network. It is neither at a breakpoint in the transportation network nor surrounded by a region rich in raw materials. Bearing these facts in mind, let us examine the locational pattern of industries in Lahore.

In the absence of census tracts, or any other standardized subdivisions, the study divides the city into nine areas according to their periods of origin, densities, land uses, and physical layouts. (See Map 5.1.) Chart 5.1 gives brief descriptions of the

neighbourhoods included in each area and their dominant characteristics.

CHART 5.1

No.	Divisions	Dominant Characteristics
1	Walled City	Pre-British, very high density, commercial and residential land uses.
2	Northern Communities (BadamiBagh, MisriShah, etc.)	Mostly post-British, medium density, industrial and residential and local commercial. Poor and middle class residences.
3	Civil Lines (The Mall, McLeod Road, Lawrence and Queen's Roads)	Post-British, relatively segregated but divergent land use, medium density, commercial, and institutional activities dominant. Middle and upper class residences.
4	Western Communities (Ravi-Road, Krishan Nagar, Mohni Road)	Late-British Low density, residential and local commercial land uses. Dispersed development. Working and middle class areas.
5	Southwestern Planned Schemes (Samanabad, Shah Jamal Wahdat colony, Iqbal Town, Multan Road)	Mostly post-Independence. Low density. Residential and local commercial land uses. Middle and upper class areas.
6	Northeastern Communities (Railway Colony, Moghalpura, SultanPura, G. T. Road)	Post-British. Heavy industrial and residential land uses. Some old villages. Medium density. Moderate income housing and industries.
7	Southeastern Planned Suburbs (Gulberg, Garden Town, Model Town)	Mostly post-Independence. Upper class residential and local commerce land uses. Low density.
8	Peripheral-Ribbon Development (Kot Lakhput, Ferozpur Road, G. T. Road)	Mostly post-Independence. Linear development. Low density residential and industrial activities. Low income housing.

9   Cantonment   British period military town.
                                    Low density. Residential and
                                    institutional land uses.

Note: Dominant characteristics referred to above are highly gen-
       eralized features.

Cross tabulating data about registered factories by the above
described nine areas, the following pattern of industrial location
can be observed:

   (1) Civil Lines (Area 3) and BadamiBagh/MisriShah (Area 2)
   had the largest concentration of registered factories in
   1978. Together they contain about 46 percent of Lahore's
   total industrial establishments. Along the southwestern axis,
   Multan Road (Area 5) and, along the eastern axis, G. T. Road
   and Baghbanpura (Area 6) are two linear, though less intensive, clusters of factories. The railways complex (the
   station, workshops, warehouses) is the locational spine for
   Lahore's industries, though, since the 1960s, ribbon-like
   industrial development has appeared along the three highways
   leading out of Lahore, i.e., G. T., Ferozpur and Multan
   Roads.
   (2) The largest cluster of small factories, mostly small and
   medium (on Railway Road, RamGali, and McLeod Road), in the
   Civil Lines area is the result of concentration of printing
   presses, metal fabrication and mechanical workshops. The
   nuclei of these operations were established in British days,
   when proximity to the railway station was the prime con-
   sideration in the location of workshops. With truck transport
   this pull has weakened, yet these industrial clusters have
   acquired agglomeration economies and are thus now well
   entrenched. Most of these clusters consist of bazaar establishments, interspersed with homes of owners, and complementary commercial markets. Often, these workshops are also
   retail outlets for their products.
   (3) Mechanical workshops producing a variety of goods
   ranging from steel bars to diesel pumps are the foundation of
   Lahore's industrial base. Not only did they constitute 32
   percent of all factories in 1978 but they also employed about
   40 percent of the work force in factories. If the number of
   workers in transport-related activities, such as railway
   establishments and auto repair workshops, is added to the
   above categories, it becomes obvious that a majority (54
   percent) of the industrial labour force is engaged in
   mechanical trades. Such factories are located in three concentrations: Railway Road, BadamiBagh, and MisriShah-Baghban-
   pura. BadamiBagh in particular has become a prominent industrial enclave. The Small Industries Corporation has built an
   industrial estate here, and a number of large plants have

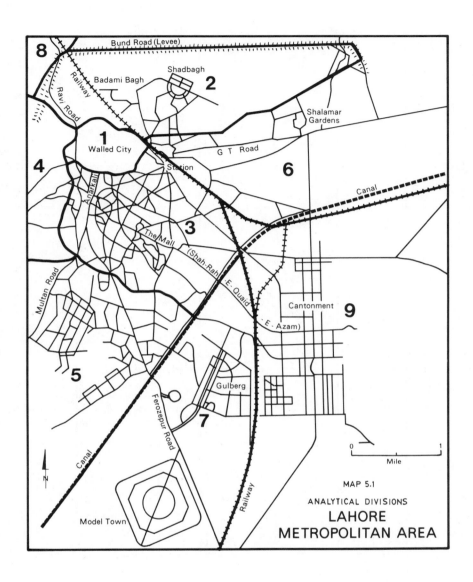

8

Bund Road (Levee)

Railway

Ravi Road

Badami Bagh

Shadbagh

2

Shalamar Gardens

1
Walled City

Station

G T Road

Anarkali

4

6

Canal

3

The Mall

(Shah-Rah-E-Quaid)

Multan Road

- E - Azam)

Cantonment

9

5

Gulberg

Ferozepur Road

7

0   1
Mile

Canal

Railway

MAP 5.1

ANALYTICAL DIVISIONS

LAHORE METROPOLITAN AREA

N

Model Town

Railway

TABLE 5.4

Types of Factories by District, Lahore

Division*/ District	Number of Registered Factories by SIC Numbers**																			Total	Percentage
	20	22	23	24	25	26	27	28	30	31	32	33	34	35	36	37	38	39	75		
1	4	4	—	—	—	—	11	1	3	3	—	3	3	2	1	—	—	—	—	32	3.5
2	12	28	—	—	2	—	—	3	5	1	1	54	14	43	6	8	2	—	5	184	20.7
3	5	12	1	2	5	—	54	17	2	—	1	6	20	61	9	7	7	1	15	225	25.3
4	1	4	1	1	—	—	2	10	1	2	1	6	5	2	3	4	1	—	—	44	5.0
5	12	16	—	—	1	1	2	17	8	1	4	12	10	6	14	14	1	1	4	124	13.9
6	11	14	1	—	—	—	3	14	7	3	2	33	7	19	6	9	1	1	1	132	14.8
7	15	9	—	1	1	—	3	5	3	1	1	3	3	1	6	—	2	—	—	54	6.9
8	2	16	—	1	1	2	1	8	7	7	1	10	9	13	8	1	—	—	1	88	9.8
9	—	1	—	—	—	—	—	—	—	—	—	—	—	2	—	—	—	—	—	3	0.3
Totals	62	104	2	5	10	3	76	75	36	15	11	127	71	149	53	43	14	3	26	886	100.0

Notes: * District here refers to the nine areas in which the city has been divided for analysis of industrial locations. Refer to Map 5.1.
** SIC = Standard Industrial Classification.

Source: Government of Punjab, Directory of Registered Factories (Lahore: Bureau of Statistics, 1978).

located in this area. Yet, as the area was filled up, the new establishments penetrated surrounding residential districts and thus spread into Areas 5 and 6. Lahore's city planners have done little to rationalize industrial districts or to improve their situation. Often they talk about relocating small workshops but show no comprehension of their operational and locational necessities.

(4) Only upper class residential areas such as G.O.R., Gulberg, Model Town, and Cantonment are "free" from factories. In Gulberg, a strip of land was set aside for industries and has been utilized by public corporations and a few influential foreign firms.

(5) New industrial establishments of 100 or more employees requiring big lots have sought locations on the outskirts of the city. Out of 78 such establishments, 27 percent are located on the outskirts along major highways (Area 8), and another 20 percent are in Bagbanpura on the northeastern perimeter of the city.

(6) Lest it may appear that mechanical workshops are the only notable industry in Lahore, it is worth mentioning that plastic and rubber products, apparel and hosiery, and chemicals and pharamceuticals have also become significant local manufacturers. As Table 5.4 shows, factories producing these goods are not concentrated in any specific area. They are scattered along Wahdat Road, Ichra, and Moghulpura (Areas 3, 5, 6, and 8). These industries have no historical roots in the city and are not the preserve of any traditional caste or clan. They are new and hence their supply of skilled labour is more open-ended. The city offers them locational advantages in the form of trained manpower and large markets. As a pointer to the role of these industries, it may be noted that about nine percent of the industrial labour force is employed in factories producing rubber and plastic products and another seven percent is engaged in the production of pharmaceuticals and chemicals. In the number of registered factories, Lahore has 44 percent of all chemical factories and 77 percent of printing establishments in the province; this indicates as much the dominance of Lahore in these industries as the meagreness of the province's stock of such establishments.

Lahore is obviously not a city where industrial, commercial and residential activities are neatly segregated into respective zones. They are scrambled together, and that is why it looks so chaotic to Western-trained eyes.

Major factory clusters are in the core of the city (i.e., Civil Lines) and along the northern edges of the inner ring (i.e., G. T. Road, MisriShah, Baghbanpura, etc.). These are very congested areas of narrow streets, traffic-choked roads, and densely packed houses. Yet these locations have been chosen by new factories. In the early decades of the twentieth century these areas might have offered both spaciousness and accessibility, but those advantages have disappeared with the growth of the city. Presently, these sites are attractive to factories because they sustain a mode of operation that is not feasible on alternate locations; owners can live nearby and workers are also readily accessible. Small factories operate on piece work and frequently on the basis of individual orders. They need to be close to retail markets and are woven into the fabric of the social networks. Concentration of factories provides conventional agglomeration economies and possibilities of exchange of materials, labour and skills. One factory may borrow a special tool from a neighbour, and the other may expect help in disposing of excess stock of some material. Such are the interdependencies among competitive production units. Often owners and workers are members of the same clan or kin and thus are bound to each other both economically and socially. Such arrangements are possible primarily in areas where owners, workers, suppliers and sellers live in close proximity to each other. These are the locational advantages of the old, congested parts of the city.

The old sections of the city also serve the latent function of casting a veil over the operations and protecting them from the prying eyes of labour and tax inspectors. It would be an exercise in futility to attempt relocation of these factories in segregated industrial zones, in the name of rationalizing land use, without providing for their operational interlinkages. Surprisingly, city authorities often dream about launching such relocation exercises, yet they seldom succeed.

Another factor contributing to the mixing of land uses is the sheer expansionary thrust of the city. An industrial plant, even a large one, locates in what, at a given time, is the periphery of the city, but its presence attracts new homes, shops, and other forms of development all around, and soon a veritable neighbourhood springs up around a plant and engulfs it. The outcome of these wave-like processes of urban expansion is a scattering of factories amidst residential communities along major highways.

Organization of Sectors

The manufacturing establishments of the bazaar sector can be divided into three strata. At the bottom are artisans and household production units, potters, washermen, carpenters, and weavers, whose economic viability has depended on individual association with a set of clients, relations with whom spanned generations. In recent times, these relations have been commercialized, and the bonds of mutual obligations have been eroded.

The middle stratum of the bazaar sector consists of small family workshops which are spatially as well as operationally separated from households. At any one time they may specialize in producing a specific item, though they switch quickly to another line if and when the demand shifts. Usually these workshops pro-

duce on order and not to stock. Their products are not trademarked
and are often individually crafted. The upper layer of the bazaar
section is mostly a post-Independence evolution. Its distinguishing characteristic is a greater degree of commercialization, on the one hand, and differentiation of business operations
from production activities on the other. At this level, products
are trademarked and manufactured for stock; sales are routed
through designated retailers and financing is arranged through
banks. In proceeding from lower to higher strata, the operations
become compartmentalized, products standardized, and dealings commercialized. Yet the common structural features of the bazaar
section are:

> (1) owners are also the workers (or foremen, to be more
> specific); (2) the organization is kin-based and the opera-
> tions are relatively small; (3) the lines of production are
> flexible and opportunistic; (4) dealings are highly per-
> sonalized.

It would be a mistake to assume, at least for Lahore, that the
bazaar is the refuge of the poor. Workshops that crank out a
diesel engine a month or bottle distilled water, or manufacture
undergarments on a few powerlooms afford an affluent living to
their owner-operators. The upper layer of the bazaar sector is
relatively well off. It merits repetition that data reported
earlier on registered factories essentially refer to the upper
layer of the bazaar sector and a small proportion of the middle
layer establishments.

The firm sector also has an internal hierarchy, though not as
clearly delineated as the bazaar sector. The firm sector is
characterized by a corporate mode of operation wherein organizations are deliberately planned, and tasks are differentiated by
functions and formalized into departments such as management,
accounts, production, sales, etc. The firm sector establishments
differ according to size and degree of corporateness. They are
also differentiated according to their power: i.e., the degree to
which they can control their situation and free themselves from
market accountability. The firm sector is vertically structured
according to these criteria. There are two broad layers. The upper
layer consists of public enterprises and large private corporations. Such establishments are bureaucratic, oligarchic and capable of commanding the state's powers for their ends. Public
agencies and establishments dominate the firm sector in Lahore.
Out of 57 registered manufacturing corporations in Lahore in 1978,
about half were public enterprises. The railway workshops, the
Pakistan Engineering Company, the milk, Roti plants, and vegetable
ghee (cooking oil) plants are the largest industrial establishments of Lahore, and they are public enterprises. They have
evolved, over the past 20 years, into replicas of civil services
rather than commercial establishments responsive to the market.
The lower layer is comprised of relatively small and competitive

corporate enterprises. These are conceived in the idiom of modern organization with a hierarchical division of labour and power. They are explicitly person-centred bureaucracies presided over by owners. Generally, the labour in the firm sector establishments is unionized on a plant basis.

Technology and Finance

Both sectors essentially rely on mechanical and electrical technologies for manufacturing. The bazaar sector may rely more on the appropriate technology but it certainly is not pre-modern. In fact, low capital overheads make bazaar establishment more adaptable to new production procedures and tools. The main difference between the two sectors lies in the way they respectively acquire any new technology.

Firm sector establishments generally consist of imported turn-key plants which are dependent on direct foreign advice and assistance. The bazaar sector operates by copying new products and tools. It does not mass produce, but crafts its products. Semi-literate craftsmen are the mainstay of the bazaar sector, and there are seldom any graduate engineers, chemists or technologists working there.

The bazaar sector's ingenuity and flexibility has allowed it to adapt new lines of production whenever those have appeared profitable and not monopolized by the firm sector. For example, since 1947, the bazaar sector in Lahore has successively taken on the production of lathes, hardware, engines, pumps, pipes, heaters, cookers, fans, nuts and bolts, carpets, refrigerator parts, radio and television cabinets, chemicals, and prefab building components. Most of these products are imitations of foreign items. Yet the bazaar sector has also shown ingenuity and inventiveness in updating many traditional products such as new forms of indigenous air coolers, washing machines and furniture.

The sources of finance for the two sectors are also significantly different. The firm sector relies on bank loans, governmental subsidies, and stock exchange, whereas the bazaar sector's sources of finance are, essentially, personal savings, loans from kin and friends, and advances from suppliers and buyers. A section of bazaar sector owners may even shun paying or receiving bank interest on religious grounds.

Sectoral Ecology

How are the markets and fields of operation divided between the two sectors? How have their relations evolved over time? These questions about the interrelations of the two sectors require some probing to illuminate the dynamics of Lahore's industrial economy.

On examining the data about size and ownership of registered factories, it becomes evident that there is a ceiling on growth in the bazaar sector establishments. An establishment starting small seldom grows over time into a large industrial plant. Only five or so cases could be identified where a small establishment grew into a plant employing 50 or more persons. Shezan Fruit Drinks, a few hosiery factories, and one foundry are the only examples. Owners of bazaar sector establishments seldom venture into large enterprises.

Most firm sector establishments start large. This is understandable because the procedures to establish an industry require resources, knowledge and contacts that are significantly different from those required to run a bazaar establishment. The mere fact that negotiations and correspondence for a firm sector establishment are conducted in the English language and involve complex legal, financial, and technical arrangements would restrict most of the bazaar operators.

The two sectors seem to have shifting but defined spheres of operations. The firm sector defines the opportunity area for the bazaar sector. Yet there are complementarities between the two which, if disturbed, tend to be restored in new forms. An example will illustrate this point.

The Case of Colas

Up to 1960, Lahore had a thriving indigenous aerated soft drink industry with banana and rose sodas being manufactured by a score of small factories in the city. The establishment of Seven-Up and Coca-Cola plants in 1962-63 knocked out these factories. As prestigious drinks from abroad Colas swept the market. Of course, foreign sponsorship and the Government's commitment to sustain them proved to be the main assets of these plants. They were given liberal import licences, quotas of sugar, and tax concessions, while indigenous manufacturers were left to fend for themselves. Though most of the local soda factories folded up, a few survived by manufacturing in times of shortage, imitations of "the real thing." Since the mid-1970s, prices of Coca-Cola and Seven-Up have risen steeply and have thereby freed the lower end of the market for relatively cheap local sodas. Now, in fashionable households, visitors are classified according to their suitability to be served Coca-Cola or indigenous soda.

This is a revealing illustration of the dynamics of relations between the two sectors. By its power and prestige, the firm sector takes over a product and a market. Some operators turn to the production of counterfeits if the firm sector cannot meet the demand. In time, the market becomes sectorized, into upper and lower circuits renewing opportunities for the bazaar sector to emerge as supplier of the lower circuit.

Milk Plant

The fate of the Lahore Milk Plant is another illustration of these dynamics, though the outcome was different. Lahore's milk

supply comes from herdsmen who live within and around the city,
since, in the absence of refrigeration and on account of
large-scale adulteration, households prefer to obtain milk from
them. In 1967, the Government established a milk plant to
modernize the supply and to make up any scarcity. Initially, the
Plants seemed to penetrate the market, and herdsmen felt
threatened. Yet inefficiences of production resulted in irregular
and substandard supply. Consumers complained of a foul smell in
the plant-supplied milk and gradually turned back to the traditional suppliers. The Milk Plant survives as a bureaucratic
bungle.

These examples illustrate two points about the firm sector:
first, its products have an aura of modernity and prestige and can
thus easily sweep the market; second, its establishments enjoy
state support and thus have considerable hold over the market. As
for the bazaar sector, it has to carve a niche for itself in the
unmet needs of consumers. It is evident that the Government has a
significant influence on the industrial activities of the city.
How the two sectors tap this influence is another basis of distinguishing between them.

The Government and the Two Sectors

Although Pakistan is said to be a mixed economy, the Government has played a central role in industrial development. the
five-year plan set the industrial priorities: fiscal and tariff
policies established the terms of trade; import licenses, foreign
exchange quotas, tax holidays, and emasculation of labour set the
framework of industrial development; foreign firms are brought in
under governmental auspices. All in all, the federal and provincial governments define the opportunity area and not infrequently
provide resources for new establishments. In all these matters,
the firm sector has a distinct advantage. Governmental policies
and programmes are primarily meant for the modern industrial
sector, while the bazaar sector is viewed as residual. This outlook sets the stage for two distinct modes of influencing the
Government by each of the two sectors.

The firm sector is not only a direct extension of the governmental institution (public enterprises), but it is also fostered
and protected by the state. There are many bonds that link the
two. Industrial owners, managers, and professionals, on the one
hand, and politicians, army generals and bureaucrats, on the
other, are members of the same class with common class interests.
Many private owners of industrial establishments are retired
generals and senior officers, and, of course, a large segment of
the upper middle class are stockholders of limited companies.
Industrial managers and government officers interchange positions,
oblige each other and otherwise support the common subculture.

There are also formal links between the Government and the
firm sector. Chambers of Commerce, advisory boards, Rotary and

Lions Clubs, the Stock Exchange, and, since the mid-1960s, the proliferation of Seminars and Conferences bring the two together formally. Bribes, job offers, and stock shares are subterranean links binding the Government and the firm sector together.

The bazaar sector is another matter. It is run by petty bourgeoisie-craftsmen turned entrepreneurs. Its working conditions are socially unattractive, and the language and culture are purely local. Usually it deals with the Government through lowly officials such as inspectors, head clerks, and overseers. Its primary mode of influence is bribing the individual officials. Yet there is an evolutionary trend in the bazaar sector towards organized lobbying for favourable policies. Trade Associations organized on the basis of lines of production or geographical market (such as the Association of Nuts and Bolts Manufacturers or the Association of Glass Manufacturers of Lahore) have emerged to lobby for favourable policies. These associations, run by "graduate" sons of entrepreneurs, present memoranda to presidents and governors, hold receptions for dignitaries, buy advertisements in newspapers, or sponsor special inserts in magazines to assert their presence. Yet their approach is that of supplication, whereas Chambers of Commerce (firm sector representatives) make demands on the Government. These are the two styles of influencing the Government.

Reprise of Industrial Trends

The preceding pages present evidence of Lahore's impressive industrial development since Independence; about 90 percent of registered factories started after 1947. Yet this development has not made Lahore into the Manchester of Pakistan. By the criterion of location quotients, it is not a city specialized in manufacturing. Indices such as size of establishments and type of goods produced show that Lahore's industrial strength seems to be in its bazaar sector. Social imperatives as embodied in occupational caste structures encouraged enterprising craftsmen to start workshops and factories for producing modern goods, e.g., fans, coolers, engines, chemicals, and shoes. Even the industrial and locational patterns bear out this conclusion: the core of the city has the largest number of industrial establishments. It is evident that the secular trend in industrial activity is towards smaller factories and reduced capital investments, as the following figures suggest:

	Before Independence	1947 -1958	1959 -1969	1970 -1978
Mean No. of Employees per registered factory started in respective periods	100	87	53	51

Mean amount of fixed
assets (capital) per
worker (1978 Rupees)   Rs. 12,198   11,870   10,889   9,022

The bazaar sector is internally divided into three strata. It
does not consist merely of poor transient artisans, as the literature in informal economics would suggest. It is a vigorous,
highly patterned, and evolving mode of operation whose flexibility
and adaptability are its assets. It is a life-style almost to the
point of being a distinct subculture.

The firm sector is fashioned after modern organizations. It
is dependent on foreign technology and the Government's patronage.
Through its political and social power, it sets the terms of relationship with the bazaar sector, and the latter often operates in
the opportunity field left over by the firm sector. While the firm
sector has become bureaucratized, the bazaar sector generally is
being commercialized, incorporating those organizational forms and
practices that are financially beneficial. However, there is a
ceiling beyond which bazaar sector establishments do not grow,
either in size or in complexity, and a bazaar sector establishment
seldom enlarges into a firm. The two have different origins, and
their fields of operations are compartmentalized by social class
and product. The bazaar sector produces modern goods to meet indigenous needs, and it has a greater affinity to lower-lower middle
class life-style. The firm sector is, on the other hand, the pur-
veyor of modern middle and upper class values.

The Government has the central role in manufacturing activities, as supplier of finance, regulator of imports, or the conduit
for foreign aid. The powers of the state are the principal assets
of the firm sector.

TRADE AND FINANCE

From time immemorial, Lahore has been the regional market for
grains, leather, gold, jewellery, glass, and other household
items. Recently it has become the centre of trade in automobiles,
machinery, tools, radios, televisions, fabrics and apparel,
hosiery, medicines, and books. Here are regional offices of major
import-export houses, industrial corporations, banks, insurance
companies and the stock exchange. The city's cinemas, hotels,
restaurants, and kebab shops have earned it the epithet that
"anyone who has not seen Lahore hasn't savoured life." Lahore is
the New York of Pakistan, where fun is business and business is a
game.

The scale of the commercial activities can be assessed from
Table 5.1. Almost 27 percent of Lahore's labour force in 1979 was
engaged in trade, and another two percent was occupied in banking
and finance activities. Despite all the limitations of the data,
it can be safely inferred that trade and banking have expanded
proportionately far more than other activities. The labour force

in these activities almost doubled over the period 1961-78, indicating a faster rate of increase than that of the work force in other activities. The question, then, is how this impressive expansion came about.

Trade is an activity that is bound to expand with population growth. Even the poor buy food, clothes, or shelter, and so sheer demographic growth stimulates the expansion of trade. Pakistan, though remaining very poor, has experienced some increase in per capita incomes (90 percent in constant prices over a 30-year period) which in turn translates into enhanced purchasing power and further expansion of trade. Over and above these expansionary thrusts, Lahore, like other Third World metropolises, has become the consumption capital of the province. It is the distribution point for imported goods, industrial products, entertainment, and tourism. Since the mid-70s, remittances from Pakistanis abroad have further inflated the demand for all kinds of goods. For these various demands, the city is the supplier of goods and services. The multiplier effect of regionally-oriented business further strengthens the city's commercial base, and so, the more the city grows economically and politically, the more it dominates the region. This phenomenon is well known to the observers of Third World cities, in which a local economy expands at a faster rate than the national economy by soaking up resources from the surrounding areas. There are no longitudinal data to illustrate the expansion of commercial activities over time, and therefore pieces of cross-sectional data and observational accounts will be relied upon to compose the evolving picture of Lahore's trade and related activities [15].

An impression of the volume of commercial activities may be derived from the survey of shops carried out by the city's planners as a background for the master plan in 1962. The survey indicates that there were 31,286 shops (stalls or hawkers not included) in the city, yielding an overall ratio of one shop per 41 persons [16]. This ratio seems to be in line with similar figures from other cities of Punjab [17]. It contrasts sharply with Western standards, where a ratio of one store per 150-300 persons has been used for allocating commercial sites. It would be logical to expect more persons per shop in poor countries where consumers have little to spend, yet the situation shows the reverse. Seemingly, this condition arises from two factors: (1) scarcities of financial resources and materials which call for numerous small shops, and (2) the spatial organization of the city. These factors will be probed in the following section.

Sectoral Organization

In Lahore, commercial activities are primarily carried out in the bazaar mode. The city's supplies of grain, meat, milk, vegetables, shoes, clothes, fans, hardware and some items of machinery come from the bazaar sector. Shops and stores are mostly family

owned, conducting business primarily through oral and personalized
transactions. They are embedded in intricate social networks, and
their operations are carried out through bargains and deals that
extend beyond a single transaction. Although the trade is now
fully monetized, prices and quality of goods vary (within a certain range) according to the social characteristics of buyers and
sellers. A nephew, an influential official, or a regular customer
gets a discount or goods of reliable quality. These favours are
expected to be returned in the form of similar privileges in the
clients' spheres of influence. This is a trade of power,
privilege, and mutual obligations. It is highly patterned, not ad
hoc, yet quite profitable.

The firm sector has a limited presence in commercial activities. Banks, insurance companies, foreign firms, public corporations, Bata or similar chain stores (very few in number), and some
markets of the rich residential areas constitute the bulk of the
firm sector. On the surface, these tend to operate according to
impersonal rules and modern business practices. Usually, English
is the language of records and correspondence. A firm sector
establishment is generally run by employees, and there is a distinct separation between "owning and managing" and "operational"
functions. As trade is primarily a face to face activity, it is
inevitable that, even in the firm sector, a certain degree of
personalization takes place. Social obligations and the power
exchange also influence the operations of the firm sector. For
example, given compelling social bonds, a bank manager cannot
overlook the recommendation of a future son-in-law, no matter how
much he may be a stickler for the rules.

Historically, trade has been a labour-intensive activity in
which risk is spread out among numerous buyers, sellers, brokers
and stockists. By segmenting and compartmentalizing the process of
transferring a commodity from producers to final consumers, layers
of middlemen reduce the time period for which anyone's capital is
tied up and personal pledges substitute for cash outlays. Furthermore, the supply comes from a large number of small producers, and
this requires relatively numerous contact men. For example, the
fruit supply for Lahore passes through four to five hands before
reaching the consumer, i.e., from grower to broker to investor to
wholesaler to broker-auctioneer to retailer/hawker. From such an
array of intermediary traders comes the proliferation of shops.
From the consumer's perspective, there are equally strong imperatives for relatively small and numerous shops. An overwhelming
majority of consumers are poor, and have neither cash on hand nor
refrigerated storage capacity to buy necessities for a week or
even a day. For example, vegetables and meat are purchased almost
at the time of actual consumption, morning or afternoon. This
means shops have to be nearby and must remain open for most of the
day. These functional requirements turn much retail trade into a
chain of personalized transactions and, in turn, establish a
ceiling for the size and distance (from consumers) of shops.

On the supply side, the entrepreneurship of the poor and

unemployed also contributes to the proliferation of shops. In the
face of high unemployment and lack of skills and resources, the
poor turn to hawking and selling. Often, with a nominal amount of
help from kin and friends, a young man can be set up to sell pen-
cils on a street corner or hawk peanuts.

These are the economic imperatives that necessitate multiplication of shops. Underlying them are general conditions, such as
scarcity of capital, plenty of labour, and a fragmented and decentralized process of production. How, then, are different parts of
the city served by this relatively diffused system of distribution? To answer this question, we turn to data about the intracity
distribution of shops.

For analysis of the commercial structure, the city has been
divided into the same nine districts as are used in industrial
location analysis (refer to Chart 5.1). Table 5.5 presents the
district-wide distribution of shops in 1962.

TABLE 5.5

Distribution of Shops in Lahore, 1964

District/Area	All Shops		Food Shops Only	
	Number	Per-centage	Number	Per-centage
1. Walled City and circular road	3,669	11.7	834	7.3
2. Northern communities (BadamiBagh, Misri-Shah, etc.)	3,452	11.0	1,534	13.5
3. Civil Lines	14,806	47.3	4,772	42.0
4. Western communities (Krishan Nagar, etc.)	1,997	6.4	758	6.7
5. Southwestern Planned Schemes (RehmanPura, Wahdat colony, Samanabad)	2,508	8.0	1,199	10.5
6. Northeastern communities (Moghalpura, SultanPura, Shahlimar Town)	2,874	9.2	1,302	11.5
7. Southeastern planned suburbs (Gulberg,				

Model Town)	619	1.9	337	3.0
8. Peripheral-Ribbon development	286	0.9	131	1.2
9. Cantonment	1,075	3.4	500	4.4
Total	31,286	100.0	11,367	100.0

Source: Government of West Pakistan, Master Plan for Greater
         Lahore (Lahore: The Master Plan Project Office, 1964),
         Appendix 7.

About half (47.3 percent) of all shops were located in District 3,
the post-British part of the city. It may also be noted that this
district has clusters of specialized markets and the largest concentration of registered factories. This suggests two points, (1)
the interdependence and proximity of markets and factories, and
(2) the concentration of most of the economic activities in this
section of the city. In anticipation of the findings of the next
section, it may be pointed out that most public and private
offices and service establishments are also located in this district. Yet all these economic activities are not concentrated
within a few blocks or along any one road, to constitute a downtown. It is a sprawling district which though "old" (dating to the
late nineteenth century) is "new" for a city that is more than
1,000 years old.
     The distribution of shops in the rest of the city more or
less follows industrial location patterns. The Walled City and the
northern New Indigenous Communities are respectively the second
and third districts of commercial concentration. The elite residential areas, such as Gulberg, Cantonment, have lower proportions
of shops.
     Assuming food to be the lowest order of goods and food shops
to be a neighbourhood commercial activity, columns 4 and 5 of
Table 5.4 have been compiled to reveal the structure of commercial
activities. First to be noted is that almost 37 percent of
Lahore's shops are stores for food, uncooked and cooked. These
figures do not include hawkers and stalls, which, if added, could
easily bring the proportion to almost half. Obviously, food is the
most common commodity to be purchased in a city of the poor:
according to surveys of consumption expenditures, almost 50
percent of an urban household's expenses were incurred by food and
drinks in 1968-69 [18]. Second, the distribution of food shops is
at variance with the district-wide proportions of all shops. Civil
Lines and the Walled City have comparatively lower proportions of
food shops, compared to all other districts. This pattern shows
that the more commercialized districts have fewer food shops,
while relatively residential districts have more.

Structure of Commercial Activities

Unlike Western cities, Lahore's hierarchy of commercial establishments is not immediately evident. To a casual observer, Lahore may appear a hodge-podge city where almost all activities mix randomly, but this impression may not reflect the reality. Because of the wide disparities in living conditions and consumption patterns of Lahoris, goods are initially distinguished by two broad categories: imported-modern versus indigenous-traditional. The second distinguishing characteristic is the order of goods, i.e., whether it is of daily use (food items) or a luxury of infrequent demand. Commercial activities in the city are organized along these lines. The Mall is the commercial spine for modern, higher order goods (imported china, cosmetics, toys, etc.). Shops in Shah Alam Market and Lohari Gate (at the edge of the Walled City) specialize in essentially indigenous higher order goods (trunks, utensils, cloth, ceramics, locally manufactured toiletries). Retail establishments for food and other items of daily use (lower order goods) are to be found everywhere, but here again class distinctions operate. A grocery shop in the Walled City has rows of sacks and tins arranged in front of a squatting owner, but in upper-class residential areas such a shop is transformed into a grocery store with showcases and walk-around display stands manned by salesmen who write out memos to be presented at the cash register. Although the goods remain the same, the shop is turned from a lower to higher level operation. This is how class characteristics define the commercial order of the city.

The level of an establishment or a market is determined as much by the order of goods being offered as by the social status of the buyers and the neighbourhood. In Lahore, it would be difficult to discern a clear hierarchical order of shopping establishments. Instead commercial clusters must be classified according to continuums which oppose modern versus indigenous and upper versus lower circuits. This also means that there is no one downtown area, but only focal points in the modern city and focal points in the traditional city. Anarkali Bazaar, where historically, modern goods have been retailed by local traders, comes closest to being the bridge between the indigenous and the modern, and it therefore serves as a surrogate for a downtown.

Apart from these commercial clusters there are numerous specialized commodity markets (Mandis), e.g., leather, grain, iron, hardware, paper, books (see Map 5.2). They dot the eastern-southeastern perimeter of the Walled City and mostly operate in the bazaar mode. The proximity of these markets to each other and to clusters of workshops and warehouses has the effect of creating localized commercial-industrial complexes.

Sectoral Dynamics

By now it should be obvious that commercial activities have

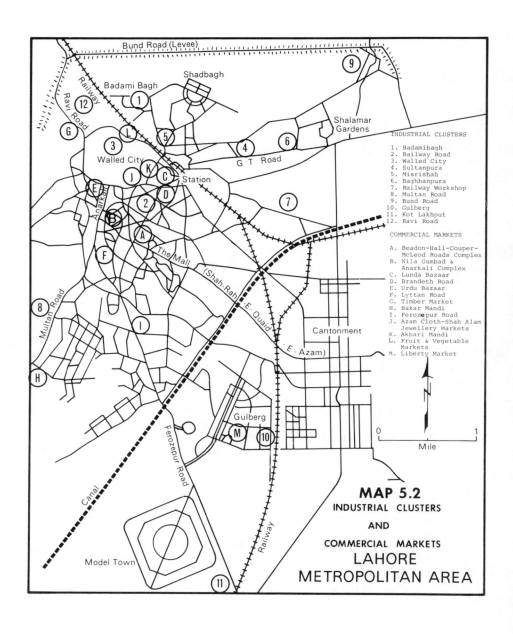

INDUSTRIAL CLUSTERS

1. Badamibagh
2. Railway Road
3. Walled City
4. Sultanpura
5. Misrishah
6. Baghbanpura
7. Railway Workshop
8. Multan Road
9. Bund Road
10. Gulberg
11. Kot Lakhput
12. Ravi Road

COMMERCIAL MARKETS

A. Beadon-Hall-Couper-
   McLeod Roads Complex
B. Nila Gumbad &
   Anarkali Complex
C. Lunda Bazaar
D. Brandeth Road
E. Urdu Bazaar
F. Lyttan Road
G. Timber Market
H. Bakar Mandi
I. Ferozepur Road
J. Azam Cloth-Shah Alam
   Jewellery Markets
K. Akbari Mandi
L. Fruit & Vegetable
   Markets
M. Liberty Market

0   1
        Mile

MAP 5.2
INDUSTRIAL CLUSTERS
AND
COMMERCIAL MARKETS
LAHORE
METROPOLITAN AREA

140

boomed in Lahore since Independence. This boom has not merely meant an arithmetical multiplication of existing types of commercial establishments, but it has also led to the emergence of new modes of operations. Structurally as well as functionally, Lahore's commercial activities manifest evolutionary trends. By responding to new demand and selectively incorporating new technologies, the traditional commercial forms continue to predominate. For example, at the mundane level, such practices as packaging of commodities, monetization of transactions, and adaptation of lucrative banking and insurance practices have been readily adopted. On the deeper structural level, there are tendencies towards formation of mutually supporting cliques and alliances as operational units, emergence of formal associations as regulators of collaborative competition in the market, and segmentation of the market (demand and supply) by social class. These trends are evident in the operations of both sectors and in their interrelations. As the bazaar is the historically predominant mode of commercial operation, it offers more vivid examples of the evolutionary trends. A few case studies will illustrate these points.

Fruit Market

Lahore's fruit supplies come from Kabul, Quetta, and Multan, towns ranging in distance from 100 to 1,500 miles. The fruit comes to the market, where it is sorted, graded, and divided into batches to be sold to retailers or bulk-buying households. The market essentially has remained the wholesale distribution point, although there is some retail activity. The key actor in the market is an Arhati, who, though essentially acting as a commission agent for producers, is also a financier, stockist, and speculator, depending on opportunity and individual resouces. Arhatis are kingpins of the bazaar mandis (markets). In the fruit market, Arhatis primarily come from the Arian clan and, though competitive among themselves, they have effectively blocked the entry of newcomers.

An Arhati contracts with growers and distant suppliers for the supply of fruit before the season. He establishes highly personal relations with a set of suppliers and buyers through complex financial arrangements and good will. He may advance money to a grower for next season's crops and thus tie up his produce years ahead. At the same time, the Arhati is a sort of bank for growers and other suppliers. He sells produce on commission, and proceeds are given to suppliers as they come in, so that at any one time an Arhati may have made an advance to a grower and yet owe him money for produce already supplied.

On a typical day, fruit is brought to the Arhati's stand and auctioned in batches to brokers acting on behalf of retailers or stockists. Not infrequently, the auctioned bulk is further subdivided and sold on the spot to small retailers, households, and hawkers. Over time, each Arhati develops a social network consisting not only of dealers, growers, and buyers, but also of

loaders, drivers, refrigerated warehouse owners, delivery van and
carriage operators. The latter are paid on a piecework basis by
buyers, yet their affiliation with an Arhati's ada (seat) is a
guarantee of reliable service. A retailer can bid for a batch of
fruit and leave it at an Arhati's stall with the assurance that it
will be delivered at his shop by a certain time. These highly personalized arrangements are essential to the operation of the
market. Overall, the fruit goes through four or five middlemen and
registers almost 400 percent mark-up before it reaches a consumer [19]. With the expansion of trade, the fruit market has
expanded in size. City authorities have twice moved it to
peripheral locations, and in 1981 there was renewed talk of
shifting it once again or starting new Mandis. These shifts are
necessitated by the crowding of the market, as each successive
location has been surrounded by new homes and neighbourhoods,
resulting in traffic congestion, insanitary conditions, and
general choking of the market.

Commercial considerations permeate all transactions, yet the
market operates through clusters of interdependent actors who
develop personal loyalties and mutual trust. The local name for
the physical locus of such a cluster is an ada, and each ada is
headed by an Arhati. They may compete among themselves but to the
outside world they present a united front. To deal with the
Government and local authorities, a formal association of fruit
traders has been formed which functions as the umbrella for pursuing common interests, resolving mutual disputes, and laying down
ground rules for competition. The association is an evolution from
informal leadership patterns of bygone days when senior members of
dominant clans used to perform such functions. The formalization
of the association has been necessitated by the legalistic and
political modes of dealing with the Government that are required
with the proliferation of rules and licenses.

Technologically, the operations of the market also have
undergone noticeable change. A new resource, cold storage, has
emerged. Expansion of the city has increased distances and necessitated dealing through intermediaries, thereby introducing a new
layer of functionaries such as buyers, delivery van operators,
etc. The telephone has proved useful in maintaining long-distance
contacts. All the beneficial technology has been readily incorporated into the market. Yet it may be noted that, as the operations
became more complex, reliance on personalized cliques became all
the more necessary.

Azam Cloth Market

This is the specialized wholesale market for cloth, bed-
sheets, laces, and other related items, and is one of the main
distribution points for cloth in the province. It is located in
the narrow alleys of the old city. It is an interesting case study
because it has developed since Independence. After Partition,
about 40 cloth shops gradually appeared around Wazir Khan Mosque

in the Walled City. As the mosque was the centre of a major anti-government religious movement in 1953, General Azam Khan, then martial law administrator of the city, cleared the surrounding area to allow easy access to the mosque by the army and police. As a result of this clearance operation, the cloth dealers were relocated at the present site, which then consisted of burnt out and abandoned houses, remnants of the 1947 communal riots. The traders preferred to locate in these two-feet wide alleys crisscrossed by open drains instead of a multistorey structure that the LIT had built to accommodate them. By 1979, the market had spread into every corner of this residential neighbourhood and had spilled over into the surrounding areas.

As the boundaries of the market are diffused, estimates of the number of these shops vary considerably. According to the President of the Azam Cloth Market Traders' Association, there are 800 wholesale and 700 retail shops in the market, not counting stalls, hawkers, and similar shops in neighbouring streets [20]. Over a 25-year period, the market physically expanded 50 times or more, an expansion which has paralleled the growth of the textile industry in the Punjab. According to a number of real estate brokers, this area of dark, narrow, inaccessible, and crowded alleys in the Walled City paradoxically commands the highest land prices in Lahore.

Major stockists and Arhatis of the cloth market operate in two ways. With large mills producing brand-name popular fabrics, they contract to lift the whole output well in advance and thus they corner the market. For this privilege, they advance large sums to these mills. On the other hand, small mills and handloom weavers seek out Arhatis to stock their products, on commission without any advance. These stockists are suppliers for small shopkeepers in the market. Buyers mostly order through brokers, who stalk the streets and who have information about stocks of various merchants in the market; they may also have influence with some, so that a buyer can obtain materials of his choice openly or in the "black market." Sometimes a transaction may involve more than one stockist, in which case a broker is all the more necessary to put together a deal. A variety of ancillary service workers, such as dyers, folders, and loaders have also appeared to serve the market. They are attached to a set of stockists and Arhatis and thus become part of a network centred around a dealer.

Most of the established Arhatis and dealers of the market belong to three main clans/castes: (1) Narowali Shiekhs, (2) Amritsari Kashmiris, and (3) Memon. Most new dealerships spin off from existing family operations, though, in lower categories of operations, there is relatively more openness and mobility. As with the fruit market, a formal association of traders has emerged which regulates internal competition and lobbies with public agencies for market interests. A shop in the market commands Rs. 200,000 to 300,000 as key-money, and entry is difficult on account of the social cohesion of the existing merchants, who jealously guard their prerogatives and resist any attempt physically to

extend the market. It appears that during the 1970s some People's
Party hacks managed to set up new shops at the periphery of the
market with the assistance of public officials. These intrusions
and expansions were a source of the bazaar's disaffection toward
Bhutto, and it found expression in the agitation that brought down
his government. Yet the use of politico-administrative powers to
promote the fortunes of the favourites of a regime is a common
pattern in Pakistan. It was being said in 1979 that many Islamists
were infiltrating markets with the backing of the public authorities. Upper-level merchants of Azam markets are reputed to be
millionaires, yet they are invisible. This is another characteristic of bazaar operations. Wealth and power are hidden,
life-styles are modest and traditional, appearances shabby, and
labour and enterprise interwoven, e.g., merchants lend a hand in
loading and storing their merchandise. The bazaar is as much a
mode of operation as a life-style. Here labour and enterprise,
modesty and shrewdness, religiosity and technology are cannily
combined. Public attempts to control and direct these markets have
failed. Officials are bribed; scarcities created to pressurize the
Government; regulations of imports, and foreign exchange, are
mastered by illiterate merchants, whenever required. In these
respects, labyrinthine quarters, personalized operation networks,
oral dealings, and paucity of records are very functional practices.

Firm Sector in Trade

    The division between the bazaar and firm sectors runs roughly
along the lines of traditional-consumable versus modern-industrial
goods. The sectors overlap in the supply of luxuries, particularly
the traditional, such as jewellery, and furniture. Also, their
spheres of operations are not cast in stone. There is considerable
filtering down and floating up of commodities between the firm and
bazaar sectors. As a commodity becomes standardized, packaged, and
brand-named, it tends to gravitate towards the firm mode of trade,
or, if the supply of a commodity is closely regulated or appropriated by public agencies, the trade also tends to take the form
of firm transactions. Commodities that have floated up from the
bazaar to the firm sector since 1970 are cooking oils, cement, and
flour, primarily through nationalization of the respective industries. Numerous public trading corporations operating with almost
the same air of authority as a government department have come to
be part of the firm sector.
    The private component of the firm sector consists of multi-
national corporations, managing agencies of large industrial
units, and distributors and depot holders of industrial products.
A quick recount of the firm sector commercial establishments in
Lahore would include such organizations as Bata Shoes, Glaxo
Pharmaceuticals, United Bank, Pakistan Cement Corporation, Lipton
Tea Company, Burmah Shell, and Coca Cola. The example of the trade

in cement is particularly illustrative of the evolutionary changes
in the firm sector's operations.

Distribution of Cement

Up to the 1950s, cement factories were privately owned, and
any shortfall of the supply was filled with imports. Almost every
factory had a wholesale dealer in Lahore who in turn established a
string of distributors and retail depots to cover most of the
city. The retail price was fixed by dealers and depot holders were
given a fixed percentage of sales. This system worked fairly
smoothly in normal times, but in periods of scarcity, the dealers
would horde stocks to sell at black market rates. By the early
1950s, the Government established a few cement factories which
followed, more or less, the well-honed existing mode of distribution. Dealers and public agencies periodically resorted to issuing
permits to ration the supplies. This gave rise to much
influence-peddling and trade in permits.

On the public take-over of cement factories, the state Cement
Corporation was established to organize distribution, but was soon
bulging with executives and sales personnel recruited to man the
distribution network. The Cement Corporation's retailing arrangements have gone through two cycles of reorganization since then.
Initially, numerous, but relatively small, depots were established, but soon the difficulties of supervising the large number
of retailers became evident. In the second round, twenty big
traders were appointed as distributors for Lahore. This system
proved to be inconvenient for consumers and did not restrain black
markets or nepotism. In the late 1970s, distribution was once
again decentralized and large numbers of small retail outlets were
reestablished. The monopoly held by the Cement Corporation proved
to be detrimental to the public interest, particularly in the
absence of institutionalized accountability. In 1981, Viewpoint, a
liberal-left magazine, commented editorially on the situation:

> No extraordinary wisdom is required to realize that
> either the authorities should rely on the normal
> channels of trade and distribution or take over the task
> themselves. Attempts to combine the two channels often
> leaves us with the disadvantage of both and advantages
> of neither [21].

Dealerships, Depots and Permits

The above example not only illustrates the changing organization of trade but also reveals the general structural framework of
the firm sector's commercial practices. This framework consists of
establishing a hierarchy of territorial monopolies headed by a
city-wide dealer. The underlying characteristic is a hierarchical
chain of command and responsibility that links together producers,
dealers and retailers (depot-holders). As public control of

distribution of a commodity increases, the structure tends to be
overtly bureaucratic and reliant on state powers. In the case of
scarcity, a system of permits and quotas comes into play to
complement the distributional network. In Lahore, sugar and flour
have been rationed goods since World War II. After Independence,
cars, scooters, bicycles, cement, and vegetable oil have been
added to the list of depoted commodities.

This system of distribution readily becomes the preserve of
the privileged and influential. The Government officers particularly benefit from this, since they can always get a permit, no
matter what may be the rules. The rich can buy from the black
market, but most ordinary consumers must stand in line for hours
or pay bribes to obtain supplies for their meagre demand. Thus the
firm sector's apparently rational system of distribution has
inherent in it scope for influence-peddling bribery and black
market activity. The superficially impersonal arrangements function primarily with the grease of personal contacts and on a "who
knows whom" basis.

To be a depot-holder of flour, sugar, or cement is a privileged business with a guaranteed market, requiring relatively
little capital and negligible commercial skills. Since 1970,
depots have become a form of political reward assigned, for
example, to party workers to assure their loyalty. As city-wide
dealerships are larger business enterprises, they have always been
the preserve of the influential businessmen. The secular trend of
the post-Independence evolution of the firm sector is toward
increasing dependence on the Government and reliance on state
powers to sustain monopolies. Generally the firm sector adopts any
practice or technology that enhances its control of the market and
provides an aura of modernity. However, modernity is usually in
form rather than function. For example, corporations feel obliged
to promote their products through advertisement, although there
could be extreme scarcity of supplies; banks have switched to com-
puterized accounts without any noticeable improvements in service;
weekly dinner meetings of Chamber of Commerce or Rotary Clubs have
become a mark of modernity though there may not be any agenda.
These symbols of modernity constitute a subculture of the firm
sector and help keep it as a preserve of the influential.

Summing Up: Structure of Trade

By now the broad contours of Lahore's commercial activities
have been bared. It is a bifurcated, multilayered structure whose
parts are loosely integrated. Commercial activities have expanded
since Independence and they are the primary source of employment
in Lahore. Commercial activities have not only multiplied but have
also undergone noticeable structural changes.

The bazaar type establishments predominate numerically. They
prevail in the trade of commodities in daily demand such as
fruits, vegetables, cloth, and grains. The firm sector essentially

dominates the trade of brand-name goods, imports, and modern
industrial products. Banking and insurance are its preserves. One
marked evolutionary change in the firm sector since Independence
has been its increasing indistinguishability from Government
departments. The State trading corporations have proliferated and
private firms are fed upon licences and State protection. These
privileged links with the State confer on firm sector establishments oligopolistic characteristics. The process of the linking of
the State and the firm sector started soon after Independence, but
it accelerated in Bhutto's era and has continued at the same pace
since his downfall. The Government and the firm sector are bound
together by the same class interests, i.e., those of officers and
corporate managers. As business enterprises, firm sector establishments turn official authority into cash through bribes and
black market sales of licences and permits. At the personal level,
Government officials circulate between bureaucracies and public
corporations and their kin and friends obtain coveted appointments
in commercial establishments. All in all the Government and the
commercial firm sector are bound together by the shared interests
of the elites.

The bazaar sector operates on margins with little capital,
high leverage and quick turnover. A commodity passes through four
or five middlemen before reaching a consumer. Stocks are seldom
bought on cash. Most of the transactions are on a commission
basis. These arrangements allow the bazaar sector to be
self-financing and capable of expanding with the addition of
operators. In recent times, banks are occasionally called upon to
underwrite business but are essentially used for the safekeeping
of cash. The bazaar sector is its own financier to a large extent,
and this, particularly in a capital-short economy, is its
strength, making it relatively independent of governmental intervention. This mode of business has been honed over centuries:
there are well-defined roles for various actors, and the necessity
of maintaining bazaar goodwill ensures conformity. The bazaar is a
unique institution where cooperative competition rules. The system
works in the context of a bazaar's social structure. A specific
caste or clan-group dominates a commodity market, particularly its
lucrative upper echelons. The lower echelons of the bazaar sector
are relatively open to new entrants. Since Independence, the
bazaar sector has changed enough to maintain its cohesiveness in
the face of new demands. With changing technologies, new layers of
actors have been added. Increasing governmental control of the
economy has led to the emergence of formal associations to lobby
for the bazaar's interests, yet bazaar operations have remained
labour-intensive, modest in appearance and demanding of intense
personal attention. Lest we may be romanticising the bazaar
sector, it should be understood that its working conditions are
poor, wages low, jobs irregular, and child labour rampant.

The firm sector is organized like a modern bureaucracy based
on division of labour by tasks and credentials. It is pyramidi-
cally arranged, with power residing in distant managing agencies

and national dealers. A commodity may go through two or three
hands before reaching consumers. Firm sector establishments tend
to carve out territorial monopolies and manage demand through
permits and licences. By relying on State powers, the firm sector
has increasingly immunized itself against competition and market
accountability.

The two modes of operations also have similarities, such as
business strategies and structures that are not apparent. Both
operate by mopping up finances through commissions and advances
from a large number of small operators. In different ways, both
operate on the principle of reducing capital demands and spreading
the risk among a large number of actors. The firm sector achieves
this objective through a hierarchical system of dealerships and
distributors, and the bazaar sector attains similar results
through <u>Arhatis</u> operation wherein personal guarantees substitute
for upfront cash and dealing on margins is the rule. Both are
resistant to new entrants particularly at the lucrative upper
levels. The firm sector, being more formally organized, is more
closed, even at lower levels, than the bazaar sector, where
hawking and retailing are activities of last resort for the unemployed. Both have oligopolistic tendencies which have increased
rather than attenuated with expansion. The fields of operation of
the two sectors shift back and forth as a commodity floats up or
filters down from the bazaar to the firm modes, and vice versa.

A tendency towards compartmentalization of Lahore's market by
social class has become evident with development. The same commodity is distributed in the bazaar mode for the poor and in the
firm mode for the affluent. Increasingly, the upper and modern
middle class circuit of buying and selling tends to be separated,
even physically, from the corresponding circuit of the traditional
middle and lower classes. These compartments of the market are
distinguishable by type and quality of goods, setup of shops,
pricing practices, and locations.

Commercial activities manifest a trend towards the formation
of personalized networks of traders as well as buyers and sellers,
and such social clusters, not individuals, constitute operational
units of the market. The expansion and development necessitate a
certain degree of impersonalization of institutions, which is cir-
cumvented with the practice of constituting friendship cliques and
social networks. The resources of impersonal institutions are the
prizes for which these cliques compete: import licences, a seat on
the auctioneer's row, or a supply of sugar at rationed prices.
This privatization of public assets on a group basis is the latent
function of nepotism, bribery, and the black market. Obviously,
the impoverished and disenfranchised masses bear the cost of this
trend in the form of scarcities, high prices, and deprivation.

All in all, Lahore's commerce has been a source of employment
and a significant contributor to its economic base. Its tremendous
expansion has met the challenges of the city's growth. Yet it has
been increasingly fractionated in its upper and lower circuits.
Commercial development has led not to an integrated hierarchy of

commercial establishments, but to segregation of shopping establishments for the poor and rich respectively.

SERVICES

The economies of Third World cities are said to be undergoing
tertiarization without being first sufficiently industrialized.
Peattie succinctly describes the process of tertiarization as
"large expansion of employment in commercial and service sectors,
relative to employment in manufacturing." [22] These trends have
been viewed with consternation by neo-Marxists who regard tertiary
activities as unproductive, while other liberal-left observers
find them reassuring expressions of poor people's entrepreneurship
and of the "small is beautiful" theme. These divergences of
opinion, even within the scope of radicalism, indicate the paradoxical nature of urban economies. Obviously, our first task is to
analyze the scale and organization of service activities in
Lahore.

Table 5.2 provides an overview of service employment in
Lahore. These data point out that community and personal services
were modal employment activities for the city's labour force in
1961; by 1977 they still constituted almost the largest employment
sector, though trade shared this status (more than half of the
city's work force was engaged in these two activities). When
figures for employment in finance and transport are added to data
for services, the preponderance of tertiary activities in Lahore's
economy is indisputable. On the surface, there are some pointers
towards slackening of the rate of increase in service employment
during 1961-77: e.g., the work force of community and personal
services increased by only 59 percent compared to an increase of
109 percent in the overall work force of the city. Yet this is
something of a statistical illusion. Employment in trade activities expanded by almost 200 percent over this period. Relatively
more of this increase occurred in the lower-level trade activities
(such as hawking) which are as much service functions as trade
activities. All in all, it can be concluded that employment in
tertiary activities constituted about 50 to 55 percent of Lahore's
work force, a proportion which remained unaltered over the period
1961-77, though there was almost a doubling of the work force. It
suggests that Lahore's economy experienced a balloon-like expansion where relative proportions of constituent elements remained
the same, an indication of the consistency of the basic structure.

Sectoral Organization

It seems that terms such as "tertiary" or "service" activities mask the precariousness of many workers' livelihood. Women
who pick through garbage piles to recover pieces of broken glass
for recycling or sort out unburnt coal from ashes in rail-yards,

boys who mop up spilled oil and wring it out for sale, men who
trail bidders at fruit auctions to load their purchases, or
barbers who ply their services on the curbside are among the
self-employed tertiary workers of Lahore, and they constitute the
bulk of the work force in service activities. Table 5.6 on the
sectoral composition of the services work force bears out this
observation.

TABLE 5.6

Sectoral Composition of Services

Activity	Percent of Workers in Unorganized Sector
Construction	80.6
Trade	97.2
Tertiary services – finance, transport and community services	53.7
Total employed labour force	53.0

Source: Lahore Urban Development and Traffic Study, Mansooba-E-
         Lahore Interim Report (Lahore: Lahore Development
         Authority, 1979), p. 9.

The term "unorganized sector" came into vogue in the mid-1970s,
and is approximately synonymous with informal or bazaar character-
izations. Implicit in this term is the notion of nonsalaried,
self-employed workers whose services are measured by volume of
work (piece-work) rather than by the time-units which are typical
of wage labour. The figures cited in Table 5.6 show that
self-employed workers constitute the majority of workers in trade,
construction, and services. The figures also show the predominance
of the low-level bazaar mode. What may be worth examining is
whether there has been any change in relative proportions of
self-employed bazaar workers and the salaried firm workers in service activities.
       The 1961 census data categorized occupations into self-em-
ployed and salaried workers. Assuming that self-employed workers
in service activities constituted the unorganized sector, we can
compare the 1961 data with the figures in Table 5.6. In 1961, 85
percent of workers in trade, 59 percent of construction workers
and 24 percent of the service labour force were self-employed.
Discounting for disparities of data it can still be safely concluded that at least the proportion of self-employed remained
unaltered over this period. This observation implies that the sec-

toral profile of Lahore's economy remained intact despite the doubling of the work force.

It seems that the lower-level, bazaar-mode service work force (loaders, drivers, washermen) increased proportionately more than the total labour force. The proportion of independent workers increased from 24 percent in 1961 to almost 54 percent in 1977. The difference between these two figures is so wide that, even if the data were somewhat incompatible, there could still be no reservations about the foregoing observation. This is not an exceptional finding, but confirms the overall national pattern. The gross value of services in Pakistan increased by 73 and 108 percent during 1960-1970 and 1971-1981 respectively, whereas corresponding increases in Pakistan's GDP were 92 and 55 percent. Obviously, service activities expanded almost at twice the rate of increase in GDP in the 1970s.

The expansion of services in newly independent countries is often a necessary and productive trend. Increased education, and improved health and welfare facilities are fruits of independence, and they are urgently needed. Similarly, an infrastructure of roads, utilities, and housing must preexist for industrial development, and therefore such services are bound to expand. Some degree of tertiarization, particularly of the firm mode, is unavoidable. These developmental requisites materialize in the form of burgeoning bureaucracies and multiplying public agencies. If these developmental predispositions are also accompanied by political preferences for increased public participation in the economy, then governmental establishments are bred like larvae. Lahore (and Pakistan as a whole) experienced all these expansionary pressures.

It is estimated that in Lahore about 75,000 officials were employed by the provincial government alone in 1974, representing a manyfold increase since Independence [23]. When federal and local government employees, officials of the railways, WAPDA, and various public corporations are added to this number, a conservative estimate of public employees in Lahore may come to 125,000 for 1977. Excluding those engaged in trade and manufacturing activities, about 100,000 can be assumed to have been employed in administration, community services, transport, and finance activities. They would constitute almost 80 to 85 percent of the corporate service work force in Lahore. Obviously the firm sector of service activities in Lahore has come to be dominated by public agencies.

This conclusion is, indirectly, affirmed by the following table reporting the distribution of employees in establishments employing 20 workers or more, by the type of agency. By 1978, public agencies almost completely dominated the medium- and large-size (more than 20 employees) establishments in all economic activities except manufacturing and trade. This suggests that the public component in the firm sector of service actitities was very dominant, an observation that confirms earlier findings.

TABLE 5.7

Distribution of Workers by Type of Establishments, Punjab 1978

Activity	Percentage of Employees		
	Public	Private	Total
Manufacturing	29.2	70.8	100.0
Utilities	99.7	0.3	100.0
Construction	97.6	2.4	100.0
Trade and tourism	17.9	82.1	100.0
Transport and construction	99.5	0.5	100.0
Finance and real estate	94.6	5.4	100.0
Community and social services	98.3	1.7	100.0

Source: Government of Punjab, Development Statistics of Punjab
(Lahore: Bureau of Statistics, 1978), Table 145.

Lahore is known to be a city of babus (white-collar workers), and it has become all the more so since Independence. Development has meant exponential multiplication of public agencies and corporations which are highly visible. A walk along a residential street in Gulberg shows a string of offices housed in bungalows: Board of Economic Inquiry, Vegetable Ghee Corporation, Ground Water Survey Agency, Drugs Control Bureau, Narcotics Court, architectural consultants. Obviously Lahore is not short of fashionable developmental institutions. Public agencies have expanded with Parkinsonian zest.

For example, according to a newspaper account, one municipal engineer and two technical supervisors used to look after 100 tube-wells for Lahore's water supply until 1967, when the task was entrusted to a new autonomous public agency (WASA) to accelerate development of water supplies. By 1980, the agency employed 300 officials, including one director and seven deputy directors, while the number of tube-wells to be looked after increased only to 143 [24]. Such a top-heavy organization for public services has become the administrative norm of development. Employment opportunities for graduates have expanded and jobs have increased, but the apparent provision of services does not reflect corresponding actual improvement. The Governor of Punjab in an annual review of the education department acknowledged that in the province 350 schools existed on paper only and 2,000 schools had no teacher [25]. These figures reveal that increased employment in service activities does not ensure an enhanced output of services.

Private establishments in the firm mode are not numerous, and, in fact, these have dwindled with nationalization of schools, colleges and banks. Only the foreign banks, insurance firms, and missionary schools and hospitals have continued to operate, because these were exempted from nationalization.

Other significant elements of private activities delivered in the firm mode are individual practitioners of modern professions, such as doctors, lawyers, accountants. A mild trend towards corporate practice in the form of private clinics and hospitals has been evident since the late 1960s.

Lahore's economy has been greatly inflated by remittances from workers abroad, particularly in the Middle East. It is almost impossible to estimate the value of these remittances or the number of Lahoris working abroad, but, by all indications, remittances sustain a significant proportion of local expenditures. In a way, remittances represent export of invisible services. Apart from their direct income effect, remittances have induced a significant local multiplier effect in the form of a construction boom, real estate speculation, and enhanced consumerism. Apart from these economic effects, remittances have induced far-reaching social structural changes, which, in turn, have produced large-scale realignment of production as well as consumption patterns.

Organizational Changes in Service Activities

Historically, subcontinental communities were highly localized, self-contained, and bonded together. A system of mutual obligations bound one family with others of complementary occupational castes for services and supplies that were not produced by a household. A person was entitled from birth to the services of a specific barber, matchmaker, cook (for festivities), weaver, etc. This is the outline of the famous <u>Jajmani</u> system that underlies Indo-Pakistani social structures. Lahore's traditional social organization was rooted in this system, though, in the city, the payment for obligatory services took the form of cash, clothes, and seasonal gifts instead of, as in villages, a share of the harvest. Of course, this system began to be eroded long ago, almost since the beginning of the British rule, yet it was prevalent in the Walled City and other old neighbourhoods. It has been the foundation of the bazaar sector, i.e., caste-aligned occupations, and clusters of clients and providers of services.

The arrival of large numbers of refugees from India in 1947 was a major jolt to the caste-based system of occupations. Their social network was rent asunder, and services had to be contractually obtained. Expansion of the city's population, migration from rural areas, and spatial spread of the city further weakened the traditional <u>Jajmani</u> bonds. Thus cooks, barbers, matchmakers, washermen, and domestics have been disassociated from their hereditary clients, and they now ply their occupations on a commercial basis. This is the evolutionary trend in the bazaar segment of service activities.

This commercialization has resulted in the stratification of service activities by social class. Depending on the social status and economic resources of the client, services are available in forms ranging from deluxe salons to curbside stalls. One further element of this evolving system of service delivery remains to be identified. Despite pervasive commercialization, the delivery of many personal services still proceeds through a social network that is carefully nurtured by clients as well as providers. This point can be illustrated with a specific example.

Matchmakers

Conventionally, marriages have been arranged through family matchmakers who served a family through generations. They were recompensed in the form of customary seasonal payment and special rewards for an errand. Since Independence, matchmaking has become a semicommercial service, particularly in New Indigenous Communities and upper income suburbs. A matchmaker, usually a woman, cultivates acquaintance with a number of families and makes rounds of their homes periodically, both to size up their needs and to maintain a pool of potential clients. An eligible boy or girl becomes the focus of her attention and she may begin to look for a suitable match. If the search leads to successful negotiations between two families, not only is she amply rewarded but she also earns goodwill and introductions to new clients. Although monetary considerations are the prime motivation, all these transactions occur in the context of patterned personal relations and mutual regard that precedes and survives any single act of matchmaking. Similar arrangements have emerged for the supply of the services of domestics, washermen, water carriers, and barbers. Such services are obtained and delivered within carefully cultivated and long lasting social networks, mutations of traditional interlinked caste groupings. Social networks have evolved from obligatory-bonded to voluntary coalition-like structures.

Another trend in the demand and supply of services, evident in the firm sector more than in the bazaar, is compartmentalization by social class. Education, recreation, medical, and even shopping facilities tend to be organized to serve a specific social class. Exclusive facilities for the upper class are not unknown in other cities, but Lahore (and other cities of Pakistan) are unique in that this segregation has emerged as a reciprocal of the attempts to expand community services to the masses. As soon as a service begins to be available on a large scale, its upper circuit splits apart into exclusive facilities for the influential, thereby draining the resources and accelerating the decline of quality for the masses.

CORRUPTION

The preceding explorations of economic activities have uncovered an extensive substratum of corruption in almost every case. Manufacturing has producers of counterfeit products and dealers in permits and quotas, commerce is rife with hoarding, and black marketing, services and administrations are ridden with bribery and nepotism. Doctors use public hospitals as private fiefs to treat fee-paying patients, landlords ask for key-money, and smugglers operate under police patronage. Such instances can be recounted almost endlessly. This does not include unearned wealth that the influential derive by devising favourable policies to benefit themselves such as distributing state lands at nominal prices among themselves, or setting aside special quotas for scarce commodities. Whether clothed in favourable rules or manifestly illicit, corruption has become a way of life. Conservatively, it can be estimated that 30 to 40 percent of local income circulates through the channels of corruption [26].

Corruption not only has direct economic effects, but also, by eroding the reliability of administrative and market institutions, it exacts high social costs. Public policies cannot be implemented, rules cease to be effective, influence-peddling and kickbacks become operational norms. Predictability and credibility go out of the public order. These conditions create economic uncertainty and distort social priorities.

Economically, corruption has effects both on growth and distribution, but predominantly on the latter. Smuggling and unauthorized manufacturing may add to the national stock of goods and services but the distributional effects of corruption are far more numerous. The black market deprives the poor of necessities and allocates them to the middle- and upper-class groups. Another wall is erected around the upper circuit of economy to insulate it from the demands of the masses. Similarly, bribery or kickbacks benefit officers and cause suffering to the community at large. Permits, quotas, allotments, and other rationing devices lay the ground for corruption and establish the process of regressive transfers.

Two rings of corruption come into play. First, for obtaining permits and quotas, and second, for cashing these privileges. Thus, bribery, nepotism, and the black market are linked and constitute a parallel economy within the local economy. Law enforcement agencies, such as taxation authorities, police, courts, and customs take their respective cuts and wink at such transactions, thereby completing the circle. Although corruption permeates the lower strata of officials and traders, the prime beneficiaries are higher-ups. A stall holder may gain a few rupees a day by covertly peddling smuggled Indian whiskey, but it is the big crook who makes hundreds of thousands in a single smuggling deal under the patronage of police and taxation authorities. Similarly, a peon may accept a cup of tea to let a client see the big boss, but the boss himself may appropriate hundreds of thousands of rupees from a construction project. Thus corruption acts as the resource mopping-up process for the influential. The cost ultimately is borne by the community, in the form of poorly constructed roads or battered buses, flooded drains, and exorbitantly high prices of food, rent, and housing.

An example of the functioning of Lahore's local transport will illustrate the intricate web of public and private forms of corruption and their social consequences.

Local Transport

The difficulties of finding a bus, taxi, rickshaw, or any other means of public transport are legend. Long waits, exorbitant charges, unsafe vehicles, high-handedness of operators, and police arbitrariness are parts of this syndrome. Undoubtedly, increasing population and expansion of the city have drained the facilities and increased the demand, but corruption, mismanagement, and poor planning have taken away all possibilities of amelioration of transportation difficulties. Lahore inherited a limited but reliable public bus service from the British era. The explosive development after Independence triggered voluminous demand which was not matched by a corresponding increase in the service. Buses in actual service are much fewer than need because of mismanagement. Seldom more than 50 percent of the Urban Transport Corporation's fleet of buses has been on the road on an average day. The rest remain in workshops or stockyards for want of pilfered parts [27]. The Corporation cannot even collect the revenue from bus fares because conductors, in collusion with their supervisors, take the cash and do not issue tickets. Periodically, a major breakdown of the system or some other catastrophic event triggers hurried acknowledgements of corruption and mismanagement. Taxi and rickshaw services and minibus operations fare not much better.

It is not for lack of regulations or enforcement agencies that vehicles are poorly maintained, fare meters tampered with, or rules of the road ignored. Vehicles are periodically examined, drivers are expected to undergo vigorous road tests, and an army of traffic policemen are in evidence on the roads, yet each agency makes its authority and powers into a saleable commodity to be exchanged for favours or bribes. Policemen charge for overlooking traffic infractions and not infrequently catch innocent drivers to shake them down. Vehicles can be found fit without ever being brought for inspection. Long lines and the authorities' harassing procedures discourage people from getting drivers' licences; instead, they pay or plead their way out if caught driving without a licence. These practices are so wide-spread that they almost could be called operational norms. Periodic public campaigns to enforce laws and take stringent actions have no lasting effect. Often they increase the suffering of the general populace because taxis and buses refrain from plying the roads for as long as such campaigns last, and, thereafter, the fares usually go up on the ground that severe measures have increased bribe rates. The outcome of this process has been visible on Lahore's roads for decades. Minibus operators stuff 18 passengers in a nine-seat vehicle and charge exorbitant fares. Taxis are hard to find, and a ride has to be individually negotiated in disregard of the meter readings. Noisy motor rickshaws spewing black smoke weave through the traffic disregarding rules of the road.

The so-called modern notions and new ideas transplanted without understanding the local situation also help sustain corruption. An example is the plan to phase out tongas from Lahore. Tongas are an old, efficient, and economical means of transportation for short distances. They carry almost a hundred thousand rides every day around the Walled City and between different points of Civil Lines. Since the 1960s, however, tongas have begun to irk Lahore's traffic planners and administrators, who regard them as slow-moving vehicles which impede the flow of automobiles and thus deserve to be banned. Foreign experts declare a ban on tongas immediately on arriving to advise about the city's traffic problems, and it is seldom that anybody bothers to gather facts and examine their functional necessity [28]. In the early 1970s, the municipality instituted a policy of not issuing new licences for tongas, thereby ensuring their slow phasing-out through attrition. The response has been predictable. Officially, the number of tongas has dwindled from 8,000 in the 1970s to 4,025 in 1981, but unofficially it is known to everyone concerned that their number has increased by almost 50 percent [29]. The "new" tongas use counterfeit number plates and are "free" to operate after paying dues to the checking staff. This is an illustration of how ill-advised policies lay the ground for corruption.

The plight of an average citizen faced with such a transportation system is hard to imagine. It is a daily battle to get a ride, pay no more than yesterday's charges, arrive safely, and not lose hours in waiting. These conditions, paradoxically, have made a private vehicle almost a necessity in this city of the poor.

This detailed description of the subterranean river of corruption in local transport illustrates the pervasiveness of such practices. This example shows clearly that corruption is patterned almost as an institution embracing all segments of the society, i.e., public agencies as well as private enterprises, senior officers as well as the lowly workers. It has the characteristics of a system in which practices are persistent and interrelated; actors may change but the system survives. A taxi driver who rigs the fare meter and browbeats passengers feels as much a victim of the system of corruption as the rider.

The pervasiveness of corruption and its systematic nature can be further appreciated from the following sample of paraphrased news accounts embracing a five-year period (1975-80) that included two different regimes of diverse policies.

(1) Test papers for various degree examinations were leaked to candidates by the secrecy branch of Punjab University (obviously in return for favours and bribes) [30].

(2) The provincial Inspector General of Police ordered the police officials not to rely on touts and tutored witnesses for prosecuting an accused [31].

(3) Forty-two police trainees were charged for forging educational diplomas to enter the police service [32].

(4) Over 7,000 cars were falsely imported into the country under a gift remittance scheme [33].

(5) During monsoon rains, recently constructed roads simply disintegrated, evidently proving the poor quality of construction, design and supervision [34].

(6) Faisal Town, a locality recently built by the LDA, "looks like a part of Mohenjodars. Lanes have cracked and drainage busted." [35]

(7) About 50,000 applications for building permits remain unattended in the municipal offices [36].

(8) Lahore Contractors Association (Buildings & Roads) alleged that 20 percent of funds earmarked for development are taken as commission by engineers (supervising the works) [37].

(9) After a crackdown on the sugar black market, Pepsi, Coke, and other drinks disappeared from the market [38].

(10) Cows and buffaloes to be shifted to the outskirts of Lahore before May 14, 1980 [39]. . . . Development work on cattle colonies has been suspended for three months. However, shifting of cattle for the city will proceed as per government policy [40]. Gowallas (cattlemen) have collected letters of allotment for plots in the cattle colony but have not shifted cattle [41]. Cattlemen (Gowallas) are keeping cattle in northern residential colonies of Lahore such as Shad Bagh, BadamiBagh, awaiting the slowdown of the shifting campaign [42]. . . . Buffaloes are back in the city [43].

(11) About 300 telephones have been installed in shops and houses of influential persons on the pretext of being available for public use [44].

(12) The Mayor of Lahore wrote to the WAPDA chairman that 75 percent of the street lights in the city were missing bulbs or otherwise not working [45].

(13) About two-thirds of the meat supply every day comes from irregularly slaughtered sheep, ostensibly as sadqas (religious charity) to avoid official inspection and control [46].

The examples cited above illustrate several points. First, corruption is pervasive and highly structured. Second, though corruption is a moral crisis of the whole community, it is not a matter any more of immorality of a few individuals; its systematic nature has made it a functional necessity for almost all. Third, corruption is a form of tax that wielders of economic, political, and administrative powers exact from the people. It is a premium received for authority, and it is derived in direct ratio to the insularity and unaccountability of those who wield power. Fourth, the ground for the corruption is laid by scarcities and maldistribution of basic necessities, resulting from mismanagement, and inappropriate policies. A feedback effect ensures that, once corruption takes hold, it exacerbates mismanagement, abuse of authority and ad-hocism. Fifth, corruption seems to have been immune to ideological shifts. Loudly-proclaimed Socialist or Islamic orders have been equally susceptible to corruption. Sixth, corruption permeates all strata of the society (from lowly rick-shaw drivers to tax commissioners), though gains are proportionate to social status; overall corruption functions as a mechanism for influentials to "mop up" resources from the masses. Seventh, cor-ruption results in substituting personalized wheelings and dealings for impersonal rules and institutions. Eighth, corruption is a process of privatizing and commercializing public authority and facilities.

Although it may not accord with the scientific outlook to be prescriptive, it seems that corruption can be reduced only by alleviating glaring disparities of power and authority, by instituting people's participation in decision-making, by bringing down the walls of unaccountability surrounding the public offices, by ensuring a fair and efficient distribution of basic public services, and by restoring citizens' rights. Otherwise corruption will continue to be the mechanism to reward the rich and influential.

Corruption not only affects costs and output of production in the local economy, but it also distorts the consumption profile. Unearned incomes promote conspicuous consumption which has a demonstrative effect. All in all, demand for luxury goods, propped up by corrupt earnings, distorts production and import priorities. For example, tikka shops (skewered-meat restaurants) in Lahore, primarily patronized by officers on kickbacks and by black-marketeers, are said to take up such a large proportion of the scarce meat supply of the city that meat has become a luxury meat. (In 1981, meat was selling at Rs. 24 per kilo, about two days' salary for a clerk.) How consumption has changed since 1947 is the last question requiring to be probed to complete the analysis of Lahore's economy.

CONSUMPTION AND LIVING STANDARDS

Myrdal rightly maintains that in poor countries increased consumption should be viewed as an investment [47]. By reducing malnutrition, by improving housing, and by raising educational levels, productivity can be increased and the quality of life enhanced. This point of view has, after a decade, found acceptance even among conservative international bankers. The basic-needs approach to development is an acknowledgment of this posi-tion [48]. People have always identified development with increased provision of health, education, food, jobs, and housing. After all, production of more goods and services is only a means to enhance general welfare, so the ultimate objective of develop-ment is greater satisfaction of people's needs. Undoubtedly the economic inspiration for independence movements in the Third World was rooted in expectations of enhanced consumption and a higher

standard of living, and Pakistan was not an exception to these
expectations.

Chapter 3 gives an overview of the secular trends in levels
of living in Pakistan since 1947. Substantial gains have been
registered in per capita income, food consumption, and health and
educational facilities, yet these gains cannot mask the persistence of mass poverty and sharpened social disparities. Lahore
encapsulates national trends in bolder relief.

Chapter 4 describes at length the changes in housing conditions and the availability of public facilities in Lahore. It suggested that, while a substantial number of new houses and community facilities had been built, the overall living conditions
had not improved much. Proportions of ill-housed, jobless, and
malnourished people have remained almost the same, despite visible
development. Development has made possible accommodation of a
larger population and has even affected the material base, but the
relative positions of various classes have not changed to any notable degree. Post-Independence achievements are the maintenance of
the social order, the accommodation of a larger population at a
subsistence level, and the emergence of indigenous professionals,
officers and capitalists. Yet, as the living conditions of
influentials changed and a larger population was maintained with a
semblance of sustenance, it was inevitable that there should be
some threshold changes in the consumption patterns of the city as
a whole.

Development is not a process of arithmetical multiplication.
Systems of production and distribution of food, vegetables, and
other necessities for half a million people are likely to undergo
substantial changes on being required to serve a population of
three million. New activities and institutions are bound to arise,
as thresholds for higher order goods are precipitated. Lahore has
witnessed a steady expansion of fun-food outlets, both in the
variety available and the numbers: e.g., kebab and tikka shops,
skewered, broiled, and fried chicken restaurants, fruit salad and
green tea stalls, have proliferated to make Lahore a delight for
eating out. These trends are manifestations of the critical mass
effect of a large number of poor consumers whose once-a-year
splurges can sustain these establishments, without the demand of
the affluent.

                          Household Incomes

There are no regional accounts or census data providing
information about household incomes of the city. How the income
has changed over time is a question that can be answered only
imprecisely. The two estimates prepared for successive master
plans of Lahore in 1964 and 1979 respectively are the primary
indicators of the change of income. In 1964, the average (median)
monthly family income was Rs. 120, which in 1979 rupees equals
342 [49]. The median household income in 1979 was Rs. 700 [50].

The 1979 figures represent almost a doubling of the average income
over a 15 year period in constant rupees. During the same period,
individual incomes in Pakistan increased by 47 percent in constant
factor prices. Apparently, Lahore's household incomes increased at
about double the rate for the country. What standard of living did
such income afford? This question can be answered by citing prices
of a few basic necessities. In 1979, a kilo of meat, milk, and
wheat flour were Rs. 18, 3.5 and 1.5 respectively [51]. At these
prices, staples such as flour, milk, and cooking oil could cost up
to 50 percent of the average monthly income of a household of six
persons. Obviously, meat would be a luxury and clothes, housing,
and medicines almost unaffordable. The point is obvious that an
average income of Rs. 700 per month would afford a life of filling
the belly with cereals and little more, and could barely sustain
the subsistence of a family. What would have been the fate of 30
to 40 percent of the households who lived below the poverty
line [52]? Their situation is almost unimaginable. Lahore has
remained a city of the poor. Yet a visible minority of affluent
households had also emerged and this was also the fruit of Independence.

Social Class and Consumption

Lahore's population can be broadly divided into four social
classes of distinct consumption patterns. At the bottom are domestics, unskilled workers, hawkers, and peons, whose earnings are
meagre (Rs. 300-400 in 1979), sporadic, and uncertain. They live
in abject poverty, without adequate food, shelter, or security.
Undoubtedly, there is more money in the hands of members of this
class, but its relative buying power may, in fact, be lower than
it was in the early 1950s. This class survives on mutual help,
charity, and other traditional entitlements of the service castes
from their patrons (discarded clothes, leftover food, etc.). One
source of change in the consumption patterns of this class is the
change in the material base of their patrons. If discards from the
master's house are jeans, Hush Puppy shoes, and European bread,
then obviously a peon or watchman will be consuming these items.
Witness Ved Mehta's poor uncle, "Chacha Ji," showing up every
morning to get the discarded shaving blade of his rich cousin, a
vivid portrayal of how the poor survive [53]. Undoubtedly, more
bicycles and radios have come to constitute possessions of the
poor, signalling a change in consumption functions. In part, these
items have become functional necessities, and in part, they stand
for a process of filtering-down of new material acquisitions.
    The second distinguishable group of consumers consists of
clerks, craftsmen, supervisors, small shopkeepers, and other members of the lower middle class. These are traditional sofad posh
(respectables) whose social status, as well as economic standing,
have declined after Independence. In comparison with that of the
upper classes, this group's level of living has declined since

Independence, because of the excessive advantages amassed by the new elite. Incomes in this group ranged between Rs. 500-1,000 in 1979, while the obligations of respectability preclude any supplementation of earnings by charity, or similar means. This group manages to live by borrowing and shuffling debts from one generation to another. Post-Independence symbols of modernity such as bicycles, coffee, mopeds, and transistors have become this group's preferred possessions, thereby altering their consumption pattern. On the other hand, the lower middle class has lost ground in the consumption of milk and meat, and in standards of dress and housing. Until the late 1950s, house rents were affordable for this class in older sections of the city, but lately such possibilities have been priced out of reach. By the late 1970s, a craftsman or clerk could afford only to live in Katchi Abadis or to double up with some other family in an old house. In dress also there has been a visible decline of standards. Up to the early 1960s, a white-collar worker or small shopkeeper used to be recognized by his clean dress. It was not uncommon to see railway officials in the train station in spotless white uniforms. But by the late 1970s it was rare to find a clean uniform on an official. Babu (clerk) used to be a term of respectability, but, in two decades, it became a form of putdown. A babu waiting to be noticed for a quarter-kilo of meat at a butchery has a pathetic presence amidst Shiekhs, Hajis and Begums ordering sides of mutton without concern for the price.

At this juncture, it may be pointed out that, within each of the two lower classes, there are wide horizontal disparities depending upon specific jobs and affiliations. For example, peons or clerks who could obtain official quarters to live in are substantially better-off than their compatriots who do not have this privilege. In these cases, corruption makes all the difference between levels of living.

Another group distinguishable for its consumption style is the upper strata of the bazaar sector. Arhatis, merchants, stockists, and owners of small factories are inconspicuous but avid consumers. They maintain a traditional and self-effacing life-style often indistinguishable from that of the lower middle class. They live in older parts of the city, though they own property in fashionable areas, and the consumption revolves around food, feasting, and conventional symbols of respectability. They may spend Rs. 100 per day on fruit, yet they will wear a simple cotton shalwar and kurta that may bear marks of manual work. This is the class whose conception of the good life consists of being able to get pure milk from one's own cow, to slaughter a lamb, or to distribute a Degh (a utensil to cook food for 50 persons) of rice as an offering on a shrine. They tend to imbibe the ways of the traditional (rural) elite; an ample supply of good food, comfortable living without ostentation, assertion of prosperity, and the status that comes with it. Social checks and balances rooted in caste and clan expectations have been eroding. Religious practices that legitimize the good fortune (e.g., charity, pilgrimage, etc.) of individuals have had an upsurge among members of this class. Those modern goods which enhance comfort have been readily adopted, such as refrigerators, and scooters, but conspicuous modernity is shunned. Members of this class do not hold receptions in the Hilton Hotel or send families to the hill station in summer.

The fourth, conspicuously visible, class of consumers consists of bankers, industrial and commercial executives, senior civil and military officers, politicians, managing agents, and other top echelons of the firm sector. Obviously food, clothes, and housing have been always plentiful for them. Since Independence, they have acquired new needs, such as cars, palatial bungalows, private schools and clinics, home movies, trips abroad, evenings in theatres, clubs, or Hilton Hotels. Whatever new product sweeps the West, this class is not far behind in adopting it. Imitative Westernism is the hallmark of this class, and the glitter of their life-style stands in sharp contrast with the abysmal living conditions of the masses. What is noteworthy is that this class also revives traditional practices and goods that the lower classes may be shedding, for example, lavish feasting at marriages has become a status symbol of this class. The custom of dowry, against which social reformers have been railing for decades, has been elaborated by this class since Independence, to the point where some of them are being crushed by this burden. The same is the case with Niaz, AQiQa and other quasi-religious occasions. The secular trend in this class is towards conspicuous consumption to assert status; modern goods provide convenience and the status of being up-to-date, and cultural revivalism serves to consolidate social position through lavish hospitality and shared symbols of prosperity such as holding AQiQa (obligatory distribution of food and meat for a newborn) receptions at the Intercontinental Hotel [54]. New prosperity has led to a resurgence in the popularity of many traditional forms of jewelry (e.g., nose rings), foods (sugar candies, etc.) and entertainments (illuminations, singing, etc.).

Cutting across these four classes is a category of indulgent consumers whose presence has become noticeable since the mid-1970s, i.e., Pakistani workers abroad and their families. Relatively high earnings from the Middle East and Europe allow these families to eat and live well, by the standards of their respective social classes. A large proportion of remittances goes into daily consumption: dowries and buying of consumer durables and houses. By 1980, an average Lahori who had no Dubai income (as the local refrain was) almost could not compete for taxis, rickshaws, homes, and entertainment against those who had some income from abroad. Remittances from abroad have turned Lahore into a city of conspicuous consumption and have further fractionated its social structure.

Economic Effects of Consumption

Scanty though the data are, it would still be valid to conclude that consumption levels in Lahore have changed both in
composition as well as on relative proportions of goods and services. Since Independence, household incomes have more than
doubled, and the range of goods available for consumption has
expanded many times. Substantial numbers of middle- and
upper-class households have emerged whose life-styles rely on the
use of fashionable Western artifacts as well as an enactment of
the traditional rites of good living. The affluent have imbibed
Western consumption patterns in the form of labour-saving machines
or revels in Singapore on New Year's Eve, yet they retain conventional conveniences, i.e., servants, feasts. Illicit earnings,
windfall gains, and incomes from abroad have given further impetus
to extravagant consumption. Undoubtedly, the levels of living have
improved en masse, at least in Lahore, but social disparities
among various groups have sharpened. These disparities are most
visible along the class lines, yet there are intraclass differences that distinguish the modern from the traditional, the educated from the uneducated, the influentials from the ordinary,
those with possibilities of black market earnings from those who
have no such means. These cultural and social enclaves are a consequence of development, and constitute distinct economic circuits
whose consumption and production pattern is both sui generis and
self-preserving.
Does, then, this fractionation of the city's economy into
circuits (or enclaves) of divergent levels of consumption represent market rewards for varying purchasing powers, a condition
that neoclassical economists regard as both necessary and efficient? The evidence produced in this chapter makes the answers
negative. Unusually high incomes are largely premiums for influence-peddling and economic oligopolies, but it also seems that
indulgent consumption in one circuit preempted others' opportunities and led to a lopsided development. This conclusion
requires elaboration.
Given a limited production capacity, over-consumption by one
segment of the population is bound to put others at a disadvantage, both through physical scarcities and abnormal increases in
prices. Take the supply of meat as an example. Despite a threefold
increase in the supply of meat between 1977 and 1980 [55], the
price increased from Rs. 18 to 24 per kilo, and availability
became erratic, particularly in the poor sections of the city.
Much of the supply was consumed by the affluent, who could stock
their freezers to bypass officially mandated meatless days, and by
the ever-increasing kebab and tikka shops. An average household
could neither afford nor obtain meat easily. Meat supplies were
diverted to the neighbourhoods of the rich, where butchers could
clear the daily stock at the asking price in large batches without
the hassle and labour required to serve customers buying small
portions. Meat shops in poor areas lost out to the stores in the

neighbourhood of the affluent. The pecuniary externalities thereby reorganized the distribution system to the advantage of the affluent. This is an illustrative example of how the overconsumption by one circuit not only disadvantaged others but also led to further consolidation of the preemptive position of the circuit.

Increased private consumption by a select group also leads to the appropriation of corresponding public goods to sustain its consumption. The supply of water, electricity, telephones, and other community facilities is a case in point. These facilities are necessary for the economic and social well-being of all groups, yet their supplies cannot be increased indefinitely, due to resource constraints. This means that air-conditioned homes of the well-to-do exact the opportunity cost in the form of unlit neighbourhoods and unserviced workshops. Such disparities in the availability of public services have self-reinforcing effects. The poor lack clean water and adequate drainage, and thus suffer from ill-health, which in turn reduces their capabilities of learning, employment, and job security, and thus perpetuates their misery. It must be noted that it is not the price which keeps out the poor from making use of public services; it is the over-consumption of the affluent and the resulting maldistribution.

These self-serving patterns of consumption feed back on production priorities. Through demand linkages (and political influence), production of luxury goods for the rich gains priority over the basic needs of the poor. For example, as the number of cars increased, the import bill for oil increased correspondingly, locking the national economy into enduring commitments in imports. In Lahore, the television stores, car dealers, and cassette hawkers have thrived, while the weavers, soap makers, and cobblers have lost out. The point to be noted is that excessive consumption of some commodities alters the demand schedule of the local economy and correspondingly leads to a gradual revision of the production schedule. This is how one circuit comes to dominate others and to widen social disparities.

The emergence of numerically small but economically dominant groups of conspicuous consumers has laid the path of development in the city. These social and economic enclaves are transposed on land in the form of residential areas and housing estates of divergent quality of life. They constitute the competing units for the provision of public facilities and for the city's meagre resources, and, in this competition, the poor and those lacking in influence lose out. The market and the public allocative processes preempt goods, services, and resources for the influential. All these are serious social costs, but perhaps the most deleterious consequence of indulgent consumption by the influential is the demonstration-effect it has for the local population in general. Thrift, prudence, and hard work are proving to be handicaps in the race for the good life; instead, social status, wheeling-dealing, bribery, and influence-peddling are increasingly becoming the signposts of success.

INFERENCES

Although two major sections of this chapter have concluded with a résumé of findings, an overall picture of the city's economic development remains to be composed. A convenient starting point are the propositions set out in Chapter 2. By reflecting on those propositions in the light of the findings of Chapter 5, it is possible to identify the structure of the city's economy. The following are significant themes that have surfaced through the analysis.

(1) This chapter points out that the city's economic base has remained remarkably consistent over time. Lahore has continued to be a multifunctional city, where trade, administration, education, and light industry provide the bulk of employment. Relative proportions of these activities, as measured by the work force, have remained almost unchanged over the two decades for which data were available, and they seem to accord with the historical accounts. This consistency and stability of economic activities indicates the city's ability to capitalize on its dominant position and reflects the multiplicative capabilities of established activities. The analysis of the post-Independence industrial development trends reveals that the city did not recapitulate the national patterns of industrial growth, a fact which further reinforces the conclusion that the city's economy has manifested a structural stability. Its growth has proceeded by building on its historical advantages such as concentration of political and administrative powers in the capital, and the traditional entrepreneurial talent of the bazaar sector.

(2) Population growth and economic expansion in the city have proceeded in tandem, so much so that the net rate of increase of employment is approximately zero. The city's economic production may not be getting ahead of population growth, but, without the latter, the momentum of economic expansion could not have been attained: the increasing population encourages production through enhanced demand, stimulates the multiplication of productive activities catering to daily needs, and precipitates the threshold for higher order goods and services. Such demand linkages help to enhance the productive capacities of the economy and bring into play new technologies and modes of operation. Given a reasonable institutional base for production, the demand creates its own supply which in turn enhances the productive capacities of the economy. To some extent this is what has happened in Lahore. The city acquired new industrial, commercial, and service activities. Its economic growth did not outpace the rate of population increase but the demographic explosion did not bring about the doom that the literature on Third World cities is wont to predict. These conclusions were anticipated in Proposition 6 of Chapter 2, which has been generally upheld.

(3) It is apparent from the findings of this chapter that development led to fractionation of the city's economy. The local

economy has been not only divided in sectors but also it has been splitting up into circuits (or enclaves) distinguished by social class, consumption patterns, modes of operation, and organizational arrangements. This has turned out to be one of the most persistent processes of the city's internal dynamics. The explanation is evident. Economic development has occurred in the idiom of the middle and upper classes. Foreign aid and public expenditures primed the demand of the upper classes and gave impetus to the development of corresponding production activities. Bungalows, air travel, and colour television became priority items, and development came to be measured in terms of their availability. So the production schedule shifted towards such items, thereby creating a circuit of demand and supply. The emergence of this upper circuit induced the formation of other circuits for respective life-styles and income levels.

(4) A cohesive economy splits up into little economies of distinct clientele and operations. Propositions 2, 3, 7 and 9 anticipated this phenomenon through such concepts as duality, dependence, polarization, etc. This chapter, while upholding those propositions, has revealed that the circuits came into being as much through fission processes set into motion by bombardment of the economy with new technology and production priorities as by the interjection of a modern mode into the domain of a traditional one. Two specific characteristics of the fractionation in Lahore deserve to be mentioned. One, the upper echelons of the bazaar sector tend to constitute an economic enclave (or circuit) of their own which is affluent but indigenous. Second, the dominant modern upper circuit is essentially state supported. Politicians, army officers, civil administrators and professionals are the primary participants in the upper circuit. The authority inherent in their statuses sustains this circuit. It might be mentioned that the process of fractionation began with British colonial rule, but it has accelerated since Independence, though still along the tracks laid in the Colonial Era.

(5) Propositions 4 and 5 of Chapter 2 reviewed current models of Third World urban economies and suggested that the bifurcation of a local economy into firm-bazaar sectors is a widely acknowledged phenomenon. In Lahore, the firm sector establishments are large in size, and organized as bureaucracies, and fashioned in the Western mode. The bazaar sector tends to fall on the other end of these continuums of values. What came as a surprise was to find that the two have different bases for internal division of tasks. Firm sector establishments are internally differentiated into hierarchies of specialization, whereas bazaar establishments are relatively more homogenous, operating as teams where owners can double up as loaders if the occasion requires additional hands. As a whole, the bazaar sector is stratified according to earnings, power, and size of operations. Cloth wholesalers, grain merchants, Arhatis of the fruit market, or owners of small workshops constitute the upper strata of the bazaar sector, which is neither poor nor informal. It is also revealed that the bazaar sector has

patterned ways of substituting labour for capital, spreading risk
through a chain of middlemen, operating on margins, and financing
its operations mostly from internal resources without much
recourse to banks. Such structural features of the bazaar sector
must be stressed, because the literature about the bazaar sector
is overloaded with notions derived from studies of hawkers. The
bazaar sector of Lahore is an expression of indigenous
mercantilism which is rooted in traditional caste/clan division of
labour. It is a form of indigenous urban capitalism. Its workers
are self-employed, and owners are also workers; it does not replicate property relations embedded in rural polity.
(6) In Lahore, the firm sector has increasingly become indistinguishable from the State. It is comprised of banks, insurance companies, foreign franchises and managing agencies. It has always
depended on the government for guidance and support. With progressive socialization of large industries, utilities, and even trade,
the firm sector has become almost an arm of the State. This
finding has far-reaching implications. It means that the State has
come to centre-stage in the drama of postcolonial development. It
contracts for foreign aid, invites Hilton and Coca-Cola corporations through favourable licences and concessions, channels
foreign aid and provides protection to employers from labour
demands. This also means that the State is conduit for whatever
external influences penetrate into the local economy. The significance of this is that the social classes which are now responsible
for perpetuating dependence consist of officers and professionals
as much as of landlords and capitalists. It also suggests that
simplistic solutions of nationalizing industries and trade or of
expanding the sphere of public production are not enough. It seems
that economic and social outcomes remain unaffected, whether a
factory is run by a private capitalist or by civil servants, as
long as both enjoy monopolistic powers and are immune from
accountability. In both cases, the influentials remain the beneficiaries of the development.
(7) Although Chapter 2 explicitly identified the role of illicit
activities in an economy, still that exposition did not prepare us
for what has been uncovered in this chapter. Corruption has been
revealed to be so interwoven into the fabric of local economy and
so patterned that it is an institution and not merely a phenomenon
of widespread delinquencies. Corruption is a premium exacted by
wielders of public authority and private monopolies (black market,
etc.). It is essentially an exaction over and above normal profits
or fees for discharging responsibilities of an office. As a charge
for social powers, it is a rent. It is regressive in incidence and
is an instrument of transferring resources from public to private
realms, from the relatively powerless to the influentials, from
consumers to providers of goods and services, from the poor to the
rich. Undoubtedly, corruption permeates all social strata, producing the situation in which a peon or rickshaw driver shakes
down poor clients as much as the affluent. Yet, as gains are proportionate to the authority inhering in one's position, it stands

to reason that the elite are the main beneficiaries of institutionalized corruption.

Corruption requires personalized dealings, and because of
this, it subverts impersonal institutions and policies. It contributes to the failure of public policies, reduces the reliability of the decision-making process, and promotes ad-hocism and
wheeling-dealing. Normatively, it needs to be eliminated but functioning as the instrument of encashing one's authority, it has
become the mainstay of the good life for the elite. It might also
be mentioned that corruption points towards the primacy of state
functionaries (upper middle class) as beneficiaries of post-
colonial urban development, along with other groups such as black-
marketeers and monopolist industrialists and politicians.

(8) From the data and case materials presented in this chapter,
it appears that household incomes in Lahore more than doubled over
the last two decades. Unmistakable evidence of the artifacts of
development can be seen in rush hour bicycle and motorbike jams,
in the skyline dotted with TV antennas, and in strains of transistor music from huts. Yesterday's luxuries, e.g., bicycles and
motorbikes, have become today's common necessities, as the city
has expanded and expectations have risen. Some new goods are
modern substitutes for conventional needs. Sui gas and kerosene
oil have replaced firewood as fuel, vegetable oil once considered
unhealthy has supplanted butter oil (Ghee) as a cooking medium,
and increased travel distances between relatives lend an aura of
necessity to telephones. All in all, more goods and services are
being consumed in the city, compared to the early days of Independence.

(9) The city has become a showcase of indulgent consumption. The
process of fractionation is also at work in this sphere.
Life-styles range all the way from modern-upper- via indigenous-
affluent- classes to abysmal poverty. Life-styles distinguished by
language, dress, food, and housing have emerged which combine
functional elements of the old and the new preferences as well as
goods. This variety of life-styles has turned the city into a
crazy quilt of social patches. Its cultural coherence and consumption discipline have been lost. The city is splintered into circuits corresponding to income and occupational enclaves.

It would be a mistake to regard modern life-styles as a con-
verse of tradition. One of the most intriguing observations of
this chapter is that it is the modern-affluent (doctors,
engineering, officers, etc.) households who revive old traditions
and reenact them with new materials, whereas the poor, who are
supposed to be tradition-bound, have long abandoned such customs
because of the expense involved.

Indulgent consumption by the affluent classes counteracts the
propensities of capital accumulation and redefines production
priorities, to the disadvantage of basic needs. As most indulgent
consumption seems to be sustained by unearned or windfall incomes,
e.g., corruption or remittances from abroad, it should not come as
a surprise that investment and capital accumulation have been

largely neglected. The social costs of indulgence by select groups
are borne by the community at large.

(10) Throughout this chapter, the theme of personalized institutions emerged recurrently from empirical observations. The clan-
and caste-based bazaar sectors, the friendship networks and
power-exchange cliques of the firm sector, and the personalized
dealings required by corruption are obvious manifestations of the
supremacy of primary relations in economic transactions. An operational unit in Lahore is more commonly a group than an individual.
One's economic success depends on building contacts and developing
capacity to mobilize power and influence. Even as a buyer, one has
to rely on an obliging butcher or helpful grocer, over and above
the asking prices, and these obligations must be reciprocated in
one's own sphere of influence. This is how socially rooted networks of economic exchange are constituted.

The above description shows that it is a person's social
standing that defines his entitlement to income and consumption.
Development has essentially proceeded along the lines of such
entitlements. By producing or importing goods preferred by
influentials, by favouring the educated and influential for jobs
and incomes, by promoting life-styles that require Western tastes,
development has expanded the opportunities of those who were
already entitled to rewarding economic standing.

Development has disproportionately expanded opportunities for
professionals, bureaucrats, importers and commission agents. There
are some new rules of entitlement; credentials and paper qualifi-
cations have gained significance, while ability to mobilize state
power for personal benefit through wire-pulling, nepotism, and
corruption has become a primary mode of advancement. Obviously,
some erosion of caste and clan entitlements has taken place in the
public realm, though in the bazaar sector they still count.

(11) All in all, economic success in Lahore requires association
with a clique that can mobilize, influence and confer mutual
advantages. Such cliques are essentially formed along sectarian,
clan, and linguistic lines, yet social class and educational and
occupational status have also come to constitute significant
bonds. Compared to clan and caste obligations, bonds based on
common educational and professional statuses are more ephemeral.
They are continually being reconstituted, and individuals must
always be establishing contacts and banking good will to maintain
a stock of influence. These are the changes brought by development. A certain degree of ad-hocism and particularism becomes
unavoidable as the cliques and networks continually change.
Lahore's economic order has increasingly come to operate on the
principle of "who knows whom," and rules underlying this principle
favour the influentials, both old and new.

(12) Only the poor bear the burden of the market in Lahore. Whatever resources are not appropriated through monopolies and state
power are distributed competitively. Thus thrift, enterprise and
ingenuity are generally seen in the lower circuit. The family
workshops of Lahore have demonstrated the capability of manufac-

turing new products without foreign assistance. Lahore's pro-
letariat are, by and large, self-employed and it is a tribute to
their ingenuity that they eke out a living from such meagre
pickings.
(13) Lest the foregoing discussion has created an impression that
a group of select families appropriated most of the economic
gains, it must be pointed out that Lahore has not been an oligarchic community. There has been considerable social mobility and
frequent cases of rise from poverty to riches. The process of
fractionation identified above created numerous routes to prosperity. One's economic status could be improved by entering professions, finding a position of public authority, mastering the
art of wheeling-dealing, linking up with ruling elites, learning
to give and take bribes, successfully dealing in permits and
quotas, mobilizing friends and relatives' influence, going abroad
to work or seizing opportunities by enterprise and hard work. This
variety of routes enabled many to afford comfortable living. Yet
the most common denominator of all these opportunities has been
the access to the governmental authority: the more one could
command, the greater were the economic gains.

NOTES

    1. For example see Harry W. Richardson, Urban Economics
(Harmondsworth: Penguin, 1971).
    2. For a critical view of the present state of urban eco-
nomics, see Michael Ball, "A Critique of Urban Economics," International Journal of Urban and Regional Research 13 (1977):
309-332.
    3. Thompson pointed out that urban economics should appro-
priately be a discipline to study processes, interlinkages, as
outcomes of productive and distributional activities in a local
community. Wilbur R. Thompson, A Preface to Urban Economics
(Baltimore: The John Hopkins Press, 1965), pp. 1-14.
    4. T. A. Broadbent, Planning and Profit in the Urban Economy
(London: Methuen, 1977), p. 91.
    5. The term "economic base" refers to the goods and services
produced in a community, though conventionally such activities are
divided into basic and non-basic components. Those goods and services which are sold or exported outside an area are classified as
basic, while local consumption and supportive activities are
designated as non-basic. At best this dichotomy should be viewed
as a procedure to unfold the circular flow of goods and services
and thus a convenient classificatory device. For the conventional
view of "economic base" see, Charles M. Tiebout, The Community
Economic Base Study (New York: Committee for Economic Development,
1962), pp. 11-14.
    6. Syed Muhammad Latif, Lahore: Its History, Architectural
Remains and Antiquities (Lahore: New Imperial Press, 1892), pp.
261-263.

7. Location Quotient (LQ) is a widely used measure of the economic specialization of a community in relation to nation or a region.

$$LQ = \frac{\frac{C_i}{C_T}}{\frac{N_i}{N_T}}$$

where C_i = Employment in activity i in a community.

C_T = Total employed labour force in a community.

N_i = Employment in activity i in a nation or region.

N_T = Total employed labour force in a nation or region.

when LQ > 1 is indicative of a community's specialization in activity i.

LQ < 1 is indicative of a community's shortfall in activity i compared to the nation.

(Avrom Bendavid, Regional Economic Analysis for Practitioners (New York: Praeger Publishers, 1974), pp. 93-95.

8. The term "tertiarization" emerged from studies of squatter settlements to describe predominance of self-employed, service workers among the resident work force. The term has steadily acquired more precise meaning and now refers to high ratio of employment in tertiary to secondary activities. Richard Morse, "Recent Research in Latin America Urbanization," in Latin American Research Review, Volume 1 (Beverly Hills: Sage Publications, 1965), pp. 35-74.

9. Lahore Urban Development and Traffic Study (LUDTS) Final Report, Vol. I, Urban Planning (Lahore: Lahore Development Authority, 1981), Table 4, p. 42.

10. A registered factory is defined as a manufacturing establishment employing five or more workers and which is registered with the Chief Inspector of Factories. By this definition, household manufacturing units and craft shops are excluded. Bureau of Statistics, Directory of Registered Factories in the Punjab (Lahore: Government of the Punjab, 1978).

11. Stephen Lewis, Economic Policy and Industrial Growth in Pakistan (London: George Allen and Unwin, 1969).

12. Stephen E. Guisinger, "Patterns of Industrial Growth in Pakistan," The Pakistan Development Review 16 (1976): 11.

13. Jajmani refers to the traditional system of reciprocal obligations in economic and ceremonial affairs among various castes. It is also the basis of division of labour and occupational specialization by castes.

14. Small craft shops and household manufacturing units producing furniture, utensils, jewellery, carpets, blankets, building
materials, etc., and repair shops for cars, cycles, radios and
television are among the unregistered establishments constituting
the lower layer of the bazaar manufacturing sector. The Walled
City alone had about 5,000 such establishments. Lahore Urban
Development and Traffic Study, Final Report, Volume III, Walled
City (Lahore: Lahore Development Authority, 1981), p. 29.

15. Unlike factories, there is no official register of shops
and offices. Hence data about commercial establishments are almost
nonexistent, special surveys being the only exception.

16. Government of West Pakistan, Master Plan for Greater
Lahore (Lahore: The Master Plan Project Office, 1964), p. 51.

17. Government of the Punjab, Gujranwala Outline Development
Plan (Gujranwala: Directorate of Physical Planning, 1972), p. 35.

18. Government of Pakistan, Pakistan Statistical Year Book
1977 (Karachi: Statistics Division, 1978), Table 18.5, p. 257.

19. Mahmood Zaman, "Lahore Market: Much fruit, much filth,"
Viewpoint, September 20, 1980, pp. 18-19.

20. These estimates of the number of shops and stalls in
Azam cloth market were offered by the President of the traders'
association in a personal interview with the author in August,
1979.

21. Viewpoint, April 23, 1981, p. 2.

22. Lisa R. Peattie, "Tertiarization and Urban Poverty in
Latin America," in Latin American Urban Research Vol. 5, ed. Wayne
A. Cornelius (Beverly Hills: Sage Publications, 1975), p. 109.

23. Estimates derived from Bureau of Statistics, Development
Statistics of the Punjab (Lahore: Government of the Punjab 1978),
Table 143.

24. Pakistan Times, December 31, 1980, p. 3.

25. Ibid., August 23, 1981, p. 1.

26. This estimate that 30 to 40 percent of local income cir-
culated in the shadow economy of corruption is an extrapolation
from known rates of kickbacks on public works and from observations about the extent of black markets, etc.

27. Lahore Urban Development and Traffic Study, Final
Report, Vol. I, Urban Planning (Lahore: Lahore Development
Authority, 1981), p. 71.

28. A United Nations expert recommended elimination of
tongas within days of his arrival in the city. Pakistan Times, May
11, 1979, p. 3.

29. Ibid., May 11, 1979, p. 3.

30. Ibid., September 20, 1976, p. 4.

31. Ibid., October 11, 1977, p. 3.

32. Ibid., April 16, 1981, p. 3.

33. Ibid., May 7, 1977, p. 5.

34. Ibid., July 21, 1975, p. 4.

35. Ibid., "Letter to the Editor," August 19, 1981, p. 4.

36. Ibid., January 9, 1981, p. 3.

37. Ibid., February 18, 1981, p. 3.

38.   Ibid., October 20, 1979, p. 5.
39.   Ibid., April 6, 1980, p. 3.
40.   Ibid., April 14, 1980, p. 3.
41.   Ibid., April 19, 1980, p. 3.
42.   Ibid., "Letter to the Editor," October 13, 1980, p. 8.
43.   Viewpoint, February 5, 1981, p. 9.
44.   Pakistan Times, February 26, 1981, p. 3.
45.   Ibid., August 19, 1981, p. 3.
46.   Ibid., November 5, 1980, p. 5.
47.   Gunnar Myrdal, Asian Drama, Vol. I (New York: Pantheon, 1968), p. 59.
48.   Paul P. Streeten, "Basic Needs: Premises and Promises," Journal of Policy Modeling 1 (1979): 136.
49.   Mazhar Hussain, Socio-Economic Survey of Lahore (Lahore: Social Science Research Centre, 1964), pp. 39-42. The 1964 incomes have been converted to 1979 values by multiplication with corresponding rise of Consumer Price Index.
50.   The average household income for 1979 calculated from data in the Lahore Urban Development and Traffic Study, Final Report, Vol. I, Urban Planning (Lahore: Lahore Development Authority, 1981), Table 10, p. 50.
51.   Viewpoint, Sept. 10, 1981, "Price Indicators."
52.   The proportion of Lahore's population below poverty line (Rs. 450 in 1979) was estimated to be 33 percent by Lahore's City Planners. Lahore Urban Development and Traffic Study, Final Report (Lahore: 1981), p. 50.
53.   Ved Mehta, "The Photographs of Chacha Ji," New Yorker 56 (1980): 42.
54.   An announcement of an AQiQa reception at Hotel International appeared in Pakistan Times, December 24, 1980, p. 3.
55.   Ibid., April 3, 1981, p. 3.

6
THE SPACE AND PEOPLE

By 1981, Lahore was almost four times larger than the city left by the British in 1947. Demographic growth on such a scale could not have been accommodated by mere enlargement of the existing apparatus of the city. It meant evolutionary changes in every aspect of the city's life, i.e., social, economic, cultural and physical. The evolving mix of economic activities, changing income distribution and institutional mutations has been described in the previous chapter. We have discovered that the city's economy has been fragmented into relatively autonomous little economies or circuits, each catering to a specific sociocultural segment of the population. These little economies, reflected in land, determine the city's spatial structure. As the officers' estates, workers' colonies and Katchi Abadis are residential counterparts of the respective social segments, so bazaars, markets, and shopping plazas are manifestations of different commercial circuits. The city's spatial coherence and architectural unity have been eroded, and a wide diversity of physical forms, ranging from villages of medieval vintage to postmodernistic housing complexes has emerged.

This observation raises many questions: What are the functional components of the city? What is its evolving land-use pattern? Where, why, and how are workshops, stores, houses, and offices being located? What are the processes of spatial development? These questions require analysis of social and spatial structures and necessitate assessment of the evolving patterns in terms of personal satisfaction and quality of community life. This is an ambitious agenda for the chapter, but, even if all these questions may not be fully answered, keeping them to the forefront provides a thematic framework.

THE SPATIAL ORGANIZATION

By now it should be obvious that the distribution of land uses and the geography of housing or jobs in Lahore cannot be described in the categories commonly used in the literature of city planning and urbanization. Terms such as "Central Business

175

District", or "Concentric Zones" are not applicable because the phenomena they describe do not exist. These terms assume consistency and continuity of a character or feature, whereas Lahore is characterized by discontinuities of factors and multiplicity of sectors and circuits.

Lahore's functional components are not areas of uniform residential, commercial, or industrial activities [1]. Instead, the basic unit is a district or territorial sector of interwoven activities, mixed land uses, and interlinked social groups. It is essentially a housing submarket of specific demand preferences, a locale for a particular set of economic activities, and a natural area [2]. These are social-ecological units, rather than functionals or activity zones.

It has been increasingly recognized that Middle Eastern and subcontinental cities are comprehensible in terms of ecological districts, and not as zones of segregated activities. For example, Abu-Lughod observes that "there are not two or three subcities . . . but indeed six fairly distinctive and co-existent urban arrangements which make up the ecological structure of North African Cities." [3] King identifies six constituent units of Indian cities, of which the main three are: the native city, the civil station, and the Cantonment [4]. It seems Lahore can be divided into six distinct ecological units namely: 1) The Walled City, 2) Civil Lines, 3) New Indigenous Communities, 4) The Planned Schemes, 5) Cantonment, and 6) Katchi Abadis (squatter settlements).

The Walled City and Pre-Colonial Settlements

The Walled City and historical settlements of Mozang, Ichra, Baghbanpura, and Mughulpura, though not contiguous, constitute a distinct spatial idiom. Noe finds the Walled City to be a representative urban form of the Islamic city [5]. The narrow meandering streets, bazaars and markets wafting spicy aromas, quarters and Mohallas (neighbourhoods) serving as loci of family and clan activities, Jami Mosque as a focal point, two or three storeys of inward-oriented houses packed along alleys, are the characteristics that Noe considers to be prototypical Islamic [6].

The Walled City measures about one square mile in area. About 250,000 people lived in this area in 1980, making its residential density 445 persons per acre, higher than that of Manhattan, New York [7]. As a residential district, it has gradually become the housing market for lower-middle-class households, particularly those of bazaar affiliations. It is also a thriving commercial district. It has four commodity markets (Mandis) of metropolitan scale, numerous wholesale bazaars, and a network of mohalla shopping streets. Historically, various blocks or streets of the city have been inhabited by occupational clans specializing in specific lines of production. Coppersmiths have plied their trade around Rang Mahal for as long as anyone can remember. Chuni Mandi

has been long associated with weavers and dyers. and kite making
has remained a specialty of Mochi and Bhatti gates. With the
availability of electricity since the 1920s, furniture making,
radio repair, sawing, milling, and grain grinding operations have
spread in all parts. All in all, the Walled City has sizeable
small-scale manufacturing and repair establishments, and numerous
commercial clusters of metropolitan scale. In 1981 it was estimated that there were 5,000 industrial units and 10,000 shops,
providing employment for 30,000 people [8].

The foregoing description only illustrates the variety of
economic activities and dispels a possible assumption that the
Walled City is predominantly a high-density, older residential
area. It does not indicate the interlinkages among these activities which produce the synergy of the Walled City. Not only do the
commercial and industrial activities have historical bases, but
they are viable in these crowded quarters because of their typical
modes of operation.

Most workshops and stores are family enterprises in which
members of a family, adults as well as children, have assigned
tasks and must take turns. There is continual traffic between
homes and shops, necessitating their close proximity, if not coin-
cidence. Since they operate on work orders by word-of-mouth, and
through intricate borrowing and lending practices, these establishments require not only frequent face-to-face contacts among
sellers, buyers, and suppliers, but also a level of mutual trust
that arises only by being acquainted with each other's places of
residence. Such modes of operation thrive in crowded, pedestrian
precincts. and the Walled City provides the necessary intimacy and
propinquity.

The building block of the Walled City is an activity cluster
of complementary establishments. It could be a kucha or katra (a
residential cul-de-sac), where rich and poor, clients and patrons.
servers and served, live side-by-side in houses of widely varying
size and quality, and where as much eating, sleeping, and playing
goes on in the street as inside the home. Alternatively it could
be a mandi or commercial-craft cluster such as the jewellery
market, where goldsmiths' retail stores, brokers' shops, apartments (Bathaks), and tea-stalls are inextricably mixed together.
The diversity of activities and the variety of their combinations
is such that the streetscape in the Walled City changes almost
every few hundred yards. For example, the gaiety of the mohalla of
dancing girls and courtesans is only a few score yards from the
staidness exuded by the Bazaar of Physicians. Such apparently
divergent activities are tied together by economic, social, and
cultural links making the Walled City a cohesive whole.

The Walled City has progressively become the distributive
centre for indigenous luxuries and conventional goods. and a place
of historical and cultural significance. It is also the housing
district for babus and bazaaris. These are the functional roles of
the Walled City in the metropolitan system.

Over the 30-year period since Independence, the Walled City

MAP 6.1
THE WALLED CITY

has evolved from being the core of the city to being the territorial base of a sociocultural segment of the metropolis. Increasingly it has become the centre of indigenous life-styles and
activities. The difficulties of bringing vehicles into residential
streets, the increasing congestion resulting from the natural
increase in population, and consequent doubling-up of homes,
filthy and open drains, and a general decline in sanitation have
prompted the exodus of the gentry from the Walled City. Doctors,
engineers, bankers, executives, etc., particularly those
affiliated with the firm sector, have been leaving ancestral homes
for bungalows in the suburbs and are being replaced by bazaar merchants or lower-grade professionals. Despite this turnover of
residents, the Walled City has remained a close-knit community.
Strangers seldom come to live in a mohalla here, and much of the
transfer of houses and movement of households occurs laterally
among those who are already residents of the Walled City.

Commercial and manufacturing activities here have expanded
since Independence. The wholesale market for toiletries in Shah
Alam, the famous Azam cloth market, and the candy and sweets Mandi
of Mochi-gate are other post-Independence commercial developments
which have promoted the growth of linked manufacturing and repair
activities. All in all, the Walled City has undergone many economic and social changes to keep in step with the evolving
metropolis.

Physically, the Walled City reflects the usual paradoxes of
Lahore. In 1980, about eight percent of houses were so dilapidated
that they were judged structurally dangerous, and another 12
percent were unoccupied because of their extreme disrepair. On the
other hand, 120 to 150 houses per year have been rebuilt since
Independence [9]. The contrasts are such that a new four-storey
mansion may be next to a house that collapsed during the last
rains, taking a toll in human life and limb. Some of the finest
specimens of carved wooden balconies are to be found along the
city streets, but frequently they are safety hazards because of
their weakened moorings. There are 20 national monuments in the
Walled City (Fort, Shahi Mosque, Wazirkhan Mosque, etc.), and
another 4,000 buildings of historical and cultural interest, yet
most of the latter are crumbling [10].

These paradoxes do not make the Walled City a slum. There is
little crime, a high degree of neighbourliness, and there are frequent reminders of riches and tradition. Perhaps Lahore's highest
property values are in the Azam cloth market where gutters pour
down into open drains and streets are so narrow that even a hand
cart cannot be brought in.

Our preoccupation with the Walled City has not allowed any
discussion of other historical settlements, such as Mozang, Ichra,
Baghbanpura. This is not a serious omission, because, physically
and socially these settlements resemble the Walled City. They are
characterized by similar intermixing of activities, narrow
streets, and pedestrian precincts, and even evolutionary trends.
These settlements lack historical heritage, and tend to be

lower-order replicas of the Walled City.

The Civil Lines

The term Civil Lines refers as much to an idiom or model of community layout as to an area in Lahore bearing this name. The Civil Lines in subcontinental cities were laid out as the British Precinct in the mid-nineteenth century. They recreated Victorian suburbs and, as King says, were characterized by low-density, horizontal, single-storey development, and broad treelined roads which gave access to a system of large compounds, each containing a roughly centrally sited bungalow [11]. The Civil Lines model is significant because it consecrated such town planning practices as segregation of land uses, standardization of lots, clustering of housing blocks by social rank, differentiation of homes from work-places, and separation of transportation modes. Breese says that "The Civil Lines street pattern, lot arrangement and separation of land uses are formal and spacious importations." [12]

The colonial English society consisted of officials and their families on tours of duty, who were unencumbered by filial bonds and kinship obligations. As a physical form, the Civil Lines catered to this truncated social structure and was in sharp con-trast with subcontinental urban traditions. The indigenous urban living required proximity to relatives and friends, but Civil Lines emphasized insular individualism.

The bungalow, a detached house, was a new artifact introduced by the British. In pre-Colonial Lahore, a freestanding house sur-rounded by a garden was usually the summer house of a prince or notable, whose regular residence would be in the Walled City. After Independence, on being occupied by indigenous people, the bungalows of Civil Lines began to lose their serene majesty and spaciousness. A Pakistani judge could not live alone. His elderly parents and unmarried brothers and sisters lived with him, and his home would often be full of visiting relatives and clansmen. All these social patterns prompted a large-scale infilling of the Civil Lines and initiated a process of adaptation.

In Lahore, the Civil Lines extend approximately from the McLeod Road in the west to the Canal in the east, and from the railway station in the north to Jail Road in the south. Here are the Government Officers' Residences (GOR), the Governor's house, the Gymkhana Club, the Race Course, the Cricket Ground, and until recently (1960s), the Civil and Military Gazette's offices where Kipling did a journalistic stint. With such a base, the Civil Lines remained an area of public officials' housing estates and governmental institutions till the mid-1960s.

With the settlement of evacuee properties, large tracts of vacant land in the interstices of Civil Lines became available for development. Inspired by such new symbols of development as the Intercontinental Hotel, WAPDA House, and the United States Infor-mation Centre, the treelined residential roads of Civil Lines began to be turned into ribbons of multi-storey office buildings, automobile showrooms, and air-conditioned shopping plazas. The commercialization of Queen's Road and Egerton, Davis. Lawrence, and Montgomery Roads signaled a new stage in the evolution of the Civil Lines. It meant that Civil Lines had become a district of mixed functions, the locale of the new breed of activities emerging with economic development. The multinational banks and international agencies have sought choice locations in the Civil Lines area. The public corporations have built edifices that now dwarf the High Court and the Cathedral. Even the obelisk raised to commemorate the first meeting of the heads of the Islamic State has found a place in front of the Assembly Building. These are symbols of the Civil Lines' new status as the commercial district of the expanded Lahore.

There is, however, some continuity with the past even in these evolutionary trends. Civil Lines has evolved with the changing structure of power and authority, and has remained the dominant centre of the modern segment of the city. The Civil Lines began as a British transplant, but has been Americanized, as the saying goes in Lahore, with the accelerating tempo of post-Independence development. Yet the Civil Lines model survives intact despite its incongruence with local conditions and social structures. It continues to guide town planning policies and beckons as a symbol of status and modernity to the affluent and the successful. Yet both public and private hopes fail to materialize, because they assume a social reality that has long gone.

New Indigenous Communities

The third sociospatial idiom in Lahore is that of the upgraded indigenous neighbourhood. Such an area has certain characteristics. 1) Streets are wide enough (12-15 feet minimum) to provide vehicular access, yet so narrow that three-storey houses cast a cooling shade over them. 2) Blocks and streets are laid out in discernible geometric patterns, rectangular or semi-circular. 3) House designs combine modern and traditional features in a harmonious blend. The houses are sunnier, airier and built around atriums or enclosed backcourts, yet unlike bungalows, they cover whole lots and are attached to each other, presenting a street facade of continuous high walls punctuated by screened windows and balconies. 4) Land uses are not deliberately segregated, and a sprinkling of artisans' workshops, bakeries, firewood stalls, and warehouses can be found amidst homes. The main thoroughfares become major shopping strips and the buildings are designed to accommodate shops at ground level. Generally, land-use patterns resemble the Walled City rather than Civil Lines, in that shops are so close to homes that for almost every meal groceries can be conveniently bought and households can do without stocking or refrigerating food.

All in all, the New Indigenous Communities combine modern

conceptions of public health, accessibility, and land subdivision
with traditional preferences for propinquity, utilitarian mixing
of activities, and proximity. They represent an evolved form of
the historical neighbourhoods. They are based on local cultural
norms and design elements of proven utility while selectively
incorporating contemporary architectural forms, planning principles, and building materials. No authority or person can be
credited with their creation. They remain unnoticed idioms of the
urban development in India and Pakistan.

By 1981, the New Indigenous Communities (NIC) were spread
over almost half the city. Neighbourhoods that have evolved in the
idiom of the NIC range from almost a century old Gowal Mandi to
the newly built Shalimar Town. Such communities began to emerge
soon after Civil Lines was laid out, when the first generation of
natives absorbed into the British administration began to seek
convenient locations and spacious quarters outside the Walled
City, and their demand spurred the expansion of Anarkali, Gowal
Mandi, and MisriShah in the NIC mode.

A NIC typically began with the surveying of land and demarca-
tion of streets and lots, often by municipal engineers or private
surveyors. Thereafter, the market took over. Houses were custom
built according to the prospective owner's preference and the
mason's conceptions of utility or beauty. Usually, municipal services were nonexistent at the start of a NIC. They were extended
fitfully when an area filled up, but sometimes even streets
remained mere dirt tracks for decades. From such beginnings, these
neighbourhoods evolved into areas of distinct identities and
physical coherence, a sequence of development which has largely
continued to the present time.

The second stage in the process of NIC development was
reached by the 1930s, when corporate groups became active in
developing exclusive residential areas for Hindus, Sikhs, or
Muslims. Krishan Nagar, Sant Nagar, and Mohammad Nagar were the
outcomes of such initiatives. Even the names of these communities
are revealing. The term nagar means "community" or "town," and has
an aura of urbanity and autonomy. These nagars were conceived as
large, self-contained neighbourhoods where sites were set aside
for parks, schools, mosques or temples, and clinics; a step
towards planned neighbourhoods. Krishan Nagar was the epitome of
this stage of development. It was a Hindu neighbourhood of
spacious attached houses, arranged in rectangular blocks and
served by a commercial spine from which residential streets
radiated. Provision was made for parks, schools, and sewerage and
drains, and arrangements were also made to build and maintain
these services. For a while, it was a model of the indigenous but
modernized neighbourhood (see Map 6.2).

The third stage in the evolution of New Indigenous Communities began after Independence. Hindus and Sikhs departed for
India, and thus the socioreligious distinctions among neighbourhoods disappeared. On the social scale, the NIC slipped down a few
notches. Now the middle class could aspire to bungalows in the

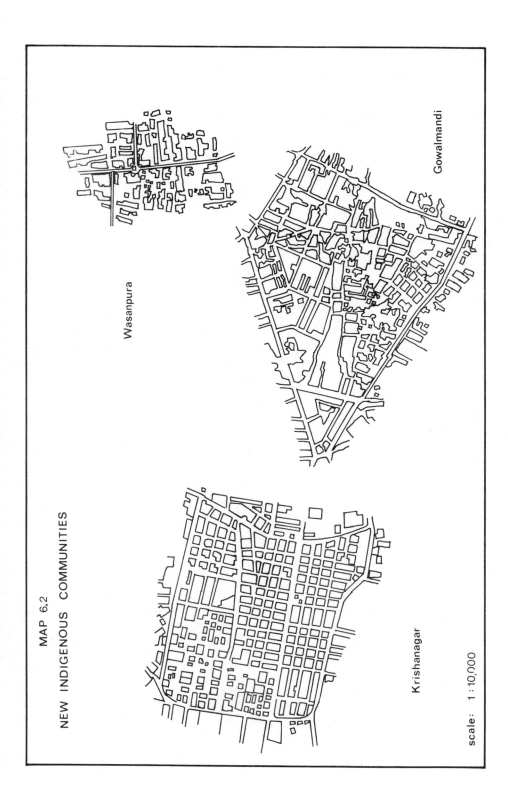

MAP 6.2

NEW INDIGENOUS COMMUNITIES

Wasanpura

Gowalmandi

Krishanagar

scale: 1 : 10,000

Civil Lines and Planned Schemes, leaving the less glamorous and underserviced NICs to bazaar merchants or lower-level professionals and officials. Differentiated according to location, lot size, and availability of facilities and services, the New Indigenous Communities acquired specific social images and became individually specialized in serving a specific segment of the population. The NICs of the northern axis (Wasanpura, the new Shad Bagh, GujarPura, etc.) have become lower-middle and working-class neighbourhoods, whereas the western communities (Data Durbar, Mohni Road, Chota Ravi) are identified with middle-level professionals, junior executives, and small businessmen. To a great extent, this phenomenon of neighbourhood specialization is the territorial counterpart of the economic and social fractionation observed earlier.

A large number of NICs have developed since Independence, yet the old communities have not remained unchanged. With increasing congestion and declining standards of public services, many respectable neighbourhoods of yesteryear have turned into veritable slums. This is particularly the case in northern parts of the city, where such areas as MisriShah, Chah Miran, and Farooq Gunj have become crammed, filthy, and blighted districts. Many older communities have also undergone an invasion-succession sequence. Centrally located neighbourhoods (such as Ram Gali, Gowal Mandi, Royal Park) have been invaded by commercial establishments, and have become Mandis. Some peripheral NICs have been swamped by squatters and small workshops.

In conclusion, it may be said that New Indigenous Communities as urban forms represent a creative adaptation of the traditional spatial idiom to modern requirements. They represent an appropriate idiom of development both sociologically and climatically if properly nourished. Yet this idiom has been eclipsed by the prestigious importations.

The Planned Schemes

Comprehensively planned residential estates are the fourth category of spatial units in Lahore. The "scheme" is a statutory term describing a real estate project undertaken by a local authority. It originated with the Punjab Town Improvement Act (1922), which authorized Town Improvement Trusts to prepare development or expansion schemes for a designated vacant tract of land, or a redevelopment area. A statutory scheme requires the preparation of a plan for land uses, street layouts, and the subdivision of land, accompanied by building bylaws and policies for acquisition of land and disposal of lots. The Lahore Improvement Trust (LIT) and its successor, Lahore Development Authority (LDA), had developed 5,300 acres of land in about 60 schemes, producing approximately 38,000 plots up to 1979 [13]. Numerically, it is an impressive record, though in light of the city's need it appears very limited: these schemes contributed only seven percent of

housing lots in the city. It is not the numerical contribution
that makes these schemes so significant; their most pronounced
effect is as examples of high-class living.

Generally the Planned Schemes are low-density (50 to 100
persons per acre), and spaciously laid out housing estates. They
are usually composed of bungalows and detached houses set on large
lots. As these are public schemes, streets, roads, and water and
sewer lines are constructed before people move in, and sites are
set aside for schools, shopping areas, parks, mosques, and ceme-
teries. The high space and service standards and physical designs
of these schemes have an aura of Western suburbia, modernity, and
(high) status. They essentially follow the Civil Lines model,
though without the imperial grandeur (see Map 6.3).

A Planned Scheme is often a distinct neighbourhood or district of the city with identifiable boundaries, an autonomous
system of facilities and services, and a physical unity arising
from preplanning and singular sponsorship. Other attractive
features are the public guarantee of the provision of facilities
and services, and an assurance of clear property titles.
Altogether, a lot in a Planned Scheme is a highly prized possession for living, as well as for speculation.

The Planned Schemes are essentially the neighbourhoods of the
modern affluent, i.e., those who follow modern life-styles. They
may be from the old Civil Lines crowd, or may have recently
graduated to this status. This concentration of a specific segment
of the affluent occurs as a result of deliberate policies
affecting the market operations and social image of these schemes.
The influentials, particularly the officers, have reserved quotas
of lots. Doctors, business executives, lawyers, village landlords
seeking city residences, and, recently, Pakistanis abroad, have
been able to buy into these schemes. Together these groups make
the bulk of the residents in Planned Schemes. Modest- or
lower-income households cannot even aspire to live there, while
Arhatis, jewellers, grain dealers, truckers, or others have generally stayed out. They are financially capable of living there,
but, for them, the bungalow culture, the suburban locations, the
separation of work and home, and the Western ambiance of these
neighbourhoods are inhibiting.

Areas such as Shadman, Gulberg, or New Garden Town not only
have high-priced houses, but are expensive to live in. Separation
of shopping areas and homes makes refrigerators, domestic servants, and automobiles necessities. Long distances, wide roads,
and the absence of sidewalks or pedestrian paths produce the need
for transportation, of a child to and from school, or a woman from
family errands. The freestanding concrete bungalows and the wide
roads get so hot in summer that air-conditioning is not a luxury.
Even the Punjabis' habit of sleeping on rooftops in the cool of a
summer's night has to be abandoned on moving into the Planned
Schemes. All in all, sanitation, spaciousness, and modernity of
Schemes are offset by increased costs of living.

Planned Schemes can be found in all parts of the city, but

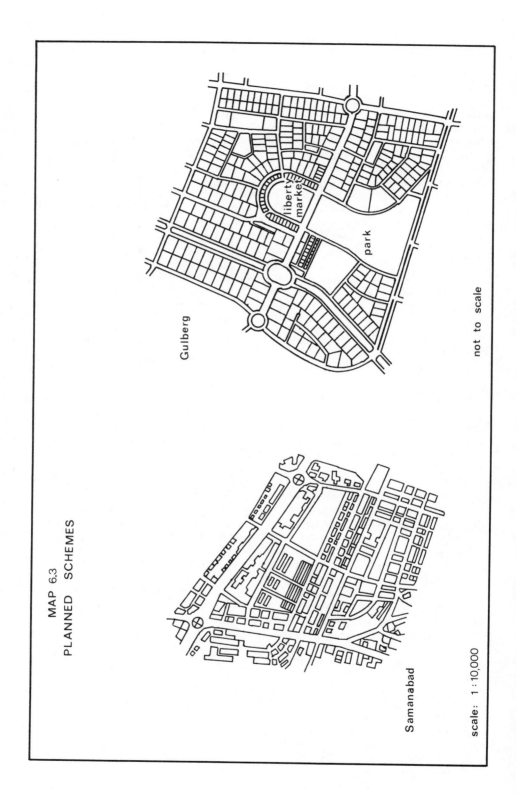

MAP 6.3
PLANNED SCHEMES

Gulberg

liberty market

park

not to scale

Samanabad

scale: 1:10,000

the southeast sector has become the main axis of this form of development (Map 6.4). This is where Shadman, Shah Jamal, Gulberg, New Garden Town, Iqbal Town have been sited, and they constitute a continuous outward-spreading band of Planned Schemes. The southeast is also the logical axis for the extension of the city as identified by two successive city plans. This means that the upper-class residential estates have preempted the choice locations, and are benefitting from investment for the expansion of the city.

So far, only a generalized account of the structural features of Planned Schemes has been given. The description may suggest that the Planned Schemes are conceived as finished and they do not change over time, but this would be an erroneous impression. The Planned Schemes have retained the above-outlined general features but they have also evolved according to a discernible pattern. One source of change is the evolving official doctrine of community planning.

Earlier schemes closely followed the Civil Lines standards. They had lots as large as half an acre to one acre and were expansive in the provision of infrastructure, though neglectful of public services and amenities. So episodal has been the planning process that personal predilections of successive town planners are evident in the schemes of the respective periods.

By the 1960s, the disutility of whole- or half-acre lots had become obvious, and small lots (8 to 16 lots per acre) were in great demand. Accordingly, the schemes conceived in this period incorporated these lessons. By the 1970s, social values had undergone another change, and provision for public amenities in residential neighbourhoods could not be overlooked. The schemes developed in this period, namely New Garden Town, Iqbal, and Faisal Town, were designed around a hierarchical system of public amenities and provided a variety of house types, including apartments and town houses.

Overall, the official planning doctrine has accommodated market realities in matters of lot size and housing densities, but the basic assumptions about distribution of activities and organization of land uses have not been critically examined despite persistent indications of their inappropriateness. Almost every Planned Scheme has undergone such large-scale modifications that a second layer of land uses and activities has emerged beneath the official facades. These adaptations have an evolutionary pattern which is sketched below in general terms.

Phase I

Some time after the first batch of households settle in a Planned Scheme, shacks or temporary stalls of bakers (tandoors), tea sellers, sweepers, etc. begin to dot the vacant sites and buffalo herds make their appearance. In the beginning, there is some fluidity about these activities. They are periodically shifted from one vacant lot to another until a site is found which

is not likely to be built over for a long while, e.g., a public
open space or a lot whose ownership is disputed. These stalls or
herds should not be regarded as unwelcome intrusions. They are
drawn by demand for their services, since it is the bungalow-walas
who prefer pure and fresh milk or need a sweeper to clean and
dust. Economic and social interdependencies link together the
sanctioned and the unapproved activities.

Phase II

As a Planned Scheme nears completion and acquires a sizeable
population, a network of Khokhas (kiosks) and stalls emerges in
residential areas. Also, bazaar-like clusters of vegetable and
fruit stands, meat and fish stores, and minor repair establishments are formed at intersections and along alleys and open spaces
around the designated commercial areas. Two factors contribute to
the formation of these bazaars. First, the official practice of
separating commercial from residential areas goes against local
behavioural patterns. Given large households, a flow of visitors
and guests, and periodic shortages of various consumer items, it
is almost impossible to avoid daily shopping. Under such conditions, proximity of daily provision stores is a basic requirement.
As planners have consistently ignored this fundamental relationship between homes and shops, the unofficial development comes
into play to correct such gross shortcomings of planning. Second,
property values and rents in the designated commercial zones are
so high that butchers, fish sellers, tailors, or vegetable vendors
cannot survive. They are thus forced into back alleys and
unplanned bazaars behind the shiny commercial markets.

Phase III

By the time a Planned Scheme matures, the parallel process of
unofficial development comes to the forefront. Ironically, the
principal violators of land-use and density arrangements are often
public agencies. New ones seeking office accommodation or established departments having to expand rent large bungalows in
Planned Schemes for offices.

The scale and range of these modifications can be judged from
the array of public offices found on a residential block of
Gulberg in 1981: Provincial Labour Court, Protector of Immigra-
tion, Social Security organizations, Medical Store, Directorate of
Production and Publicity, Directorate of Family Planning, and the
local office of the Cabinet Division.

While the public agencies infiltrate the residential streets,
Kebab shops, clinics, showrooms, restaurants, and schools appear
along the main boulevards. A drive through Samnabad and Gulberg,
the older of the Planned Schemes, verifies these observations. It
may be worth noting that this unofficial commercialization of
residential properties works to the advantage of homeowners who
happen to be the influentials of the city. The LDA's attempts

merely to collect the conversion charges and regularize commercialization of bungalows along Gulberg's Main Road ran into powerful resistance from judges, ex-mayors and ministers, doctors and
generals, who were the property owners. So the unapproved conversions are not as unofficial as they may appear.

The combined effect of the two evolutionary processes, official and unofficial, is a progressive indigenization of Planned
Schemes. The Planned Schemes remain prestigious neighbourhoods of
upper-income housing and modern life-style, but, while maintaining
this broad function, each substantial scheme assumes a specific
identity and character through unofficial developments. Samnabad
began as a high-class modern suburb, but it evolved into an expensive housing district particularly suited for merchants and
second-rung firm sector executives. It did not acquire a special
city-wide function, whereas Gulberg's indigenization has not
lowered its social standing and, if anything, has added to the
convenience of the area. Its Liberty Market has become the foreign
fashion centre, and the main boulevard has turned into the
dining-out strip of the city. Shad Bagh, in the north, was planned
as a middle-income modern area, but it has evolved into a spacious
New Indigenous Community. Thus, each Planned Scheme becomes a
special housing market for a segment of the affluent classes, and
thereafter, for associated commercial activities.

The Cantonment

Indo-Pakistani cities have inherited from the British a
unique spatial idiom known as the Cantonment. It originated as
"the institutionalized form of settlement for the military representatives of British Colonial power in India." [14] Since Independence, Lahore's Cantonment has continued to be a distinct and
autonomous unit, physically, socially, and administratively. The
Cantonment is distinguished for its precise geometric layout, spacious grounds, arrangement of residences, offices, clinics,
schools, and even shopping areas, according to rank and official
status. Ruddick describes Lahore's Cantonment as "a Garden City
built half a century before this concept of planning became
popular in England." [15]

Even in British days, the Cantonment had a native bazaar.
After Independence, racial and ethnic distinctions disappeared,
but class and rank differences remained intact. The Sadar Bazaar
became a precinct for lower ranks, whereas Wellington Mall and the
surrounding district became officers' territory. Due to greater
administrative control in the Cantonment, its high-income areas
have not undergone the same degree of commercialization and conversion as has the Civil Lines. In the Cantonment, the indigenous
and the modern institutions have generally remained separated.
Thus, the upper-class areas of the Cantonment are some of the most
well-kept and salubrious sections of the city. Since Independence,
the Cantonment has become even more a locus of power and

authority: after all, for about 17 of the 35 years of Independence, Pakistan has been ruled by the army.

The attraction of the Cantonment as a clean, modern and
orderly area has made it a prime target for development. There
were substantial tracts of open spaces and vacant lands, and it
has been relatively easy to sever a few parcels for officers to
build private homes. Cumulatively, these new bungalows began to
fill spaces, and by 1980 the Cantonment had become a fairly
built-up area. Similarly, around peripheral villages, clusters of
modest   houses   have   been   appearing   in   response   to   an
ever-increasing demand. The development has become an organized
activity, and by 1982 the Cantonment Cooperative Society was about
to complete the first phase of developing a veritable township.
Although the Cantonment has been swept by the property development
fever, a sharp delineation of upper and modern versus lower and
indigenous areas has been maintained.

Katchi Abadis (Squatter Clusters)

Squatters have become a trade mark of Third World cities, and
Lahore fully qualifies on this score. In 1980, almost 23 percent
of the city's population was living in squatter clusters. Between
1964 and 1979, squatters increased at a yearly rate of about 17
percent per year, which was almost three times the rate of population growth [16]. This was also the period of accelerating house
building activity, and, odd as it might seem, the evidence
suggests that squatters multiplied in direct ratio to the increase
of housing stock. Apparently home building by middle- and
upper-income groups squeezed out the poor from the housing market,
and left them no choice but to congregate in squatter clusters or
Katchi Abadis, as these are known locally.

A Katchi Abadi is a neighbourhood of the poor or, more pre-
cisely, it consists of one- or two-room mud and timber houses
built on small lots (25-75 square yards) on lands of disputed
titles or unenforced ownership. Public amenities are nonexistent,
and a feeling of insecurity (about tenure and occupation of land)
pervades. It is the temporary nature of the tenure, rather than of
the structures, that has earned the adjective "Katchi" (dissolvable) for Abadis (settlements).

Katchi Abadis range from clusters of Jhuggis (hutments)
strung along the flood drains and rail tracks, to rectangular
blocks of semi-pacca (semipermanent) homes, apparently laid out
with considerable preplanning and deliberation. While the former
conform to the conventional image of squatters' abodes, the latter
are almost indistinguishable from New Indigenous Communities. Such
a variation of layouts and physical conditions is itself a reflection of the evolutionary trends among Katchi Abadis.

There are two processes at work in bringing about changes in
the physical and social make-up of Katchi Abadis. First, with age,
a Katchi Abadi is stabilized and little by little gains acceptance

from authorities and surrounding communities. It becomes a part of
the overall scene. Relatively influential residents manage to get
an electric connection from the WAPDA, and, when the wires are
strung to oblige a few, the rest cannot be excluded for long.
Similar sequences of events take place for other facilities.

When a whole generation grows up in a Katchi Abadi, it is
inevitable that a few youngsters qualify as doctors, lawyers, or
engineers. Such changes in personal fortunes begin to be reflected
in the physical conditions of the area. Individuals may move out
eventually, but their ancestral homes are improved along the way.
Other less spectacular changes in social status and economic fortune over a generation result in the establishment of small businesses and craft shops in a Katchi Abadi, thereby contributing to
its prosperity, as well as stability.

The second source of change in Katchi Abadis is their progressively increasing political power. Earlier, Katchi Abadis grew
incrementally and timidly. A new shack would unobtrusively appear
next to an existing one to avoid being discovered, and thus, one
by one, they clustered into an Abadi. With the heating up of the
housing market, the poor were squeezed out from normal channels of
supply and large numbers of households had to find shelter in
existing Katchi Abadis or form new ones [17]. Katchi Abadis thus
became a development business. By the mid-1960s, Katchi Abadis
were being developed as whole sites divided into cheap lots by
clever entrepreneurs, with the tacit cooperation of local officials. Some Abadis were also developed by cooperative groups or
clans for their members.

Katchi Abadis of this vintage have straight streets, rectangular layouts, and standardized lots. By the 1970s, Katchi
Abadis were the only choice available to low-income households
looking for shelter. In a regular neighbourhood, almost nothing
could be had for a rent of less than Rs. 200-300 per month (equal
to 60 to 70 percent of the salary of a clerk). Such persons as
peons, clerks, primary school teachers, and police constables
turned to Katchi Abadis for affordable accommodation. A survey of
Katchi Abadis in 1977 revealed that although a majority of residents were labourers, craftsmen, and hawkers (68 percent), most of
whom were self-employed and worked from their homes, yet a sizeable minority (27 percent) were white-collar employees and supervisors [18].

As the number of Katchi Abadi residents increased, they began
to be vociferous about their needs. Their associations or anjumans
(corporations) could field a noisy demonstration or bring out a
crowd to resist eviction. Thus, Katchi Abadis have evolved from
the shacks of the pitiable to the neighbourhoods of the aroused
poor.

The official attitudes towards Katchi Abadis also have undergone change with the rise of their political clout. Instead of
viewing Katchi Abadis as illegal eyesores to be demolished and
dispersed, the LDA and the Municipal Corporation have acknowledged
the futility of such an approach. During the People's Party rule

(1971–77), proprietary rights for residents of <u>Katchi Abadis</u> were promised, and an attempt was made to promote a self–help organization, Awami Rehashi Tanzeem, for the improvement of <u>Katchi Abadis</u>. In 1978, the Martial Law government created a directorate within the LDA, to improve and regularize about 97 <u>Abadis</u>. Obviously, <u>Katchi Abadis</u> have come to be an accepted component of the city.

The six spatial units described above constitute the pieces which combine in various arrangements to make the physical mosaic that is the city. These are not zones or sectors in the usual meanings of these terms, i.e., territorial districts of uniform land uses and densities. Each one represents a complex of uses and activities articulated around a specific function and life–style. They are distinct community types and specialized housing markets.

Lahore's sociospatial structure cannot be described in terms of consistent arrays of variables, densities, incomes, house types or land uses. The sociospatial permutations arising from factors such as incomes, social statuses, roles of operations, sectoral affiliations and life–style are so wide–ranging that it would be inappropriate to treat them as variations of the same theme. Lahore was originally a confederation of communities, and its economic and physical development has further segmented its sociospatial structure. To observe the territorial distribution of these segments and their interrelations, we will next examine the land use patterns.

THE LAND USE STRUCTURE

Lahore has generally expanded along a north–south axis, creating a rectangular built–up area. It has fanned out along highways such as G. T., Ferozpur, and Multan Roads. Within broad swaths of land enclosed by these highways, the expansion has proceeded along major traffic arteries laid out by the British, i.e., The Mall, Jail, Canal Bank, Lytton, and Mayo Roads.

The city has grown through a combination of leaping out and filling in processes. The leaping out of development is often initiated by a Planned Scheme. It opens virgin land for settlement and serves as the pole for further development. The possibility of tapping the utilities extended for a Planned Scheme stimulates the infilling of intervening areas, and raises the developmental potential of lands further out. Thus the planned and officially sponsored development extends the urban frontier, while the unofficial building activity fills up the leaped over areas and brings the more distant countryside under urban influences. This sequence of development has been repeated for almost all major Planned Schemes. Samnabad spawned the filling up of New Mozang and Islamia Park, and even accelerated the building up of Nawan Kot and Bank Colony further out on the periphery of the city. Shad Bagh became an anchor for Bhagatpura and other northern exurbia, while Gulberg precipitated the filling in of Shah Jamal and Canal Bank, and brought into the city orbit areas across the railway line.

The unofficial development activity usually takes one of two forms: a New Indigenous Community or a <u>Katchi Abadi</u>. On particularly valuable sites, such as leftover lands along the canal or a major road, bungalows, upper-class residences, or commercial buildings may also be built. These cross-processes of development result in the patchwork of Planned Schemes, New Indigenous Communities, and <u>Katchi Abadis</u> which distinguishes Lahore's land use pattern. Along any one-mile length of a road, one may pass by elegant bungalows, squatters' huts, workers' quarters, and clusters of indigenous houses. The variations of activities and building styles in this rapidly changing streetscape often give the impression of haphazardness. Its underlying order requires to be elaborated.

Organizational Framework

Land uses in Lahore are organized at two levels, dominant and subordinate. The functional specializations of an area, its reputation and imagability lay the bases for its dominant land use, whereas functions which are either complementary or contributory to dominant activity constitute the subordinate land use. A subordinate land use is not defined by the quantity of activities, but by their functional role in a neighbourhood's economic specialization and sociocultural standing. A few examples will illustrate this point.

Mayo Gardens or Government Officers' Residences (G.O.R.) are housing estates for senior officers of the Government. They are elite residential areas of exceptional charm and exclusivity. Yet tucked away behind palatial bungalows are servants' quarters where clans of cooks, peons and gardeners are crammed five or ten to a room. Numerically, members of servants' households are usually double or triple the number of patrons, but this fact has not affected the standing of the area, because the servants' housing is a subordinate land use. Similarly, a close look at Anarkali, Gulberg, or any other area reveals the duality of land uses. The used-clothes hawkers and <u>chat</u> (spicy fruit salad) sellers of Anarkali constitute a subordinate land use complementing its dominant activity as a market for fabric, hosiery, garments, and toiletries. The former have become prosperous businesses in their own right, yet the main draw of Anarkali remains its regular establishments. Similarly, by the late 1970s, Gulberg's main market had become a place for hiring construction labourers. Every morning, little was visible in the street except men waiting for contractors' agents, and yet this activity remained a subordinate land use amidst restaurants, supermarkets, and banks. How this two-layered structure defines the city's land-use patterns is a question to be explored further.

TABLE 6.1

Land Uses, Densities and Public Utilities by Neighbourhoods

Neighbourhood	Area (acres)	Density (persons per acre)	Dominant Land Use	Subordinate Land Use	Water Supply	Sewerage	Drainage
BadamiBagh	2,272	31	Industry	Workers' housing Squatters	Poor	Poor	Poor
Wasanpura	543	101	New Indigenous housing	Household workshops	Poor	Poor	Poor
Shad Bagh	4,730	24	Middle Income modern housing	Commerce Squatters Dairy Herds	Adequate	Poor	Poor
Faiz Bagh	161	485	Old settlement Workers' housing	Household workshops Industry	Adequate	Poor	Adequate
Kot Khawaja Saeed	692	73	New Indigenous and traditional housing	Industry Dairy herds Squatters Vegetable gardens	Adequate	Poor	Adequate
University of Engineering	780	104	Institutions Industry	Modern housing Squatters	Adequate	Poor	Adequate
Nabipura	545	85	Old settlements Peripheral villages	Industries Vacant	Poor	Poor	Poor
Baghbanpura	852	70	Traditional housing Local commerce Old settlements	Household workshops Fodder and grain markets Vacant	Adequate	Poor	Poor

TABLE 6.1 (continued)

Land Uses, Densities and Public Utilities by Neighbourhoods

Neighbourhood	Area (acres)	Density (persons per acre)	Dominant Land Use	Subordinate Land Use	Water Supply	Sewerage	Drainage
Shalimar Town	1,110	32	Modern middle and lower income housing	Industry Squatters	Poor	Poor	Poor
Walled City	763	335	Old settlement Traditional, mixed housing Markets	Bazaars Household workshops	Poor	Poor	Poor
Anarkali	852	67	Commerce Institutions	Tenements	Adequate	Poor	Poor
Data Durbar	568	118	New Indigenous housing	Commerce Institutions Squatters	Adequate	Poor	Poor
Hall Road	2,025	25	Commerce Institutions	Apartments Offices	Good	Poor	Poor
Qila Gujar Singh	123	242	Old settlement	Commerce Workshops Squatters	Good	Poor	Poor
Gawal Mandi	209	316	New Indigenous housing	Workshops Commerce Squatters	Good	Poor	Poor
Simla Hill and G.O.R.	1,235	91	Modern bungalows Planned Schemes	Institutions Park	Good	Poor	Adequate

TABLE 6.1 (continued)

Land Uses, Densities and Public Utilities by Neighbourhoods

Neighbourhood	Area (acres)	Density (persons per acre)	Dominant Land Use	Subordinate Land Use	Water Supply	Sewerage	Drainage
Ghori Shahu	703	44	New Indigenous housing Bungalows and Quarters	Workshops Institutions Squatters	Good	Poor	Poor
Allama Iqbal Road	852	64	Modern bungalows and Quarters Planned Schemes	Institutions Squatters	Good	Poor	Poor
Mozang	271	205	Old settlement	Commerce	Good	Poor	Adequate
Samanabad and Islamia Park	2,050	61	Planned Schemes Bungalows	Commerce Workshops	Good	Good	Poor
Ichra	716	124	Old settlements New Indigenous housing	Commerce Industry Squatters	Poor	Poor	Poor
Rifle Range Krishan Nagar	2,630	38	New Indigenous housing Bungalows	Commerce Vegetable gardens	Good	Poor	Poor
Gulberg	1,496	30	Planned Schemes Bungalows	Commerce Industry	Good	Adequate	Adequate
Garden Town Model Town	2,852	34	Planned Schemes Bungalows	Commerce Institutions Workshops	Good	Adequate	Poor
Shadman	815	93	Planned Schemes	Commerce	Good	Good	Adequate

TABLE 6.1 (continued)

Sources: 1) For area, density and public utilities, Lahore Urban
          Development and Traffic Study, Final Report: Volume I.
          Urban Planning (Lahore: LDA, 1981), Table 22, pp.
          158-159.
          2) For land uses, field surveys by the author.

Neighbourhoods and Residential Densities

Table 6.1 portrays, albeit crudely, both the social ecology
and distribution of land uses of the city in 1980. A number of
observations can be gleaned from it. First, it appears that Lahore
is a city of mixed land uses. Almost every constituent area has
not only residential and commercial activities, but also, within
these broad categories, wide ranges of architectural styles and
types of establishments. Second, the character of a residential
neighbourhood seems to be as much the product of the style of
houses as of the social characteristics of the residents. And the
social image of an area depends on residents' incomes, as well as
on the manner in which they were earned (sectoral affiliation).
Covenanted officers and Halvais (sweets sellers) might have
similar incomes, but the former are likely to live in Planned
Schemes of governmental housing estates, while the latter gravi-
tates towards neighbourhoods of traditional or New Indigenous
houses. A combination of these physical and social characteristics
turns an area into a housing submarket, and lays bases for the
dominant land use. Third, it seems that the second layer of land
uses is subordinate only in the sense that it does not conform to
the special character and image of a district. In many cases, the
subordinate uses are autonomous and tangential to the main functions of an area, though spatially fully integrated in it, for
example, the Mandis of the old city, the tenements of Anarkali, or
railway offices. Fourth, the age, social standing, and cultural
orientation (Western versus indigenous) of the neighbourhoods are
correlated with their densities, conditions of services, and
general quality of life. Overall, the older, the indigenous, and
the poorer areas are crowded as well as inadequately serviced,
even by the relatively low standards of the city as a whole.

It appears that the organic unity of the historical city has
given way to the shifting equilibrium of sociospatial units. There
is little internal uniformity of activities and land uses within a
neighbourhood. Only on the scale of a mohalla (5,000-10,000
people) or of a block can a reasonable degree of uniformity be
found. This means that most Western-inspired notions and models of
spatial structures cannot encompass Lahore's reality. Nor can conventional city planning measures be applicable. For example, how
can zoning as a regulatory device be applied when there are no
sizeable areas of uniform land use?

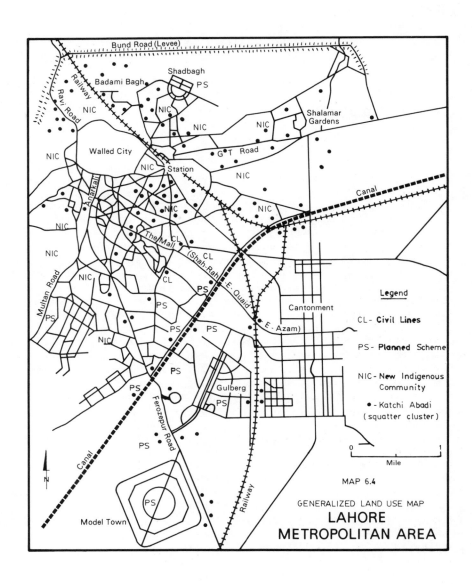

Bund Road (Levee)

Shadbagh

Badami Bagh   PS

NIC   NIC

NIC

NIC   Shalamar
            Gardens

Walled City   NIC

NIC   Station   G T Road

NIC   NIC

Anarkali   NIC

NIC   The Mall   CL

NIC   CL

Multan Road   NIC   CL

PS   PS   PS   Cantonment

NIC   PS   PS   E Azam)

(Shah-Rah   E. Quaid

PS   E Azam)

PS

PS   Gulberg

PS   PS

Ferozepur Road

PS

Canal

N

PS

Model Town

Railway

Railway

Ravi Road

Canal

Legend

CL- Civil Lines

PS- Planned Scheme

NIC- New Indigenous
      Community

• - Katchi Abadi
    (squatter cluster)

0   1
        Mile

MAP 6.4

GENERALIZED LAND USE MAP
LAHORE
METROPOLITAN AREA

Map 6.4 gives a generalized picture of the city's spatial structure. It shows that most of the Planned Schemes have been sited along the south and southeastern axes, whereas the New Indigenous Communities have evolved in the northern sector, which is poorly serviced, prone to floods, and accessible only through three passages under the railway line. Paralleling Multan Road on the west, and along G. T. Road toward the east, old settlements have fanned out to merge with each other and produce a continuously built-up area of Katchi Abadis, industrial estates, and NICs. The core of the city consists of the New Indigenous Communities, and Civil Lines. It is an area where markets, bazaars, workshops, hospitals, colleges, and offices are sprinkled among crammed houses.

Examination of Map 6.4 in conjunction with the residential densities map (6.5) brings the structural features of the city into bold relief. The high density of the Walled City is a legend, but, surprisingly, Faiz Bagh, Gowal Mandi and Ram Gahi constitute an arc of almost similar residential densities (more than 200 persons per acre) to the east-southeast of the Walled City. These areas were largely developed during the early days of British rule in the idiom of New Indigenous Communities. The density gradients drop precipitously beyond the core, though there are pockets of high density around old settlements and suburban Katchi Abadis. Another notable pattern is that, along the axis of Planned Schemes, starting from the Mall and proceeding in a southeasterly direction towards Model Town, residential densities are markedly low (100 persons per acre), whereas equally new but unofficial development to the north and paralleling the G. T. Road towards the east has high densities. This contrast of residential densities is not merely a reflection of differences in layout and design. It also stands for the distinctions between the modern and traditional life-styles, upper and moderate incomes, official and unofficial modes of development. Finally, the differences in residential densities are as much indicative of social class standings as of life-styles and cultural orientations (modern versus vernacular).

So far this analysis of land use patterns has focussed on the organization of neighbourhoods and residential land uses. This emphasis has been necessary because of the fact that a neighbourhood or district is the basic spatial unit of the city. A separate analysis of commercial and industrial locational patterns is required to complete the account of Lahore's land use structure.

Distribution of Commercial and Industrial Activities

In Chapters 4 and 5, the evolutionary trends in commercial and industrial activities were examined, and their respective locational tendencies were uncovered. The present discussion of the locational patterns of these activities must, therefore, begin with a résumé of the earlier findings. Here is a brief recount.

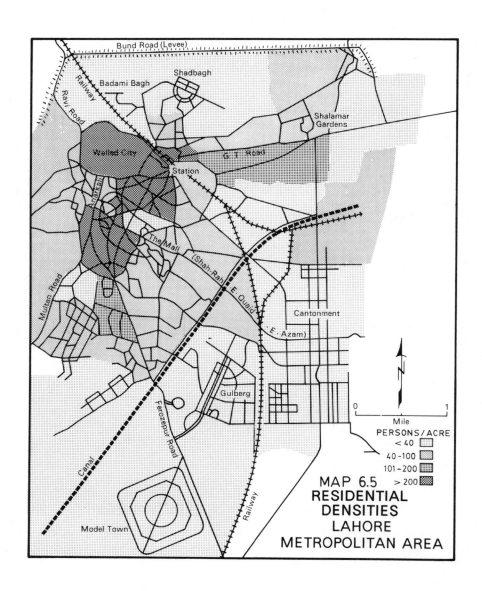

Bund Road (Levee)

Shadbagh

Badami Bagh

Railway

Ravi Road

Shalamar
Gardens

Walled City

G. T. Road

Station

Markazi

The Mall

Multan Road

(Shah-Rah E. Quaid

E. Azam)

Cantonment

Gulberg

Ferozepur Road

Canal

Railway

Model Town

0   1

Mile

PERSONS/ACRE

< 40

40 - 100

101 - 200

> 200

MAP 6.5
RESIDENTIAL
DENSITIES
LAHORE
METROPOLITAN AREA

(1) Stores and workshops are everywhere in the city. With the exception of three industrial Estates (BadamiBagh, Railway Workshop, and Kot Kakhpat), there are no segregated commercial or industrial districts.
(2) The core area (from Anarkali to Empress Road) has almost 50 percent of the shops and the largest concentration of small industries in the city.
(3) The Civil Lines has been swept by the process of converting spacious bungalows into offices and stores during the 1970s. The main roads are steadily becoming commercial strips and ribbons of office complexes.
(4) A similar but less varied commercialization has occurred in other parts of the city, particularly in northern and southwestern sections.
(5) Although most commercial development everywhere, even in the Civil Lines, has been unofficial in the sense that it was seldom planned or approved by the LDA, yet hawkers, stallholders, and other sidewalk purveyors of services and goods constitute the distinct form of spontaneous commercialization known locally as encroachments. They serve the lower circuit and permeate all parts of the city.
(6) Commercial markets and nodes are specialized by commodities as well as by the social standing of prospective customers. A variety store in Kashmari Bazaar specializes in catering to veiled women and Dhoti-clad men, while in a similar store on the Mall or in Liberty Market they would be out of place. Even the language of transaction would be Punjabi in the former case and Urdu in the latter.

     The findings cited above point out an intrinsic order among what the casual observer may think is haphazard development. The interpenetration of shops and homes, the pervasiveness of commercial establishments, and the permeation of encroachments are not random phenomena. They are the territorial imprints of the multiple circuits and divergent, but interdependent, modes of operation. The locational pattern arising from these processes is discussed below.

     There are two basic forms of commercial development: (1) strips of shoplined streets with wide ranges of stores, and (2) nodes of a specialized commodity market. The shopping strips radiate from the city's core and have already captured major roads in Civil Lines and in the New Indigenous Communities of the north. The main arteries of the older Planned Schemes such as Samnabad, Gulberg, or Shad Bagh, have also been turned into commercial strips. The specialized commercial markets are concentrated in the Walled City and in the triangular territory formed by Anarkali, Railway Station, and the Assembly Chambers on the Mall. It may be noted that half (11 out of 22) of these commodity markets have been formed since 1947. As soon as a new commodity came into wide use, a specialized Mandi for its supply emerged. For example, Hall Road became the centre for television sets and cassette players, as these items became a part of local consumption. Similarly, increasing numbers of motorbikes, cars, and auto rickshaws spawned markets for parts at Montgomery-Queen's Road and Lytton Road. The increasing tempo of construction activity in the southeast section of the city prompted the formation of markets for sanitary fittings at Qartba Chowk, for hardware and electrical goods on Beadon Road. These examples illustrate that the formation of commodity markets for higher order goods remained a basic mode of commercial organization.

The commercial establishments in Lahore are arranged in a three-tiered hierarchy. At the base are milk and grocery stores, vegetable and fruit stands, Halvis, Tandoors, and butchers. Shops selling goods for common needs are distributed almost everywhere in residential areas. The second tier consists of fabric and general stores, tailors and druggists, etc. Such establishments are found both in neighbourhood shopping strips and in special nodes of city-wide significance, e.g. tailors on Dani Ram Street, druggists around Mayo Hospital and on Temple Road, and Tikka shops in Mozang, Gowalmandi and Gulberg. The third tier consists of the specialized markets, discussed earlier. Although commercial establishments at all levels could be further distinguished by their modes of operation, i.e., indigenous versus modern, this distinction becomes a significant criterion of specialization at the third tier. Liberty (of Gulberg) is not a commodity market consisting of only electrical goods or fabrics or toy shops. It is known to be the fashion centre of the city. Whether one is looking for the newest imported styles in shoes or garments, or packaged goods, Liberty is the place to go. Its up-to-dateness is its specialization.

Another interesting example is the so-called "puthan market" in Shadman. The shopping area of Shadman was developed by the LDA as a showpiece suburban shopping arcade, but it evolved into a fabric market with a specialization in smuggled foreign cloth. Similar fates befell other shopping plazas privately developed on the Mall, Ferozpur Road, and Queen's Road. Instead of attracting a variety of stores to replicate a modern shopping centre, these buildings have evolved into specific commodity markets catering to a well-defined clientele. All these examples point to an organizing principle of Lahore's commercial structure unanticipated in Western theory, i.e., specialization by social status and life-style of buyers on the one hand, and/or by commodities on the other. Lastly, it may be noted that the specialization of a market may change over time from one commodity or taste to another, but the result is seldom a multipurpose shopping area.

There is an evident clannishness of commodity markets and small industries. Map 5.2 shows that workshop clusters were mostly located in close proximity to commercial nodes. Large plants were sited along major highways towards the outskirts of the city, whereas workshops infiltrated the residential sections of Gujjarpura, Shad Bagh, and Multan and Ferozpur Roads. It may be noted that small industries manifest the same locational tendencies as the commercial establishments, i.e., intermixing with

other land uses, or in linear strips and nodes of workshops producing a specific item, e.g., fans, shoes, etc.

By now it should be evident why Lahore has become a city of
multiple foci and diffused physical form. Economic development has
sharpened the differences between the modern and the indigenous
institutions, and among various social strata. These differences
are reflected on the land in the form of an array of divergent
neighbourhoods. Institutionally and operationally, the city has
come to be characterized by discontinuities which militate against
the formation of a hierarchy of commercial nodes and the emergence
of a focal point, i.e., a central business district. Instead, a
number of parallel special-purpose markets have emerged which
serve as centres of respective social and economic segments of the
city.

SUMMING UP

This chapter attempts to describe the distribution of homes,
stores, workshops, and industries in the city, and tries to
explain the reasons for their locations. These are not static
phenomena, yet there is some continuity of overall patterns.
Although the chapter primarily presents a picture of the city as
it was in 1980-82, yet, by probing the evolutionary trends of constituent units, it has uncovered the continuing organizational
framework underlying the ebb and flow of land uses. The task was
complicated by the inapplicability of many Western models and concepts to the empirical realities of Lahore. The local situation
deviates from the assumptions of these models to such a degree
that it would have been pointless to persist with them. The
coexistence of two modes of operation and the institutionalization
of corruption militate against any assumed functional uniformity
of activities. For example, the indistinguishability of family and
business operations among artisans, hawkers, and bazaaris contradicts the assumption of separability of activity on which land use
categories are based. Similarly, if only about 12 percent of new
construction was proceeding with the approval of local authorities, it made little sense to treat unapproved land uses as devia-
tions from public norms. In fact, the unofficial development was
the norm. These examples point to the inadmissability of concepts
such as gravity, gradients, or zones of uniform land uses. Due to
these conceptual limitations, we have let the empirical facts
define the analytical categories.

Lahore has become a city of diffused land uses, punctuated
with markets, shopping centres, office clusters, and historical
monuments. There are marked variations of crowdedness and inten-
sity of activity from one part of the city to another, but there
is a pervasive familiarity. Shops and stalls are sprinkled among
residences, cows roam over open spaces, encroachments block sidewalks, and loud speakers blare from mosque minarets. These are the
sights and sounds of Lahore, and not even the new suburbs are

without them. Scarcely any area could be called exclusively residential, commercial, or industrial, except for the officers' residential estates.

There are shopping streets, industrial clusters, institutional complexes, and other nodes of intense activity, but they
are seldom singular in character. The success of one activity at a
location attracts others to take advantage of its drawing powers
and ultimately leads to a complex of linked land uses. Such commercial or institutional nodes constitute focal points in the
city, e.g., (1) Lohari gate, Anarkali, Vila Gumbad, (2) Hall,
Beadon and Mall Roads, (3) Mozang Chungi, (4) Shah Alam and
Kashmiri Bazaar, (5) the Bus Stand and BadamiBagh. These nodes do
not have clearly defined boundaries, and at their peripheries they
are indistinguishable from surrounding neighbourhoods, yet each
one has an individual character and their variety makes Lahore so
interesting.

The basic unit of spatial organization in Lahore is a neighbourhood or district of distinct social and economic functions. It
is a sort of ecological unit which serves as the territorial base
for a particular sociocultural group. Whether it is the
bazaar-oriented working-class area or a colony of low-grade public
officials, a neighbourhood includes linked activities that contribute to its sociological specialization. The term neighbourhood
here means a relatively large area which constitutes a housing
market and has a distinct identity. It is not merely an area
within which daily residential activities are carried out, as
Perry originally defined, and as city planners now routinely lay
out.

This chapter identified six constituent units of the city,
namely (1) the Walled City, (2) the Civil Lines, (3) New Indigenous Communities, (4) the Planned Schemes, (5) Cantonment, and
(6) Katchi Abadi. Lahore has grown as a patchwork of alternating
New Indigenous Communities and Planned Schemes interspersed with
Katchi Abadis and old settlements. The economic functions, social
statuses, and physical images of those spatial units differ
markedly. Yet they coexist in close proximity to each other, so
much so that there is hardly any part of the city where artisans'
sheds, tandoors, stalls, indigenous homes and Western bungalows
cannot be found. Undoubtedly there is a more or less dominant
social function and architectural idiom in each district, but they
are composites of diverse elements. The economic and social interdependencies are so deep-rooted that living in an upper-income
area would be unimaginable without sweepers, washerwomen, or
watchmen, not to mention hawkers, cooks, matchmakers, etc. In the
absence of appropriate housing for the latter, it is inevitable
that alongside posh bungalows will be huts and hovels. This is how
apparently disparate land uses come to exist side by side.

All in all, the Planned Schemes have appropriated the more
salubrious south-southeastern axis for the affluent and the
influential, while the moderate-income, traditional housing
development, taking the form of New Indigenous Communities, has

converged to the northern and western peripheries. Although the
two groups are concentrated on opposite sides of the city, it
still is not a situation of class apartheid, as Abu-Lughod found
in Rabat [19]. Lahore's neighbourhoods are differentiated along
class lines, but they do not constitute spatial monopolies. In
fact, a more pronounced effect of north-south differentiation is
the preempting by the Planned Schemes of public investments and
infrastructural facilities and services. Inequalities of water
supply, sewerage, public transport, schools, and clinics between
the southern Planned Schemes and the rest of the city are evident.
Interestingly, such spatial inequalities are the direct result of
the practice of town planning in Lahore.

A district in the city has two layers of land uses, (1)
dominant and (2) subordinate. This two-tiered land use structure
is another manifestation of the dichotomous processes of development and the multiplicity of modes of operations. A dominant land
use is essentially rooted in the economic and social specialization of an area. For example, Shadman is a residential area of
modern affluence. It specializes in a housing market for a
specific social segment, and that is its dominant land use as well
as preeminent image. Yet, there are also fashion boutiques,
clinics, and governmental offices here. Such land uses are
permanent but subordinate.

The Civil Lines has, since Independence, undergone commercialization and become the core district of the city. Yet it is
not a central business district in the sense of a contiguous
shopping area. It is a sprawling district dotted with specialized
markets, shopping plazas, public buildings, and workshop clusters.
The Walled City may have lost its position of centrality for the
city, but it has become the focal point of the bazaar sector. New
Mandis have evolved since Independence, namely Azam cloth market
and Shah Alam market. As a residential area, it has been losing
households of professionals and modern affluents whose places are
being taken by prosperous bazaaris. Despite congestion, dilapida-
tion of buildings, and unsanitary conditions, the Walled City has
remained a thriving community. The Planned Schemes, such as
Samnabad and Gulberg, manifest an evolutionary sequence which
brings about their indigenization through conversions of properties and encroachments on public spaces.

The most extensive idiom of physical development is the New
Indigenous Community comprised of updated indigenous houses and
incorporating contemporary standards in street layouts and site
allocations. This form of development emerged soon after the
British built the Civil Lines and was an experiment which blended
Western urban forms with indigenous house designs and activity
systems. WasanPura through Krishan Nagar to the more recent Nia
Mozang and Islamia Park are examples of an evolving genre of New
Indigenous Communities.

Finally, the Katchi Abadis began as temporary settlements of
refugees, but they have gradually become the primary source of the
low-income housing supply in the city. Although about a third of

Katchi Abadis are in the northern section, there is no part of the
city that does not support one or more such clusters. Such a widespread distribution of Katchi Abadis is also an indication of the
intertwining of various land uses.

The distribution of industrial activities repeats the pattern
of commercial land uses. Artisan units and craft shops can be
found in almost every district of the city. A large historical
concentration of machine shops on Railway-Brandeth Roads makes an
industrial node, but this location also testifies to the complex
web of interlinkages between these workshops, and the nearby tool
and hardware market and the residential enclaves of blacksmiths:
New small industrial nodes such as those at the Bus Stand, Badami
Bagh, and Ferozpur Road also manifest similar complex characteristics incorporating complementary but distinct activities. These
complexes suggest that the locational determinants of industries
are not so much the transport costs as the operational externalities. Crowded and out-of-the-way streets seem to be attractive for
small industries as long as they facilitate operational linkages.

Large industrial plants have gravitated towards the periphery
of the city along major highways, though it is not uncommon to
find a factory in the middle of a residential area or commercial
strip. The latter situation might have arisen from residential or
commercial development following and swamping an industrial plant
in what once was open land, or vice versa. The textile mill in
Garhi Shahu and the rolling mills in Nawan Kot are examples of
such arrangements.

From the above discussion, the contours of the city's spatial
structure are discernible. Lahore has evolved in the post-Independence period through a dialectic of diffusion-differentiation processes. While homes, stores and workshops have followed each other
in all parts of the city, producing a diffused mixture of land
uses everywhere, commodity markets, industrial clusters, and
special interest housing have been emerging as site-differentiated
enclaves of specialized activities. These two tendencies working
simultaneously have created a basic homogeneity of physical form
throughout the city, overlaid with a lattice of special areas and
markets. For the historian, it is not an unfamiliar pattern. The
old Lahore was similarly structured. It seems that underneath the
impressive modern transformation, there are persistent historical
patterns. The main fissure that divides the city is the distinction between bungalows and indigenous housing districts. This distinction not only symbolizes architectural differences, but also
signifies divergences of life-styles, incomes, and cultural orientation. It is the divide between the modern and the indigenous.

Perhaps of equal significance are the negative findings of
this chapter. Lahore is not a city of separable land uses, except
for higher-level special activities. It cannot be meaningfully
divided into residential, commercial, or industrial zones, nor can
it be explained by a familiar model of urban structures. It has
become a federation of neighbourhoods, special districts, and the
social-economic interests they stand for. There is no one central

area, and not even the transport networks converge to any single focal point. These features underlay the colonial Lahore, and post-Independence development has proceeded more or less along the same grooves. Fission rather than fusion characterizes the recent evolution of the city.

NOTES

1. Implicit in this statement about the expected uniformity of functional areas in a city are assumptions of Western land use models such as Burgess and Park Concentric Zone (1925), Homer Hoyt's Sector Model (1939) and Harris and Ullman's Multiple Nuclei Model. Accessibility, land value, and tendencies of similar activities to agglomerate are assumed to be the factors which sort out activities into zones, sectors or districts of internal homo-geneity and external contrasts. Shaped by these forces, a city is expected to be organized into areas of uniform activities whose overall configuration may take the form of concentric zones or sectors or districts. For an overview of the internal structure of cities see B. J. Garner, "Models of Urban Geography and Settlement Location," in Socio-Economic Models in Geography, ed. Richard J. Chorley and Peter Haggett (London: Methuen, 1967), pp. 338-343. Obviously these models and assumptions are statements of ideal types. Empirically many divergences are found even in the European and North American cities from these models.

2. A natural area in an ecological unit serving as the habitat of a differentiated group and becoming identified with the character and quality of its inhabitants, e.g., an Italian neigh-bourhood, slum, wholesale district, etc. For a description of the concept of natural area see Camilla Lambert and David Wier (eds.), Cities in Modern Britain (Glasgow: Fontana, 1975), pp. 37-38.

3. Janet Abu-Lughod, "Developments in North African Urban-ism: The Process of Decolonization," in Urbanization and Coun-ter-Urbanization, ed. Brian J. Berry (Beverly Hills: Sage Publica-tions, 1976), p. 202.

4. Anthony D. King, Colonial Urban Development (London: Routledge and Kegan Paul, 1976), pp. 7-8.

5. Samuel V. Noe, "In search of 'the' traditional Islamic city: an analytical proposal with Lahore as a case example," Ekistics 280 (1980): 74.

6. Ibid., pp. 74-75.

7. Manhattan's residential density in 1960 was 172 persons per acre, and it has declined since then. New York 1960 density derived from Edgar M. Hoover and Raymond Vernon, Anatomy of a Metropolis (New York: Anchor Books, 1962), Table 24, p. 129.

8. Lahore Urban Development and Traffic Study (LUDTS), Final Report: Volume III. Walled City (Lahore: Lahore Development Authority, 1981), p. 29.

9. Ibid., p. 20.

10. Ibid., p. 29.

11. King, Colonial Urban Development, pp. 6-7.

12. Gerald Breese, Urbanization in Newly Developing Countries (Englewood Cliffs: Prentice-Hall, 1966), p. 65.

13. Lahore Urban Development and Traffic Study (LUDTS), Final Report: Volume I. Urban Planning (Lahore: Lahore Development Authority, 1981), p. 87 and p. 209, Table 27.

14. King, Colonial Urban Development, p. 97.

15. G. Rudduck, Urban Biographies (Karachi: Government of Pakistan, Planning Commission, 1965), p. 111.

16. Estimates of squatter population growth have been derived from data in Government of West Pakistan, Master Plan for Greater Lahore (Lahore: The Master Plan Projects Office, 1964), p. 55; and Mahmood Zaman, "Katchi Abadis: How did it all begin?" Viewpoint, October 19, 1980, p. 18.

17. Prior to the emergence of Katchi Abadis, the poor used to find a quarter (one-room house) in Ahatas or in tenements in the Walled City. Low-income rental housing almost disappeared with the escalation of property values.

18. M. A. Qadeer and A. Sattar Sikander, "Squatter Settlements: A functional view," in Proceedings of the National Seminar on Planning for Urban Development in the developing counries with special reference to Pakistan, ed. A. Sattar Sikander (Lahore: University of Engineering and Technology, 1978), Table 1, p. 173.

19. Janet L. Abu-Lughod, Rabat (Princeton: Princeton University Press, 1980), p. 305.

7

THE WORKING
OF THE URBAN SYSTEM

A city is a community and not merely an aggregate of activities and people. Inherent in this truism is the idea that a city is a collectivity whose needs and requirements are over and above those of any individual. A household may be able to do without a water tap, but a neighbourhood must have a source of water. Similarly, no individual may demand traffic regulations, but almost everybody's safety and well-being depends on the observance of the rules of the road. To function effectively, a city requires a transportation network, communal systems of water supply and waste disposal, an organized mode of land division and house building, and provisions for schools, hospitals, parks or mosques. Apart from these physical facilities, laws, rules, and norms are also essential for civic order. These are examples of collective goods considered necessary for the working of a city [1]. One city may vary from another in terms of its specific set of collective goods and the type and quality of civic services may vary in the same city over a given time period, but all cities have to provide for common needs. Such collective facilities and services, and institutions are the elements constituting an urban system, and their efficiency, equitability, and relevance determine the quality of life in a city.

The functioning of an urban system is also reflected in the experiences and satisfaction of its citizens. Where and how is public transport provided, and for whom? What does a citizen have to do to get water supply or electricity? Where are the schools, and whom are they serving? The answers to such questions illuminate the quality of life in a Third World city. One must also ask how people cope with endemic shortages of collective goods and inequities of distribution. Obvious shortfalls in basic services may arouse alarm, but they may also attest to the marvel of human ingenuity, that somehow millions of people manage to live with so few facilities. Whatever attitude one takes, the fundamental question remains: how does the system work? In answering this question, both perspectives ("organization of collective goods" and "how people cope") can be combined, and this will be the approach in the present chapter. For each facility or service

209

examined here, we will also explore the patterns of its use and access.

TRANSPORTATION AND COMMUNICATION

Until 1947, and even a few years after, Lahore was a leisure-ly paced city. Traffic was limited; distances between homes, work-places, shops, and kin's abodes were so short that walking was the most common mode of transport. A tonga (horse-carriage) ride was a treat and a bicycle a luxury. Even perceptions of distances were conditioned by the compactness of the city. Tonga drivers used to call out, "Going to the city," while going from WasanPura or MisriShah to Delhi gate (a distance of 1 to 3 miles). Automobiles were generally limited to Civil Lines, and Lahore Omni Bus (public transport) connected the core areas to the outskirts. As the popu-lation of the city expanded, transportation needs multiplied exponentially.

The city's territorial expansion has lengthened travel dis-tances, but its pattern of growth has also been such that neigh-bourhoods and clan quarters have been rent asunder. Jajmani groups have been dispersed and linked activities scattered. This pattern of sociospatial develoment has precipitated a disproportionately large travel demand. Also, lack of rentable office space and the lure of modern neighbourhoods have prompted public corporations, private firms, and government departments to fan out in Planned Schemes and in fashionable parts of Civil Lines. For example, the main offices of the LDA are at the Mall, the planning section has moved to Lawrence Road, and the Water and Sanitation Directorate has settled in Gulberg. These offices are branches of the same agency, and a citizen pursuing his file or peons and clerks carrying files and messages must go back and forth over a distance of five miles, creating a large stream of traffic. Such locational dispersal has precipitated extraordinary needs for transport, and it is no exaggeration to say that, if only public agencies were clustered together, the trip demand in the city would decrease by 10 to 20 percent. In addition, travel within the city is necessi-tated by clan and filial obligations characteristic of the local social structure and by commuters whose homes and workplaces are no longer close together. It thus becomes evident that transporta-tion needs have increased proportionately more than the growth of the city necessitated.

Lahore is a city of personalized dealings. Even payment of taxes or electric bills has to be made in person. This means that every chore involves a trip. If the city's development had been accompanied by some impersonalization of transactions without necessitating mutual acquaintance between buyers and sellers or a service being available by calling or writing to an agency, trans-portation needs would have been lower. In fact, the reverse has been the trend. With more goods and services available, more visits to market and offices are needed. These demands are so

pressing that one person is required by a family just to carry out
daily chores, such as taking a child to school, going to the
"right" shop for whatever happens to be in scarce supply, or
running after WAPDA to get the electric supply restored. Usually,
officers depute a clerk or peon for daily chores, merchants or
industrialists have an errand man, and those lacking both
authority and money rely on jobless relatives and friendly neigh-
bours for necessary transactions, or else make do without them.

These examples illustrate the point that both the land use
pattern and the mode of transactions have contributed to transportation needs. A substantial proportion of traffic in Lahore was
avoidable, given appropriate planning and relevant policies. While
needs have multiplied, transportation facilities such as buses,
taxis and bicycles have also been increasing, but the way in which
the resources have been used is another story. The operational
patterns of transportation facilities deserve to be explored,
because they reveal underlying structural conditions.

The local bus service has expanded both in organization and
in resources since Independence. It has been a public monopoly
from the beginning, but a threshold change occurred when it was
modernized by merging Lahore Omni Bus service into a provincial
public body called the Punjab Urban Transportation Corporation
(PUTC). What this reorganization meant in the actual performance
of the service is difficult to discern. Like its predecessor, the
corporation has not been able to keep more than 50 to 60 percent
of its bus fleet on the roads throughout the 1970s, despite two
substantial injections of capital from the federal government [2].
With an enlarged system of routes and growing demand, buses have
steadily become so overcrowded that passengers routinely hang out
from doors and windows. As the bus service has grown bigger it has
become unreliable, unsafe, and inconvenient. Some management problems are so persistent that they are now considered to be features
of the bus system, e.g., cannibalization of buses for the black
market in spares, overcharging and intimidation of passengers,
leakage of revenues and continual staff increase. Tension between
discount-seeking students and resentful conductors and drivers
periodically flares up as violent clashes; it is a perennial condition. These operational features became permanent despite three
shifts of national governments and socioideological stances, and
it made little difference whether national policies emphasized
public management or private enterprise. This point deserves to be
noted. It suggests that broad socioideological stances have little
effect if they do not take into account specific local conditions.

The steady decline in the quality of local bus service means
that it has become the transport to the poor; those who have no
alternative. For slightly higher social strata, such as clerks or
shopkeepers, private station wagons operating along designated
routes appeared in the early 1960s, and have become an element of
the city's transportation system. These minibuses ("minis," as
they are locally called) began as comfortable transport with
assured seats and fast services, but they have steadily become

crowded as well as hazardous, particularly as the vehicles have
aged. By 1981, packing five or six passengers into a seat for
three had become the norm. Although many regulations existed for
setting fares, designating routes and requiring tickets or
receipts to be issued to passengers, in actual practice few were
observed [3]. Yet minis remain a relatively regular and frequent
mode of transport for the lower-middle and middle classes.

A notch higher on the social scale as mode of public transport are scooter-rickshaws which emerged as cheap cabs in the late
1950s and have since become the staple of the city's taxi service.
Over time, some familiar malpractices have evolved in this mode
also. Rickshaws soon became noisy, smoky, and jolty, due to over-
use and poor maintenance. Each ride has to be individually bar-
gained, since fare meters are either rigged or not turned on.
Overcharging is common but the demand for rickshaw rides is almost
incessant. Lahore had a sizeable Yellow taxi (car) fleet which
dwindled after 1973, apparently because of the sharp rise in
petrol prices. Since then rent-a-car business has picked up to
serve primarily foreigners and executives on expense accounts.

Apart from the four types of auto transport described above,
tongas (horse-carriages) have continued to carry 100,000 rides a
day or more, particularly in the core area, despite an official
policy of phasing them out. For goods transport, the city also
exhibits a similar mixture of old and new modes, ranging from
porters who carry loads on their backs, through handcarts, rehras
(seatless horse-carriages), oxcarts for heavy materials, up to
trucks. Recently Suzuki vans have appeared as commercial delivery
vehicles.

As distances become greater, the motorcycle is increasingly
replacing the bicycle as the minimum need of a family, particularly in view of the expense, unreliability, and hazards of public
transport. It is a developmental paradox that, in a city of the
poor, a motorcycle has become a necessity. This paradox also
explains a phenomenon commonly seen on Lahore's roads: a family of
five or six persons, including infants, perched on a motorbike.
What appears to be indifference to personal safety and convenience
turns out on closer examination to be the optimal solution to
transportation needs.

In 1981, motorcycles constituted about half the licensed
motor driven vehicles in Lahore, and during the previous five
years their number had increased at the phenomenal rate of 20
percent per year [4]. Overall, about 33 percent of total motorized
traffic in the sprawling core area was carried by buses, 22
percent by minibuses, 11 percent by rickshaws, and the rest by
private vehicles [5]. Yet motorized traffic represents only 20
percent of the total flow in the core area and the predominant (80
percent) modes of transportation were bicycles, tongas, and feet.
When these figures are compared with the findings of the Lahore
master plan of 1964, it appears that motorized traffic, particularly scooters and motorcycles, has been increasing very rapidly
mostly as a substitute for public transport.

The bazaar and firm sector dichotomy is discernible, even in the traffic patterns. The fact that cyclists, tonga riders, and pedestrians comprised 80 percent of the core area traffic illustrates that markets and bazaars have continued to operate on an intimate human scale. They have retained compactness, intertwining homes, workshops, and stores. These characteristics have kept the bazaar sector relatively immune from motorized transport, while the firm sector manifests a diffused locational pattern. Long commuting journeys and frequent trips necessitated by the separation of activities have rendered the firm sector largely dependent on automobiles.

The emerging costs and inconvenience of transport have made the congestion and filth of old quarters bearable. The bazaar sector in particular has continued to thrive at locations inaccessible by vehicle, and the LDA's periodic campaigns to shift markets have been strenuously resisted by bazaaris [6]. The Walled City and the older sections of the core area present the smallest transportation costs, in terms of money, time, and convenience, while the Planned Schemes are the most expensive and exhausting on these scores. Sample surveys (1978) of the Walled City and Gujjarpura (a working-class New Indigenous Community) revealed that in both areas about 60 percent of residents walked to work and another 12 to 20 percent used bicycles [7]. An earlier survey (1972) in Lahore Township (a working-class Planned Scheme) pointed out that about 58 percent of residents daily travelled seven or more miles in one direction to their workplaces [8]. One can see a veritable parade of cyclists twice daily snaking its way through Gulberg and along the Mall or Allama Iqbal Road. Such long commuting journeys cannot but affect workers' efficiency and productivity. A clerk who arrives in the office after pedalling for seven miles will have little energy to work, and his inability to perform effectively further reduces the efficiency of his agency, which in turn lays the ground for personalized dealings and corruption. This is an illustration of how the inequities and inefficiencies of the system feed on each other.

Some other transportation-related trends emerged with the development of the city, such as increasing indifference to traffic rules, poor road conditions, proliferation of regulatory agencies, and imitative and often irrelevant public policies. These conditions have been so persistent that they can be termed the characteristics of the transport system. These characteristics should not be viewed merely as temporary operational shortcomings. Though these conditions are socially unacceptable and administratively acknowledged as problems, their persistence suggests that they serve some latent functions of the urban system.

They also represent people's coping mechanisms. The constable who shakes down a rickshaw driver, the cab owner who tampers with the fare meter, the gentleman who drives without a licence, the cyclist who disregards traffic signals, the bus conductor who pockets fares, and the road-repair crew that seldom leaves the office are undoubtedly individuals of compromised morality, yet

their behaviour is the response of the individual to imperatives
of living in a fractionated system. Almost everyone is both a
culprit and a victim. The privatization of collective goods, the
self-serving policies of the ruling classes, the domination of
borrowed perceptions, and the disregard of indigenous reality have
contributed to the equilibrium of inefficiencies that characterizes the evolving urban system.

COMMUNITY FACILITIES AND SERVICES

     The city's supplies of water and electricity, its sewerage
network, and the number of schools, colleges, hospitals, telephone
lines, and radio channels have increased by factors of four to six
since Independence. Increases of such proportions in the provision
of community facilities and services have brought them, to varying
degrees, within the reach of about 60 to 70 percent of the population. Yet these gains have not resulted in noticeable improvement
of the quality of life in the city or of individual satisfaction
levels. Expectations have risen more rapidly than satisfactions,
and new needs arose as the city grew. Many facilities that could
once be privately arranged or omitted have become necessary. For
example, the domestic water supplies in northern New Indigenous
Communities (WasanPura, Chah Miran) came primarily from hand pumps
and private wells until the mid-1950s. As these areas have been
filled up, wells have dried and the quality of water has deteriorated, making the municipal water system a necessity. A much more
illuminating example is the one of telephones. In a city of the
poor, telephones were a rare novelty available only to administrators and corporate executives. As distances in the city increased,
the utility of telephones became evident. Even the man-in-
the-street could save a trip if the condition of an ailing relative on the other side of the city could be ascertained by telephone. Thus the telephone has evolved over a 30 year period from a
luxury to a widely-felt necessity of daily life, though its availability remains a matter of privileged status and/or money.
     Increasing provision of community facilities and services has
yielded less than the expected satisfaction because of operational
shortfalls resulting from policies and procedures followed. If by
design or cooptation a service is made available to select groups,
if the policies are capricious, and management is susceptible to
corruption, then obviously the service will have limited utility.
This is largely what has happened in Lahore. A community facility
worked effectively as long as it was meant for a small select
group. On its expansion for mass consumption, its quality declined
and useability eroded. In transformation from a privilege of the
few to a necessity for all, a community service ceases to be
reliable and effective. The result is that the hardships of the
poor are seldom reduced, while the privileges of the rich cannot
be taken for granted any more. This is the pattern of development
in community facilities and services. An example will illustrate

this point concretely.

Schools

Primary education has been compulsory in Punjab under the Provincial Act of 1940, though there have never been enough schools to accommodate all the children. Lahore has always led the province in educational facilities. Since Independence, the number of schools in the city has progressively increased to the point that, in 1979, about 80 percent of primary school age children were enrolled [9]. There were 370 primary schools in the city in 1965, and the number increased to 1,078 by 1979, a 13.6 percent per annum rate of increase [10]. High schools, polytechnics, colleges, and other institutions of higher learning have also increased in the same scale. These impressive numerical increases in educational facilities should have brought a sense of adequacy on this score. The overall effect has been almost the reverse. Finding a decent school for children and getting them admitted has become a parents' nightmare [11]. The government-run schools in general, and municipal schools in particular, have steadily declined in quality and service. Concerned parents pull all possible strings to get their children into a "model," or, if affordable, a foreign missionary school.

About 50 percent of schools in Lahore are housed in rented dwellings, and a substantial number of municipal schools do not even have any quarters and are held in parks or open spaces. Zaman notes that "the majority of the schools are in very congested localities . . . Their buildings have no main gates and are often used as cattle barns when no education is going on." [12] So abysmal were conditions in some municipal schools that they could not attract even the children of the poor, their normal clientele. Municipal schools in Anarkali, Lytton Road, Jain Mandar, and other areas were experiencing student shortages in 1981. Apart from inadequate, sometimes dangerous, buildings, schools generally lacked furniture, trained teachers, play fields, and books. Generally, capital investments to establish new facilities enjoy higher priority among decision makers than the maintenance of existing institutions. In 1981, the Lahore municipal corporation spent about Rs. 1.50 per enrolled child per year on operational expenses [13]. With this allocation not even a year's supply of chalk could be bought. The quality of schools has steadily declined, though the number has been increasing. These trends have persisted through all swings of national policies, right, left, or Islamic.

After the nationalization of schools (1973), private educational institutions were disallowed, except foreign "mission" schools. This was purportedly a step to indigenize and standardize education for the rich and the poor alike, but in reality, the policy only took a bit of shine off the elite schools (e.g., St. Anthony, Crescent Model, Government College) without improving the

conditions of the large number of schools taken over from educational trusts, associations, and private entrepreneurs. By
assuming responsibility for mass education, the Government essentially enlarged the empire of the Ministry of Education. There was
little relief for the common man in the form of access to better
schools, and conditions in the ordinary institutions have kept on
deteriorating. As public education became indigenized, an upper
layer of modern schools and English-medium institutions emerged to
cater to the rich and the influential. The duality of the urban
system observed in other instances also came to characterize
public education. Since 1977, private enterprise has been
reallowed to establish educational institutions. This shift in
policy combined with further indigenization and Islamization of
school curriculums have further stimulated all the more the demand
for schools of English as a medium of instruction. Almost everywhere in the city, expensive nurseries, schools, and tuition
centres have sprung up. Privately managed, these institutions
charge substantial fees and promise European education. It is
evident that the enlargement of the educational system has been
accompanied by its differentiation into two or three streams. As
the common man's access to educational facilities increases, their
quality declines, and a parallel stream of exclusive schools for
the influential emerges, largely supported by public funds or subsidies. An interesting phenomenon is that leaders and administrators who so loudly proclaim the need to indigenize education are
the ones who send their own children to exclusive schools. This
dualization of facilities has a direct bearing on the spatial
structure of the city.

The differentiation of educational institutions by quality
and social standing militates against the neighbourhood principle
on which modern cities are organized [14]. The old Lahore used to
be organized on this principle. Within the Walled City, each
Mohalla had a primary school, and four or five of these schools
fed into a high school. A similar principle was followed in early
New Indigenous Communities. Such a spatial organization is
feasible if the facilities are of uniform quality, a point worthy
of notice for city planners. Schools of divergent quality and
curriculums do not lend themselves to neighbourhood institutionalization.

In metropolitan Lahore, the neighbourhood principle has
evaporated. First, the planners and developers paid little attention to this principle. In fact, Planned Schemes generally made no
provisions for primary schools: the planners must have felt that
the rich did not need municipal schools nearby. Second, the
quality-differentiated demand for schools further scrambled the
locational discipline. The rich from the Walled City send their
children to Samanabad or Gulberg for appropriate education, and
the children from Katchi Abadis in Gulberg go to primary schools
in Mozang or Ichra. This pattern of distribution of educational
facilities has exacted heavy social costs in the form of long,
arduous, and expensive travel, even for the children of the

influential. Transportation of children to school and back is a
major task of the day. The poor cope with it by suffering depriva-
tions, for the middle class, it is a constant hassle, while the
upper strata have to spare official vans and family cars to bring
children back and forth. The neglect of the commonweal victimizes
even those who appear to be self-sufficient.

From British times, high schools and colleges were strung
along the periphery of the Walled City and located in older sections of the Civil Lines area. Even the University was located at
the southern end of Anarkali. This concentration of educational
institutions in a narrow band of territory did not cause noticeable inconvenience or expense, because the city was small and its
various parts readily accessible. However, with the expansion of
the city, new institutions, particularly the more prestigious
ones, have converged towards Planned Schemes and salubrious areas.
An expansive new campus for the University was built along the
canal, and a string of colleges emerged along Gulberg Road, establishing another locus for educational institutions. These locational tendencies have resulted in spatial disparities in the distribution of schools and colleges. The south-southeastern section
of the city has most of the institutions of higher learning, while
the greater proportion of the population lives in the northern and
western New Indigenous Communities. This spatial imbalance in the
distribution of educational facilities is not altogether acci-
dental, since the main concentration of upper-class residences
lies along the southeastern axis. Thus, the spatial disparity is
an expression of social privilege as well as a reinforcing
mechanism to perpetuate the privilege.

Hospitals, Clinics and Parks

Health and recreational services are characterized by the
same trends and processes as are observed in the provision of educational facilities. By now, the disparities in the distribution
of health and recreational services should be self-evident as the
new and higher-income residential areas are better served than the
old and lower-class neighbourhoods. Examination of these services
brings out vividly the phenomenon of floating up. Just as the
cream floats to the top on churned milk, similarly, in Lahore,
public improvements in the provision of services tend to separate
out to minister to the private preferences of select groups. This
is generally the outcome of public investment in the provision of
services operating in tandem with favouritism and corruption at
the operational level.

The evolving system of parks and open spaces in Lahore is a
vivid illustration of the floating up process. From historical
times, the Walled City was encircled by a park including an exclusive arboretum for ladies. There were also Madans (playing fields)
and Akharas (wrestling gymnasia), which were supplemented with
sports grounds, cricket fields, golf clubs, and the race course

after the British took over. All in all, open spaces and play areas were close by for all sections of the local population. Undoubtedly, the elite areas were very amply provided for. In 1946, there were 2.6 acres of recreational open space per 1,000 persons in the city. By 1964, however, only 1.8 acres of open space per 1,000 persons were left [15].

Two factors contributed to the decline. First, the population growth outstripped the rate of park development. Second, the new parks were developed in the Planned Schemes on the periphery, whereas the existing parks, particularly around the Walled City, were indifferently maintained and often were allowed to be built over through official conversions or unofficial encroachments. This trend continues to the present. For example, in 1981, LDA built a market for displaced hawkers from Anarkali on a section of park space outside Lohari gate [16]. The Punjab University's proposal (1981) to build a shopping plaza on the lawns of the old campus was halted only by the personal intervention of the provincial Governor; otherwise, another scarce but central patch of green would have been turned into private property. The LDA has developed new parks in Gulberg, Iqbal Town, and other bungalow estates where almost every house has a lawn of some kind. By the mid-1970s, almost one-fifth of public park space was concentrated in Gulberg alone [17]. These examples illustrate how, through policy and operations, amenities financed from public funds are made to benefit a small section of the populace.

The social costs of ill-conceived public policies and operations are evident. Along the narrow bazaars of the Walled City and in the residential alleys of New Indigenous Communities, on a typical weekend, gangs of youths can be found playing cricket or flying kites. These recreations take their toll in the form of smashed windows, broken limbs, traffic accidents, and gang fights. The governmental response to these problems is to announce a ban on playing cricket or flying kites in the streets, a ban that cannot be enforced but does provide another justification for the police to harass youths and shake down their parents. A pattern is discernible, underneath these events, of public resources and powers used for the private benefit of the select. This pattern is another manifestation of recurrent processes, such as segmentalization of the urban system, encashment of public authority, expansion of community service accompanied by declining quality, privatization of facilities that ought to be shared by all.

These processes are equally evident in health services. Historically, three systems of medicine have been practised in Lahore. Doctors, Hakims, and homeopaths have provided private medical treatment, while the municipality, the Cantonment Board, the Provincial Department of Health, and recently the Social Security Department maintain public dispensaries for those who cannot afford private practitioners. For indoor treatment and diagnostic investigations, hospitals have been the main facility. Public Health has been the joint responsibility of the municipal corporation and the Provincial Ministry of Health. Briefly, these are the broad contours of the local health system.

In 1964, there were 42 public dispensaries and maternity and child-health centres in the city [18]. By 1979, dispensaries had increased to 98 and the child-health centres to 61 [19]. Most of these dispensaries are located in the older sections of the city and in new industrial areas. Obviously, it was not felt necessary to have public dispensaries in Planned Schemes. Although the number of hospitals has remained the same (17) over this period, the number of beds has increased. In 1981, two new hospitals were under construction, one a gift from the ruler of Dubai, and the other a charitable trust hospital near Baghbarpura. Once again, facilities increase, but the population also increases. Between 1961 and 1979, the number of beds per 1,000 persons decreased from 3 to 2.3, despite the substantial expansion of hospitals.

The number of medical institutions is an essential, but not the complete, index of the state of health services. What happens in these institutions and what they offer (operational variables) are equally significant elements of the health system. On this score, the situation of health facilities has deteriorated, despite numerical increases. Hospitals and dispensaries functioned reasonably well as long as they catered to small and select clientele. After Independence, the demand for hospitals increased as the general public became more aware of modern treatment, but the quality of service deteriorated sharply. Up to the 1950s, hospitals provided essential medicines, clean beds and reasonable care. By 1980, medicines had to be bought from the market, specialists consulted at their private clinics, and, to ensure proper care in a "free" hospital, a friend or relative had to stay to look after the patient. Up to the 1960s, one could expect to get a public ambulance in an emergency or hope to be supplied blood if transfusion was needed. Now it is almost inconceivable. Public hospitals have been shorn of these services in direct relation to the emergence of expensive private blood dealers and ambulance suppliers; often, these are unofficial businesses of the relevant public functionaries. By the late 1960s, x-ray and clinical laboratories had become thriving businesses, and, during the decade of the 1970s, clinics where major operations can be done also emerged. Thus hospital service in Lahore has evolved from a public monopoly to a dual framework of private clinics and mass hospitals. The rich and the expense-account executives rely on private clinics, and the ordinary people line up outside public hospitals.

Public health conditions have largely been neglected, and the development has meant the creation of legions of officers for malaria control, family planning, and environmental research, but the city sewerage continues to be pumped untreated into the river Ravi [20]. The Provincial Governor recently listed "pools of stagnant water" as a major civic problem [21]. The black smoke spewed by public buses, private cars, and rickshaws has been added to dust and dried cow dung as the air pollutants. Traditional environmental deficiencies (open drains, piles of wet garbage,

crowded quaters) have not been overcome, while the health hazards
of the industrial era have been added, such as chemical pollution,
automobile accidents, and diseases of affluence. By one estimate,
about "two thirds of cases dealt with in hospitals are
attributable to environmental factors." [22]

Water Supply and Waste Disposal

Public water, sewers, and drainage networks are the veins and
arteries of a city. In a city, individual arrangements for water
supply cannot be long sustained as population expands and densities increase. Similarly, dirty water or garbage from one house
cannot be dumped in front of neighbouring houses without
imperilling everybody's health and safety. A city requires these
facilities to be jointly operated. This is the physical manifestation of a city's communal nature. The public health and environmental well-being of a city is indivisible and public arrangements
for water supply and waste disposal are among the basic needs of
urban living. Their quality cannot be ensured for those "who can
pay" without embracing those "who cannot afford." Therefore it is
inevitable that infrastructural facilities will expand as a city
grows, even if the public agenda is dominated by the concerns of
the influential. Lahore has undergone a similar experience.

As described in Chapter 4, the capacity of Lahore's water-
supply network has increased by about 400 percent since Independence, and almost 60 percent of households were being served by it
in 1979. The sewers, which were almost nonexistent before 1947,
have also expanded, though not to the same extent as the water
supply. By 1981, about 20 percent of households were being served
by sewers. Storm-water drainage has been still less developed, and
the system of garbage collection and disposal has lagged farthest
behind. On the other hand, organizational development has been
spectacular. Evidence of what in official circles is called
development can be found in the formation of a separate autonomous
public corporation, the Water and Sanitation Authority (WASA),
with a large payroll and substantial budget, the master plan to
spend Rs. 750 million on capital works over three phases, the
zestful pursuit of World Bank loans, the parade of foreign
experts, international conferences, national seminars, and trips
abroad (for administrators and planners) [23].

Even from this brief recounting of developmental trends of
utility systems in Lahore, a pattern can be discerned: those
facilities which conferred individualized benefits have boomed,
whereas the inappropriable services have languished. Jobs,
budgets, and perks for officials have expanded most, followed by
water supply for domestic use, whereas garbage collection and
storm-water drainage services have received the least attention.
This pattern is again explicable as the result of self-serving
administrative policies and organizational procedures which allow
the pursuit of the individual's interests at the cost of common

welfare.

Given the severe limitation of financial and technical resources, shortfalls of water supplies and waste disposal are understandable. The more crucial issue is the manner in which these limited resources are deployed. By giving high priority to new capital works while neglecting maintenance and upgrading of existing facilities, and by precluding citizens' input in decision making, the public agencies have become self-serving. The areas where the officers live have turned out to be the best serviced by public utilities. Shadman, Gulberg and other Planned Schemes have received the bulk of public investments. Civil Lines has witnessed considerable expansion of water and sewer facilities, but it remains a partially served district, whereas the New Indigenous Communities of the north and west are poorly served, and the availability of utilities has declined in the Walled City since Independence (Map 7.1). Katchi Abadis have scarcely been noticed. This pattern of distribution has emerged after four to six times increase in the capacities of utility systems. Overall, development has provided public subsidies for influentials and self-help for the people.

The arrangements for water supply, sewerage, and storm-water disposal in Lahore are highly localized. Water is supplied from about 150 tube wells scattered throughout the city. From these tube wells, the water is pumped directly into the distribution network. There are no reservoirs, and even the 30 or so water towers recently constructed are for purposes of pressure rather than storage. The water supply of an area depends on the drawing capacities and conditions of its tube wells, which vary considerably. In older and densely built-up areas, the ground water table is being drawn down while the condition and upkeep of tube wells are being neglected. The new Planned Schemes have modern tube wells of high capacity which are maintained in good repair. In Gulberg, about 118 gallons of water per day per person are available, while in the Walled City only 40 gallons are delivered [24]. Even areas equipped with water-supply networks vary widely in adequacy and regularity of supply. Most of the new suburbs have round-the-clock running water, whereas the Walled City and New Indigenous Communities get only a few hours of flow from taps. In these areas, the water pressure is too low to deliver water to upper stories, and pipes in the ground have been left unattended so long that they have been reduced to 50 percent capacity by silt deposits [25].

It appears that the tasks which do not directly benefit officials (from kickbacks, favours, etc.) or have not been pressed for by influential groups command low priority on the public agenda. There is not even a systematic measuring of the water yield for tube wells in new areas. The WASA concedes that about 50 percent of the water leaks out from cracked pipes and joints [26]. As there are no individual interests tied to these tasks, they remain mere footnotes in consultant reports.

Foreign advice and demand also distorts priorities, as is

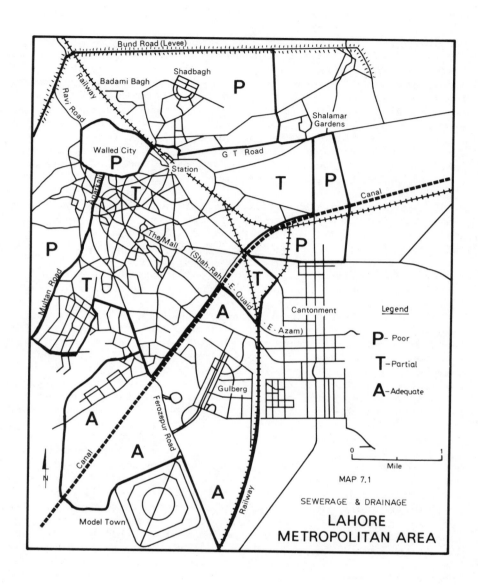

Bund Road (Levee)

Badami Bagh

Shadbagh

Railway

Ravi Road

Shalamar
Gardens

P

Walled City

P

Station

G T Road

Anarkali

T

Canal

T

P

The Mall

P

(Shah-Rah)

E. Quaid

P

Multan Road

T

T

A

(E. Azam)

Cantonment

Legend

P – Poor

T – Partial

A – Adequate

Gulberg

A

Ferozepur Road

Canal

A

A

N

0   1

Mile

A

Railway

MAP 7.1

Model Town

SEWERAGE & DRAINAGE

LAHORE
METROPOLITAN AREA

illustrated by the case of "levying water charges." The capital
works of the WASA's master plan have been funded by a World Bank
loan. As the World Bank insists on introducing the discipline of
the market, it has directed the local authorities to start
metering domestic supplies and levying rates [27]. For the World
Bank experts, water charges are a key policy instrument for
promoting efficient use of water, but it is ironic that the simple
fact of "50 percent leakage" indicative of the WASA's mismanagement has been overlooked. Would not Lahore's water supplies
improve immediately if these leaks were plugged?

The city is divided into seven sewerage districts, an
arrangement that represents a substantial advance since 1947, when
there was hardly any sewer network. The Planned Schemes of the
south-southeastern quadrant have the most developed networks. In
other parts of the city, it is patchy and not infrequently discon-
tinuous. Even in fully serviced areas, not all houses are
connected to the sewer lines. A house or street is connected with
trunk sewers by lateral pipes which are often too expensive for
moderate-income households and which in narrow streets may not be
feasible to lay out. This means that in New Indigenous Communities
where sewer trunks have been laid, a majority of houses cannot
take benefit. In most of the city, night soil continues to be
transported through open drains that empty into underground
sewers. The disposal of the sewage has been given the least attention, and the age-old practice of irrigating vegetable gardens
around the city with effluents and of pumping untreated sewage
into the river continues [28].

Storm-water drainage is a perfect public good. To protect one
house from rain flooding, the whole street or neighbourhood has to
be properly drained. In Lahore where privatization of public goods
has been the trend, storm-water drainage remains at a very rudimentary level. Five drainage districts have been delineated in
accordance with the natural lie of the land. The three northern
districts drain near the flood protection Bund from which the
storm water is pumped into the river. The two southern districts
drain into a natural channel (Hudiara) which empties into the
river. Generally, roads and streets serve as channels for rain
water, which eventually seeps into the ground, flows into sewers,
or collects as pools of stagnant water in various depressions. The
indivisibility of the ruled and the rulers in the matter of
drainage can be observed from the fact that, during heavy rain-
fall, even the Governor's House becomes inaccessible, while the
Mall road submerges under water [29]. With the expansion of the
city, the surface run-off has increased, and thus areas which
seldom used to be flooded now are submerged during monsoons. About
2,000 ponds of stagnant water had come to be a permanent feature
of the city by 1981 [30].

Garbage collection and solid waste disposal are also shared
needs which have to be communally provided. Lahore has progressed
relatively little on this score. There has been an increase in the
number of sweepers (5,500 in 1981) and bins, but collection opera-

tions have remained desultory. Solid waste is mixed with night soil brought out manually from most of the city. This slimy and hazardous mixture is deposited in bins and collection points to be carried to two designated city dumps. Yet actually "there are no specific and organized dumping sites and no treatment of the wastes . . . Much of the waste is dumped in depressions and in low lying areas." [31]

Garbage collection and disposal are poor even in bungalow estates. These services require operational management, not capital works, and they have remained a low priority. In Gulberg or Garden Town, garbage from homes is dumped on whatever lot happens to be vacant nearby, and, when it gets built over, another distant one is put into use. It is not uncommon to see, on the threshold of an immaculately tended bungalow, stray dogs rummaging through the house's garbage, a symptomatic spectacle of private opulence and public squalor. These fashionable areas are saved, however, from becoming stinking holes by the flush toilet. Their low density also helps in minimizing health risks, though small piles of garbage are visible all around. In the older parts of the city, garbage often litters the streets, but, as they are compact, manual sweeping and night soil collection prevents the situation from turning into a public health disaster.

LAND AND HOUSING

Land is the absolute necessity for human beings. Man as a physical being must occupy land. This is the human condition. Even in a situation of homelessness, one remains lodged on a piece of land. In a well-functioning city, mechanisms for development and distribution of land allow the vast majority of citizens legally to find livable space. Ironically, if these mechanisms do not work well, those who are exluded continue to occupy land illegally, and often free of rent.

The term "land" subsumes improvement put over it, and is a code word for sites as well as buildings. It is a very special commodity. It is both a necessity and a property. As a necessity, some minimum supply must be available to all, and to ensure this minimum is a public responsibility. As a property, land is a source of financial gain, social prestige, and personal satisfaction, and thus falls in the private realm. Often, the public interest in ensuring the basic necessity for all and the private drive for individual gain come into conflict. This is why, even in capitalist societies, urban land markets operate under stringent public controls. In fact, the term "land market" refers to a mode of individual transactions taking place within the framework of public regulations. Almost everywhere in countries of market economies (the U.S., Britain, or Japan), the rights that constitute land ownership (rights to use, hold possession, derive income, build or destroy, inherit or bequeath) are severely constrained by property laws and tax and zoning regulations. Further-

more, urban land is itself a social creation. It is the concentration of people and activities that lends values to individual
parcels and public investments in the form of facilities and services convert the "gift of nature" into usable urban land. These
are the imperatives of the nature of urban land. They require that
the land-development process in a city must fulfill basic needs in
all segments of the community and promote an efficient pattern of
land use. Whether these objectives are met through controlled
market operations or public enterprise is immaterial from a practical point of view.

Whatever the process, it should work efficiently and equitably for the general welfare. Many problems that have come to
characterize Third World cities arise from the failure of land
development and allocation processes. Lahore is not an exception.

The infusion of British land laws into the customary system
of rights and practices in Punjab dating back to Mughal times
resulted in a wide array of tenurial arrangements ranging from
Western-style freeholds to inalienable Waqf lands. The British
reforms diluted the historical land-tenure system, which was
essentially based on private (not state) but communal ownership
principles, and introduced individual ownership. Of course, the
old system was not completely supplanted by the new, and many
traditional rights and relationships were left untouched. Thus the
following trends emerged from this situation.

On the one hand, the land became a commodity to be appropriated as individual property, and historical tenancy claims and
community obligations were eroded. This tendency gave rise to
ruinous litigations among contending claimants. On the other hand,
the traditional arrangements for residential uses of land remained
unaffected, particularly in villages. Members of a community could
stake out land for residential use from common grounds. There was
no price on residential land, and it seldom traded in the market.
To some extent, this continues to be the situation, even today, in
remote villages. These social values and arrangements did not
prevail in the city, but the notion that a shelter was not a commodity remained entrenched in urban ethos.

In Lahore in pre-Independence days, residential land was
cheap, even by the criterion of incomes of those days, and readily
available. Home ownership was a mark of respectability and a
source of security, but renting was not entirely a commercial venture. It was not uncommon for a family to have rented the same
shelter for generations, and landlord-renter relations were often
circumscribed by social obligations. Renters were usually widows,
poor relations, or members of service castes who were tied to
landlords through multiple bonds of obligations and rights. Generally, while commercial properties were considered as business
investments, housing did not become a commodity. The availability
of cheap and plentiful land at the periphery of the city further
inhibited housing from becoming a lucrative investment.

Even in this brief description of Lahore's residential land
market, glimmers of regional ethos are discernible. Before being

swept by the winds of development, Lahore was a commun-
ally-oriented city. Yet the British rule had laid the ground for
individualization.

After Independence, land and housing took on more and more of
the character of merchandise. Real property steadily became an
object of speculation, a source of windfall gains, and a riskless
investment. It became a means of converting personal authority or
status into tangible assets and an opportunity to acquire unearned
wealth. Lahore's property market became intertwined with the
shadow economy of corruption. While economic functions and social
meanings of land (and houses) were changing, housing needs multiplied geometrically. The increasing population precipitated the
need for an unprecedented number of houses, but the supply did not
increase correspondingly. The housing imbalance has been further
exacerbated by the erosion of clan or neighbourhood responsibility
for housing its members and the breakdown of conventional modes of
supply. The conventional arrangements would not have sufficed for
such a colossal demand, but they could have evolved to meet contemporary needs if housing had not been turned into a commodity.
This opportunity was preempted by post-Independence development
trends.

The first major disruption of Lahore's land and housing
markets resulted from the necessity of allotting evacuee properties to refugees from India. This phase lasted almost a decade and
a half (1947-1960). The entitlements for allotments were meant to
be based on claims of properties left in India, but, as the claims
could not be easily verified, the allotment process turned into an
entrepreneurial exercise, and those who could bribe, influence, or
forcefully pursue their case were rewarded with allotments of
houses or stores. The evacuee properties became a sort of bonanza
which could be obtained by suitably manipulating rules and procedures. This phase fostered a new set of expectations regarding
properties, which became prizes for the clever and the influential
rather than rewards of earnings. Furthermore, the pursuit of
housing became an individualized act of serving oneself instead of
a collaborative enterprise of a joint family or clan. These expectations gradually became the norms of the local real estate
market.

The second phase began around 1960, though it started
building up earlier. By this time, house lots were badly needed
for increasing numbers of households, and the relentless demand
could not be met by a few Planned Schemes undertaken by the LIT.
The land market split into an upper circuit, consisting of lots in
Planned Schemes, and a lower circuit, comprised of unofficial subdivisions in New Indigenous Communities. The poor, priced out of
both circuits, resorted to squatting on unclaimed evacuee lands or
public open spaces. Since their emergence, the three submarkets
have steadily diverged from each other in terms of operational
practices as well as prices. They cater to different social segments, but they are not segregated geographically. Often, all
three circuits can be found coexisting in the same neighbourhood,

yet the upper circuit of Planned Schemes sets the tone for the other two.

Phase three of Lahore's real property market began around 1971. It has been characterized by corporatist tendencies in each of the three submarkets. Land development has become a big business. The LDA has accelerated its land development activity, but a host of private companies has also emerged to float townships, communities, and schemes. Home-building has become an organized business practised by contractors instead of a personal endeavour of a prospective home-owner, and real estate brokerage has become a rewarding enterprise. Such changes have been more visible in the upper circuit, but other submarkets have reflected similar trends. Katchi Abadi residents have formed locality associations to lobby for public improvement and to demand rights of land ownership.

Similar trends are observable in the middle and lower middle-class circuit of New Indigenous Communities. A note of caution must be sounded about the tendency toward corporatism identified here. It is not a phenomenon of mutual help or an expression of community sentiment, but it is the outcome of two processes. First, it is a market-induced tendency to incorporate real estate business, and, second, it is a tactical device to promote the interests of a specific group. Within the group, benefits, once obtained, continue to be distributed according to social standing and individual entrepreneurship. An example will illustrate this point.

It has become a common demand of associations of doctors, enginers, journalists, etc., that special quotas of housing lots in public schemes be set aside for their members. A house lot obtained at the official price is a bonanza. Even the allotment letter can be sold on the black market at three or four times the official price of a lot. Obviously, applying collective pressure to increase the probabilities of such windfalls is in the interest of everybody in a select group, although, even when a quota is increased, only the more influential members of the group benefit. The foregoing description suggests that a few themes and trends underlay the three phases and steadily evolved to full bloom, e.g., splintering into circuits, rising expectations of acquiring real property through influence peddling and manipulation of regulations and quotas, and increasing imbalance between the demand for and supply of housing. These are structural features of Lahore's evolving land and housing markets, and represent the consistent evolutionary trends of the system as a whole.

Two questions remain. First, how have these trends affected land prices and thereby the affordability of housing in Lahore? Second, if public regulations and quotas are the ground over which the market forces are played out, then how have those been evolving? Those questions will be taken in the above order.

Land Prices

Observing land prices in Lahore is unusually difficult. It is
not that sales records or assessment data are nonexistent but that
although modern procedures of land records are followed in the
letter, they are not followed in meaning or intent. The property
values recorded on sales deeds tend to vary widely from what is
actually paid or received. They may be inflated to launder black
money or deflated to avoid transfer taxes. Payment may be made in
foreign exchange abroad or in under-the-table cash as key-money
for vacant posession. These crosscurrents of under- and overstate-
ment of values make the data on official records both inconsistent
and unreliable. This brief digression into data problems also
illustrates the considerations which enter into land transactions.
For land-price studies in Lahore, it has been found that data
collected on generalized bases from brokers and informed persons
were the only reliable source. Even Lahore's planners relied on
interviews with brokers to compile maps of land-value contours of
the city (1981).

Map 7.2 suggests a pattern in the distribution of land values
which, if read in conjunction with knowledge of the socioeconomic
characteristics of a district, becomes very illuminating. First,
nowhere within the metropolitan district could a piece of land be
bought for less than Rs. 82 per square yard (Rs. 50,000 per kanal
- i.e. one-eighth of an acre), which means that the smallest
feasible house lot would have cost Rs. 8,000 or more in 1981. This
price would preclude almost three-quarters of the population from
owning a lot in the city. Second, the peak of land values seems to
be centred in the Walled City (Rs. 660 per square yard). As
Chapter 5 shows, it is understandable, because the Walled City has
become a centre of the bazaar sector, where some of the biggest
wholesale markets of the country are located. Third, the southeast
quadrant including the core area, Civil Lines and Shadman Gulberg,
is the locus of high values. This observation is also
self-explanatory in view of the concentration of commercial functions and bungalow estates in this area. As Map 7.2 shows, land
values do not decline with distance from the core area, since the
absence of a concentrated centre militates against the dis-
tance-decay of land values phenomenon normally observed in Western
cities. Fourth, a positive correlation between public services and
land values can be observed.

So far we have described a cross-sectional distribution of
land values, as observed in 1981. Table 7.1 provides some idea of
how the values changed over time. It has been composed from data
collected specifically for this book, by interviews with a sample
of brokers.

Table 7.1 points out that residential land prices in almost
all parts of Lahore increased at double or triple the rate of the
consumer price index. Obviously, land was a good hedge against
inflation. From the table, it appears that land prices in a district do not rise continually but follow a rhythm, seeming to

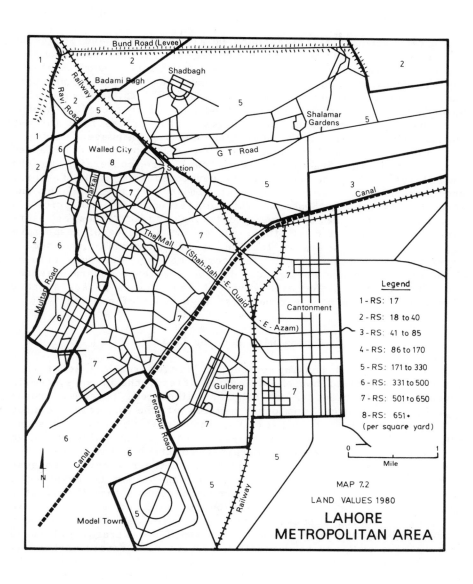

Bund Road (Levee)

1

2

Railway

Ravi Road

Badami Bagh

2

5

Shadbagh

Shalamar
Gardens

5

2

5

5

1

6

Walled City

8

G T Road

Station

2

Anarkali

7

3

Canal

5

The Mall

7

7

2

6

(Shah-Rah-E-Quaid

7

Multan Road

E-Azam)

Cantonment

7

6

7

7

Legend

1 - RS: 17

2 - RS: 18 to 40

3 - RS: 41 to 85

4 - RS: 86 to 170

5 - RS: 171 to 330

6 - RS: 331 to 500

7 - RS: 501 to 650

8 - RS: 651+

(per square yard)

7

Gulberg

7

4

7

Ferozepur Road

6

Canal

6

5

N

5

Railway

0   1

Mile

MAP 7.2

LAND VALUES 1980

5

**LAHORE
METROPOLITAN AREA**

5

Model Town

229

accelerate after a district opens up to settlement and before it is filled up, and steadying when it is filled. For example, Gulberg underwent a sharp rise in prices in the years 1965–70, whereas Shadman, New Garden Town, and the New Indigenous Communities went through similar stages in 1970–75, a period when Gulberg's rate of price increase steadied, and in fact fell behind the rate of CPI increase. This suggests that prices rise fastest when supply is at its peak, during the filling in phase.

Table 7.1 further suggests that land prices in Planned Schemes (Gulberg, Shadman, Garden Town) were converging to the same level, while the unofficially developed lots in Haji, Pura, and GhoreShah Road were selling at almost half the price of the land in Gulberg or Shadman. This difference in land price is attributable to the relative provisions of facilities and services, environmental conditions, and social standing of respective areas. Land prices are reflective of the livability and social attraction of an area, and also serve to sort out the affluent from moderate-income households and the people of modern orientation from bazaaris. The high level of land prices raises another question: how have people coped with high costs of housing?

Coping with Housing Costs

When land and housing prices in a city reach a level that almost 75 percent of households cannot afford, the urban system is severely inefficient. In Lahore, displaced persons, rural migrants, unemployed, and other members of the underclass cannot afford decent shelter, but clerks, industrial workers, and shopkeepers, who constitute the bulk of the local population, have also been steadily rendered marginal to the housing market. The joint family system obliging sons to pool their earnings to sustain and improve a family's situation has helped to maintain a semblance of order in matters of accommodation. A family waits for years for sons to grow up and become arms of the father in building or buying a house. Recently, working abroad has become a route to ownership for a section of the lower strata. All these factors have combined to maintain a buoyant real estate market. As was estimated in Chapter 4, almost 12,000 new houses per year, of varying quality, were constructed on average during the period 1961–73, and since then the rate of construction has accelerated. To a visitor, the city would appear to be a busy construction site with houses, shops, and sheds going up everywhere. Such pervasive building activity suggests a vigorous housing demand, despite high prices. Similarly, rents had risen to such a level that newspaper advertisements (in 1981) routinely suggested Rs. 1,500–2,000 as a bargain for monthly rent for a three-bedroom bungalow. The question, then, is to ascertain who were sustaining this buoyant market.

It is a fact that real income in the city has almost doubled since Independence. Yet it is the upper segment of the local popu-

TABLE 7.1

Residential Land Prices

Year	Land Prices (per square yard)								
	Northern New Indigenous Communities (Ghore Shah, Haji Park)		Gulberg		Shadman and Shah Jamal		New Garden Town		Consumer Price Index
	Price	Percentage Increase	Price	Percentage Increase	Price	Percentage Increase	Price	Percentage Increase	
1960	---	---	Rs. 7- 10	---	---	---	---	---	---
1965	Rs. 5- 7	---	Rs. 20- 23	120	Rs. 33- 85	---	Rs. 13- 20	---	---
1970	Rs. 10- 17	130	Rs. 100- 132	536	Rs. 123- 165	150	Rs. 33- 66	200	100
1977	Rs. 83- 165	837	Rs. 250- 415	185	Rs. 413- 580	242	Rs. 206- 290	400	260

Source: Survey of Real Estate Brokers, 1978.

lation which has gained proportionately far more from economic development: industrialists, politicians, merchants, contractors, officers, and professionals. In 1978 about 20 percent of households in Lahore were earning more than Rs. 20,000 per year. And this is the distribution of the reported income. By adding illicit earnings to these figures the proportion of households who can afford high housing prices (and rents) could be as much as 30 percent. Furthermore, a steady trickle of rural landlords seeking city residence and a sizeable expatriate community have stimulated additional demand for expensive houses.

As with most happenings in the city, the Government subsidizes a substantial segment of the high-priced housing demand through generous house rent allowances for officers and the provision of free furnished accommodation for senior executives. The equivalent of 50 to 100 percent of a senior official's salary has been paid as house rent, which can amount to Rs. 1,500-3,000 a month. While subsidizing the high rents of executives, the Government has also been helping them to become landlords through concessional house-building loans and quotas for housing lots. At times, officials who own houses rent them to the Government for substantial amounts while themselves living in subsidized rental accommodations. Thus a self-sustaining current of demand and supply for expensive housing at public expense has been maintained. Apart from the government, banks, corporate industrial establishments, and foreign missions make lavish housing provisions for their executives. It is symptomatic of the dependent development that Americans are the preferred tenants in post-colonial Lahore.

Another way in which publicly conferred unearned gains sustain upper circuit housing is through allotments of prized lots at one-fifth of market prices to selected groups. The prices charged from allottees by the LDA for lots in Planned Schemes have been as follows [32]:

    1975-76 - Rs. 25,000 per Kanal (one-eighth acre)
            - Rs. 41 per square yard
    1978-79 - Rs. 50,000 per Kanal (one-eighth acre)
            - Rs. 82 per square yard
    1980-81 - Rs. 55,000 per Kanal (one-eighth acre)
            - Rs. 91 per square yard

Corresponding market prices for these lots averaged Rs. 250 and Rs. 413 per square yard in 1976 and 1981 respectively. It is no wonder that allotment letters are the most prized pieces of paper in Lahore, and that every association, union, or cooperative society routinely demands reservation of housing lot quotas in Planned Schemes. City property has thus become another instrument for turning influence and authority into cash, and such windfall gains have also enabled many salaried persons to sustain conspicuous consumption. This pattern has remained unaffected through all phases of national political change and ideological shift.

Only the symbols and eligibility criteria changed, while the practices remained the same. Each phase brought forth another section
of the upper circuit to profit from the public authority. If at
one time cadres of one political party were the beneficiaries, in
the next round the other reaped the rewards of wielding the state
powers, but through all these phases, officers, military as well
as civilian, have remained at the centre stage of such rewards.

  This account of land market operations would be incomplete
without an examination of the low-income housing schemes. Sodiwal
Quarters and Lahore Township were schemes of 1960 vintage for
low-income housing. During the 1970s, a province-wide programme of
giving residential lots to low-income households, particularly in
rural areas, was implemented, known as the Five Marla Scheme. This
programme was primarily meant to alleviate the residential needs
of landless peasants and non-agricultural rural workers. In Lahore
district, about 5,000-6,000 lots were distributed among low-income
households, mostly in villages at the periphery of the city [33].
Also, attempts to give proprietary rights to residents of Katchi
Abadis alleviated the land squeeze on the poor of the city. These
programmes delivered too little in comparison with the need for
about 200,000 lots. The gaping chasm between the supply and demand
produced the familiar phenomenon of floating up. From among the
poor, those who could muster influence, political power, or bribes
won, while the rest remained at the mercy of the market. Even in
this lower circuit, the resale of allotted plots at double or
triple the official price was common. Thus, a two-layered land
market appeared in both circuits, one controlled and subsidized
for the influentials and the other high-priced and uncontrolled
for the rest. Advantages conferred through public programmes
floated up through policies and programmes which lent themselves
readily to manipulation. This observation will be validated in the
following section, where the second question raised earlier may be
answered, i.e., the role public policies have played in the local
housing market.

Land and Housing Policies

  Constitutionally, housing is a subject of provincial jurisdiction in Pakistan, though political as well as administrative
authority has been concentrated at the federal level, where
five-year plans are prepared, annual developmental allocations are
decided, individual projects approved, and foreign aid disbursed.
In a country where provincial autonomy remains an unresolved
political issue, it is understandable that local governments would
have little authority, and Lahore, being the provincial capital,
is all the more under the command of provincial and federal
governments. An account of land and housing policies in Lahore
inevitably refers to decisions taken by the higher levels of
government.

  Pakistan treated housing and physical planning as a development sector of the Five Year Plan as early as 1955. Since then, the scope of work and allocations of this sector have continually increased. Initially, the emphasis was on institutional development. Separate federal and provincial Ministries of Housing and Town Planning were established, a school for architectural and planning studies instituted, Urban Development Corporations and the House Building Finance Corporation formalized, and Building Research and Public Health Laboratories developed. Whatever procedures seemed necessary or modern such as master planning, feasibility studies, or metrication of weights and measures, were adopted. In Chapters 3 and 4, details of such institutional development have been given. At present, it is enough to reiterate that a wide-ranging array of policies, programmes, and practices has come to characterize public efforts in housing development. The results have been less than satisfactory. Despite these efforts, housing needs have accumulated and prices have risen beyond the means of almost three-quarters of the population. These conditions occurred, not for lack of policies and programmes, but despite them. Most national and provincial policies and procedures have affected the housing situation in Lahore, but it would be beyond the scope of this brief review to attempt to evaluate most of them. Our exploration will be limited to those policies that have a direct bearing on land and housing markets in Lahore.

Institution Building

Mere existence of an institution is not a satisfactory indication of its output. How does it operate? This question is the key to assessing the impact of a policy. Lahore is the seat of many housing-related institutions and agencies, and therefore it would be logical to expect that their contributions would be very visible here. On this score, however, institutions such as the Building Research and Public Health Laboratories have had little effect. For example there is not a single product or procedure in common use that can be credited to these laboratories and directorates; at best they have served as rudimentary testing laboratories. Much-proclaimed international and national seminars are organized by these fashionable institutions, but environmental degradation or water and sanitation deficiencies have continued unabated. Functionally, these institutions represent rituals of development, and they symbolize the preemptive and self-serving tendencies of the upper circuit. They have provided jobs for professionals, and little else.

After about 20 years of operating, the House Building Finance Corporation was disbursing about Rs. 70 million per year in Lahore, most of which went as loans to middle- and high-income groups, as even the city planners concede [34]. By now this should not be a surprise. What needs to be asked is how the Corporation manages to exclude the bulk of the population despite explicit policies of serving low-income households. The answer lies in its operational procedures. Loans are given only to persons who have regular and attestable (by income tax authorities among others) sources of income, building permits, site plans, and an approved house lot. Obviously, hawkers, self-employed weavers, casual labourers, and other lower echelons of the bazaar sector would not qualify because they have no "attestable" incomes and they are seldom likely to have an approved lot. The Finance Corporation may be a useful institution, but its procedures confine its usefulness to a segment of the firm sector. As if procedures were not enough of a barrier, an informal practice of commissions to be paid to Corporation functionaries for loan approval further excludes the ordinary citizen from its preview loan. This is an illustration of the multilayered structure of an institution and its operational proclivites. What appear to be progressive policies turn out to be protective walls around the upper circuit.

Rent Control

A rent control ordinance was enforced in Lahore during World War II, and it has remained on the books since then. Ostensibly it is a measure that protects poor tenants from greedly landlords, but in Lahore it has created strange inequities. In older parts of the city where rents were set down long ago, many houses and shops remain rented out at one-tenth or less of the market rent. Rented premises are hard to get vacated except through long litigation and not infrequently with the help of local toughs. The rent control ordinance cuts both ways in that it shields an affluent shopkeeper against a widow or pensioner who may happen to be the landlord and vice versa. Overall, the law has made possession a marketable commodity. Shops change hands among tenants for key-money, and houses remain occupied for decades at peppercorn rents. The process favours the influential and the powerful whoever they happen to be, tenants or landlords. The rent law becomes the instrument with which the strong beat down the weak. The new Planned Schemes are relatively immune to the effects of rent control legislation. Rents are high, and repossession of properties is difficult but not impossible. It appears that one of the unintended consequences of rent legislation is the neglect of properties in older parts of the city.

This example illustrates how a policy in actual operation gets coopted by the market and produces contrary results. A mere legislative edict about rights of tenants, if it is not accompanied by monitoring mechanisms and review procedures, quickly degenerates into an obstacle that the influential and powerful can negotiate but which victimizes the rest.

Land Acquisition for Housing

Almost three years before the HABITAT Conference (1976) recommended public recapture of unearned increment of urban land values, the Punjab Provincial Government legislated that urban land acquired for housing schemes would be compensated at the rate

Rs. 20,000 per acre maximum and conferred almost unquestionable powers upon housing and city planning agencies to expeditiously acquire land whenever needed [35]. the Land Acquisition Act (Housing) of 1973 supplanted earlier procedures where compensation was based on market value and land acquisition could be stalled through arguments over purpose and value. by all indications it should have been a progressive measure. Yet it has turned out to be another source of unaccountability of public agencies and an instrument of regressive transfer. It was conceived hurriedly with little regard to the objective conditions of the enforcing agencies or of the city.

Under this Act, land is acquired from farmers or other private owners at Rs. 20,000 per acre (often a quarter or less of the market value), developed, and subdivided into lots to be allotted to a selected few at highly subsidized prices. A proportion of lots is sold by auction, and they command fabulous prices. Through this sequence, one set of landowners is deprived of market values, and they are transferred through allotments to another set of property owners. It is no wonder that the Act has turned into a political and administrative tool to enrich influentials.

Interestingly, the Act has produced a response that typically arises in packaged land reforms. The Act provides that an owner whose land is acquired is entitled to one housing lot out of the surrendered acreage. This "exemption" was raised in 1977 to 30 percent of the original holding. This provision of the Act prompted a widespread break-up of large land parcels into smaller units registered individually under the names of family members. Thus the "exemptions" became so numerous that, in some of the recent schemes, more lots reverted to original owners than became available for public disposition.

Reprise of Land and Housing Analysis

The conclusions emerging from the preceding section and examined in the context of earlier findings about the evolutionary trends in the land and housing markets of the city suggest the following patterns.

(1) Land and housing have progressively acquired the characteristics of a commodity which is to be parlayed into financial gain. They have evolved from properties hedged by social values of public trust and community welfare to profitable possessions. The trend towards commercialization of interests and values that has characterized Pakistan's economic development is evident in this case.

(2) Seemingly, policies and institutions are borrowed from abroad without any regard to their social context and stripped of the necessary operational checks that ensured their effectiveness in their original settings. Thus, they turn out to be instruments serving the interests of wielders of

authority. A subterranean but entrenched layer of illicit deals and exchanges evolves around almost every policy or institution, and this second layer mops up whatever little benefits tend to trickle down. Land and housing markets have increasingly become sources of unearned gain and tools to profit from public authority. Through compulsory land acquisition, rent control, lot allotment procedures, and other public programmes, the influentials are being subsidized to the detriment of general welfare.

(3) The land and housing markets have evolved from an organically singular entity to multiple circuits serving divergent interests. The poor and working-class housing market has been strained out into an autonomous circuit. In this lower circuit, the supply comes from doubling up in older areas or through incremental additions to marginal lands. Information about available accommodation and rents is passed by word of mouth, and transactions flow along channels of mutual acquaintance and clan obligations. The upper circuit is served by real estate companies, rental agents, and newspaper advertisements. Transactions are in writing, and dealings are businesslike, though a vestige of personal relationships persists. Public policies and procedures have promoted the differentiation into circuits. The House Building Finance Corporation's operational procedures, described earlier, are a case in point. Even progressive policies implemented through procedures that assume certain prerequisites of income, knowledge, status, and occupation turn out to be self-serving for those in authority. Developmental thrusts in the idiom of modern, educated, upper middle class can serve only the upper circuit. This is a phenomenon where the mode in which supply is provided creates its own demand.

CITY PLANNING

Although city planning is an ancient art, in contemporary times it has become a public institution to guide and coordinate multifarious decisions that affect the livability of a city. City planning is an ongoing process in which actions of individuals as well as groups are regulated and directed to promote the health, convenience, and welfare of all. By convention, city planning is concerned with ensuring an orderly and efficient pattern of land uses and adequate provisions of housing, transportation, utilities, and services, though both its scope and procedures vary from country to country according to social conditions and constitutional provisions. City planning practice has evolved from an exercise in beautifying a city to a process for managing its development. The new version of city planning comes close to being an intelligence and control function of an urban system, and this concept has come to be widely practised both in the East and in the West.

The modern phase of city planning in Lahore began in 1936 with the creation of the statutory body, Lahore Improvement Trust (LIT), to prepare development schemes, and draw up area improvement plans. The formation of a statutory, nonelective body, independent of the municipal corporation, put the planning and development functions into a professional and bureaucratic realm, shielded from citizens' input and insulated against public accountability. This beginning laid the path along which city planning in Lahore has evolved. Another original feature that has become a characteristic of local planning is the emphasis on development schemes. Plot development is what city planning has come to mean in Lahore.

Soon after the LIT was established, a town planner was appointed who became preoccupied with subdividing land for housing estates and with approving building permits. These tasks have remained central to city planning through various phases of post-Independence development. The supplanting of the LIT by the LDA in 1975 was a public acknowledgement that development of residential projects was the main task of city planning in Lahore.

With greater financial resources and more power than the LIT, the LDA has become the main agency for public works in Lahore. Typically, the term "development" has meant focussing on capital expenditures, not on operational efficiency or functional transformation of the city. The LDA has wide powers of comprehensive development planning and has the authority to prepare, implement, and enforce schemes for environmental improvements, housing, solid waste disposal, transportation and traffic, and health and educational facilities [36]. With the formation of the LDA, the scope of city planning has expanded to include sanitation, transportation and other essential urban functions.

Judged on the criterion of lot production, city planning has an impressive and steadily improving record. Up to 1975, the LIT had developed 8,470 lots of which about 90 percent were meant for middle- and upper-income groups. The formation of LDA quickened the tempo of development, and about 28,610 lots were developed in the next four-year period (1975-79), including 15,550 that LIT had initiated [37]. In this period, the proportion of small lots meant for moderate income groups has increased to constitute about 30 percent of the total output [38].

Apart from these planned schemes, LIT/LDA also approved about 575 small (1-4 acre) and large private land subdivisions over the 30 year period [39]. Despite such an impressive record of lot production, city planning could not meet the demand, and the gap was so wide that a majority of new houses were built on unapproved lots. City planning practice in Lahore has increasingly come to mean developing capital works and focussing only on profitable aspects of land use controls, such as rezoning properties for commercial uses. No effective legislation or suitable procedures have been evolved to regulate land uses in general. There are building regulations and site approval procedures, but both have been ineffective as well as irrelevant. Generally construction proceeds

without permits, and, in cases where approvals are sought, regulations and standards are not followed in implementation. Even in
planned schemes, where one would expect vigorous enforcement of
building regulations, front yards extend over sidewalks, setbacks
are built over, and buildings are sited on lots in disregard of
the prescribed building line.

This is the situation in prestigious areas like Gulberg or
Garden Town. What happens in unplanned New Indigenous Communities
or Katchi Abadis needs little elaboration. This state of affairs
has arisen from the corruptability of officials as well as from
the inconsistency and irrelevance of the regulations. For example,
in a city where mixing of activities is an economic necessity,
segregation of land uses in residential or commercial zones is
impractical. Such regulations primarily become a stick in the
hands of officials to shake down those who happen to get caught in
the net of rules. Little objective, indigenous thinking has been
done about the approaches to and instruments of city planning.
Western idioms and packaged policies are continually being
imported, lately with the assistance of the international
agencies, irrespective of their relevance and applicability to the
local situation. These borrowings are mere outward forms of
Western practices without the meanings, internal checks and
balances, or the context of their origins. For example, regulations requiring site-plan approvals have been instituted, but the
citizens' rights, the appeal procedures, the burden of having
well-defined preexisting plans and mechanisms to monitor and
modify the implementation of regulations remain unnoticed. Whatever rule or practice confers powers on public officials or
increases an agency's budget is adopted while obligations that
accompany such procedures are ignored. Thus city planning in its
control functions becomes a ritual exercising powers without any
attempt to identify issues and evolve criteria. The rules become a
sort of obstacle course that citizens go around by mobilizing
their contacts or buying their way out. The overall result is a
high degree of adhocism in formation and implementation of
policies, despite a facade of systematic approaches.

In form, not function, city planning has kept abreast with
up-to-date practices. Since Independence, two major mas-
ter-planning exercises have been undertaken. First, in 1963-65,
the Provincial Town Planning Department prepared a master plan for
the city. It was a local effort managed by two professionals with
the assistance of a few geographers and sociologists. The master
plan was a pictorial document outlining the form and pattern for
the expansion of the city. Its proposals were structured on the
neighbourhood principle, and it was a reasonable physical plan. It
took various committees of the Provincial Government seven years
formally to approve the master plan in 1973. However, the master
plan was largely irrelevant to the pressing problems of the city,
though it provided a framework for expansion. Its identification
of axes of future development (i.e., south, southeast, and north)
was a signal to entrepreneurs and public agencies to build new

subdivisions there. Thus it served as a guide for capital works and land speculation.

By 1975, city planning in Lahore had become a development exercise, and development in Pakistan has generally meant scrambling for foreign aid and advice. One of the first acts of the newly constituted LDA (1975) was to negotiate with the World Bank to fund the preparation of the Structure Plan called the Lahore Urban Development Traffic Study (LUDTS). What had been done only seven years ago entirely by local efforts was now to be redone (with some new elements added by foreign consultants) funded from a World Bank loan. This transformation brought city planners to full bloom in the contemporary idiom of development. It also became fully integrated in the dependency network of foreign advice and aid. This dependency was not entirely an external imposition, but was invited by local city planners and administrators whose vested interests were served by associating with the international agencies. Foreign aid makes an agency relatively free from resource constraints and enhances its power base vis-à-vis other departments. It also confers substantial material benefits on executives in the form of trips abroad, jobs in international agencies, and perks at home. The LUDTS is a case in point, serving various latent functions for city planning, such as lending prestige and status to city planning, gaining media exposure, and access to the highest authority (president, governor) in the country through foreign advisors, and making trips and attending conferences abroad for senior staff.

The foregoing examination of city planning in Lahore illustrates how external dependence is internally induced. It also shows that the path of development in Lahore has led from modest self-help to state-sponsored extravaganzas incurring foreign debts and the burgeoning of public agencies. However, the foregoing comments should not detract from the intrinsic merit of the LUDTS. The structural plan produced by the study updates the outlook and approach of local city planning. It comments on the past neglect of housing for the poor, points out the lagging provision of community services, and puts forth credible proposals for the amelioration of these conditions. Yet the plan-making is only a step towards policies and programmes. Implementation of the structural plan had already begun to reveal the characteristic patterns of Lahore's development, i.e., that only those proposals were getting to the programme stage which entailed capital works and expansion of bureaucratic empires or enhanced official powers, or served the interests of the influential.

In Lahore, city planning has expanded its jurisdiction and increased its authority and visibility in the daily life of citizens. Numerous functions or activities have been brought under its jurisdiction, such as city beautification, road widening, encroachment control, Katchi Abadis upgrading, granting of tenural rights to squatters, lot allotment and environmental and public health services. Not all these activities have yet received appropriate attention from city planners, but there has been

steadily increasing talk about these matters in city planning
circles.

   As earlier sections of this and the previous chapter have
amply demonstrated, living conditions in Lahore have not registered any noticeable improvement despite the sustained development
of every element of the urban system. This outcome is also an
indication of the ineffectiveness (on social indicators) of city
planning. The most noticeable change is that city planning has
become central to the property market, in that large windfall
gains can be reaped only by working through the city planning
organization. City planning presents the characteristic
"double-face" in the form of an institution: objectives, policies,
and structures proclaim one state of affairs, and operations
deliver another. City planning operates in the same manner as any
other public institution, dispensing benefits to the influential,
through favourable policies as well as power exchange and
merchandising of public authority.

                    THE GOVERNMENT AND THE CITY

   The probing of almost every institution and process has
revealed that governmental programmes and operations have steadily
become the dominant elements of the urban system. Even apparently
autonomous sectors (e.g., bazaar) operate on the ground laid by
governmental policies and regulations. The state has become the
preeminent institution. This tendency emerged during the colonial
era, when capturing and strengthening state authority was the
strategy to maintain rule, but Independence did not counter the
trend. Soon after Independence, the drive for social and economic
development became the justification for strengthening the state
apparatus. Political groups soon discovered that the short cut to
power was to capture the state authority without seeking the
people's mandate. A peculiarity of Pakistan is that expansion of
the state's authority and role has not been accompanied by the
development of political institutions; this, in turn, has made the
state into a self-sustaining, insular organization. A situation
has steadily arisen where the state's policies and programmes
arise independent of people's needs or objective conditions. At
the operational level, the objectives, notions (borrowed or otherwise) and the whims of state functionaries have become criteria
for decisions.

   There are almost no institutional means for people to register their demands and appraise authorities of the effects of
public policies [40]. The only recourse left to a citizen is to
seek the intervention of somebody influential or to bribe. Those
who cannot mobilize any of these two resources have to bear the
consequences. The conventional mechanisms of accountability by
public officials have been eroded, and few new arrangements have
been instituted to balance the expanding governmental institutions. These are the evolutionary trends of governmental opera-

tions in Pakistan as a whole. Lahore is not an exception.

At the time of Independence (1947), two local bodies looked after Lahore's civic needs. The Lahore Municipal Corporation, headed by a Mayor and consisting of an elected council, had primary responsibility for conservancy, street maintenance, public health, and primary education. The Cantonment Board, comprised of nominees of the Defence Ministry and a few elected representatives, had jurisdiction for similar community services in the Cantonment area. Apart from the two local bodies, the Provincial Government exercised direct control over the affairs of the city. The Deputy Commissioner, the Superintendent of Police, and the Sessions Judge constituted the triumvirate which ruled the city. The Federal Government's presence was evident through the department of railways, the telephone and post office, and the army. In this set-up, the management of the city essentially remained with provincial civil servants, while the municipality was limited to maintenance of civic facilities. The people's perception of the relatively subordinate position of the local municipality can be measured by their name for the local councillors, the Mori Members (members to look after drains).

Independence has had a ballooning effect on the public agencies. They multiplied many fold, but the overall structure remained unchanged. There is hardly any aspect of city life where some public agency is not involved. Over and above the expanded state role in the production of goods and services, civil servants remain the effective rulers of the city. It is the Deputy Commissioner who decides the price of meat or gives and takes away permission for gatherings of more than five persons. If there are cement shortages in the city, the Commissioner may order the executives of the Cement Corporation to remedy the situation. The Provincial Public Works Department issues safety and occupancy certificates for cinemas, and a committee of heads of concerned departments demarcates industrial sites or allots sites for petrol stations. Area magistrates carry out raids to remove encroachments and to curb traffic abuses. These examples indicate the extent to which provincial and federal officials run the city. This situation is little different from that of colonial days, except that the magnitude and range of governmental presence have increased vastly.

There is one structural effect of this expansion of public activities. Authority is not concentrated in a small clutch of officers, but has become dispersed among large numbers of functionaries. Even the state apparatus has evolved from unitary character to the multiple nuclei of authority. In 1980 there were about 100 governmental agencies involved in the development and management of the city [41].

While the jurisdiction of civil servants have waxed, the role of elected local councillors has waned. Elections have been few and far between: in fact, for almost twenty years, there were no direct elections to the local councils. The municipal council was formed through indirect elections and nominations during the Ayub

era, and then it remained suspended up to 1979. While the local
council languished, new agencies and bureaus have continued to be
formed, both to look after new activities and to reorganize
existing functions. The processes of centralization of public
authority and concentration of powers in the hands of civil
servants have gained momentum with development. The local
councillors have lost so much of their authority that even the
topics of discussion in the council have been prescribed by the
Commissioner. Recently, the Lahore Municipal Corporation seemed to
have strained the patience of the officers and was barred from
discussing the performance of various departments and even
employees of the municipal corporation.

Power Structure and Decision-Making

With the ballooning of state authority, civil servants and
political appointees have become the primary decision makers. The
city's power structure has, thus, been realigned. As well, the
ethos of development has affected the relative standings of power
groups.

In the British era, the officers were the government, but
they stood above the local power nexus. The city's power align-
ments ran along clan and Baradari lines, with Jats, Arians,
Kakizais and Lohors the powerful clans. Both local and provincial
elections brought forth leaders from these clans who acted as
power brokers and patrons. If one wanted a water connection for
the municipality or required to bail out a relative from police
custody, one turned to the elders of the clan or the leaders of
the neighbourhood for help. Since Independence, the clans have
steadily been diluted, though not dissipated. Marriages have continued to be arranged within Baradaris (clans), and this practice
has helped maintain some cohesiveness. However, the clans have
lost both the territorial propinquity and political clout. They
have become instead a loose social network for mutual support. One
turns to a relative who happens to be in a position of authority
for getting a child admitted to a good school or obtaining a
cement permit. Such favours are sought as barter for corresponding
help in matters over which a seeker may have jurisdiction or
authority. Obviously, barter occurs between equals in authority,
though poor relatives are looked after in exchange for emotional
support or even help in physical chores. It is access to state
authority that has come to determine the power status of an individual in a clan. These trends have affected the city's power
structure, which has evolved from an assembly of clan (and caste)
leaders to a confederation of social coalitions comprised of
mutually supporting officers, businessmen, and politicians. This
shift in the bases of power is reflected in the social backgrounds
of municipal councillors. Up to the late 1950s, the Council was
dominated by semiliterate clan leaders, but the 1979 elections
brought forth merchants, contractors, fledgling lawyers, and small

industrialists of considerable formal education [42].

Parallel to the realignment of power structures are corresponding trends in the decision-making processes. The concentration of authority in the hands of governmental functionaries, political as well as administrative, resulted in centralization of the decision-making process. Yet, within this decision-making stratum, authority has dispersed among ever increasing numbers of bureaus and corporations. Functionally, decision-making has been diffused, while institutionally it has been centralized. The result of these two tendencies is the emergence of distinct cadres or networks of doers and getters for each significant public activity. Whenever a major policy decision is to be made, a loose coalition of various networks has to be put together. At the institutional level, it means a tendency towards operational ad hocism masked by administrative rituals. For individuals, it means that to get something done, one has to mobilize and apply pressure at every stage through which the desired decision has to be processed. The most common practice in dealing with public agencies is to follow the file; whether a chief engineer wants a grant of foreign exchange to build a bridge in the public interest or an individual applies for a passport, both have to follow more or less the same procedures, i.e., call on relevant officers and pressure them through barter of favours. This is how the government operates. In this evolving system, there is little that can be taken as a matter of right or procedure. One cannot even expect a reply to a letter sent to governmental departments. The rich and the powerful are capable of mobilizing the necessary resources, but they are also not relieved from the necessity of expending time and energy for every task.

How have the evolutionary trends in decision-making and power structure affected the functioning of the city? The centralization of authority and monopolizing of power by the state has elevated local decisions to the provincial and national levels. Furthermore, mechanisms through which citizens could register their needs, influence officials' perceptions, and provide feed-back on public policies have been steadily neutralized. Institutionally and operationally, there are almost no interest groups or power blocks left which may bargain for the city as a whole. The state functionaries charged with the responsibilities of managing the city, i.e., deputy commissioners, chairmen of the LDA, or administrators of the municipality, seldom remain posted for more than three years and they are judged on their alacrity in executing orders from the higher quarters. The result of all these processes is an erosion of the city's capacity to manage its own affairs.

Revenues and Expenditures

According to the LUDTS, an average of one billion rupees per year was being spent on development projects during the late 1970s [43]. In Pakistan, this is a substantial investment. About

37 percent of this capital expenditure was directly incurred by federal and provincial agencies operating in Lahore. The LDA undertook another 37 percent of capital expenditures, but about 43 percent of its revenue was from grants and loans from the two governments. Altogether, about 50 to 55 percent of city development funds came directly from federal and provincial governments, and a substantial proportion of the rest was also underwritten by them. Obviously, Lahore was dependent for development funds upon the largesse of higher levels of government and they in turn relied on foreign aid and loans. Through this chain of grants and loans, city developmental priorities have come to be decided in Washington.

With about three-fourths of development funds coming from the two higher levels of government, civil servants have come to be the masters of the city, and it comes as no surprise that the provincial secretaries and governor personally decide whether the racecourse grounds should be turned into an amusement park or apartment complex. Almost every significant decision about the city, from land uses to riot control, quickly becomes a matter of provincial or federal choice. The Lahore Municipal Corporation has remained a low-key, resource-starved local body. Its per capita annual revenues and expenditures averaged Rs. 53 and Rs. 55 (about $5.00) respectively during the late 1970s [44].

TABLE 7.2

Average Revenues of Lahore Municipal Corporation
1975-76 to 1979-80

Source of Revenue	Four Years Moving Average (Million Rupees)	Percentage
Octoroi (toll tax)	118.1	67.0
Property Tax	19.7	11.1
Government Grants	11.5	6.5
Fees, Rents & Others	27.4	15.4
TOTAL	176.7	100.0

Source: Lahore Urban Development and Traffic Study, Final Report: Volume I, Appendix 11, p. 376.

Almost 70 percent of municipal revenue came from a toll tax levied on goods coming into or going out of the city. It is notable that the property tax contributed only 11 percent of the revenue, which is very low by any standards [45]. With these meagre revenues the corporation ran 256 schools, 54 dispensaries, and two hospitals, employed 5,500 sweepers to collect refuse, and carried out other necessary civic works in 1979. It is also interesting to note that the municipal corporation periodically acknowledges the pocketing of octoroi tax by city officials and auctions tax collection to private contractors for a lump sum amount.

In contrast with the municipal corporation, the Lahore Development Authority (LDA) appears to be bathed in riches. The per capita expenditure of the LDA in 1979-81 was Rs. 400, almost eight times the municipal expenditure. About 58 percent of LDA revenue came from the sale of lots and from development charges, and the higher levels of government also lavishly supported its projects with grants and loans (37 percent of the revenue) [46]. The contrast between the revenue-expenditure patterns of the municipal corporation and those of the LDA is a reflection of the high priority assigned to capital works (development) and the indifference to maintenance and operational activities. Furthermore, in the case of development funds, supply creates its own demand in that the availability of aid and loans becomes an incentive to propose projects, whereas maintenance requires self-help and mobilization of local resources, hence it remains a neglected task.

FINDINGS AND IMPLICATIONS

In this chapter we have explored the workings of schools, hospitals, water supply, housing, and other elements of Lahore's institutional system. As the quantitative account of the development of these goods and services has been given in Chapter 4, here we have concentrated on examining their operations, i.e., how they actually work and whom they serve. This study has amply demonstrated that Lahore has witnessed continual institutional development and change since Independence. Our explorations have also revealed that the crucial question is how the new institutions, organizations, and facilities operate, because it is only at the operational level that the factual contributions of these elements can be observed.

The true but trite observation that development has primarily benefitted the upper classes is an inescapable conclusion, no matter what aspect of the urban system is probed. The question, then, is how this happens. Despite public policies and programmes that have progressively come to recognize the necessity of improving the living condition of the masses, the chasm between the intention and the outcome has remained unbridged. The key to the internal dynamics of the city lies in the answer to this question. The following summary of findings will illuminate this issue.

(1) The extension of a facility or service to a broader
spectrum of population leads to its dualization into an exclusive,
high quality provision for the privileged and an overused, low
quality, corruption-ridden burden for the rest. For example, while
public education has been indigenized and nationalized for the
masses, special model schools and private academies offering
"English-style" education have emerged for the middle and upper
classes. When the hospitals became crowded and the quality of care
declined, private clinics made their appearance. As public buses
became both unreliable and inconvenient, minibuses and company
vans came into operation as modes of public transport. This
phenomenon of "streaming" or "tracking" of collective goods by
social strata is a counterpart of the segmentalization of social
and economic structures observed previously.

(2) The streaming of community facilities and services into
distinct tracks for respective social strata arises from, and in
turn reinforces, processes of privatization of public goods and
floating-up of resources. Even in countries with market economies,
education, public health, water supply, sewage, drainage, and
shelter have come to be viewed as public goods whose supply is
fairly and equitably available for both rich and the poor. In
Lahore, streaming helps to segregate the provision for the upper
strata and thus differentiates between their interests and those
of the rest. Provided separately, schools, clinics, sewage, and
water supply for the influential command high priority and receive
prompt attention among the decision makers. Even if policies are
progressive, implementation turns them into exercises in serving
the influential. Directly, through organizational and programme
biases, and indirectly, throuⁿh kickbacks, nepotism and bribery,
public resources are diverted to reinforce the identifiable upper
track. Private clinics are reimbursed from the medical allowance
of the executives. A bed in a public hospital is available only if
the specialist is consulted privately. The first phase of a
city-wide sewage plan often falls in upper-class areas and usually
the funds run out by the time the phase is completed. These are
some examples of the way in which public resources sustain private
consumption by the upper strata.

(3) To the extent that a community service is indivisible,
streaming works to the detriment of everybody, including the upper
strata. Drainage, sewage and garbage disposal, public transport,
and land uses are such collective facilities that neglect of the
public interest results in poor provision for all. For example,
every passing year has extended the area of the city prone to
flooding from the increased run-off from monsoons. The drainage of
one part of the city cannot be separated from others, and thus in
heavy rains even the Governor's house now becomes inaccessible. A
garbage heap in front of an opulent house is a health hazard even
for the rich, and long journeys necessitated by disorderly land
uses wear out car owners. These examples illustrate that on some
scores there are no private solutions to needs that are common,
and that the upper strata cannot be immune to public shortfalls.

In these matters privatization does not provide isolated heaven
for the privileged. They also find that routine chores of city
living turn into daily missions, requiring attention and expense,
be they those of children's travel to school or of finding a place
to empty the garbage pail.

(4) Community services of unequal quality militate against
orderliness of land uses and prevent formation of balanced neighbourhoods. For example, as schools, dispensaries, and parks have
diverged in quality and services, travel patterns have become
highly disordered. Some children from the southeast travel to the
north central areas for model schools, while others may head
further south towards a municipal school, and vice versa. Patients
from the Walled City may come to a doctor in Mozang, while residents of Mozang may seek medical treatment in Ichra. Such long,
diffused, and costly journeys have been precipitated by the
absence of a qualitative standardization of community services. It
is obvious that implicit in the neighbourhood principle is an
assumption about the basic uniformity of services, a point worthy
of notice by city planners and urban theorists.

(5) The public resources, physical, financial and organizational, are the common denominator of an urban system. How they
are allocated and used determines the effectiveness of the system.
In Lahore, public resources and authority are dispensed through
permits and quotas, and, at the operational level, through
influence peddling and bribes. Seemingly progressive policies turn
out in operation to be means of benefitting the influential. The
rent-control legislation and the housing-land acquisition act of
1973 are two examples that illustrate how the state authority has
been coopted to reward the wheeler-dealers and the privileged.
Land and housing have become the source of windfall gains, and
thus have served as tools to convert influence and authority into
property. Evacuee property allotments, quotas for lots in Planned
Schemes, and subsidized loans for the House Building Corporation
supplemented by expense accounts for executive housing are
seemingly fair procedures which in fact have worked to create a
subsidized and sheltered property submarket for those who have
access to public authority, i.e., politicians, party men, officers, and powerbrokers. These operations have induced pervasive
practices of double-dealing, fixing, and rule manipulation. The
net result is a situation wherein the affluent enjoy public subsidies and the poor have to be content with self-help. This
general pattern has remained unaffected, despite political changes
including Ayub's free enterprise, Bhutto's socialism, and the subsequent Islamisation of the State. The process of encashment of
the state authority goes on unabated; only the faces of the beneficiaries change.

(6) In Lahore, the tempo of development (as a process of
organizational, technological, and material change) has accelerated steadily in both public and private realms. The most marked
result of development has been the formation of new organizations,
agencies, and corporations. The State has been the promoter and

regulator of development and thus the public apparatus has expanded most conspicuously. Lahore has come to have about 100 governmental agencies directly involved in development work, not to mention the regular governmental departments. The State has become the most pervasive institution and even the bazaar sector operates within the parameters laid by governmental policies, rules and investments. Foreign aid has strengthened the government vis-à-vis other institutions, and, within the government, it has reinforced centralization tendencies. Given the political peculiarities of Pakistan, the result of these trends has been an attenuation of local self-government and further strengthening of the authority of public functionaries, which, in the absence of mechanisms of accountability, promotes corruption.

(7) The city has lost organized forums and interest groups which could articulate community needs and provide feedback on public actions. The municipal corporation has been eclipsed politically by the long suspension of elections and administratively by new developmental agencies. This means that whatever little influence the elected representatives enjoyed has been eroded. Decision-making is guided by the perceptions, interests and whims of public functionaries. If a prime minister feels that Lahore should be beautified, beautification becomes the overriding issue of the city. If a governor likes a circular railway, then it becomes the promised panacea for the ills of the transportation system. When the World Bank requires a raise in domestic water charges as a condition for a loan, the provincial and federal ministers begin to echo the demand as an efficiency measure while conveniently overlooking the 50 percent loss of water through leaks. These are examples of the perceptions that guide decision-making in Lahore. Generally, the insularity of public functionaries from accountability and the absence of institutional means for people to register their concerns have laid the ground for self-serving public policies and the shadow economy of corruption. Lahore has most of the modern institutions, but few of them operate effectively. Foreign aid tends to promote such hollow institutions which replicate borrowed forms, without corresponding functions, meaning and context.

(8) Another feature of development is that capital works are stressed while maintenance and upgrading of existing facilities receive lower priority. This pattern has been observed in almost every collective goods and service examined in the chapter. While scores of new schools are built every year, the operational budgets for the existing ones are such that they cannot even repair desks or buy books. Obviously foreign loans or federal grants preclude operational expenses, and therefore those command lower priority. Capital works have more benefits to confer on the officials in the form of jobs as well as kickbacks. A chain of dependency extends all the way from the World Bank to the municipal primary school in Lahore.

(9) The prices of houses and land in Lahore have reached levels that about 75 percent of the population cannot afford. Yet

the upper circuit has expanded enough that the market for new houses has remained very vigorous. Furthermore, Lahore's social structure has proven to be a resilient resource. The patriarchal family system has kept afloat the poor, and the sentiment of solidarity among friends and relatives has proven an asset in this city where public interest has become a ground for private gain. Friends, relatives, and acquaintances are expected to help each other with whatever happens to be within an individual's jurisdiction. Whether one has to pay an electric bill or apply for a passport, one is well advised to look around for some help from friends. Such "favour-exchanges" and "influence-swaps", like bribery or the black market, are coping mechanisms, highly individual solutions to common problems. The traditional clans have loosened but not dissolved, while the imperatives of favour-exchange have prompted the emergence of social networks and coalitions along class and professional lines.

NOTES

1. Collective goods are those goods and services considered necessary for the functioning of a collectivity but which seldom are produced privately. Collective goods partake of the characteristics of public goods which in pure form are indivisible both in consumption and production (i.e., they are available to either all or none) such as clean air, law and order, etc. By convention as well as technological necessities, water supply, sewerage, drainage, schools, land use controls, parks, police and public transportation have come to be collective goods for urban living.

2. Lahore Urban Development and Traffic Study, Final Report: Volume I. Urban Planning (Lahore: Lahore Development Authority, 1981), p. 71.

3. Hussain Naqi, "Lahore Diary," Viewpoint, July 13, 1980, p. 11.

4. Lahore Urban Development and Traffic Study, Final Report, p. 70.

5. Ibid., p. 70.

6. The Lahore Development Authority's periodic attempts to shift the cloth market or Akbari Mandi, often end in abandoning of such programmes.

7. Lahore Urban Development and Traffic Study, Summary of Findings of Socio-Economic Survey of Walled City, Lahore and Summary of the Findings, Socio-Economic Survey of Gujjarpura, Lahore (mimeographed) (Lahore: Lahore Development Authority, 1980).

8. Department of Social Work, Punjab University, A Study of Lahore Township Scheme Kot Lakhpat, Lahore – A Socio-Economic and Evaluative Study (Lahore: Punjab University, 1972).

9. Lahore Urban Development and Traffic Study, Final Report, p. 77.

10. Ibid., p. 77.

11. Mahmood Zaman, "The School you want is not the School

that wants you," Viewpoint, May 20, 1982, p. 22.

12. Mahmood Zaman, "Schools no one wants to join," View-point, April 29, 1982, pp. 24-25.

13. Ibid., p. 23.

14. The neighbourhood principle in city planning originated with Clarence Perry and since then it has become a common prac-tice. Houses are clustered around a school, park and shops to con-stitute a super block within which day-to-day living can be carried out without the intrusion of through traffic or outside demands.

15. Government of West Pakistan, Master Plan for Greater Lahore (Lahore: The Master Plan Project Office, 1964), p. 73.

16. Pakistan Times, January 18, 1982, p. 3.

17. Gulberg had 179 out of 930 acres of open space for public use in Lahore. Saleem Shakir, "Two Lahores 2 Gulbergs," Viewpoint, June 1, 1980, p. 8.

18. Government of West Pakistan, Master Plan, Appendix 12, pp. 144-145.

19. Lahore Urban Development and Traffic Study, Final Report: Volume I. Urban Planning, p. 74.

20. Ibid., p. 69.

21. Pakistan Times, May 13, 1979, p. 5.

22. Lahore Urban Development and Traffic Study, Final Report: Volume I, p. 74.

23. M. A. Kamran, "The WASA Myth Shattered," Viewpoint, July 16, 1981, p. 13.

24. Pakistan Times, April 19, 1979, p. 6.

25. Lahore Urban Development and Traffic Study, Final Report: Volume I, p. 56.

26. Ibid., p. 57.

27. Pakistan Times, December 31, 1980, pp. 3 and 5.

28. Lahore Urban Development and Traffic Study, Final Report: Volume I, p. 64.

29. Viewpoint, April 31, 1980, p. 18.

30. Ibid., p. 18.

31. Lahore Urban Development and Traffic Study, Final Report: Volume I, p. 68.

32. Pakistan Times, April 13, 1980, p. 3.

33. There are no reliable data for Five Marla lots allotted in Lahore district. Figures for the whole province were often cited by the Housing Minister in the Provincial Assembly, but they seldom were consistent. See the Minister's statement in Pakistan Times, September 15, 1974, p. 5, and April 16, 1975, p. 10.

34. Lahore Urban Development and Traffic Study, Final Report: Volume I, p. 93.

35. The Punjab Acquisition of Land (Housing) Act, 1973, Sections 9 and 10.

36. The Lahore Development Authority Act (xxx of 1975), Section 6.3.i.

37. Lahore Urban Development and Traffic Study, Final Report: Volume I, Table 27, p. 209.

38. Ibid., p. 210.

39. Figures about private land subdivisions given to the author by the Town Planner in LDA during an interview.

40. Pakistan has almost continually been under censorship and press control. Long periods of martial law rule and brief spells of controlled democracy have weakened procedures of registering response to public policies and officials.

41. Lahore Urban Development and Traffic Study, Final Report: Volume I, p. 83.

42. The observations about social backgrounds of local councillors have been derived from their life sketches published in newspapers. Pakistan Times, December 20, 1979, p. 5.

43. Lahore Urban Development and Traffic Study, Final Report: Volume I, Table 11, p. 102.

44. Bureau of Statistics, Development Statistics of the Punjab (Lahore: Government of the Punjab, 1978), Table 179, p. 301.

45. Property taxes are the primary source of revenue for cities in Europe and North America. About 40 to 50 percent of local revenue is raised from these taxes.

46. Lahore Urban Development and Traffic Study, Final Report: Volume I, Appendix 10, p. 375.

8
OVERVIEW

As the HABITAT declaration affirmed, the development of a
city (or for that matter any human settlement) should lead to "the
rapid and continuous improvement in the quality of life for all
people, beginning with the satisfaction of the basic needs of
food, shelter, clean water, employment, health, education, training, social security without any discrimination as to race,
colour, sex, language, religion, ideology, national or social
origin or other cause, in a frame of freedom, dignity, and social
justice." [1] (Emphasis added). Although this is a statement of
goals for human settlement development, it mirrors current
thinking about development in general.

Three notions underlie this statement: (1) development is a
process and not a product or state; (2) benefits of development
must be available to all, or at least there should not be any
institutional barriers to improvement in the quality of life of
any section of population; (3) development must encompass
physical, institutional, economic and social improvements and not
be merely a matter of capitol works. These notions are particularly relevant to cities.

Cities are communities whose well-being is largely indivisible. One segment of a city's population cannot enjoy clean
air, plentiful water, smooth flow of traffic, or freedom from epidemics and disturbances without others being extended the same
benefits. Similarly, the development of one element of an urban
system without parallel growth of others is not usually beneficial. For example, if more houses are built without a corresponding increase of facilities for water supply, sewage disposal, or
transportation, and education, the livability of a city may even
decrease. Consequently, even in countries with market economies,
contemporary thinking has come to view urban development as the
process of establishing a common floor of institutions, regulations, facilities, services, and administrative practices. For the
Third World, provision for the basic habitational needs of the
whole population of a city should be the overriding goal of urban
development and the criterion by which the performance of an urban
system is to be assessed.

LAHORE – A JUDGEMENT

Since Independence, Lahore has undergone explosive growth and notable transformation of its material, technological, and institutional bases. Yet, like most Third World cities, it continues to be ravaged by poverty, inequality, and mismanagement. Housing shortages have remained unabated despite two decades of building boom. Transportation has progressively become unreliable, costly, and risky, though the numbers of cars and scooters have increased at rates as high as 15 to 20 percent per year. Such contradictions can be recounted almost endlessly. Lahore's quality of life has registered little improvement; in fact, despite an accelerating tempo of development, it may have declined. Socially and physically, it has become a city of contrasts: colour televisions and open drains; air-conditioned bungalows and mud huts; grandiose master plans and administrative inability to enforce traffic rules. These contrasts are symptoms of misdirected development. They indicate that common facilities, services, and institutions necessary for urban development have been neglected to the detriment of all. Even the upper classes do not escape the social costs of this neglect. Roads flooded by rain, bureaucracies rife with corruption, and an electrical supply that frequently breaks down detract from the comfort and satisfaction of rich and poor alike. Neglect of the welfare of the majority reverts to erode the quality of life for all, including the dominant minority. This lesson has emerged from probes of almost every aspect of Lahore's life. Why, then, has development been so misdirected?

IMPULSIONS OF URBAN DEVELOPMENT

This study has sought to probe the reasons for misdevelopment in Lahore, but it has proceeded with a deliberate stance. Accepting the role of neo-colonial external factors as the determining and constraining elements, it focuses on the internal dynamics of the city. The question, then, becomes that of the internal preparation of ground which lets the forces of external domination prevail, and of the particular social structures and economic processes which emerge to maintain poverty and inequality. The study has given as much attention to the actual operations and patterns of activity in the city as to its structures and institutions.

Like any other social phenomenon, cities are worthy of abstract theorizing to illuminate their abiding characteristics. But they are also places where decisions are made and actions are taken daily, regardless of the state of theory. Cumulatively, these actions give rise to conceptual stances and policy outlooks which also acquire the status of a theory of a kind. Often the two theoretical streams do not blend well. One is a highbrow attempt to explain the basis of urban life, while the other has the practical objective of solving immediate problems. This study has steered a middle path. Its analysis is guided by theoretical propositions, but it has not shied from examining the urgent practical issues. A somewhat similar approach has been followed in articulating conclusions. They consider theories but do not withhold judgements and opinions on appropriate policies for city development. Each preceding chapter concludes with a résumé of main findings. In the following sections, significant conclusions will be recapitulated, and their respective theoretical and practical implications will be commented upon.

Development Without Social Progress

There is an alarmist strain in the literature concerned with Third World cities. These cities are portrayed as expanding without undergoing development and are presented as victims of public indifference and private inaction. Lahore's example contradicts both these assertions. Over a 15 year period (1964-1979) the city has registered a doubling of household incomes which is almost twice the rate of per capita income increase for the country as a whole. Some 90 percent (about 800) of registered factories in Lahore have been established since Independence, though, admittedly, 87 percent of those are small (less than 10 workers). New goods and services have come into common use. Out of 22 mandis in Lahore, 11 have been founded since 1947.

There is almost no contemporary, internationally favoured idea, proposal, or programme which has not found its way into Lahore. Sites and services, the current World Bank panacea for squatter settlement, have been provided, with varying degrees of enthusiasm, for a long time; acquisition prices for urban land were fixed in 1973; rent control has been in operation since World War II; banks, insurance companies, schools, and large industries have been nationalized.

This evidence should dispel the assumption that the city has not developed. The city has undergone technological, institutional and social transformation, not mere multiplication of old structures under population pressure. Yet, in spite of this, the city shows little progress using such criteria as noticeable reduction of poverty, improvement of quality of life for all people, meeting of basic needs, or establishment of smoothly functioning administrative and social systems. It appears that the so-called remedies of Third World urban problems are exacerbating their maladies. But the example of Lahore invalidates the notion that Third World cities are passively witnessing their own race to disaster. One should look at the origins and biases of the remedies to understand the reasons for this paradox.

Prepackaged Institutions and Policies

In practice, the development process has come to be a matter of implementing a set of prepackaged policies and programmes. Ideologies of the Left and the Right give rise to different packages, respectively reflecting Russian, Chinese, American or Swedish models, but each one has a fairly standardized set of proposals. The United Nations and the World Bank also create their own packages of policies and programmes, which sweep through the Third World, propelled by financial aid and technical assistance. Thus, in contemporary times, the Third World has a wide choice of ready-made policies to match with an individual country's ideological preferences, but the cost of this choice is token service to local conditions and disregard of indigenous institutions. The ineffectiveness of one set of policies does not lead to a search for causes or to attuning to local situations. Instead, other readily available packages are pressed into action, thereby maintaining a momentum without any triggering of the process of social learning [2].

Pakistan has undergone four ideological-political swings (from parliamentary democracy to martial law, populist socialism, and Islamic state), but functionally and operationally it manifests remarkable consistency and continuity. Each political shift brought new faces to the fore, but they came from the same class through remarkably similar routes. In Lahore, a new policy or ideological thrust has always meant the formation of another set of directorates, corporations and agencies which in turn provided more jobs, status, and authority to one or other of the middle- and upper-class segments. The civil servants, army officers, business executives, professionals, and contractors have remained the primary beneficiaries as one imitative institution after another has swept through Lahore. When banks and industries are nationalized, their efficiency does not improve, but job opportunities for the middle class expand; if Islamic courts are established, they may not ensure fairness and speedy justice, but they certainly enhance the entitlements of lawyers of appropriate persuasions and religious scholars for high paying jobs [3]. This focusing on structures and organizations instead of functions and operations has led to the formation of "hollow institutions," i.e., the creation of borrowed institutional forms without regard to their context, meaning, or function. An example from housing and physical planning will further illustrate this point.

One of the first public initiatives in the field of housing and physical planning was to establish the Building Research Institute and to form the Housing Agency which later was transformed into the Provincial Department of Housing and Town Planning. To date, however, there is not one visible construction technique or product that can be credited to almost 25 years of building research. Similarly, the Department of Town Planning quickly became a land subdividing agency to produce lucrative house lots and let out construction contracts. It produced master plans for various cities, but this function was so unimportant that most of these plans remain unapproved and unread. This emphasis on forms rather than functions has been greatly facilitated by the present international order where aid and advice are the instruments of ideological war.

The Preponderance of the State

The state has emerged as the dominant and pervasive social institution in many Third World countries. This is undoubtedly the case in Pakistan, where the process of development has strengthened the state apparatus, to the detriment of the general polity and local communities. The government regulates trade, distributes foreign aid, seeks external advice, contracts debts, decides developmental priorities, and sponsors industrial development, among many other activities. These economic powers, combined with conventional political and administrative authority, have given state functionaries almost a monopoly in decision-making. The dominance of the state in the national institutional framework has inhibited the development of political organizations and has precluded the evolution of suitable social mechanisms for registering the popular will, providing feedback on governmental policies, and maintaining the public accountability of officials. These features have created a self-serving state apparatus and have fostered a mode of decision-making based on the interests and whims of the officers' class. The government operates almost as a sectional interest promoting the well-being of the modern middle and upper classes.

The dominance of the state among social institutions and the guidance of state policies by the interests and values of the modern middle and upper classes have profoundly affected the structure of social entitlements. Affluence has largely come to be a function of access to the powers of the state. Public offices, contracts, licences, permits, or quotas have become the routes for economic success. As cities are the locales where such privileges are concentrated, so they have become foci of contemporary development. Undoubtedly, the pattern of Lahore's development can be largely attributed to the opportunities afforded by easy access to the public authorities. Even the economic contrasts and social contradictions emerging with development are explicable by the extent to which different social segments can mobilize public powers for their respective benefits.

Although the state has become the preponderant institution, it is generally ineffective and frequently indistinguishable from the interest groups controlling it. The example of Lahore seems to show that public decisions are largely unresponsive to the needs of the common weal, policies are seldom guided by understanding of objective reality, and governmental operations are frequently ritualistic exercises in enforcing the whims of decision makers. How else can we explain the banning of tongas, although they carry almost 100,000 rides a day, or police raids to shift buffalos from the city, although these herds provide 45 percent of the city's milk supply [4], or attempts to beautify the city with fountains

and obelisks, although 10 to 15 percent of the population lack
even latrines? Such policies indicate the extent to which the
values, interests, and perceptions of state functionaries are out
of tune with local realities. What may also be noteworthy is that
such programmes seldom work. Buffalos have remained in the city,
the number of tongas continues to increase despite raids, and campaigns of beautification last barely a week [5]. There is yet
another side to such irrelevant measures, as each turns into a
source of bribes, wheeling and dealing, and unquestioned authority
for public officials.

Corruption has become central to the operations of the
government as well as of the market. The study of Lahore reveals
that corruption constitutes an economic sector and a patterned
social practice. It cannot be treated as an exceptional situation
as its absence from the literature of development seems to
suggest. Corruption is largely a mode of encashing public or private authority. As the state has assumed a preponderant role in
Third World countries, corruption has come to constitute a
parallel track for public transactions wherein governmental powers
become a commodity to be traded. Obviously the primary beneficiaries of this trade are the rulers, the administrators and the
influentials who gain at the cost of public interest and common
good (leaving aside the regressive influence of its financial
burden). Corruption exacerbates the unresponsiveness of the state
and makes it all the more ineffective. In Lahore, almost every
public programme, law, or regulation constitutes ground for
influence-peddling, nepotism, and kickbacks. Thus, public objectives turn into cynical clichés, and programmes become a hunting
ground for enterprising officials and their business cohorts.
Development has expanded the scope of corruption through increased
public investments and controls, particularly as these activities
are undertaken without corresponding mechanisms for accountability
and feedback. The concentration of authority in the hands of state
functionaries has reinforced their inclination to serve their own
interests with impunity, and corruption is the most vivid expression of this tendency.

State agencies are also the channels for foreign aid and advice, which relieve a government from the discipline of raising
resources internally and thus makes it oblivious to countervailing
political forces. As well as fuelling corruption, foreign aid also
tilts the balance of power in favour of the central government and
against cities and provinces. Local communities cease to feel
responsible for their own needs. In Lahore, even the decisions
about water rates have come to be made in Islamabad and Washington. United Nations missions are now needed to inform a city that
it lacks an efficient bus service or that sewage should not be
dumped untreated. It is not that these matters cannot be handled
locally; UN involvement ensures trips abroad for executives and
managers, and, therefore, why not seek its advice! These considerations guide decision-making. Local autonomy and self-
reliance are the first victims of aid dependency, and the state

becomes the crucial link in a chain that shackles a Lahori household to Washington.

The City, the State, and the Market

A city is a piece of the national fabric, and its economic,
social, and political structures are components of broader institutions. Yet a city is distinguishable from the rest of a society
in a number of ways. It represents in accentuated forms the
characteristics and contradictions of the society at large. The
concentration of large numbers of people and activities in relatively limited space precipitates many technological and
behavioural thresholds that make cities a distinct genus of
societal species. To take the more obvious examples, water supply,
waste disposal, streets, schools, traffic regulations, or police
and fire protection are facilities and services which either would
not be needed or could be privately provided in the countryside,
but which must be supplied collectively in cities.

The necessity for collective provision makes good government
a prerequisite for an efficient and satisfying city. When, as in
many countries of the Third World, the state becomes preponderant,
then obviously cities become all the more dependent on a fair and
effective system of government. Ineffective and corrupt state
apparatus bears considerable responsibility for the misdevelopment
of Third World cities.

Paradoxically, the increasing role of the government in
Lahore also stimulates the expansion of the market economy. This
situation arises from a complex interplay of the two institutions.
First, the government in fact operates as a sectional interest of
the modern middle and upper classes, thereby leaving the vast
majority of the local population to the mercy of the market, both
for their livelihoods and for their needs. Inevitably, the homeless build Katchi Abadis and the unemployed turn to hawking and
petty trade. This is, of course, the response of only one segment:
the illiterate trader, the propertied craftsman, and other members
of the traditional middle strata must also rely on the market.
Second, the government's control of the commanding heights of
local economy stimulates consumption and thereby triggers expansion of milk stores, grain mandis or craftshops which operate in
the bazaar mode of the market. Third, corruption introduces a
layer of market process in governmental decision-making. The
interpenetration of market and public activities along these lines
detracts from the effectiveness of both: ad hocism and authori-
tarianism characterize public decisions and inconsistency and
power play become the rules of the market. The overall effect of
these processes is to make life routines, such as taking a bus,
sending children to school, or buying daily necessities, into
missions requiring investment of time, energy and influence. Particular and personalized arrangements must be struck for activities which, in a city, should be possible as impersonal routines.

Neither the government nor the market can be relied upon consistently to deliver expected services and products. Even the rich
and the influential are not immune to these social costs.

The Vitality of the Vernacular

Duality has come to be widely recognized as a feature of
Third World cities. One does not need much theoretical illumination to observe contrasts such as squatters' shacks alongside
bungalow estates, or hawkers lounging in the shadow of an air-conditioned shopping centre. These are the manifestations of the two
divergent modes of living; yet there is more to it than meets the
eye. Such contrasts should not be taken merely as the symptoms of
the coexistence of two separate life-styles. The two are intertwined and are the two sides of the same coin. Together they
represent an evolving balance among social classes as well as
modes of operation.

This study reveals that indigenous modes of operation and
traditional social organizations have proven to be both functional
and adaptable to contemporary demands. The traditional ways,
though harking back to earlier times, have evolved in conjunction
with the society in general through various colonial and
post-colonial phases. For example, the bazaar sector is revealed
as both vigorous and evolving and seems to have contributed substantially to post-Independence economic development. It has
remained the main supplier of daily needs, despite quantitative
increase in demand and qualitative change in preferences. The
small workshops and the backyard manufacturing establishments of
Lahore have been responsive to emerging consumer demands and are
cannily aware of unmet needs. No matter what happens to be on the
restricted imports list, these local producers attempt to fill the
gap, manufacturing goods of diversity and technical complexity,
from washing machines to pharmaceuticals. The bazaar merchants
have been equally enterprising. For most of the new goods that
have come into use recently (e.g., sanitary fittings, foam
beddings), mandis organized in the conventional ways have come
into being. This is vivid evidence of the vitality and entrepreneurship of the bazaar mode of operation.

We have discovered that the vitality of the bazaar mode
arises from its adaptability to new technology and practices. It
has remained functional by continually going through evolutionary
changes. The distinguishing features of the bazaar mode have been
discussed at length in earlier chapters. Here it is enough to
reiterate that it is a mode of operation which is labour-intensive
and risk-sharing (through subdivision of tasks and personalized
relations) and which has assimilated advantageous new practices
and procedures (e.g., the use of the telephone, intricacies of
import and foreign exchange regulations). However, it must also be
noted that the bazaar mode has its shortcomings. It is permeated
with practices that are frowned upon by contemporary ideals: child

labour, piece work, job insecurity, and poor working conditions.
Despite these limitations (which incidentally also characterize
firm sector and government operations) the bazaar mode is neither
feudal in organization nor informal in operations. The somewhat
romantic preoccupation among observers of Third World cities with
hawkers and peddlers has not led to full appreciation of the
structural evolution of the bazaar sector. Observers continue to
look upon it as a pre-capitalist mode which is bound to dissolve
in the face of modern economic thrusts, but Lahore's example
suggests that the bazaar mode represents an indigenous capitalist
form which has been evolving in the cities of the subcontinent and
which can live up to new challenges.

Similar resilience and evolutionary adaptability in indigenous forms are evident in the physical city over the last half century. The New Indigenous Community (NIC) has evolved as an urban
form combining the compactness and social relevance of traditional
residential designs with modern requirements for sanitation and
vehicular access. Initially, it was the preferred residential area
for local professionals and executives, but Independence brought
its social standing down a few notches, as the design doctrines of
the Western city became the unquestioned official policies and
bungalow estates became the mark of good living. The NIC has now
become the residential mode of junior officials, salaried workers,
and bazaar merchants.

The foregoing account should dispel any notion of the dis-
solvability of indigenous institutions and practices. There are
discernible evolutionary trends in the indigenous modes of economic and physical development which enable them to meet the
challenges of growth. After all they are based on the proper
labour-intensive factor mix in economic terms and are in con-
gruence with local social organization. Yet the official indifference (even lack of understanding) to evolving indigenous practices
stands in sharp contrast to their pervasiveness and persistence.
This contrast itself indicates the extent to which the sectional
interests of state functionaries and ruling classes make them
oblivious to the objective reality around them and enhance their
willing subservience to external influence.

Social progress in the Third World will be attained through
self-reliance and the encouragement of indigenous experiments.
Such an approach does not exclude foreign ideas and technology but
insists on adopting and assimilating them within a progressive,
indigenous framework.

INTERNAL DYNAMICS

A fairly accurate generalized picture of the structural
features of Third World cities can be gleaned from the writings of
McGee, Abu-Lughod, or Santos [6]. There is broad consensus that
these cities are differentiated into two or more sectors, each
representing a distinct mode of operation and performing a

specific role in the urban system. Contemporary urban literature debates with fervor whether this differentiation indicates the existence of duality, is a manifestation of the over-arching neo-colonial umbrella, or is a symptom of peripheral capitalism characteristic of Third World countries but there is seldom any question about the fissured nature of the city per se. The present study also made its starting point the picture of the city structure outlined above.

Lahore has been found to be a city characterized by two sectors (three, if corruption is also treated as a separate category), namely, firm and bazaar. The study has further refined the structural model by pointing out that sectors are internally stratified into layers of uniform economic roles and social rewards. Furthermore, it has been suggested that corresponding layers of various sectors are laterally linked to constitute operational (distributional) circuits which function as socially differentiated markets and provide a mechanism to insulate the rich from the poor and the influential from the ordinary people. Thus the picture of the urban structure has been further filled in with details about the internal organization of sectors. Important though these findings are, the main thrust of this study has been in uncovering the process, particularly the internal one, which sustains unequal development and retards social progress. The two key elements in this process are discussed in the following sections.

Segmentalization

Just as a diamond splinters into fragments with a cutter's blow, Lahore's economy and social structure seem to fracture into enclaves, sectors, or segments on the injection of developmental thrusts. These segments are subsystems of uniform social standing and similar economic roles. They are differentiated by multiple criteria, such as social class, education, life-style, and access to the state's authority.

The process of segmentalization proceeds through two phases: (1) unhinging of established economic interdependencies, and erosion of conventional privileges and obligations; (2) reorganization of splintered groups into economic enclaves and social segments on the basis of mutuality of interests, shared life-styles, and modes of operation. It is a simultaneous process of detribalization of the old order and retribalization along lines of mutual support, power exchange and social class. The emerging social units (segments or enclaves) continue to be groups, with one marked difference from the traditional order in that they are relatively free from interlocking obligations and privileges with other groups. It may be noted that the process of segmentalization does not result in the individualization and impersonalization of social organizations so often associated with urbanism. In fact, Lahore has progressively become a city which operates on the basis

of personalized cliques, with face-to-face dealings and exchanges of power and influence. "Who knows whom" is the operational order of almost all transactions, public or private, and social segments and economic enclaves channel personalized dealings and provide a framework for mutual help.

Differentiation and fractionation appear to be the fundamental features of the internal dynamics of development. They create economic enclaves and social preserves for the purpose of distributing the benefits of development, they legitimize the varying entitlements of different groups, and sustain the inequalities. The contemporary form of development (i.e., with emphasis on bureaucratic institutions, corporate enterprises, and borrowed technology) confers exceptional premiums on the one hand on the educated, regardless of their output, and on the other the capitalists, wheeler-dealers, and dispensers of the state authority. The prerequisites to benefit from development become the basis for fractionation. Social segments arising from development are differentiated by mode of operation (firm versus bazaar), by life-style (modern versus traditional), by social class (upper versus lower), and by access to state authority (influentials versus ordinary citizens). Various permutations of these criteria produce a kaleidoscopic variety of social units. As an illustration, it may be pointed out that the prosperous bazaar merchants are a social segment clearly distinguished from equally affluent officers or lawyers by different life-styles and social standings. The phenomenon of the coexistence of "numerous cities in one" is essentially the physical manifestation of the process of segmentalization. By filtering out a group and reconstituting it into a relatively uniform enclave practising a distinct life-style, the process of segmentalization contributes to the contrasts so evident in Third World cities. It is from the splintering and fractionation of the social organization as much as from the grafting of an imported way of life that the multiplicity of urban forms in Third World cities arises.

Streaming and Tracking of Development

As Lahore's example points out, Third World cities have not lagged in developmental initiatives and have been undergoing noticeable changes. Economic growth may not have been spectacular, but it has averaged a rate twice or thrice that of population growth. Development of public facilities and services would have similarly outpaced the expansion of the city. The question, then, is why this development has not raised the quality of life. Once again, we probed the internal dynamics and found a pervasive process of streaming and tracking of the benefits of development for specific social segments. This process is an integral part of the mechanism whereby developmental benefits are directed towards the influential and resourceful segments of local population by design as well as through operational procedures. The base for the unfolding of this process is laid by the segmentalization trends, and the two fit together very well.

When development is conceived in a particular mode which conforms to the resources, preferences, and needs of specific social segments, the ground is laid for its benefits to be appropriated by the relevant group. For example, if city planning means establishing a directorate, drafting zoning bylaws, appointing enforcement officers, and inviting foreign consultants, then the first impact of such a development project will be in increasing jobs and the authority of city planners and managers. What benefits low-income households seeking affordable accommodation derive from such an exercise is hard to conceive. The point is that implicit in a development programme or project are prerequisites for benefitting from it, and they constitute the tracks along which the outcome will be delivered. This is an example of the propensity for streaming and tracking implicit in the design of development. More systematic bases for sectionalizing the benefits of development are laid in operations and administration.

The process of streaming and tracking of public facilities and services is rooted, on the one hand, in the system of quotas, permits, and rules of eligibility, and, on the other, in corruption, power exchange, and self-serving administrative procedure. For example, in Lahore, schools were nationalized to ensure equal quality of education for all, but, soon after, English-medium and model schools proliferated, often with public subsidies, ostensibly for the talented, but effectively streaming the children of the privileged to better schools. Similar effects result from a city-wide sewage development project, financed from foreign loans, whose first priority is to serve the new suburbs being developed by the local authority. By the time the foreign loan is expended, only the areas of executives' residences will have been serviced with sewers. Another example is the case of telephones. The number of telephone lines available in Lahore has increased by almost 700 percent since the day of Independence. As more telephones became available, even second- or third-tier civil servants became eligible for telephones at home; yet the number of operative public telephones has remained the same over a 30-year period. These are examples of the streaming and tracking process, and they illustrate the mechanism by which basic needs remain unattended while so-called development proceeds impressively. This process largely lays the ground for uneven development and promotes private opulance amidst communal squalor.

INFERENTIAL PROPOSITIONS

This study began with a set of propositions (Chapter 2) deduced from the current literature. These propositions were meant to provide an analytical framework for the study, but were not set forth as formal hypotheses which could have constrained the exploration of the topic. Generally, the propositions served well

in disciplining and guiding our probe. Now, before concluding this
study, another set of propositions will be formulated to pull
together themes and notions emerging from the empirical analysis.
They are offered as much to round off our findings as to point out
areas for the attention of policy makers and researchers.
Following is a summary of the inferred propositions.

(1) Development that aims at raising the quality of life for all
and at meeting essential human needs requires self-reliance,
inventiveness, and creative adaptation of technology and ideas
from abroad. It must evolve from indigenous institutions and
accord with local conditions. There is seldom a universal solution
to problems that appear to be similar. The same problem can arise
from different combinations of factors in various situations and
it requires situationally specific solutions within the framework
of universal objectives.

(2) Development as presently practised stimulates processes of
internal differentiation in a city, and sorts its population into
enclaves and preserves of divergent entitlements. The sectional-
ization of local polity and economy lays the ground for unequal
development and imbalanced growth.

(3) After Independence, the state has emerged as the preeminent
social institution. It commands most of the resources and has
amassed authority. As the state becomes an autonomous institution,
its functionaries are less and less constrained by political and
social checks and are increasingly immune from accountability.
This concentration of authority without institutionalized responsiveness to the people breeds corruption.

(4) Foreign aid releases a state from the restraints associated
with raising resources locally. Being a distributor of foreign
aid, the central government becomes stronger at the cost of provincial and local authorities. Cities become vassals of the state,
and their problems become items on a national agenda awaiting
their turn for attention.

(5) The state and the firm sector have steadily merged. Overall,
the affluence and success of an individual (or group) have come to
be a function of his capacity to mobilize the state's powers.
Bankers, corporate managers, and industrialists depend on permits,
quotas, and subsidies for their success, and rulers and administrators make use of their authority to enjoy a life of opulence.
In one way or another, the state confers the affluence. These outcomes suggest that theoretical debates about private versus public
modes of economic development are irrelevant under present operational arrangements. Not only a mode of development is significant, but the method of organization in a given mode must also be
considered in determining its relevance.

(6) Dependency is externally induced, but a receptive ground for
its infiltration is internally laid. Through the process of
differential development, social enclave and economic preserves
emerge whose entitlements and welfare are linked with the flow of
external aid and ideas. They constitute the internal base for

external dependency.
(7) How does a city operate as a community? How is it structured?
What ˋoperational arrangements, acknowledged or illicit, emerge
with growth and change? These questions point towards the functioning of the city, and they should guide urban planning.
Analytical emphasis should be on processes, not formal structures;
on operations, not policies alone. (Lahore at least is littered
with the debris of policies and institutions, which seemed beneficial but which produced the opposite results.)
(8) A common base of facilities, services, and institutions is a
prerequisite for the efficient and equitable functioning of a
city. The unequal development of various parts of a city precludes
the formation of such a common base and exacts pervasive social
costs from which even the ruling elite cannot escape, e.g., piled
garbage, flooded streets, mismanaged schools, undisciplined
traffic.
(9) Urban land is a public resource but is used to confer windfall gains on the privileged with an air of legitimacy. City
planning largely serves as the process of delivering expensive
lots to the well-connected at subsidized prices. Many problems of
the physical layout of a city arise from the use of land as a
speculative commodity.

The foregoing propositions outline the present reality of a Third
World city yet it is possible to leap from this theory to the
suggestion of some feasible lines of urban development.

                              THE ATTAINABLE CITY

     A city's fate is tied to the fortunes of its society. It may
fare better than the nation, but it cannot long remain an island
of prosperity in a sea of poverty. Ultimately, it is the development of a society that ensures a decent quality of life for its
cities. The Third World is not likely to be an exception to this
rule, no matter how much optimism the international aid agencies
breathe into their latest urban programmes. Do Third World cities,
then, have to wait passively for the general progress of their
respective societies? Cannot there be planning approaches that
would help meet the basic needs of these cities in the immediate
future? These questions reflect the impatience of policy makers
with sweeping theories, and call for the necessary leap from
theory to action.
     Undoubtedly, the relationship between a city and a society is
neither a one-way street nor a mechanical following of a pre-
determined path. Cities reflect national conditions, but they also
harbour forces of change which transform a society. Thus, appropriate policies and programmes to raise the quality of life in
cities would reinforce and accelerate processes of national
development. Therefore, it seems logical to respond to the questions articulated above by suggesting that self-contained pro-

grammes to improve living conditions in Third World cities are both conceivable and necessary. Of course, such objectives assume a prior national commitment to economic progress and social justice. Our judgements about a feasible approach to the development of Third World cities are derived from the case study of Lahore, and thus the proposals are primarily applicable to that city.

If a decent quality of life is equated with individual homes and private facilities, then there is no hope for a city which has a backlog of 300,000 houses and whose housing supply is falling short by 15–20,000 dwellings per year, and in which about 40 percent of the population lives without piped water and 10–15 percent does not have access even to a shared latrine. If modern middle-class standards were norms of livability, the city might easily consume the total national budget for decades. And financial resources are only one of the constraints; other obvious ones are the paucity of developable land, exhaustability of water sources, and limitations of environmental capacities. Yet all these constraints exist for every city. Even New York and Tokyo are plagued by both financial and physical limitations. What seem to be the preponderant constraints in a city like Lahore are imitative institutions, irrelevant policies, corrupt organizations, and ineffective administration. These have partially stifled human ingenuity and obstructed mobilization of people's energies which would have helped overcome financial and physical limitations.

Lahore has been held back by irrelevant institutions and corruptible organizations. Resources that have promoted fractured development could have, if effectively deployed, made Lahore a city where an overwhelming majority would have enjoyed convenient, healthful and satisfying living. Even with existing resources such a city is attainable but only if there is public commitment to pursue the common good. To meet the basic needs of a city, the first step is institutional reorganization.

Institutional Reorganization and Administrative Reforms

The example of Lahore suggests that the top priority in attempting to ensure a minimum quality of life to all in a city should be given to streamlining decision-making processes and to reforming administrative operations, and reducing corruption, particularly in the public realm. It is almost a revolutionary task, easier said than done. The lines along which institutional reorganization should proceed are an issue worthy of a separate book, but indisputably among the required steps would be restitution of people's fundamental rights, political and social checks and balances, and public visibility and accountability by decision-makers – in sum, a mechanism which makes public agencies responsive to public needs and removes authoritarian insularity of functionaries.

The urgency of institutional reform is borne out by developmental experiences. It is pointless to develop elaborate housing standards and regulations if only 12 percent of houses are built with official permission. What is the relevance of the UN-sponsored fad for computerization of land records when every step of the land development process is tailor-made for graft. In the same vein, can there be an adequate public transport as long as managers cannibalize buses for spares and drivers pocket fares? These examples illustrate the point that, without an efficient and dependable operational system, grandiose programmes and progressive policies have little effect.

The objective of institutional reorganization should be the creation of a city where basic facilities and services are available to all without let or favour. A citizen should be able to get a reply to his letter or be able to pay a tax bill without having to bribe; to register a complaint with some assurance of fair response; and to expect to be treated as a human being in accordance with the rule of law, not the caprice of officials. Routines of life should not become missions requiring undue investment of time and energy, when they could be accomplished in standardized, fair, and impersonal ways. These are the preconditions for ensuring effective and equitable urban development. Creation of such conditions should be the first step in dealing with the urban crisis of the Third World.

Collectivization of Basic Services

Traditionally, the Third World's social structures are communal and familistic in nature. Families and clans live in close proximity and share latrines, water wells, or guest quarters. A house itself is often a cluster of rooms or huts around a common compound. While shared living arrangements continue to be the way of life for the majority, contemporary development has been officially defined as individualizing and privatizing basic facilities and services.

On privatized bases, latrines, water taps, baths, garbage collection, and even electricity are unlikely to be available to a substantial majority in the foreseeable future. Yet, with some ingenuity and by making imaginative use of traditions, such services can be extended on shared or joint ownership bases to almost everybody. As an illustration of this point, it may be suggested that two latrines (for men and women separately), a water stand-pipe, and a common shed may be provided to a cluster of say three to four houses. On a joint ownership basis with a policy of recovering the cost, such arrangements to provide facilities on low cost (per capita) shared bases will help stretch the existing resources so that an overwhelming majority may be ensured of a minimum quality of life [7]. Furthermore, through personal ownership, the maintenance and upkeep of facilities could be ensured and the neglect that often characterizes communal taps or latrines could be avoided. For middle- and upper-class households, such

facilities might be made individually available, but at prices
that recover the cost of private consumption. The principle of
clustering and collectivizing basic services need not be limited
to water taps and latrines. It could be extended to telephones,
television, refrigerated storage, and other requirements of modern
city life in accordance with emerging preferences.

The principle of shared facilities and services and of joint
ownership ensures efficient use of resources, but it also serves
other purposes. First, it illustrates the feasibility of anchoring
development in traditions and using historical social practices
for modern ends. Second, it makes a concrete suggestion about
delivering basic services in a form that inhibits their streaming
and tracking for influential groups, thus preventing the presently
pervasive process of the "floating-up" of benefits of public
investments. By reducing appropriability of social goods for individual use, propensity towards corruption would also be curbed and
the tendency towards segmentalization restrained.

Indigenizing City Planning

One consistent observation emerging from every aspect of the
case study is that often the so-called solutions exacerbate the
problems of the city. Such outcomes from policies and programmes
based on borrowed perceptions and on ruling class interests should
not surprise. Neglect of traditions and indifference to local conditions underlie the contemporary institutionalized modes of
apprehending and solving urban problems. The city planning process
is a case in point. Despite intellectual protestations, city
planning in the post-colonial era has become a practice of
enforcing prepackaged precepts and faddish policy clichés. Such
predispositions have turned city planning into an instrument of
misdevelopment in the Third World.

City planning in Third World cities should rationalize,
strengthen, and build upon the developmental potential of traditions and historical practices. For example, in Lahore, the bazaar
sector has continued to be central to the economy of the city. Yet
the land use plans, housing schemes, or transportation policies
reflect little of this reality. Even problems are perceived
through the haze of such inapplicable precepts as segregation of
land uses, clustering of (similar) activities, and priority of
motorized traffic. The fact that the spatial order of Lahore consists of mixed land uses and intertwined activities has not been
registered in the city planning practice. Similarly, by focusing
on fashionable policies and by laying stress on organizational
structures (bureaus and agencies) to the neglect of operations and
outputs, city planning has become a ritualistic process of rationalizing the whims and self-interests of the decision makers. A
formal process of solving the city's problems is necessary, but it
should be based on objective understanding of the local situation.
To illustrate how indigenous and specific such a process should

be, we will describe a few key factors around which effective, pragmatic, and economical programmes can be devised.

Transportation

For a Third World city like Lahore, transportation needs can be met as much by extending road networks and building mass-transit facilities as by reducing travel demand. If the services rendered by schools, dispensaries, etc., could be standardized and their locational distribution rationalized, if operations of public agencies could be streamlined and normal transactions impersonalized, if public offices could be concentrated at a few accessible points, travel demand in Lahore would probably decrease by 10 to 20 percent. These are all measures requiring administrative and locational rationalization and efficient use of present resources. From the transportation point of view, the city could be a safe and convenient place within a few years, if public attention is focused on factors that really count in Lahore instead of on grandiose capital works.

House Design and Community Layout

The official city planning doctrine has been steeped in the Western suburban model of detached bungalows, standardized blocks of similarly sized lots, and segregated land uses. Such layouts and house designs have turned Lahore into a sprawled city which promises only to spread out further as the proposals for building satellite new towns materialize. In this brief account of official city planning practice, the Howard's garden-city idea is fully evident. Unofficially, however, in the evolved residential form of the New Indigenous Community, traditional house designs and community layouts have been upgraded to be more commodious and readily accessible without sacrificing compactness and proximity of activities and social groups. Nevertheless, despite its functional appropriateness and economic suitability, the New Indigenous Community idiom has not found room in official planning practice. Not a single planned scheme has been designed to offer attached houses and compact layouts according to the historical urban forms. Yet people on their own have built large expanses of the city in such an idiom. These are the incongruities that borrowed ideas promote. Indigenous solutions to housing problems remain unacknowledged, while precious resources are squandered on imitative development.

The preceding brief accounts show possibilities that wait to be grasped to make Lahore a city where decent shelter, assured access to basic facilities, convenience, healthful living arrangements, and fairness could rule. It may not be a city of skyscrapers and exciting designs, but it could be a place where the whole population could have a basic minimum quality of life. This is not a Utopia, but it is a dream whose realization depends on a genuine national commitment to progress, development and equality.

As long as the national commitment remains unfulfilled, Lahore will remain an unrealized city.

NOTES

1. HABITAT, United Nations Conference on Human Settlements, "Declaration of Principles," in Third World Urbanization, ed. Janet Abu-Lughod and Richard Hay Jr. (Chicago: Maaroufa Press, 1977), p. 342.

2. Social learning is a concept used by policy researchers to describe the capability of an organization (or community) to absorb its experiences and to evolve new paradigms by observing effects of previous actions. For extended description of the concept see J. Friedmann and G. Abony, "Social Learning: A Model for Policy Research," Environment and Planning 8 (1976): 927-940.

3. Entitlement is a concept referring to a person's claim on incomes, outputs and rights arising from his "legitimate" possession and use of economic resources in a society. It is a socially conferred claim for income arising from market exchange, appointment and status. Sen defines entitlement as "A person's ability to command food - indeed to command any commodity he wishes to acquire or retain - depends on the entitlement relations that govern possession and use in that society. It depends on what he owns, what exchange possibilities are offered to him." Amartya Sen, Poverty and Famines (Oxford: Clarenden Press, 1981), pp. 154-155.

4. Muhammad A. Anjum, "A Note on Economic Analysis of Consumer Demand for Raw and Processed Fluid Milk in Lahore," Pakistan Development Review 12 (1978): 501.

5. By citing these examples of inappropriate policies, we do not mean to imply that buffalos in the city are not nuisances or that tongas pose no traffic obstacle. The point is that these problems are being dealt with in a whimsical and authoritarian way which fails anyway. They must be addressed with thorough and objective analyses of issues involved and by involving citizens in decision-making.

6. T. G. McGee, "Conservation and Dissolution in the Third World City: The Shanty Town as an element of Conservation," Development and Change 10 (Jan 79): 1-22; Janet Abu-Lughod, Rabat (Princeton: Princeton University Press, 1981); Milton Santos, Shared Space (London: Methuen, 1979).

7. Almost every poor country which in recent times has registered notable improvement in housing conditions has resorted to building shared facilities and services. This policy has been pursued on the one hand by socialist Russia and China and by market-oriented South Korea on the other. For the example of Seoul, South Korea, see Richard L. Meier, Urban Futures Observed in The Asian Third World (New York: Pergamon Press, 1980), p. 38.

BIBLIOGRAPHY

Abu-Lughod, Janet. "Developments in North African Urbanism: The Process of Decolonization." In Urbanization and Counterurbanization, editor Brian Berry, pp. 191-211. Beverly Hills: Sage Publications, 1976.

Abu-Lughod, Janet, and Richard Hay, Jr. (editors). Third World Urbanization. Chicago: Maaroufa Press, 1977.

Abu-Lughod, Janet L. Rabat. Princeton: Princeton University Press, 1980.

Abu-Lughod, Janet. "Contemporary Relevance of Islamic Urban Principles." Ekistics 47 (1980):6-10.

Afzal, Mohammad. The Population of Pakistan. CICRED series. Islamabad: Institute of Development Economics, 1974.

Ahmad, Saghir. "Peasant Classes in Pakistan." In Imperialism and Revolution in South Asia, editors Kathleen Gough and Hari P. Sharma, pp. 203-22. New York: Monthly Review Press, 1973.

Alavi, Hamza. "The State in Post-Colonial Societies: Pakistan and Bangladesh." In Imperialism and Revolution in South Asia, editors Kathleen Gough and Hari P. Sharma, pp. 145-173. New York: Monthly Review Press, 1973.

Amjad, Rashid. Industrial Concentration and Economic Power in Pakistan. Lahore: South Asian Institute, University of the Punjab, 1974.

Anjum, Muhammad. "A Note on Economic Analysis of Consumer Demand for Raw and Processed Fluid Milk in Lahore." The Pakistan Development Review 12 (1978):495-512.

Ansari, Yousaf Jamal. "Angrazi Dor Ki Chund Tameerat." (Some British Monuments) NaQoosh, Special Issue on Lahore, 1962, pp. 660-74.

Ball, Michael. "A Critique of Urban Economics." International Journal of Urban and Regional Research 13 (1977):309-32.

Baqar, Mohammad. "Lahore." NaQoosh, February 1962, pp. 24-33.

Bendavid, Avrom. Regional Economic Analysis for Practitioners. New York: Praeger, 1974.

Bergan, A. "Personal Income Distribution and Personal Savings in Pakistan, 1963-64." The Pakistan Development Review (1967):160-212.

Berry, Brian J. L. "Hierarchical Diffusion: The Basis of Developmental Filtering and Spread in a System of Growth Centers." In Growth Centers in Regional Economic Development, editor Niles Hanson, pp. 108-38. New York: The Free Press, 1972.

Berry, Brian. The Human Consequences of Urbanization. New York: St. Martin's Press, 1973.

Blau, Peter M. "Introduction: Parallels and Contrasts in Structural Inquiries." In Approaches to the Study of Social Structure, editor Peter M. Blau, pp. 1-20. London: The Free Press, 1975.

Breese, Gerald. Urbanization in Newly Developing Countries. Englewood Cliffs: Prentice-Hall, 1966.

Broadbent, T. A. Planning and Profit in the Urban Economy. London: Methuen, 1977.

Brookfield, Harold. Interdependent Development. London: Methuen, 1975.

Brush, John E. "The Morphology of Indian Cities." In India's Urban Future, editor Roy Turner, pp. 52-70. Berkeley: University of California Press, 1962.

Buckley, Walter. Sociology and Modern Systems Theory. Englewood Cliffs: Prentice-Hall, 1967.

Bureau of Statistics. Directory of Registered Factories in the Punjab. Lahore: Government of the Punjab, 1978.

————. Development Statistics of the Punjab. Lahore: Government of the Punjab, 1978.

Castells, Manuel. "Is there an Urban Sociology." In Urban Sociology: Critical Essays, editor C. J. Pickvance, pp. 33-59. London: Tavistock, 1976.

Chilcote, Ronald H. "Dependency: A Critical Synthesis of the Literature." In Third World Urbanization, editors Janet Abu-Lughod and Richard Hay, Jr., pp. 128-39. Chicago: Maaroufa Press, 1977.

Costello, V. F. Urbanization in the Middle East. London: Cambridge University Press, 1977.

Department of Social Work. A Study of Lahore Township Scheme Kot Lakhpat, Lahore – A Socio-Economic and Evaluative Study. Lahore: Punjab University, 1972.

Dos Santos, R. "The Structure of Dependence." American Economic Review 60 (1970): 231–37.

Eisenstadt, S. N. "Reflections on a Theory of Modernization." In Nations by Design, editor Arnold Rivkin, pp. 35–61. New York: Anchor Books, 1968.

Farooqi, Naseem Iqbal and Iqbal Alam. "Provisional Abridged Life Tables for Urban and Rural Areas in Pakistan, Based on PGS 1968 and 1971." The Pakistan Development Review 13 (1974): 335–53.

Frank, Andre Gunder. "The Development of Underdevelopment." In Dependence and Underdevelopment, editor James D. Cockcroft, pp. 3–18. New York: Anchor Books, 1972.

Friedmann, John. "Cities in Social Transformation." In Regional Development and Planning, editors John Friedmann and William Alonso, pp. 343–60. Cambridge: MIT Press, 1964.

————. "A General Theory of Polarized Development." Growth Centres in Regional Economic Development, editor Niles Hanson, pp. 82–107. New York: The Free Press, 1972.

————. Urbanization, Planning and National Development. Beverly Hills: Sage, 1973.

Friedmann, John and Flora Sullivan. "The Absorption of Labour in the Urban Economy: The Case of Developing Countries." In Regional Policy: Readings in Theory and Applications, editors John Friedmann and William Alonso, pp. 473–504. Cambridge: MIT Press, 1975.

Friedmann, John, and Robert Wulff. The Urban Transition. London: Edward Arnold, 1976.

Friedmann, John. "The Role of Cities in National Development." In Systems of Cities, editors L. S. Bourne and J. W. Simmons, pp. 70–82. New York: Oxford University Press, 1978.

Furtado, C. "Elements of a Theory of Underdevelopment – The Underdeveloped Structures." In Underdevelopment and Development, editor Henry Bernstein, pp. 33–43. Harmondsworth: Penguin Books, 1973.

Gans, Herbert J. The Urban Villagers. New York: The Free Press, 1962.

Gappert, Gary, and Harold M. Rose (editors). The Social Economy of Cities. Beverly Hills: Gage, 1975.

Garner, B. J. "Models of Urban Geography and Settlement Location." In Socio-Economic Models in Geography, editors Richard J. Chorley and Peter Haggett, pp. 303-60. London: Methuen, 1967.

Geertz, Clifford. Peddlers and Princes: Social Development and Economic Change in Two Indonesian Towns. Chicago: University of Chicago Press, 1963.

Goulding, H. R. Old Lahore, Reminiscences of a Resident, 1924. Lahore: Lahore Universal Book, 1976.

Government of Pakistan. Pakistan's Statistical Yearbook, 1977. Karachi: Statistics Division, 1979.

Government of the Punjab. Gujranwala Outline Development Plan. Gujranwala: Directorate of Physical Planning, 1972.

Government of West Pakistan, Directorate of Town Planning. Master Plan for Greater Lahore. Lahore: The Master Plan Project Office, 1964.

Guisinger, Stephen E. "Patterns of Industrial Growth in Pakistan." The Pakistan Development Review 15 (1976):8-27.

Guisinger, Stephen, and Norma L. Hicks. "Long Term Trends in Income Distribution in Pakistan." World Development 6 (1978): 1271-1280.

Guisinger, Stephen and Mohammed Irfan. "Pakistan's Informal Sector." The Journal of Developmental Studies 16 (1980): 412-26.

Gusfield, Joseph R. "Tradition and Modernity. Misplaced Polarities in the Study of Social Change." In Social Change, editors Eva Etzioni-Helevy and Amitai Etzioni, pp. 333-41. New York: Basic Books, 1973.

Hagenbuch, Walter. Social Economics. Cambridge: James Nisbet, 1958.

Haq, Mahbub ul. The Poverty Curtain. New York: Columbia University Press, 1976.

Hart, Keith. "Informal Income Opportunities and Urban Employment in Ghana." The Journal of Modern African Studies 11 (1973): 61-89.

Harvey, David. Social Justice and the City. London: Edward Arnold,

1973.

Hashmi, Waheed-ul-Hasan. "Colleges." NaQoosh, Special Issue on
    Lahore, 1962, pp. 687-714.

Hauser, Philip (editor). Urbanization in Asia and Far East.
    Geneva: UNESCO, 1957.

Heitmann, George, et al. "A Note on the Rank-Size Rule and Future
    Urban Growth Patterns in Pakistan." The Pakistan Development
    Review 16 (1977):464-69.

Helbock, Richard W. "Differential Urban Growth and Distance Con-
    siderations in Domestic Migration Flows in Pakistan." The
    Pakistan Development Review 14 (1975):53-84.

——. "Urban Population Growth in Pakistan, 1961-1972." The
    Pakistan Development Review 14 (1975):315-33.

Hodge, Gerald, and Jacques D. Paris. "Population Growth and
    Regional Development: Implications for Educational Planning."
    Demography and Educational Planning. Toronto: Ontario Insti-
    tute for Studies in Education, Monograph Series No. 7, 1969,
    pp. 249-64.

Hoover, Edgar M., and Raymond Vernon. Anatomy of a Metropolis. New
    York: Anchor Books, 1962.

Hoselitz, Bert F. "The Role of Urbanization in Economic Develop-
    ment: Some International Comparisons." In India's Urban
    Future, editor Roy Turner, pp. 157-81. Bombay: Oxford Univer-
    sity Press, 1962.

Hussain, Mazhar. Socio-Economic Survey of Lahore. Lahore: Social
    Science Research Center, 1964.

International Labour Organization (ILO). Employment, Incomes and
    Equality: A Strategy for Increasing Productive Employment in
    Kenya. Geneva: ILO, 1972.

Iqbal, Mian Muhammad. "Participation of Local Organizations in
    Planned Improvement of Katchi Abadis." In Proceedings of the
    National Seminar on Planning for Urban Development in the
    Developing Countries, With Special Reference to Pakistan,
    editor Sattar Sikander, pp. 176-85. Lahore: Department of City
    and Regional Planning, University of Engineering and Tech-
    nology, 1978.

Kamran, M. A. "The WASA Myth Shattered." Viewpoint, July 16, 1981,
    p. 13.

Khan, M. Ayub. Friends Not Masters. New York: Oxford University
    Press, 1967.

Khan, Azizur Rahman. "What Has Been Happening to Real Wages in
    Pakistan?" In Growth and Inequality in Pakistan, editors Keith
    Griffin and A. R. Khan, 224–49. London: MacMillan, 1972.

King, Anthony D. Colonial Urban Development. London: Routledge and
    Kegan Paul, 1976.

Krohn, Roger G., et al. The Other Economy. Toronto: Peter Martin
    Associates, 1977.

Krotki, Karol J. "Population Size, Growth and Age Distribution:
    Fourth Release for the 1961 Census of Pakistan." The Pakistan
    Development Review 3 (1963):279–305.

Krueckeberg, Donald A., and Arthur L. Silvers. Urban Planning
    Analysis: Methods and Models. New York: John Wiley and Sons,
    1976.

Lahore Urban Development and Traffic Study (LUDTS). Mansooba-E-
    Lahore. Preliminary Report. Lahore: Lahore Development
    Authority, 1979.

————. Final Report: Vol. I, Urban Planning. Lahore: Lahore
    Development Authority, 1981.

————. Final Report: Vol. III, Walled City. Lahore: Lahore
    Development Authority, 1981.

Lambert, Camilla, and David Wier (editors). Cities in Modern
    Britain. Glasgow: Fontana, 1975.

Latif, Syed Muhammad. Lahore: Its History, Architectural Remains
    and Antiquities. Lahore: New Imperial Press, 1892.

Lewis, Stephen R., Jr. Economic Policy and Industrial Growth in
    Pakistan. London: George Allen and Unwin, 1969.

Lipton, Michael. Why Poor People Stay Poor. London: Temple Smith,
    1977.

Little, Kenneth. West African Urbanization. Cambridge: Cambridge
    University Press, 1965.

Maddison, Angus. Class Structure and Economic Growth. London:
    George Allen and Unwin, 1971.

Mehta, Ved. "The Photographs of Chacha Ji." New Yorker 56 (1980):
    42–55.

Malik, Hafeez. "Problems of Regionalism in Pakistan." In Pakistan in Transition, editor Howard Wriggens, pp. 60-132. Islamabad: University of Islamabad Press, 1975.

Mangin, William. "Latin American Squatter Settlements: A Problem and A Solution." Latin American Research Review 2,3 (Summer 1975):65-98.

Marx, Karl and Friedrich Engles. "The Communist Manifesto." In Essential Works of Marxism, editor Arthur P. Mendel, pp. 13-44. New York: Bantam Books, 1961.

Mazmudar, Dipak. "The Urban Informal Sector." World Development 4 (1976):655-78.

McGee, T. G. The Urbanization Process in the Third World: Explorations in Search of a Theory. London: G. Bell, 1971.

————. "Catalysts or Cancers? The Role of Cities in Asian Society." In Urbanization and National Development, editors Leo Jakobsen and Ved Prakash, pp. 157-81. Beverly Hills: Sage, 1971.

McGee, T. G., and Y. M. Yeung. Hawkers in Southeast Asian Cities. Ottawa: International Development Research Center, 1977.

McGee, T. G. "Conservation and Dissolution in Third World City: the shanty town as an element of conservation." Development and Change 10 (1979):1-22.

Miner, Horace. "The Folk-Urban Continuum." In Cities and Society, editors Paul K. Hatt et al., pp. 22-34. Glencoe: The Free Press, 1957.

Moore, Wilbert T. "Modernization as Rationalization: Process and Restraint." In Essays on Economic Development and Cultural Change in Honour of Bert F. Hoselitz, editor Manning Nash. Economic Development and Cultural Change. Supplement 25 (1977): 29-42.

Morse, Richard. "Recent Research in Latin-America Urbanization." Latin American Research Review, Vol. I, pp. 35-74. Beverly Hills: Sage, 1965.

Mujahid, G. B. S. "A Note of Measurement of Poverty and Income Inequalities in Pakistan: Some Observations on Methodology." The Pakistan Development Review 17 (1978):365-77.

Musa, Hakim Mohammad. "Atbas." NaQoosh, Special Issue on Lahore, 1962, pp. 798-838.

Myrdal, Gunnar. _Asian Drama_, Vol. I, II, III. New York: Pantheon, 1968.

Naqi, Hussain. "Lahore Diary." _Viewpoint_, July 13, 1980, p. 11.

Naseem, S. M. "Mass Poverty in Pakistan: Some Preliminary Findings." _The Pakistan Development Review_ 12 (1973):317-30.

Noe, Samuel V. "In search of 'the' traditional Islamic city: an analytical proposal with Lahore as a case example." _Ekistics_ 280 (1980):69-75.

Pahl, R. E. _Whose City?_ Harmondsworth: Penguin Books, 1975.

Papanek, G. _Pakistan's Development: Social Goals and Private Incentives_. Cambridge: Harvard University Press, 1967.

Peattie, Lisa R. "Tertiarization and Urban Poverty in Latin America." In _Latin American Urban Research_, Vol. 5, editor Wayne A. Cornelius, pp. 109-24. Beverly Hills: Sage, 1975.

Perloff, H., and Edgar S. Dunn. _Regions, Resources and Economic Growth_. Baltimore: The John Hopkins Press and Resources for the Future, 1960.

Qadeer, Mohammad A. "Some Indigenous Factors in the Institutionalization of Professions in Pakistan." In _Pakistan in Transition_, editor W. H. Wriggins, pp. 136-44. Islamabad: University of Islamabad Press, 1975.

————. "Do Cities 'Modernize' the Developing Countries: An Examination of the South Asian Experience." _Comparative Studies in Society and History_ 16 (1974):266-83.

————. _An Evaluation of the Integrated Rural Development Programme_. Islamabad: Pakistan Institute of Development Economics, 1977.

Qadeer, M. A., and A. Sattar Sikander. "Squatter Settlements: A functional view." In _Proceedings of the National Seminar on Planning for Urban Development in the developing countries with special reference to Pakistan_, editor A. Sattar Sikander, pp. 163-75. Lahore: University of Engineering and Technology, 1978.

Qadeer, Mohammad A. "Issues and Approaches of Rural Community Planning in Canada." _Plan Canada_ 19 (1979):106-21.

Qureshi, Saleem. "Islam and Development: The Zia Regime in Pakistan." _World Development_ 8 (1980):563-75.

Redfield, Robert. Peasant Society and Culture. Chicago: University of Chicago Press, 1965.

Richardson, Harry W. Urban Economics. Harmondsworth: Penguin, 1971.

Roberts, Bryan. Cities of Peasants. London: Edward Arnold, 1978.

Robinson, Joan. Aspects of Development and Underdevelopment. Cambridge: Cambridge University Press, 1979.

Robinson, Warren C., and Nasreen Abbasi. "Underemployment in Pakistan." The Pakistan Development Review 18 (1979):313-31.

Rodinelli, Dennis A., and Kenneth Ruddle. Urbanization and Rural Development. Praeger, 1978.

Rotblat, Howard J. "Social Organization and Development in an Iranian Provincial Bazaar." Economic Development and Cultural Change 23 (1975):292-305.

Rudduck, G. Urban Biographies. Karachi: Planning Commission, Physical Planning and Housing Study 19, 1965.

Santos, Milton. The Shared Space. London: Methuen, 1979.

Sathar, Zeba Ayesha. "Rural-Urban Fertility Differential." The Pakistan Development Review 18 (1979):231-51.

Seers, Dudley. "The New Meaning of Development." International Development Review 3 (1977):3-5.

Shakir, Saleem. "Two Lahores Two Gulbergs." Viewpoint, June 1, 1980, pp. 8-9.

Shibli, A. R. 22 Khanawaday (Twenty-two Families). Lahore: People's Publications, 1972.

————. Pakistan Kay Dahi Khuda (Pakistan's Rural Lords). Lahore: People's Publications, 1973.

Shuja-ud-din. "Siyasi and Saqafati Tarigh" Urdu (Political and Cultural History) NaQoosh, February 1962, pp. 34-139.

Sjoberg, Gideon. The Pre Industrial City. New York: The Free Press, 1960.

Soja, Edward W., and Richard J. Tobin. "The Geography of Modernization: Paths, Patterns, and Processes of Spatial Change in Developing Countries." In Third World Urbanization, editors Janet Abu-Lughod and Richard Hay, Jr., pp. 155-64. Chicago: